# Henry James
# Goes to the Movies

# Henry James
# Goes to the Movies

Edited by Susan M. Griffin

THE UNIVERSITY PRESS OF KENTUCKY

Publication of this volume was made possible in part by a grant
from the National Endowment for the Humanities.

*Editorial and Sales Offices:* The University Press of Kentucky
663 South Limestone Street, Lexington, Kentucky 40508-4008

05  04  03  02  01    5  4  3  2  1

Library of Congress Cataloging-in-Publication Data

Henry James goes to the movies / edited by Susan M. Griffin.
    p. cm.
Includes index.
  ISBN 0-8131-2191-4 (alk. paper)
  1. James, Henry, 1843-1916—Film and video adaptations. 2. American
fiction—Film and video adaptations. 3. Film adaptations. I. Griffin,
Susan M., 1953-
  PS2127.F55 H45 2001
  813'.4—dc21                           00-012274

This book is printed on acid-free recycled paper
meeting the requirements of the American National Standard
for Permanence of Paper for Printed Library Materials.

Manufactured in the United States of America.

# Contents

# Illustrations

# Introduction

## Making Movies with Henry James

*Susan M. Griffin*

"Move over, Jane Austen: here comes Henry James," the *New York Times* declared, heralding a cluster of new films based on James's fiction: Jane Campion's *Portrait of a Lady* (1996), Iain Softley's *The Wings of the Dove* (1997), and Agnieszka Holland's *Washington Square* (1997). As Sarah Koch's filmography included in this volume reveals, James's writings have long been a resource for television and film alike. And, strikingly, movie and especially television stagings of James have been an international phenomenon, including American, British, French, and Spanish productions. Some of these productions are cinema classics, like William Wyler's *The Heiress* (1949); others, like the 1973 BBC *The Golden Bowl,* introduced some of James's most difficult work to a larger audience. The 1990s James films, starring actors like Nicole Kidman and John Malkovich, directed by both avant-garde—Campion—and more mainstream—Softley—directors, received widespread media coverage and, appearing so closely together, represent an intriguing cultural phenomenon. This latest Jamesian phase (craze?) has crossed into another century with two productions of *The Golden Bowl,* the 1999 rerelease of the BBC version and the 2000 premiere of the new Merchant Ivory film starring Nick Nolte and Uma Thurman, as well as the 2001 Masterpiece Theatre *The American.*

It is a phenomenon that would certainly have interested James himself. Despite his reputation as an artist of the esoteric, writing for and about an elite audience, James longed—and strove—for popularity. He never achieved the lucrative popular audience that he desired: his one original stage play, *Guy Domville,* flopped famously, and the summative grand New York Edition of his works was a financial failure. Nonetheless, the acknowledged literary "Master" of late-nineteenth- and early-twentieth-century literature was an astute analyst of contemporary artistic marketplaces. As critic and artist, James participated in the historical evolution during his lifetime of separate but fluctuating high and low cultures. These distinctions became a topic of James's own fictions in works like "The Death of the Lion" and "The Next Time." The author of "The Art of Fiction" who labored to elevate the novel to a high art form was also the reader, viewer, and reviewer of a wide spectrum of cultural productions from popular novels to contemporary art exhibitions to public ceremonies and rituals to the range of theatrical productions in several countries over many years. His art and literary criticism, as well as his voluminous correspondence, repeatedly evidence his acute awareness of the range and categories of cultural production.

Describing James's interest in the cultural values of art does not, however, explain the cultural capital that his own work has accrued in modern cinema. Why has James's writing proved so popular as the material for film? Popular, too, at a variety of historical moments: from the 1930s and 1940s, which saw Frank Lloyd's 1933 *Berkeley Square,* Martin Gabel's *The Lost Moment* (1947), with Susan Hayward, Robert Cummings, and Agnes Moorehead, and William Wyler's *The Heiress,* with Olivia de Havilland, Montgomery Clift, and Ralph Richardson, through a spate of American television productions in the 1950s and a BBC series based on the women in James's short fiction in the 1970s to the nineties films with their period "authenticity" in costume and setting and postmodern depictions of psychology and sexuality. Striking as well is the range of film artists who have turned to James: among the directors are, predictably, James Ivory, but also less expected figures like Peter Bogdanovich, John Frankenheimer, Jacques Rivette, and François Truffaut. And look at the variety of actors who have played James characters: Peggy Ashcroft, Nathalie Baye, Montgomery Clift, Olivia de Havilland, Leslie Howard, Agnes Moorehead, Cybill Shepherd, Vanessa Redgrave, Diana Rigg, Paul Scofield, Irene Worth.

The experiences in and of the theater that led to James's narrative use of a "scenic method" surely open his prose to filmic treatment. And those who have chosen to adapt James's intricate, difficult prose to the screen are preceded by those who translated his fiction to the stage. First among these was James himself, who reworked over a half-dozen narratives into plays, including "Daisy Miller," *The American,* and *The Other House.* James absorbed himself in the details of staging, from casting to costuming. Alas, in his lifetime, no play based on James's fiction met with unqualified success. Yet this work in some sense paved the way for later, better-received theatrical productions like Ruth and Augustus Goetz's *The Heiress,* which has been produced successfully from the 1940s to the 1990s. *The Heiress* script became, in turn, the basis for the Goetzes' screenplay for the 1947 film of the same name.

Why film James? Certainly James's acute visual sense, his near obsession with perception and point of view is one reason. Then, too, there is the richness of his oeuvre in terms of character. Perhaps most influential has been his engagement with matters central to contemporary culture: the position of woman, the workings of sexualities both hetero- and homo-, the complexities of social existence, the problems of knowing and the workings of power.

The making of movies with Henry James—the uses of his narratives, the recognition of his scenic method, the invocation of his name, the borrowing of his techniques, the recasting of his characters, the responses to his artistry as well as his roles and reputations (shifting over time) as artist— is the subject variously explored in this collection. The filmmakers and films discussed in turn revise, rebel against, and reify Henry James and his work. Over the decades, very different Henry Jameses have appeared on the screen. Analyzing these visions and versions of "The Master" informs us not only about James's rich diversity but also about the changing needs and interests of cultures and their filmmakers. The contributors to this volume explore the reasons for and the techniques involved in filming James, the ways in which his prose fosters and at times frustrates the work of making movies.

What *Making Movies with Henry James* offers, then, is a range of information about and responses to Jamesian cinema. The contributors include established senior critics, as well as newer voices. We have aimed for a wide audience: James studies as well as film studies and critics who work in cultural studies and feminist studies. The essays have been written so as to be accessible to students; we hope that the volume will prove useful in a variety of classroom settings.

James's most famous short fiction, "The Turn of the Screw," has also been his work most often adapted into film, with versions ranging from a "prequel"—the 1971 *The Nightcomers*—to filmings of performances of the Benjamin Britten opera to a 1995 television production starring Valerie Bertinelli and Diana Rigg (*The Haunting of Helen Walker*). Anthony Mazzella's essay analyzes the best known and perhaps the best of these, Jack Clayton's 1962 *The Innocents*, exploring its filmic attempt to render the radical ambiguity of James's story. Mazzella argues that the technology of cinema represents and recreates the structures of possession that ensnare both character and audience in "The Turn of the Screw." Aided by William Archibald and Truman Capote's screenplay, Georges Auric's score, and Freddie Francis's photography, Clayton creates an experience of visual and aural disorientation.

Like James's 1878 "Daisy Miller," Peter Bogdanovich's 1974 film of the same name, starring his then-girlfriend, the former model Cybill Shepherd, created a critical scandal. Peggy McCormack explores the cultural moments that set the stages for both Daisys, at the same time demonstrating the ways in which James and Bogdanovich themselves, in creating icons of the American girl, stage political, gendered dramas of American identity. These two Daisy Millers, in turn, had widely differing effects on their creators' professional careers. Encountering novella and film in the 1990s, McCormack and her students provide a third critical audience, reading the cultural meanings of the American artist and his girl.

Priscilla Walton's essay will serve to introduce many to Jacques Rivette's 1974 *Celine et Julie vont en bateau*. Walton demonstrates how this example of French New Wave cinema provides a way into James's neglected—and fascinating—1896 murder mystery *The Other House*. Dominique Labourier's and Juliette Berto's improvisational performances, Walton argues, create "a narrative about the reconstruction of narratives," a recognizably Jamesian reflexivity. The film's representation of female desire sensitizes us to James's own depiction of the power and threat of same-sex desire, its ability to undermine the conventional paradigms of heterosexuality. Walton traces patterns of transgression and containment in these sensational narratives— one filmic and twentieth-century, the other fictional and fin-de-siècle.

French New Wave cinema is also the subject of Matthew Jordan's essay, which analyzes the workings of mourning, nostalgia, and melancholia in François Truffaut's *La Chambre verte*. In setting one of James's most compelling fictions, "The Altar of the Dead," in post–World War I France, Truffaut encourages us, Jordan argues, to read the story of the protagonist's individual loss as a narrative about national trauma. Drawing on aspects of two other James stories, "The Beast in the Jungle" and "The Friends of Friends," Truffaut demonstrates the need for cultural remembrance, as well as the dangers of a pathological fixation on a private past. The result is an instance of what Jordan shows is Truffaut's own filmic "healthy piety" for James's stories.

Looking closely at another cultural moment, Leland Person takes up James Ivory's curious 1984 casting of Superman—aka Christopher Reeve— in the role of Basil Ransom, the main male character in *The Bostonians*. In the conservative political context of the first Reagan presidency, James's story about nineteenth-century feminists resonates complexly. Comparing the constructions of masculinity across genres, Person argues that the "compulsory heterosexuality" that James complicates and undercuts in the novel is stabilized and normalized in the film, in part through Reeve's casting and performance.

Nancy Bentley's "Conscious Observation of a Lovely Woman" defends the most controversial aspects of Jane Campion's 1996 *Portrait of a Lady*. In her anachronistic reading of James, her refusal to create an "authenticated" period piece, Campion actually, Bentley argues, remains true to James's narrative and cultural complexities. By underscoring and analyzing the ways in which watching a young woman serves as cultural "entertainment," Campion re-turns us to how James's realist novel explores and exploits precisely these concerns.

Julie Rivkin and Karen Chandler take up the two major filmic adaptations of James's *Washington Square:* William Wyler's 1949 *The Heiress* and Agniezka Holland's 1996 *Washington Square.* Rivkin asks why a novel with such a pointedly unattractive heroine should prove so very attractive to filmmakers. Not only is Catherine Sloper plain, she is "resolutely opaque and uncommunicative." What kind of cultural entertainment, to take up Bentely's terms, does this young woman's story provide? Rivkin suggests that the misogyny and sadism James depicts in the novel—albeit interpreted differently by the two directors fifty years apart—provide part of the answer. And she argues that the Catherines that these films make visible are, respectively, heroines for 1949 and 1999.

Chandler focuses on the workings of melodrama in James's, Holland's, and Wyler's stories of Catherine Sloper. In particular, she analyzes the ways in which novel and films use female silence—a standard melodramatic trope—as, respectively, signs of Catherine's inarticulate passivity and an expressive, generative power. That power is varyingly conveyed, Chandler demonstrates, by Wyler's and Holland's differing uses of Romantic music. Reading Holland's film as a response both to James's novel and to the earlier movie, Chandler traces the ways in which this feminist director works within and manipulates popular melodramatic form.

The next four essays treat the 1990s James films as a group, including as well discussion of other 1990s James sightings, in *Under Heaven, Notting Hill,* and *Next Stop, Wonderland.* Each essay poses in some way the question of what cultural work is performed by filming James at this late date, asking, too, what sorts of cultural capital are accrued by invoking or viewing "Henry James." Dale Bauer, Alan Nadel, Marc Bousquet, and Dianne Sadoff describe and differentiate the various audiences for James at the turn of our century.

Using the 1999 *Notting Hill* and *Next Stop, Wonderland* as instructive counterexamples, Dale Bauer focuses on Campion's *Portrait* and Softley's *Wings* in order to explore the filmmakers' task of reproduction, of mastering or being mastered by James. Is Jamesian substance accessible or even desirable in 1990s movies or is the use of Jamesian style sufficient? Particularly Jamesian is the problem of irony—what Bauer identifies as "the Master's trope"—as an avenue for cultural capital, allowing us to be part of the audience that "gets it." How to invoke that ironic knowledge and win that educated audience without losing a larger consumer base? Bauer suggests that Jamesian value as constructed in 1990s cinema often rejects a nuanced usage of Jamesian content or narrative structure in favor of the spectatorial and the sensational.

In contrast, Alan Nadel maintains current James films take advantage of James's narrative innovations and cultural investigations. Indeed, Nadel finds a fundamental resemblance between the Jamesian house of fiction and narrative cinema: "the fragmentation and reassembly of unique perceptions, acquired through an optical mechanics and creating the illusion of multiple—potentially infinite—windows on an imaginary reality." Analyzing the three nineties adaptations of James—*The Portrait of a Lady, The Wings of the Dove,* and *Washington Square*—as, precisely, products of late-twentieth-century culture, Nadel explores the ways in which Jamesian narrative qualities allow these films to address issues of money, gender, and nationality.

Marc Bousquet, on the other hand, looks skeptically at the notion that cultural capital, Jamesian or otherwise, overcomes material circumstances and class structures. Despite the role of "the James formation" in the cultural work of sustaining that notion, we can and should differentiate among different groups' experience of "Henry James." Through a detailed examination of the economic and cultural situations of Gen-X audiences, Bousquet explores the ways in which Softley's *Wings* can be seen as addressing such viewers. In Kate Croy's and Merton Densher's alienated, desiring end, he argues, young audiences can recognize their own generational experience of postmodern hypercapitalism.

Dianne Sadoff, too, views these latest three James films in their turn-of-the-century context. Sadoff focuses on the ways that Campion's, Holland's, and Softley's films appropriate James's fiction in order to depict and express cultural anxiety about the institutions of marriage and the family. Her essay explores the target audiences for these films: the cultural cohorts that each sought to reach and shape, exploring why *Portrait* and *Washington Square* failed to find the viewers they sought, while *Wings* achieved moderate success.

Essays by Lee Clark Mitchell and Wendy Graham address the latest (for now) film of a Henry James fiction, Merchant Ivory's *The Golden Bowl,* which premiered at Cannes in 2000 and was released in the United States in spring 2001. Mitchell's "'Based on a Novel by Henry James': *The Golden Bowl* 2000," a nuanced comparison of James's novel, the 1973 Masterpiece Theatre *Golden Bowl,* and the Merchant Ivory film, asks precisely what it means to "adapt" a fiction cinematically. Mitchell focuses on filmmakers' attempts to render (or ignore) the fundamental uncertainties of James's narration. Arguing that adaptations "allow a reconsideration of what it is that keeps drawing us back to the narrative, compelling a desire for it in another form," Mitchell suggests that James's own creative practice of revision, his "invitation to the reader to dream again in my company," offers his adapters an example that transcends literal-mindedness while demanding a deep readerly engagement.

Wendy Graham's "The Rift in the *Loot:* Cognitive Dissonance for the Reader of Merchant Ivory's *The Golden Bowl*" looks closely at the materialism conveyed and elided by the detailed visual richness of the film. Graham argues that Merchant Ivory's meticulously reproduced Edwardian costumes and decor work to create fantasy rather than history, insofar as they gloss over matters of economics and class. Situating the film's visual discourse within the art worlk of James's day and reading it against James's fiction and nonfictional writings on art, Graham traces the art film's complex relations with capital and its myths.

Sarah Koch's extremely useful international filmography also includes television productions of Henry James's works. Listing some 110 adaptations of James, Koch's filmography includes information on the productions' screenwriters, directors, casts, crews, and awards. This rich source for future scholarship documents the ways in which James has appeared on screens around the world.

Finally, the volume includes Sarah Edgington and Steve Wexler's detailed bibliography of critical work on James and cinema, a listing of essays and magazine and newspaper articles that, along with the essays in this volume, will work to aid and stimulate further scholarship on and discussion of Jamesian film.

Sincere thanks to Joanne Webb, who brought her impeccable editorial skills to this project, to Darci L. Thoune, who provided much-needed last minute help, and to Mary Murphy of Merchant Ivory for her generous assistance. We are grateful to the University of Louisville's Committee on Academic Publications for support and to the Johns Hopkins University Press for permissions.

Filming James, 1961–1984

# "The Story . . . Held Us"

## "The Turn of the Screw" from Henry James to Jack Clayton

*Anthony J. Mazzella*

Henry James's notorious ghost story "The Turn of the Screw" (1898; New York Edition, 1908) has been capable of sustaining a diversity of readings, often contradictory ones, as evidenced by its critical history over the past century: the ghosts are real (from the beginning through Peter G. Beidler's book-length study of 1989 and beyond); the sex-repressed, insane governess is hallucinating (starting in 1920 with Harold C. Goddard's essay, and in 1934 with Edmund Wilson's work, perhaps the best known of the early studies, and into the future); Mrs. Grose is the evil genius behind the mysteries at Bly (1964 and later, with commentaries by Eric Solomon and C. Knight Aldrich); it is not the ghosts who are corrupting the children but the text of the governess's tale that is corrupt (1980 and continuing, with an essay by Anthony J. Mazzella). There have also been Marxist and feminist studies, deconstructive and psychoanalytic accounts, as well as reader-response criticism.[1] James's tale has enmeshed readers in its coils so that once one begins the process of trying to understand its meaning(s), one is imprisoned by the story, one cannot escape, one is possessed. "The story . . . held us," indeed (*TS* 21).

Any filmmaker attempting a film adaptation of this novella is challenged with finding a visual way of rendering such apparently infinite intricacies of prose. How do you use visual images and sound constructs to accomplish in film what James has accomplished in words? How do you create a film that plays on variations of possession? Jack Clayton's 1961 film *The Innocents* comes close to answering that question. With a screenplay by William Archibald (based also on his play of the same name) and Truman Capote and additional scenes and dialogue by John Mortimer, the film, too, works its devious magic, aided by Georges Auric's mesmerizing score, as reorchestrated by Lambert Wilson, and by Freddie Francis's crisp black-

and-white photography. According to the liner notes for the 1995 wide-screen laser disc release, Francis observed that "our audiences probably didn't realize . . . that one of the things that contributed towards the horror of the film is that I had these filters made up so only the center of the screen would be fully illuminated. The edge of the screen would always be a little bit dark so that you didn't know whether there was anything there or not."

Not to know what is there, apparently, is also James's intention as expressed in his 1908 preface to "The Turn of the Screw," where he remarks, "Make [the reader] *think* the evil, make him think it for himself, and you are released from weak specifications" (reprinted in *The Art of the Novel* 175). This view is suggested also in his 19 December 1898 letter to F.W.H. Myers, where he alludes to "one thing and another that are questionable and ambiguous" in the tale (*Letters of Henry James* 299). Going back even earlier, one can examine his notebook entry of 12 January 1895, where he gives the source of the tale as a ghost story told by the Archbishop of Canterbury. In the entry, he uses such terms as "vague" and "obscure" to characterize both his source and his development of the material into a tale all his own (*Notebooks of Henry James* 178–79).

Thus, not knowing whether there is anything there or not is the name of the game for Henry James's "The Turn of the Screw." Let's start with the ghosts: Peter Quint, for example. He is certainly not present in the prologue. Everyone else is mentioned: Mrs. Grose, Miles, Flora, and "a young lady [Miss Jessel] whom they had the misfortune to lose" (*TS* 26). Included even are "a cook, a housemaid, a dairywoman, an old pony, an old groom and an old gardener . . ." (26). But not Peter Quint. He appears for the first time when the governess sees him at the top of the tower. He materializes the second time outside the "'grown-up' dining-room" window (42) and seen again "from the waist up" (43). Provided with a description by the governess, Mrs. Grose identifies him as Peter Quint, the uncle's "own man, his valet, when he was here!" (47).

Three things happen simultaneously with this identification: the ghost is real, the ghost is a hallucination, Mrs. Grose invented him. The ghost is real, because the governess had never heard of him before and yet identified him precisely. The ghost is a hallucination, because between Quint's first appearance and his second, the governess "made sure" that the stranger was "nobody about the place" and "nobody from the village" (45). She did this presumably by actually going to the village, asking questions, and describing this individual. Yet some six months before the governess's arrival at Bly in June, there was an "inquest and boundless chatter" following discovery "on the dawn of a winter's morning, [of] Peter Quint . . . , by a labourer going to early work, stone dead on the road from the village" (51).

A dead Peter Quint, an inquest, boundless chatter—and still no one from the village could identify him to the governess? How can this be, with all the gossip? It cannot be, because Quint never was. And if he never was, the governess must have hallucinated him. But Mrs. Grose identified him. Or did she? When the governess provides her account of the second sighting, she writes, "Mrs. Grose's large face showed me . . . the far-away glimmer of a consciousness more acute: I somehow made out in it the delayed dawn of an idea" (45). Mrs. Grose's idea is to invent Peter Quint. Her motive? Jealousy. The governess has displaced her in importance at Bly, replaced her with Flora, and otherwise humiliated her, assuming without justification that she cannot read (32), that she can't write (88), and "shutting her out to go by another passage to her own place" (62).

Later, after Miss Jessel makes the appearances that climax at Flora's eruption against the governess by the lake in chapter 20, with the governess feeling "justified" and adding that "no moment of my monstrous time was perhaps so extraordinary as that in which I consciously threw out to [Miss Jessel] . . . an inarticulate message of gratitude" (98), Mrs. Grose leads the child away, reassuring Flora that "*We* know, don't we, love? . . . It's all a mere mistake and a worry and a joke" (99). The joke is on the governess. The children are playing a game aided by Mrs. Grose. Despite strict orders from the governess that the children not meet after this (103), they do, and with Mrs. Grose. The governess herself writes, "I learned below that [Miles] had breakfasted—in the presence of a couple of the maids—with Mrs. Grose and his sister" (107). There, unknown to the governess, they planned what Miles should do after Mrs. Grose and Flora drove off: he should avoid the governess as long as possible and wait for Mrs. Grose's return, a scenario that explains his strange question and emphasis, "Is she *here*?" (116), at the novel's climax. The usual reading is that he has confused Jessel with Quint, since the governess puts the emphasis on "she," but *his* emphasis is on "here" (at Bly) rather than "there" (in London). When he realizes that Mrs. Grose has not yet come, he, "with sudden fury" (116), utters the name of the former governess, angry that he has been abandoned. The view that Mrs. Grose is a kind of monster on the loose at Bly is supported by James's having linked these words (or their sounds) in his revision of the tale, where the line "some one had taken a liberty rather monstrous" (40) in the New York Edition had originally been "a liberty rather gross."

A film adaptation, having to deal with just these three interpretive strands, has a large order to fill, and—in the Clayton version—in only 99 minutes. The film, for a reader coming from this disorienting encounter with "The Turn of the Screw," provides a similar experience, one that is also *literally* disorienting.

Figure 1. Flora (Pamela Franklin) saying her prayers, as the governess (Deborah Kerr) reassures her. Twentieth Century–Fox; Museum of Modern Art / Film Stills Archive.

If the novella can have a governess both twenty (when she was hired) and forty (when she wrote her manuscript), the film elects, as it must, a central character of one age only: the governess of Deborah Kerr, whose name Miss Giddens announces what will become a visual, and aural, pattern of giddiness. In her interview with Michael Redgrave's Uncle, there is a middle-distance of emptiness between the two characters. There was a tendency in the early 20th-Century Fox CinemaScope films to intensify screen width by having the performers occupy either end of the screen, a strategy that works for this film by providing a central space whose content can be both seen and imagined. As the uncle approaches the candidate during his commentary on Miss Jessel, the clock strikes when he states, "she died," adding that he was in Calcutta at the time. The jarring sound and the announcement of his own distance from the event serve to place the viewer and the candidate at an imbalance at just the time that he makes his final appeal: "Help me, Miss Giddens, for truly I am helpless," he says to her. His next words use the language of a marriage proposal—"Give me your hand. Give me your promise"—so that the new governess is treated to both a job offer and the ambiguous hint of something more. Yet the proposal comes in the context of the announcement of a death. It also occurs with the act of his clasping her gloved hand, the start of yet another visual motif—that of hands that extend but offer nothing. The patterns of dizziness and emptiness supply a context for the elusive concrete, for ghosts that are and aren't there.

The shots of empty spaces begin almost immediately. After Miss Giddens's interview with the uncle, there is a dissolve to a carriage ride taking the governess to Bly. The carriage window, to the right of the governess, provides another open space (again, as if to be filled). She asks the driver to stop, before the horse enters the archway. A shot of the lake and of more open space follows. The music is the sound of romantic strings, accompanied by the sounds of nature. Then the name "Flora" is heard on the soundtrack several times as the governess approaches the lake. The sound of "Flora" is heard a third time when it is followed by a shot of Flora's reflection in the water—a disorienting vision because the clouds reflected in the water appear to be on the ground and filling the space around Flora and Miss Giddens. Flora (Pamela Franklin) greets the governess and introduces her turtle, Rupert, saying, "But Rupert isn't the only one . . .," and then she quickly changes the subject. Here the verbal ellipsis creates a different kind of space to be filled. If Rupert isn't the only one, who else is there?

A dissolve follows to the governess and Flora's approaching the house and meeting Mrs. Grose. Again, another open space is visible, this time between the governess and Mrs. Grose (Megs Jenkins). The empty area between the governess and the housekeeper, who have just met for the first time, helps to reinforce the distance between the woman who is in "supreme authority," as the uncle phrased it, and a "base menial" (61), as Miles is assumed by the governess to have phrased it in the novella. A shot occurring soon after is one of those visual elements that mark the governess as one of the "innocents": a shot of Miss Giddens's head framed by the high oval window at Bly's entrance, through which light streams, encircling the governess as if by a halo.

Shots of disorientation and scenes of dizziness have a long preparatory gestation before Miles's arrival at Bly, which introduces the most pronounced early such sequence in the film. His arrival may be said to begin with an asynchronous sound cut (itself disorienting) to splashing by Flora in her bath, saying, "Miles is coming! Miles is coming!" A cut follows to a tour of the house conducted by Flora, who tells Miss Giddens, "Big rooms get bigger at night"—a verbal suggestion of disorientation—and that Mrs. Grose "shuts her eyes in the dark"—a condition that encourages the filling

in of a metaphorical blank space. The tour ends with a cut to Flora's bedroom (fig. 1), Flora saying her prayers, "If I should wake before—" but she
catches herself in the anomaly of waking before she dies and yet adds, in
reference to the governess's assuring her that she is "a very, very good girl,"
"but I might not be. And if I weren't, wouldn't the Lord need to see me
there to walk around? Isn't that what happens to some people?" This disconcerting question is followed by a disorienting sound. The governess
perceives it as someone being hurt, a filling in of the visuals for the sound.
But Flora attributes it to "her imagining things."

The sequence that follows is of the governess sleeping, watched by
Flora. The governess is restless. The moaning sound being heard might
come from the governess—or a ghost. Flora then looks out onto the garden
with its circle of statues. There is a cut back to Flora, gazing, smiling, but
there is no eye line shot to show what she sees—yet another blank to be
filled. Following quickly is the superimposition of a shot of one of the
garden's soldier statues, a shot implicating Miles's presence (his name in
Latin) dominating the scene before there is a dissolve to the next shot. Then
the governess is seen reading a letter from her home containing a photograph of her and her sister. Flora asks if she's in the picture too. Miss
Giddens denies this, saying it's impossible; but for a child who may consort
with ghosts who fill empty spaces, it would not be so impossible to fill a
place in the governess's photo.

When the governess opens the letter from the uncle, she herself becomes disoriented, for it contains the letter from Miles's school announcing
that he has been expelled. The governess is shown seeking out Mrs. Grose
and filling her in on the details, explaining that Miles is deemed "an injury
to the others." When the governess defines "being bad," she uses such syn-
onyms as "To contaminate. . . . To corrupt." Their discussion is situated in
the conservatory. As they converse, the camera shows them before a torso of
a nearly nude male statue at just the point when the housekeeper asks the
governess, "Are you afraid Miles will corrupt you?" The statue is not seen by
the governess (she is looking forward), so for her the space is empty, but not
for the viewing audience. The audience fills in the spaces—verbal and
visual—of the governess, the statue, and the word "corrupt."

The next series of shots is an elaborately disorienting one, for it seems
mundane on the surface—the governess with Flora meeting Miles (Martin
Stephens) in a carriage (fig. 2). But he looks strained. His gift of a small
bouquet of flowers to the governess pleases her, while his words cause her
to depict him as a "deceitful flatterer." What makes the scene disorienting is
the tension that has been building ever since Flora declared that he would
be coming home before anyone else knew that. As if to emphasize her

Figure 2. Miles (Martin Stephens) in a carriage on his way to Bly, with his sister Flora (Pamela Franklin) and the governess (Deborah Kerr). Twentieth Century–Fox; Museum of Modern Art / Film Stills Archive.

prominence in a sequence ostensibly belonging to Miles, there is a shot of her holding the flowers that Miles gave to the governess (how Flora acquired them is not shown—another ellipsis, or blank space in the pictorial content of the film). As the carriage passes exterior screen right to screen left, the camera shows Flora dropping—flinging?—the flowers out of the open carriage window. Her act disorients the viewer already apprehensive about the first visual encounter with Miles.

What occurs next is the first truly sustained dizzying sequence. Miles greets Mrs. Grose at Bly and the camera shows him spinning round with the housekeeper, the camera moving synchronously with them and the music de-intensifying. The next disorienting sequence occurs that night when Miles, hearing the governess outside his bedroom, invites her in. Unlike her prototype in the novella, the governess in the film informs Miles that he has been expelled. About his uncle, Miles says, "He doesn't care what happens to us." There is another open space between characters, the openness marking an emptiness, emphasized here by Miles's pain over his uncle's indifference. When the governess moves nearer, in an effort to fill that emptiness, and states that she cares, the camera in extreme close-up provides a shot of Miles's tear-stained cheek. When the governess declares, "I want to help you. Trust me" (echoing the uncle's words to her), there's a powerful blast of wind and the governess gasps, "My candle's gone out!" Miles's disconcerting reassurance, like that of his prototype, is contained in his closing term of endearment: "It's only the wind, my dear."

Following the first appearance of the figure, on the tower, is the powerfully dizzying depiction of Miles on horseback, enhanced by Auric's pulsating score. Miles jumps on horseback over a hedge, causing birds to screech and echoes to reverberate. Shown as being heard from the governess's perspective, they disorient the viewer because of the uncertainty concerning their objectivity, the exaggerated quality suggesting that they are the governess's subjective experience.

A quietly unsettling scene is the costume-party sequence. Background for this sequence is provided by the governess examining Quint's photograph (which means, of course, that she took it from the attic and may now be said to possess it). There are shots of her in bed and the sounds of a storm. The window is open, but she doesn't close it against the wind and the rain. There is a dissolve to the next day and a shot of a severe rain storm as seen through the window of the schoolroom. The children are writing, with Flora creating a rhythmic squeaking sound on her slate. Miles accuses her of begging for attention. She screams loudly, the governess comforts her, and Flora announces, "Everything is so horrible," qualifying her statement to mean the weather. The governess assures Flora, "You *are* good. You both are." To ease the tension, she suggests that they pretend it's Flora's birthday. The children decide to have a costume party, and depart to get dressed, while the governess says to herself, "I let them go." Mrs. Grose reassures her: "They'll come to no harm." They discuss Quint. The housekeeper states her seeing him might have been a dream, but the governess announces that she had seen him the first time in daylight. It might have been different, she admits, if she hadn't seen him. Mrs. Grose reminds her that she did see his picture in the miniature. The governess then asks how he died. Mrs. Grose explains that it was on "those very steps." It was winter. The steps were icy. He came home late and full of drink. His eyes were open, filled with surprise. According to Mrs. Grose, he was a peculiar man who had done vicious things. Unlike her counterpart in the James tale, the housekeeper adds that Miles found him, noting, "That poor little boy worshiped Quint. . . . Quint took advantage. . . . They were always together." She explains that this was inevitable, since the boy was an orphan whose uncle never visited.

When the children arrive, bedecked and costumed, Flora announces that she is Princess Pincushion and that Miles will recite a poem. The text heard on the soundtrack is a mesmerizing series of questions that culminate in the disturbing question that the governess herself asks:

> What shall I sing to my lord from my window?
> What shall I sing, for my lord will not stay?
> What shall I say, for my lord will not listen?
> Where shall I go when my lord is away?
> Whom shall I love when the moon is arisen?
> Gone is my lord and the grave is his prison.
> What shall I say when my lord comes a-calling?
> What shall I say when he knocks on my door?
> What shall I say when he speaks, "Enter," softly?
> Leaving the marks of his grave on my floor.
> Enter, my lord. Come from your prison.
> Come from your grave, for the moon is arisen.
> Welcome, my lord.

As Miles recites this poem about his lord, whose grave is his prison and whom he welcomes at last for the moon has arisen, the camera cuts between the Miles who starts out as reading lines and a Miles who gradually becomes more involved and immersed in his words, looking at the audience (and presumably at the governess, since the camera establishes Miles's gaze as in her direction) until finally, when he welcomes his lord, his gaze at the governess is almost a challenge and an acknowledgment. The governess then whispers to Mrs. Grose, "What if Miles knows?" The question is overheard by Flora, who asks, "Knows what, Miss Giddens?" There follows a slow-motion dissolve and superimposition of Flora smiling—at a blank space, for the object receiving her smile is not shown. The disorientation comes from the content of Miles's words, the manner of his delivery, but most of all it comes from Flora's benignant smile over nothingness.

Finally, the most intensely dizzying shot occurs when the governess conducts her nocturnal visit of Bly, convinced the ghosts are using the children to reach each other. The sequence begins with a cut to a shot of the governess in her room reading the Bible, light gleaming off the cross on its cover. Her hair is down. She stokes the fire and hears the tinkle of a piano, and then voices, "The children." The film here is establishing an uncertainty of sources: Is the governess imagining the sounds, or are they there for anyone to hear? Then laughter follows. The camera provides close-ups of roses, candles. But, again, it is not clear from whose point of view they are seen. The camera next shows the governess as she advances right, then left, with part of Miles's poem heard on the sound track. The camera shows the governess illuminated by the candelabra she is holding as she climbs the stairs. A creak of the stairs is heard. There is an extended murky shot of the wall tapestry, so that the uncertainty continues and all is indistinct until what materializes is a mid-close-up of the governess's face. It's as if the murkiness out of which she materializes is her own extended space to be filled by her self. The wind is heard on the sound track, followed by laughter. The governess is unable to open a locked door, as whispers and more laughter are heard. Miles's voice appears to say, "You're hurting me," followed by more laughter. An echoing sound intensifies as the governess turns left, then right. Suddenly, there is an abrupt cut to an overhead shot of the governess twisting and turning in such a way that her candles seem to follow a split-second behind—making the spinning more erratic. A cut follows to a shot of a window-shade cord with a bulbous end striking rhythmically against the window. "Love me, love me" is heard on the sound track. These various markers intensify the disorientation and dislocation, but most disorienting of all is a sudden, abrupt close-up of a devil's mask with one eye visible and another veiled (echoing visually Mrs. Grose's comment early in the film that he [presumably Quint] "had the Devil's own eye"). A scream ends the sequence.

In this elusiveness, in the form of images of dizziness, disorientation, and emptiness, the ghosts make their (non)appearance. The camera offers evidence, throughout the film, of the ghosts' subjective reality in the mind of the governess, the most definitive occurring during a game of hide-and-seek. It is the governess's turn, and as she secures her hiding place behind the drapery in the drawing room, the camera provides a distinct subjective shot from the governess's point of view, showing her tucking her shoes in so that they won't reveal her location to the children. Then, with the governess's face in extreme close-up, the camera shows her sensing an approaching figure. The camera cuts to reveal the face of a man (Peter Wyngarde) advancing to the window and gazing in. The governess gasps in horror. The figure withdraws.

While the *shot* is definitive enough, the attendant circumstances call that very subjectivity into question. For when the governess descended the main staircase to search out her hiding place, the camera showed a tapestry on the wall of a maiden with a unicorn, an emblem of sexuality and *innocence*. When she passes a vase of roses, the petals fall, an event, according to Mrs. Grose, that "always happens," suggestive of some influence in the house that is a catalyst for death and that *antedates* the governess's arrival at Bly. However, during the children's part of the hide-and-seek game, there is a passageway tracking shot, following the governess. Then, at the end of the hallway, a figure of a woman in a black dress passes, gliding, the governess calling out, "Anna?" But the figure moves on. The governess is next shown ascending the stairs to the attic. She opens the door to a room and is about to withdraw, when she notices the moving head of a toy, a clown figure. Entering the room, she stops the moving head and notices a music box. Opening it, she hears the tune Flora hums. In the music box is a cracked frame behind which is the photograph of a man, seen from the waist up— a man whose face will soon appear to the governess outside the drawing room window, seemingly supportive of the view that the governess has projected the picture in the miniature beyond the window pane. Thus, the seemingly definitive subjective shot is undercut by the circumstance of the tapestry and the falling rose petals, which, in turn, is undercut by the picture in the miniature. Equally supportive of the hallucination theory is the fear attendant upon the governess's gaze, a fear that seems to begin in the very room where the picture was found. As the governess is examining the picture, Miles enters and surprises her, putting his arm around her neck in what becomes a stranglehold, for she cries out that he is hurting her (an echo of his words during her nocturnal wanderings?). He yields his grip only when Flora interrupts them. Is Miles's choking grip part of the game? Or is it a manifestation of Quint's possession of Miles, acting as a result of the governess's having seen the picture?

Further complicating the issue is additional evidence of visual pro-jection when, after the governess's determined exit of the house following the figure's appearance, she opens the windowed door and searches out-side, finding nothing. But the camera shows the advancing figure of Mrs. Grose reflected in the window pane. If the window pane can reflect the image of Mrs. Grose, it is possible that it earlier reflected the image of the governess herself, and what she saw outside the window was her own reflection, upon which she superimposed the retained image from the min-iature with its surrounding emotion of fear induced by Miles's strangle-hold.[2] The film, then, while seemingly giving us an unalloyed subjective shot surrounds that shot with images and events that both undermine and reinforce the ghost's objective reality.

If we go back to an earlier scene in the film, the one presenting Quint's first appearance on the tower, we find a similar pattern. The governess is shown outdoors, dressed in white, cutting flowers for a bouquet. As she spreads the branches, the camera reveals the statue of a cherub, an emblem analogous to half of the tapestry's content—the innocent half. The statue also provides the other half. For in the next occasion of the hands pattern, the cherub is extending its arms, holding a pair of hands that are broken off. The extending of hands initiated by the uncle asking for help here contains nothing. Further, the camera shows an insect crawling out of the cherub's mouth—an innocent occurrence in nature, perhaps, but especially unsettling here because of the context. Suddenly, the soundtrack goes completely silent. The governess slowly glances up toward the tower where she sees, through the nearly blinding sunlight, the figure of a man. The governess drops her scissors in a basin of water, establishing visually a conjoining of phallic and vaginal images, and also of the governess's courage and aggression. For when the sounds of Nature return, the governess advances toward the tower and pushes open a gate barring the entrance (all the while, heard on the soundtrack is Flora's pre-credit "Willow" song). Intercut are shots of the tower, with several slow-motion ones of pigeons ascending. The governess climbs the stairs to the tower after forcing the door open, the sounds echoing and reverberating. Heard in intensified fashion is the sound of bees buzzing. What follows is a shot of the rectangular stairway as seen from its base and looking up at a jagged spiral—another in the series of vertiginous shots. Superimposed is her sudden entrance to the top of the tower, as if in an accelerated ascent (contrasting with that of the pigeons in slow motion)—inducing a disorientation in the viewer. The camera then reveals only Miles present, attending his pigeons. He denies that anyone else was there. When he speaks of Flora, he declares that she "invents things," she "imagines them." Thus, verbally, the film is suggesting that the governess, too, "imagines things." One of the qualifications the uncle demanded in his new governess was "imagination." Therefore, the very quality that aided the governess in securing her position is also the quality that can damage and destroy.

While the film continues its oscillation of subjective shots undercut by objectified data, it offers at the climax of the film one of the most striking instances of this pattern—this time in reverse order: a definitively objective shot undercut by a context of rich subjectivity. If closure tends to have primacy, one is tempted to consider the objective shot as finally determinant. Yet one cannot easily do so because, like the Henry James story, the film offers its own gloss on Mrs. Grose's conduct that complicates matters by unsettling them. Most of all, again like the James original, it calls the reality of its own totality into question. If the prologue to the tale provides evidence that the *text* of the governess's account of her stay at Bly is corrupt—and therefore indeterminate—then the film provides evidence in *its* prologue (not the interview with the uncle) that the visual and aural record of Miss Giddens's sojourn at Bly is equally indeterminate.

First, consider the film's presentation of Mrs. Grose. The fact of the housekeeper's not being able to read, left ambiguous in James, becomes definitive in the film. When Miss Giddens hands her the letter from the uncle to read for herself, Mrs. Grose admits, "It's no good, Miss. I—I never learned." But when the figure of Miss Jessel appears at the lake, the situa-

Figure 3. The governess, Miss Giddens (Deborah Kerr), alone after Flora's outburst, facing right in this still but facing left in the film in the scene discussed in the text. Twentieth Century–Fox; Museum of Modern Art / Film Stills Archive.

tion supporting the housekeeper's integrity begins to change. The arrival of Mrs. Grose is followed by Flora's screaming to escape from the governess, and Mrs. Grose leads her away, screams punctuating the scene as the rain lashes and the governess remains alone in the gazebo, framed by its arches, her head bowed, in profile facing left (fig. 3).

A cut follows to Bly indoors as Miss Giddens approaches the door behind which Mrs. Grose tries to comfort Flora, whose screams shatter the scene. Sitting by the fire, the governess finds Miles coming in to join her as they both extend their hands to the warmth of the flames. Eventually the housekeeper emerges, stating that she can't understand where the child "learned such language" and exclaiming, "To hear such filth from a child's mouth." When they discuss what had transpired at the lake, Mrs. Grose states that Flora asserted "there was no one there." When the governess comments, "And you pretended to agree with her," the housekeeper declares, somewhat coldly, "I didn't have to pretend."

Her manner is superior, a quality that is heightened by the low-angle shot from the governess's point of view looking up at Mrs. Grose. What does Mrs. Grose have to feel superior about? To answer, one reviews the housekeeper's numerous comments about "stuff and nonsense," explaining away the unexplainable, and her leading remarks that encourage the susceptible governess to act, as in the case of "the devil's own eye," discussed earlier and her comment, in her explanation to the governess's asking if Quint and Jessel were in love, "I suppose that's what she called it," but for Mrs. Grose, "It was more like a sickness, a fever that leaves the body burned out and dry." She states that Quint struck Miss Jessel, but that she "wanted the weight of his hand," adding that "he had a savage laugh." In the background, outside the window, the camera shows the soldiers that adorn the periphery of Bly and constitute the statues in the circular garden, like silent sentinels for the unseen and the unheard. The housekeeper adds that "rooms [were] used by daylight as though they were dark woods." In the background now the camera shows a fire burning in the fireplace, "a hellfire" in the context of the suggestive subject matter. When the governess asks if the children saw, Mrs. Grose replies, "I don't know what the children saw." She adds that there was too much whispering in the house.

During this conversation, there is a shot of white roses in a vase, casting black shadows against the wall. One gets the sense that the governess wants a black-and-white world, where events are seen clearly, where hands hold out kindness, and where blank spaces are filled not with horrors but with goodness. But this isn't the world the housekeeper offers, despite her earlier mantra of "stuff and nonsense." Instead, she says explicitly that Quint and Jessel were guilty of "using them [the children]." Not surprisingly, in this suggestive context, the governess adds, "They still are." Mrs. Grose fills in the picture, completes the blank spaces: "When Quint was found, [Miss Jessel] grieved. . . . She never slept, never ate. I used to hear her wandering about all over the house, sobbing. She couldn't go on. Finally, she died [at Bly]. . . . I suppose you might say [of] a broken heart."

When the governess wants to seek professional advice, to consult the local vicar, the housekeeper dissuades her: "I wouldn't do that," for it would cause "a scandal." Thus any third-party counsel is forestalled, with the result that the very next sequence in the film is the governess's nightmare collage: In a swirl of images and sounds, the governess dramatizes what she has heard: "Secret." Whispers. "Watch her." There is also a visual and verbal superimposition: words, tower, hands, dancing doll. The camera shows that the governess's eyes are open, watching Mrs. Grose's words come to life, seemingly creating the scene with Miles and Quint, Flora and Jessel, holding hands in close-up—holding, perhaps, the absence in the hands of the cherub statue. As though in response to Mrs. Grose's words, the governess enacts the housekeeper's scenario—a scenario that, like Mrs. Grose's Peter Quint, has no outside corroboration. In the film, then, as in the novella, there is evidence incriminating Mrs. Grose.

As the film draws to its close, Mrs. Grose and Flora have left for London. The governess is alone, shown walking the grounds of Bly, passing a line of statues of soldiers—a visual way of invoking Miles. Following a cut to the indoors, the governess is shown with tea implements. Cries of "Help" are heard, as if, in this film of reverberating echoes of doors slamming as when Mrs. Grose leaves, this were an echo of the uncle's early plea to the governess. Then there is a shot of Miles entering. A large space between him and the governess is occupied only by the piano. It's one of those shots that emphasize the separation of characters, the emptiness between them. Miles declares that the governess is afraid, then reassures her: "Don't worry, there's a man in the house." When the governess questioningly echoes him, "Is there?" he replies confidently, "Yes, me," adding, "I'll protect you." He extends his hand over the tea table to the governess, but when she responds by smiling and extending her own, he pulls away from her to slap the gelatin on the table in the shape of a rodent, all the while laughing. This is another in the series of hand shots where the offer of friendship and belonging is canceled, as when, in an earlier scene before Flora's departure with Mrs. Grose, he joins the governess by the fire where her hands are extended toward the warmth of the flames and he extends his own. Similarly, prior to the first appearance of the figure on the tower, the camera showed the cherub with arms outstretched and broken-off hands.

When Miles asserts that they have the whole house to themselves, the governess comments, "More or less," adding, "There are still the others." Miles's look speaks volumes: he knows the meaning of her allusion; he's afraid that she's insane; he's afraid of her. They discuss Flora, her sudden illness and departure. Miles states that Flora loved this house (echoing his own words earlier about himself). When the governess asks if Miles is happy

Figure 4. The governess (Deborah Kerr) and Miles (Martin Stephens) at the climax of the film, during the confrontation scene with Quint. Twentieth Century–Fox; Museum of Modern Art / Film Stills Archive.

at Bly, he does not answer but runs off to the conservatory where he picks up Rupert, Flora's turtle, remarking that poor Flora must have been upset to have forgotten him. Miles asks the governess why she wants to be alone with him. Her remarks cause Miles to comment that when she speaks as she does, it makes her look "ugly and cruel." This is said with the pair situated before a grouping of orchids, the plants that feed on the dead. The governess pleads with Miles that she wants only to help him.

She then asks him why he was sent home. Miles replies, "It must be—because I'm different." When the governess protests that he is like any other boy, he observes, "Ah, now who isn't telling the truth." He adds that he thinks she is afraid. And she answers that she's afraid *for him.* Then she inquires if he took her letter. When he admits he did, she asks why. "To see what you said about us?" "Us?" she echoes. "Oh, about me," Miles clarifies. All the while a sound of leaves rustling is heard on the soundtrack, as if someone were walking about, but the source of the sound remains undisclosed. Miles denies being a thief at school. He acknowledges that he said things. And sometimes he heard things at night, after it got dark. "The Masters heard about it. They said I frightened the other boys" (in contrast to the text's acknowledgment that he said things to "those [he] liked" and "they must have repeated them. To those *they* liked," with word getting round to the Masters, who nevertheless never told what he said). In the film, when the governess asks where Miles learned these things, Miles states that he "made them up." The governess persists in asking her questions, almost badgering Miles: "Who taught them to you? . . . Shall I tell you his name!?" Then, visible behind Miles's face, is Quint's face, advancing, outside the steaming conservatory window.

As Miles calls the governess "a damned hussy; a damned, dirty-minded hag," the camera shows a laughing Peter Quint in close-up. Miles's laughter conjoins with Quint's silent visual laughter. Then, in a surprise move, Miles hurls the turtle through a pane of glass in the conservatory and flees outside (fig. 4), then falls to the ground, telling the governess, "Forgive me." The governess soothes him: "It wasn't you. That voice. Those words." She adds, "Say his name, and it will all be over." Miles, breaking away, insists that the governess is insane. In a series of close-ups, Miles's face is seen as strained, pressured, and perspiring.

Then it comes, that extraordinary shift in point of view, away from Miles and the governess to high up and beyond the ring of soldier statues lining the circular enclosure of the garden. Peter Quint has replaced one of them and raises his hands in a kind of perverse benediction, the camera *behind* him and encompassing Miles and the governess.[3] This is the last in the series of hand images. Again, hands are extended, and again they hold nothing. In close-up Miles cries out, "Quint! Peter Quint—where, you devil!?" The camera shows Miles searching futilely for Quint, whose extended hand, fingers spread wide, occupies the space between Miles and the governess. Then Miles collapses to the ground, the camera high up and looking down, now showing not Quint but the head of the statue returned. The governess, holding Miles in her arms, says, "He's gone, Miles. You're free. I have you. He's lost you forever." Unaware of the irony of her words (to be free and yet to be had), the governess continues to hold him. The film thus provides, at the penultimate moment, an objective shot beyond all debate. Quint is real.

(Earlier in the film, during the governess's confrontation with Flora about Miss Jessel at the lake, the governess asks her doomed question, "And where, my pet, is Miss Jessel?" In a camera shot from behind the governess and Flora, Miss Jessel appears. But this shot is deliberately ambiguous. It appears to be an objective shot for both the governess and Flora, suggesting that both see the ghost, for the camera doesn't frame the shot so that Flora is excluded. But it also appears to be subjective for the governess alone, since she, in dominating the scene, may be said to be imposing her vision.)

The definitively objective shot near the end of the film recalls the definitively *subjective* world of the governess in chapter 22, near the end of the novella. There the governess is alone with Miles. The text reads as follows: "Our meal was of the briefest—mine a vain pretence, and I had the things immediately removed. While this was done Miles stood again with his hands in his little pockets and his back to me—stood and looked out of the wide window through which, that other day, I had seen what pulled me up. We continued silent while the maid was with us—as silent, it whimsically occurred to me, as some young couple who, on their wedding-journey, at the inn, feel shy in the presence of the waiter. He turned round only when the waiter had left us. 'Well—so we're alone!'" (109). Eventually, readers come to recognize that the maid of reality has turned into the waiter of the governess's fantasy honeymoon with Miles, seemingly definitively establishing that for what follows—the death of Miles—the governess is truly culpable.

In the film, Miss Giddens, holding Miles, realizes that he is dead. The camera shows her caressing his body followed by an extreme close-up of his face, his eyes wide open and seen from slightly below. Birds twitter. The governess, loudly moaning, "Miles! Miles!" kisses Miles full on the lips, reproducing his earlier kiss of her. The full-lips kiss then so startled the governess that her face twitched. Here she follows the kiss by lifting her head backwards and to the rear and left of screen while the words "The End" appear in the same font as the opening credits, a precise though jagged-edged script.

The definitive shot of Quint, the camera *behind* him and looking down at the governess and Miles so that he is objectively real to the audience, nevertheless has to play against the previous, undermining images that permeated the film—and the following shot of the statue's head in place of Quint. Even so, while the audience struggles against refusing to believe its own (the camera's) eyes, there arises a tantalizing question: the last image of Quint as an objective shot causes one to wonder if the ghosts are real and the governess now possessed. Did Quint's spirit pass through Miles through the governess's kiss and into her? The ironic juxtaposition of "You're free now. I have you" replays the theme of possession. If the dead Miles is free of Quint, then is the living governess possessed by Quint? Or by Miles—since it is the newly dead in this film who appear to possess the living? We will never know. More so since the film is circular. The darkly dressed governess to the left of the screen, against a black background, having just embraced the dead Miles, becomes the figure present at the opening credits, also darkly dressed and against a black background. Her extending hands, expressing longing and desire but clasping nothing now, next clasp each other in a kind of prayer. These shots are also accompanied by the twittering and chirping of birds. The film, then, is a never-ending nightmare, with the governess forever dissolving into a replay of her early interview with the uncle. If one tries to decipher this event, one duplicates the situation following one's reading of the passage about the "maid/waiter" in "The Turn of the Screw": the passage is a definitively subjective one *where it occurs;* it is not definitive for the work as a whole.

The circularity of *The Innocents,* ending where it begins, reminds us that the film starts even earlier than that. There is a pre-credit sequence of a totally black screen, and on the soundtrack the voice that is later identified as *seeming* to belong to Flora (since the film never shows her as actually singing these words but humming them, the singer could easily be Miss Jessel in her possession of Flora). The lyrics of the song, written by Paul Dehn, certainly seem more appropriate to Miss Jessel than to Flora, as heard (or misheard) on the soundtrack:

> We wait, my love and I
> Beneath a weeping willow.
> But now alone I lie
> And weep beside the tree
> Singing, "Awaiting, awaiting,"
> By the tree that weeps with me.
> Singing, "Awaiting, awaiting,
> 'Till my lover returns to me."
> We wait, my love and I,
> Beneath a weeping willow.
> But now alone I lie.
> A willow I die,
> A willow I die.

The association of willow and dying recalls the more famous figure of Ophelia, who also drowned herself in madness and grief, as Miss Jessel has done, if we accept Mrs. Grose's account in the film. She tells the governess that when Quint died, Miss Jessel grieved: "She never slept, never ate. . . . [Always] wandering, . . . sobbing. . . . Finally, she died [at Bly]." When asked what she died of, Mrs. Grose replies, as noted earlier, "You might say, [of] a broken heart." Later, however, she is more precise. As she and the governess are about to enter church, Miss Giddens asks her point-blank: "How did Miss Jessel die?" Mrs. Grose's answer: "In wickedness. She put an end to herself. She was found in the lake, drowned."

Like the empty spaces that ask to be filled between characters in the film, the film's opening invites the audience to fill in the blanks. And one blank is surely the empty screen, which, as the credits roll, begins to be filled by shots of the governess in the exact same setting as at the end of the film, where she is garbed in black (long having dropped her clothes of white, she now appears to have taken her dress cues from Miss Jessel) and shown through a closeup of hands outstretched, then clasped, as Georges Auric's music (flute and strings) intensifies. The next shot is of a woman's face in close-up and seemingly in ecstasy.[4] Then her hands clasp in prayer, followed by a three-quarter shot of her face showing anxiety: "I want to save the children, not destroy them," she declares, adding that "they need affection, love."

A soft focus, slow dissolve to a scene of the governess with the uncle follows. A large empty space is seen to the right of the governess (beginning the pattern of "gulfs" to be occupied by whatever one imagines). The uncle states that he has "no room for [his niece and nephew] either mentally or emotionally." He advances to the window and gazes out (the beginning of an additional pattern, this time of seeing, or not seeing, through windows). Another space opens between the governess and the uncle. The positioning of the camera is low-angle, giving a view looking up at the uncle, as he speaks of the children's needing someone to love and to whom they can belong, words that the governess is heard uttering during the credit sequence. If the words she utters *prior* to the credit sequence then turn up as part of the uncle's dialogue in a later sequence, it may be argued that the governess is editing the film, that the governess, in choosing the words, dissolving into the images of the tale, and repeating them endlessly, is controlling and, hence, corrupting the "text" of the movie.[5]

Similarly, the text of the governess's manuscript in the Henry James tale may also be said to be corrupt, on the basis of three central pieces of evidence. First, the narrator of the prologue, before declaring that "Douglas . . . had begun to read [the text of the governess's story] with a fine clearness that was like a rendering to the ear of the beauty of his author's hand" (27), we are informed of an important fact: the tale of the governess that we get is *not* the manuscript that was read "to our hushed little circle" (25). Nor are we auditors to Douglas's reading. Instead, the prologue's narrator tells us, "Let me say here distinctly, to have done with it, that this narrative, from an exact transcript of my own made much later, is what I shall presently give" (24–25).

Moreover, in the act of transcribing, a handwritten manuscript contained within "the faded red cover of a thin old-fashioned gilt-edged album" (27) somehow became a rather thick printed book. In addition to its faded cover, the original manuscript itself was "in old faded ink" (23). Yet the thick, not thin, book has no notations to indicate where the "faded" ink was replaced by legible script. Finally, the manuscript that also had no "title" (27) was given one, "The Turn of the Screw." It may be argued that the narrator of the prologue supplied not only this title, but also filled in the blanks, as the film invites its audience to do—to the extent that whatever was "faded" in the original manuscript became clear in the copy, and whatever was "thin" in the original became more substantial in the transcript, whose "exact" nature is now suspect.

If the governess's original tale is a composite ("corrupt") text, that might explain a notable contradiction in the printed account. In describing Quint as "looking like an actor" (47), the governess adds, "I've never seen one, but so I suppose them" (47). Presumably, in never having "seen one," the governess also was never in a theater to see a play. Yet in describing the change of seasons at Bly, she uses a striking, vivid image that only a playgoer could produce, a playgoer like the sophisticated London narrator of the tale's prologue: "The summer had turned, the summer had gone; the autumn had dropped upon Bly and had blown out half our lights. The place, with its grey sky and withered garlands, its bared spaces and scattered dead leaves, was like a theatre after the performance—all strewn with crumpled playbills" (77).

Both James's "The Turn of the Screw" and Jack Clayton's *The Innocents* grip their conscientious readers and viewers, individuals accustomed by inclination and training, by education and humanism, to seek the truth—what the governess in the film requires of Mrs. Grose when the latter asked what she was to tell the uncle upon her arrival in London with Flora. Yet these very same individuals are to be left unfulfilled. They are not to know. They are only to be possessed—to return again and again to the intractable mystery that is "The Turn of the Screw." At the moment that they feel they can echo the governess and Miss Giddens, that they understand these works, can nail them down and confidently declare, "*I* have you," they soon discover "what it truly was that [they] held" (116).

For it is "the stor[ies that] held *us*."

## Notes

1. See Beidler's edition of *The Turn of the Screw* (*TS*) for representative essays.
2. Recchia, citing the script of the film, asserts that Clayton is "relying primarily on mirror shots to suggest the possibility that Miss Giddens is superimposing Quint's features on her own reflection in the French windows" (31). He also cites McDougal for corroboration (151–52).
3. Chase also discusses the tear of the former governess on the slate in the school-room, arguing that "this cannot be explained by imagination (as can the ghosts' previous appearances and the governess's perceptions of the children's corruption)" (70).
4. Chase views the governess's face as "rapt, tormented" (70).
5. Recchia argues that, "in effect, we cannot be sure if we are seeing Miss Giddens's recollection of the events at Bly or the film's objective reconstruction of those events" (30). Palmer, too, comments on this construction, calling it a "flashback," and asking, is it "to indicate a kind of subjective retelling of the story . . . from her point of view? Is she to be our protagonist-narrator? Or is the flashback merely a conventional structural device of the director?" (210).

## Works Cited

Aldrich, C. Knight. "Another Twist to *The Turn of the Screw*." *Modern Fiction Studies* 13 (1967): 167–78.

Beidler, Peter G. *Ghosts, Demons, and Henry James: "The Turn of the Screw" at the Turn of the Century.* Columbia: U of Missouri P, 1989.

Chase, Donald. "Romancing the Stones: Jack Clayton's *The Innocents*." *Film Comment* Jan.–Feb. 1998.

Goddard, Harold C. "A Pre-Freudian Reading of *The Turn of the Screw*." *Nineteenth-Century Fiction* 12 (1957): 1–36.

James, Henry. *The Art of the Novel: Critical Prefaces.* Ed. R.P. Blackmur. New York: Scribner's, 1934.

———. *The Letters of Henry James.* Ed. Percy Lubbock. Vol. 1. New York: Scribner's, 1920.

———. *The Notebooks of Henry James.* Ed. F. O. Matthiessen and Kenneth B. Murdock. New York: Oxford, 1947.

———. *The Turn of the Screw.* Ed. Peter G. Beidler. Boston: Bedford/St. Martin's, 1995.

Mazzella, Anthony J. "An Answer to the Mystery of *The Turn of the Screw*." *Studies in Short Fiction* 17 (1980): 327–33.

McDougal, Stuart Y. *Made into Movies: From Literature to Film.* New York: Holt, 1985.

Palmer, James W. "Cinematic Ambiguity: James's *The Turn of the Screw* and Jack Clayton's *The Innocents*." *Literature Film Quarterly* 5 (1977): 198–215.

Recchia, Edward. "An Eye for an I: Adapting Henry James's *The Turn of the Screw* to the Screen." *Literature Film Quarterly* 15 (1987): 28–35.

Solomon, Eric. "The Return of the Screw." *The Norton Critical Edition of "The Turn of the Screw."* Ed. Robert Kimbrough. New York: Norton, 1966. 237–45.

Wilson, Edmund. "The Ambiguity of Henry James." *A Casebook on Henry James's "The Turn of The Screw."* 2d ed. New York: Crowell, 1969. 115–52.

## *Filmography*

*The Innocents.* Dir. Jack Clayton. Writ. William Archibald and Truman Capote. Perf. Deborah Kerr, Peter Wyngarde, Megs Jenkins, Michael Redgrave, Pamela Franklin, Martin Stephens, Clytie Jessop. Twentieth-Century Fox, 1961.

# Reexamining Bogdanovich's *Daisy Miller*

*Peggy McCormack*

On May 22, 1974, Peter Bogdanovich premiered his fifth film, *Daisy Miller*, at the Orson Welles Cinema in Cambridge, Massachusetts. According to Michael Sragow's *New York Times* review, the Cambridge audience responded well to the film and welcomed the appearances at the premiere of the thirty-five-year-old director and the twenty-four-year-old star of the film, Cybill Shepherd. However, published reviews of the film were decidedly mixed and often conflicting. Sragow, even as he acknowledged the audience's positive response to the film's world premiere, struggled fiercely to discount it. Overall, while there were good, even glowing, reviews, the popular and critical perception that took hold in 1974, and that has now become an accepted "fact" of the history of Hollywood cinema, was that *Daisy Miller* was a failure. Critics have primarily blamed the film's young star, Shepherd, for its lack of success, claiming she was insufficiently trained as an actor to carry out the role of Daisy (Biskind 212–13).

## *Bogdanovich and Shepherd in the 1970s: A Costly "Youthful Indiscretion"*

Bogdanovich made the film because, in his own words, Cybill Shepherd *was* Daisy: "on re-reading the book, it seemed to me that Henry James had Cybill in mind when he wrote it. I thought, if James had gone to all the trouble to write this story for Cybill, the least I could do was to film it" (qtd. in Alpert 44). However, Bogdanovich's assessment of Shepherd's unique fit for the role of Daisy was not entirely neutral. In his second picture, *The Last Picture Show* (1971), he had cast Shepherd, a prominent model with no previous acting experience, as Jacy, a rich, shallow, manipulative heartbreaker. During the filming the two fell in love and began living together in a very public way, making no attempt to hide their relationship. As a consequence of Bogdanovich's affair with Shepherd, he eventually divorced his wife, Polly Platt, who had also been the set designer for his films.

Bogdanovich's casting of Shepherd as an unfeeling heartbreaker in *The Last Picture Show* proved to be a powerfully difficult image for Shepherd to overcome. This was, in large part, due to Bogdanovich and Shepherd's eagerness to seek the spotlight, appearing on the *Tonight Show* and on the covers of popular magazines such as *People* (Biskind 209). In their interviews, the couple made a point of bringing up their love affair as well as their decision *not* to marry. The title of the 1974 *People* interview was "Peter and Cybill: 'Who Needs Marriage?'" (19). Thus, throughout the early 1970s, public perception of Shepherd was that she *was* Jacy in relation to Bogdanovich's ten-year marriage. This perception was reinforced by the Jacy-like characters—cool, uncaring, sexual manipulators—that Shepherd continued to play after *The Last Picture Show*, as in, for example, *The Heartbreak Kid* (1972).

I suggest that in 1974, then, when Bogdanovich cast Shepherd as Daisy Miller, audiences reacted not to the actual quality of her performance as James's ingenuous, young American girl, but rather to the perception created by the couple's own public performances as reckless, star-cast lovers. In particular, I would argue that the public and the members of the film industry recoiled at Shepherd's ill-considered outspokenness during this period and at her apparent casual indifference to the psychological price paid by Bogdanovich's wife and two children when her affair ended Bogdanovich's marriage.

An examination of public perceptions of Shepherd and Bogdanovich in the early 1970s reveals why, when *Daisy Miller* debuted, there was little chance that the movie would be judged on its actual merits. Not only did the movie itself go down in America's cultural perception as a failure; it also initiated both Bogdanovich's and Shepherd's downward career spirals.[1] Despite the financial and critical success of Bogdanovich's four previous films, *Targets* (1968), *The Last Picture Show* (1971), *What's Up, Doc?* (1972), and *Paper Moon* (1973), his status as a golden boy suddenly disappeared and, as of today, remains diminished (Biskind 208–11). Consider the entry for Bogdanovich in the 1972 edition of *Current Biography,* in which the director's abilities are assessed in rare praise: "*The Last Picture Show,* his second feature film, which premiered at the 1971 New York Film Festival, marked Bogdanovich as one of the most gifted, sure handed American directors of his generation" (41). From the same entry come the following praise and predictions of a brilliant career: "In his review for *Newsweek* (October 12, 1971) Paul D. Zimmerman declared in no uncertain terms: '*The Last Picture Show* is a masterpiece. It is not merely the best American movie of a rather dreary year; it is the most impressive work by a young American director since *Citizen Kane*.' He acknowledged imperfections, but felt that the minor flaws of a genuine talent still developing were far outmatched by what he called 'an avalanche of positive achievements.' Other reviewers hailed it as a work of artistic unity and as 'a contemporary American classic'" (43). Compare these assessments to the judgment of Bogdanovich in a 1997 film dictionary: "*Daisy Miller*, a period vehicle for Shepherd more redolent of Henry King than Henry James, inaugurated Bogdanovich's decline" (Baxter 96). The comparison is unfortunate for Bogdanovich, since Henry King, a Hollywood director in the 1940s and 1950s, never achieved more than second-rank stature for such films as *David and Bathsheba*, *Gunfighter*, *Jesse James*, and *Love Is a Many Splendored Thing*.

I argue that audiences in the summer of 1974 reacted negatively to *Daisy Miller* precisely because of the public way in which Bogdanovich flaunted his personal lifestyle change. Traditional Americans, including film critics—albeit perhaps unconsciously—made the young director into a scapegoat for their more widespread frustration with "the times." In 1974, American audiences were still recovering from the moral and political shocks of the late 1960s and early 1970s.[2] Clearly, Bogdanovich did not expect the public and the critics to oppose his decision to cast his girlfriend as a character who turns out to have been "innocent," after all—"innocent" being an encoded term for virgin. His deliberate cultivation of publicity about his personal life obviously backfired when audiences refused to accept Shepherd as the "poet[ical]" idealization of the American Girl James describes in the preface to the New York Edition of "Daisy Miller" (*DM*).[3]

My experience with teaching the James novella alongside Bogdanovich's film entirely contradicts the criticisms found in most of the negative reviews published when the film was released. In fact, the film works so well with the novella that I am necessarily drawn to reexamine the context in which it debuted. In particular, I am interested in studying three issues. First, the cultural baggage Bogdanovich and Shepherd brought to the film's release that caused many contemporary reviewers to dismiss the work as pretentious and to brand Shepherd as insufficiently talented to make audiences view her as an innocent girl, not as the director's mistress. Second, the film's legacy, that is, why it remains a "fact" of the history of American cinema that *Daisy Miller* is a bad film. And third, the elements that, for my students and me, make the film a success and prove that Bogdanovich successfully evokes Henry James's idealized Daisy in Shepherd's performance.

The financial context in which Bogdanovich made this film is worth noting. The film was financed and produced by the Directors' Company, a short-lived triumvirate of Bogdanovich, William Friedkin, and Francis Ford Coppola. All three were riding the crest of success in the early 1970s. Friedkin made *The French Connection* in 1971 and *The Exorcist* in 1973; both did phenomenally well critically and commercially. Coppola was even more successful at that juncture of his career. Each of his first two *Godfather* pictures, in 1972 and 1974, swept the Academy Awards and astonished the industry with their profits. The theory behind this short-lived Directors' production company (1972–1974) was that Paramount would finance them. The three directors agreed to a ceiling of $3 million for each picture they would make. In exchange, each director would choose his own pictures and have complete control over every aspect of the film's production. The directors would split the proceeds equally from the films they made (Biskind 212–14).

It is very possible that only under the umbrella of a company giving each director complete freedom to choose the movies he made could Bogdanovich have financed a film such as *Daisy Miller,* which was not likely to garner huge profits because of its literary subject matter. However, commercial considerations were completely separate from the problems the film incurred because of the image difficulties of its director and star. In an interview with Biskind, Director's Company partner William Friedkin recalls that when he first heard about the project, he was convinced that Shepherd "had no discernible acting ability whatsoever" (212). Sure that the picture would be a commercial failure, Friedkin reminded Bogdanovich that the directors had agreed not "to take projects like [*Daisy Miller*], that no other studio would make with us and dump them into this company" (Biskind 212).[4]

According to Peter Biskind's *Easy Riders, Raging Bulls: How the Sex-Drugs-and-Rock 'n' Roll Generation Saved Hollywood,* a popular rather than academic study of the rebellious and self-indulgent young directors of the 1970s, both Coppola and Bogdanovich took entirely too seriously the praise generated by their initial film successes. In particular, Bogdanovich alienated the industry, as well as the public, with two fatal gestures. The first was flaunting Shepherd as a sexual trophy and repeatedly describing her as his Eliza Doolittle:

> When Peter talked about Cybill, he patronized her. "Cybill started out as a whim, an instinct, a little voice in my ear that I listened to. I had an itch, and I scratched it. . . . She's very malleable. You can bend her in any direction. She does what she's told." It became impossible to pick up a magazine without seeing the two of them beaming toothily from the cover, winsome and smug, as if to say, We're Peter and Cybill, and you're not. Cary Grant told him to shut up. "Will you stop telling people you're in love. Stop telling people you're happy."

"Why?"

"Because they're not in love and they're not happy. And they don't want to hear it."

"But Cary, I thought all the world loves a lover."

"Don't you believe it. It isn't true. Just remember one thing, Peter, people do not like beautiful people."

Adds Bogdanovich, now chastened, "And so, an enormous amount of envy and jealousy and shit hit the fan." (Biskind 209)

The second, and I would argue more damning, flaw for which Bogdanovich has still not been forgiven was his arrogance as the self-appointed intellectual historian of American cinema:

> Unlike the other new Hollywood directors, Bogdanovich was very much at home in Hollywood, very much embraced his celebrity. He was riding high, busy—although he was too intoxicated with himself to realize it—sowing the seeds of his own destruction. Almost everyone who met him detested him. He was an inveterate name dropper. When he opened his mouth, it was "Orson" this and "Howard" that, "John" something else. He liked to parade his erudition, and had a bad habit of lecturing instead of conversing. As one junior executive put it, "The first time I met him, it was as if I were in the presence of God. I had to go up to him and introduce myself, and he wasn't about to reciprocate and say his name, because that might indicate that there was some doubt as to who he was." . . . When they were not sitting for photographers, the couple haunted the talk shows, appearing regularly on Johnny Carson, for whom Peter became an occasional replacement. He had become a bit of dandy, wearing candy-striped shirts with white collars, occasionally improved by an ascot. . . . Preening like a peacock, he told the *New York Times* in words that would come back to haunt him, "I don't judge myself on the basis of my contemporaries. . . . I judge myself against the directors I admire—Hawks, Lubitsch, Buster Keaton, Welles, Ford, Renoir, Hitchcock." Modesty required a demurral: "I certainly don't think I'm anywhere near as good as they are, but," he couldn't help adding, "I think I'm pretty good." (Biskind 209)

The industry's hostility toward Bogdanovich's self-appointment as America's film historian accounts in part for the director's continuing inability to get good scripts and make profitable films. Of course, Biskind's thesis, encapsulated in his title, requires that he initially show the major directors of the 1970s in the worst possible light—as bad boys who flaunted all the rules but nonetheless made movies that were so commercially successful and technically innovative that those who matured past their excessive lifestyles during the 1970s have now become Hollywood's ruling figures. However, his judgment of Bogdanovich as bloated by early critical praise and disliked for his pretensions is corroborated by an examination of the reviews of *Daisy Miller* upon its release. Biskind's assessment that Bogdanovich dug his own grave with his arrogant behavior recurs in the negative reviews, as if these critics, offended by Bogdanovich's airs, were eager to damn him—whether his films were good or not—as soon as one fared poorly at the box office.

Stanley Kauffmann, the formidable film critic for the *New Republic*, sets the tone for the negative but less than substantive reviews of the film. He acerbically comments, "Poor Bogdanovich, surfing along on a golden wave (the last splash was *Paper Moon*) but still poor in any artistic sense because all he knows is what he has seen in films" (20). Kauffmann derogates Bogdanovich as "all right when he can imitate film precedents," but once he "gets outside sheerly cinematic frames of reference he is utterly lost—which is to say, when he has to deal with James as James. "Daisy Miller" simply doesn't exist without recognizable and effective class distinctions, and here Bogdanovich hasn't a clue or he would not have cast the picture as he did" (20). Interestingly, Kauffmann's criticisms of Bogdanovich—that all he knows how to do is to imitate earlier works of art, that he lacks the great artist's ability to convey a sense of lived life, and that he cannot create a work that gives the audience the wisdom to live life better—were the same criticisms repeatedly leveled at James, particularly in reviews of his earlier works.[5]

Kauffmann, however, spends the majority of his review displaying *his* erudition by drawing irrelevant comparisons between the novella and the very little known play of *Daisy Miller*, which, like James's other dramas, fared poorly. Kauffmann fails to validate his assertion that Bogdanovich "hasn't a clue" about Jamesian class distinctions and is, therefore, "utterly lost" in adapting James's novella (20). Instead, again in a rather self-serving demonstration of his knowledge, Kauffmann offers a list of sequences in *Daisy Miller* that are either homages to or thefts of earlier filmmakers' works, depending upon one's point of view (20).[6] He also notes minor changes in the film's screenplay to which he objects. For example, Kauffmann laments that his favorite line from the novella, Mrs. Costello's deploring of the fact that the Millers' valet, Eugenio, "smokes" (*DM* 24) in the presence of the socially ignorant Miller family, has been dumbed down to the phrase "smokes in their faces," so that less enlightened viewers of the film understand this social error. A further opportunity to demonstrate his sophistication in reviewing Bogdanovich's literary adaptation occurs when he notes that Daisy is buried not, as in the novella, in Rome's "little Protestant cemetery" (91) but rather in "some rolling green field," thus losing "a highly specific touch of Rome" (Kauffmann 20).

These remarks serve more to display Kauffmann's knowledge than to advance a convincing argument that the film is a failure. Other than his unproven assertion that Bogdanovich is at sea in interpreting James's text, Kauffmann's chief objection to the movie is that not a single character is cast correctly, except for Randolph, played by James McMurtry, son of the novelist who wrote the book from which Bogdanovich adapted his second film and first big success, *The Last Picture Show*. Note Kauffmann's acidic, highly subjective remarks; for example, "Mrs. Walker, supposedly a social arbiter, is played by Eileen Brennan, who was a Texas waitress in *The Last Picture Show* and still is" (20). Ironically, Kauffmann's idea of bad casting turns out to be grounds for other reviewers' praise. For example, Jack Kroll in *Newsweek*, as well as Vincent Canby and Nora Sayre in the *New York Times*, praised precisely the same casting and performances that Kauffmann criticizes. Kroll describes Barry Brown (Winterbourne) as "perfect," Cloris Leachman (Mrs. Miller) as "beautifully vacuous," Mildred Natwick (Mrs. Costello) as "superbly snobbish," and Shepherd [Daisy] as "incandescent," "affecting," and "brilliant" (83, 81). Canby declares that "Bogdanovich's casting is, as always, nearly flawless" (5). Thus, Kauffmann's negative assessment of the cast is not always shared by other noted reviewers.

However, other reviewers do often agree with Kauffmann's skepticism about Bogdanovich's skill as a director. Echoing Kauffmann's statement that Bogdanovich can only imitate but not create great art is Jonathan Baumbach, who pays the director either a lukewarm compliment or a modest insult regarding his use of earlier directors' trademarks: "Bogdanovich's nostalgia—his mode and essential theme—has to do with American . . . filmmakers (Hawks, Ford, Welles, etc.) to whom he pays homage by doing serious imitations and variations on their best work. Bogdanovich has always seemed . . . a premature old master, his vision a pastiche, meticulously wrought and controlled, of great moments from classic American movies. His films have been calculatedly moving and funny, avoiding small mistakes at the expense of spontaneity, as if a talented archivist were redoing pieces of film history in case the originals were destroyed by fire" (450).

Baumbach then notes that, having recently been "Gatsbyized" (Jack Clayton's film of *The Great Gatsby* with Robert Redford and Mia Farrow had premiered several weeks before *Daisy Miller*), he expected he "could live a full life without sitting through another respectful literary adaptation" (450–51). So also, Colin Westerbeck notes that "Peter Bogdanovich is turning out to be, disappointingly, a master of atmospheres and periods," a minor talent "not to be confused with movie direction" (361). These critics' assessments in 1974 of Bogdanovich as a failed artist are repeated in Biskind's 1998 assertion that ever since the making of *Daisy Miller,* reviewers have labeled the director as too much the scholar, wanting in true ability.

However, in what is hard to see as anything but old-fashioned 1970s sexism, Shepherd engenders far more hostility in the negative reviews than does Bogdanovich. Some are no more than mild criticisms, such as Baumbach's comment: "Bogdanovich, who relies heavily on performance in his other films, *transcends the limitation of Cybill Shepherd's Daisy* through image . . . mak[ing] Shepherd's performance seem richer in retrospect than it does from scene to scene" (451; emphasis mine). These milder complaints also include the inevitable cliche about beautiful women, whom critics equate with looks alone. Urjo Kareda admits, "I could not honestly tell whether or not Cybill Shepherd could act. . . . I could with no confidence decide whether I had been responding to Cybill Shepherd's characterization of Daisy's gaucheness or simply to Cybill Shepherd's own gaucheness as an actress. . . . That pause for doubt about her as an actress, and my inability to determine whether she acted Daisy Miller or happened upon Daisy Miller [leaves] us not knowing whether she is in control of her performance, whether she knows what she's doing" (1).

The sharpest barbs directed at Shepherd appear to be reactions against precisely those elements of her performance that other critics find convincing. Their hostility suggests to me that these critics' comments are overdetermined responses to Shepherd and Bogdanovich as momentary but nonetheless notorious cultural icons of the 1970s. Jay Cocks's opinion serves to stand for many others that are equally vicious:

> Among all the flaws in this movie—the numbing literalness, the flagrant absence of subtlety—nothing is quite so wrong as Cybill Shepherd. Bogdanovich installed her in the lead as if she were some sort of electrical appliance being plugged into an outlet. Shepherd has a home-fried hauteur good enough for the one-dimensional roles she played in *The Last Picture Show* and *The Heartbreak Kid* (she used to be a fashion model, after all), but she has no resources as an actress. She runs short of breath in the middle of lines and gives no sign of understanding the words she blurts out in little hiccups. Daisy is supposed to be un-

spoiled, cunning and callow—and blithely attractive. *Shepherd*
*projects instead a taunting sexual hostility that turns Daisy into a little*
*bitch goddess on a pedestal.* (56–57; emphasis mine)

Cocks's last sentence particularly exemplifies my argument that neither Shepherd nor the film was judged dispassionately by critics who were
offended, whether they acknowledged it or not, by Bogdanovich and
Shepherd's public affair, by Bogdanovich's overt Pygmalion attitude toward
her, and by his absolute judgments about Hollywood cinema. In an interview eleven years later, Bogdanovich confirms that "Cybill took the heat for
the film and our relationship. It was unfair. People like to put her down"
(qtd. in "Shepherd, Cybill" 513). According to Biskind's account of the
1970s, Cocks was, if not a friend of Bogdanovich, certainly an acquaintance
whose vitriol may well epitomize the "envy" and "jealousy" that Bogdanovich
argues prompted the negative responses to Shepherd. Biskind refers to Cocks
during these years as the "ubiquitous Jay Cocks" (240), and the eight references to Cocks in Biskind's book portray him as a minor Hollywood figure
who sought the companionship of well-established directors, producers,
and actors for any reflected glory that might come his way (487).

Interestingly, in a 1975 column in the *New Yorker,* Pauline Kael also
argued that the combination of Bogdanovich's patronizing of Shepherd
and her own outspokenness, her initial lack of acting training, and her
physicality (both her size—she is tall, very broad-shouldered, and strong—
and her cool, blonde looks) occasioned "vindictive" male responses: "Men
wanted to get at her to wipe the jeering smile off her face. Bogdanovich
engendered these ambivalent feelings toward her: [Shepherd appeared to
be] an overgrown baton twirler, she was a projection of men's resentment of
the bitch-princesses they're drawn to. . . . She's an object, not a star; people
don't feel for her and don't identify with her" (qtd. in "Shepherd, Cybill"
513).

While criticism's usual business is to debate meaning and thereby
proliferate itself, the intensity of these judgments, ostensibly about *Daisy*
*Miller,* suggests that a widely accepted piece of conventional wisdom was at
work in contemporary reviews of the film: however simply put, Cary Grant's
remark to Bogdanovich that "people do not like beautiful people" hits home
here as a telling motivation for the extremity of the negative reviews (Biskind
209). Bogdanovich's pretensions and Shepherd's unwillingness to apologize for their lifestyle made them easy targets for free-floating hostility from
the public and from critics. The single most vicious review appeared in a
*New York Times* "Second Opinion" column by Michael Sragow on June 30,
1974. His excoriating reaction to both director and star was prompted by

Vincent Canby's positive review in the *Times* two weeks earlier. Sragow risks a stroke in his need to discredit the couple. About Bogdanovich, he fulminates the following criticism of the man, his posturing, and his movies:

> Bogdanovich may be the most shameless Hollywood celebrity since exhibitionism became a national life-style. Every piece he writes as a "film critic" is peppered with forced buddy-buddy anecdotes and reverential references about film buff favorites like John Ford and Howard Hawks. His own interviews carry ceaseless self-endorsements of his obsessive moviegoing, simple-minded art-for-art's sake stance, and grand enduring passion for Miss Shepherd. Of course, the man's films are the most damaging evidence against him as an artist: they display nothing but his overpowering ambition to make old-fashioned movies. . . . *Daisy Miller* is Bogdanovich's latest and most ambitious attempt to break into the cultural big leagues. The director laid the framework for his assault with arrogant self-serving remarks, like "Henry James wrote his book for Cybill Shepherd." (1)

Sragow obviously attended the world premiere of the film at the Orson Welles Cinema in Cambridge, for he is forced to find reasons to explain away the success of the opening night: "James's fans in attendance were too entranced by the Master's voice to scurry out aghast at [the film's] vulgarization [of James's novella]; film people were too excited from catching sight of a preview print to admit boredom" (1). Not only is he forced to read the minds of the audience to discount their openly positive reception, Sragow also criticizes Bogdanovich for the excellence of his production staff. He derogates Bogdanovich's use of respected British novelist Frederic Raphael as screenwriter and Bertolucci's "fancy photographer, Vittorio Storao, to mind his lights and colors" (1).

Pertinent to Sragow's loathing, which overburdens every sentence of his essay, is the information in his byline, which identifies him as "film critic for the Harvard *Crimson* until his college graduation in 1973. He is now a freelance writer living in Boston" (1). At the time of the movie's release, then, Sragow was a twenty-something Harvard grad who had spent a year since graduation apparently not setting the world of film criticism on fire. He then witnessed Bogdanovich and Shepherd's success at the opening—occurring, maddeningly enough, on his home turf. Here again, the couple, as a cultural icon, engender hostility, which is then displaced onto the film. In addition, the layout for Sragow's column includes a cover pic-

Figure 5. Cybill Shepherd as Daisy Miller, from the cover picture on the video box of *Daisy Miller.* Film distributed by Viacom.

Figure 6. Cybill Shepherd (in a pose very similar to the movie poster photograph) with Peter Bogdonavich in a picture that accompanied an interview with the couple in *People Magazine*. Published with permission of *People Magazine*.

ture of the couple, which epitomizes their objectionability to Sragow. In language that Biskind's book will later echo, Sragow delineates a cultural perception of Bogdanovich and Shepherd as arrogant, condescending, self-deluded, self-congratulatory, and vain—ultimately he is only a minor talent and she is a big, untalented blonde. Furthermore, in the summer of 1974, as the country watched Watergate and other serious political, economic, and social events unfolding, many reviewers and most audiences were clearly not in the mood for a film that was the second, reverent literary adaptation released within a month. The times were simply not amenable to a story from a novelist considered stuffy and elitist, a film from a director whose moviemaking seemed more imitative than original, and a performance from his young, outspoken girlfriend whom he paraded under the public's nose.

Sragow clearly believed his argument against the movie, the director, and the actress was strengthened by his inclusion of the magazine cover of the couple. His use of the photograph supports my hypothesis that *Daisy Miller* failed not because of inherent artistic weaknesses but rather because Bogdanovich's apparent need to publicize his relationship with Shepherd and to promote his reputation as a film historian made him a target of critics and of the public. In looking at two pictures—the movie poster, now turned into video tape box cover for the film (fig. 5) and the magazine cover (fig. 6)—it would be very hard *not* to conflate Cybill Shepherd with Daisy Miller.[7] Shepherd's poses are nearly identical. In each, she faces the camera, her body at a three-quarter turn; her line of vision is up and back toward the audience, and her eyes are rather seductively heavy-lidded. In the magazine cover, she assumes this pose in a two-shot with Bogdanovich behind her, smiling "toothily," as Biskind puts it (209), while she conveys an enigmatic, seductive look. The movie poster portrays her in the same pose, with the same line of vision and smile, only here she is dressed in her white muslin outfit from the opening scene, her white parasol resting on her shoulder, and the title, *Daisy Miller,* appears in captions at her shoulder level. In other words, she *is* Daisy Miller. The only difference between the two photographs, other than costuming, is that the invisible presence who made her *into* Daisy Miller in the film poster (director-lover Bogdanovich) is shown behind her on the magazine cover, smiling happily, as if to suggest that he were her creator.

*Daisy Miller* made a respectable but only modest profit—nothing like the money coming into the Directors' Company from Coppola's two *Godfathers* and Friedkin's *French Connection* and *The Exorcist*—but more significantly, the film positioned Bogdanovich for his irrevocable fall from investors' grace. The list of movies he has made since *Daisy Miller* is a cautionary tale about talent, discretion, and public reaction: *At Long Last Love; Diaries, Notes, and Sketches—Volume I, Reels 1–6; Lost, Lost, Lost; Nickelodeon; Opening Night; St. Jack; They All Laughed; Mask; Illegally Yours; Hollywood Mavericks* (an obvious irony); *Texasville;* and *The Thing Called Love.* As the 1997 film dictionary indicates, Bogdanovich's career "has continued but not prospered" (96). The best film in this list is *Mask;* some, such as *At Long Last Love* and *Nickelodeon,* have achieved legendary status for the critical and public dismissal and singular lack of profits they generated. The last two, starring Shepherd, also had the effect of officially making her box office poison. After making those films she returned home to Memphis, found acting work in little theater companies throughout the country, and performed a singing act. In the mid-eighties, she reinvented herself very successfully on television, demonstrating a comic flair in *Moonlighting* and more recently in *Cybill.* Currently, Bogdanovich remains the more obscure of the former couple, but he could always reenter the arena of serious film making; Terrence Malick's recent resuscitation with *The Thin Red Line* proves that comebacks are always possible in American culture, wherein self-fashioning and re-fashioning are identifying characteristics.[8]

## Bogdanovich's Film: A Beautiful Evocation of His Daisy

I have taught this book and film in several classes; they work very well in American literature surveys and even better in a Nineteenth-Century Fiction course since, along with Martin Scorsese's *The Age of Innocence* and Michael Mann's *The Last of the Mohicans,* the film is one of the most interesting adaptations of a nineteenth-century American text. While some American students express the familiar confusion at James's language, his psychologically driven rather than plot-driven characters, and his Austen-like preciousness, many students who have not grown up in America and who shuttle between America and another culture understand the story's theme of the consequences of cultural difference.

The movie works out a number of ideas that students do not always become interested in from reading James's text alone. The most important of these is the portrayal of Daisy as an independent subject. The film visualizes effectively moments in which Daisy freely exercises existential choice, but in doing so ignorantly—without parental wisdom to assist her—reaps quick, sharp, fatal consequences. As Priscilla Walton has demonstrated persuasively, the films made from James's stories visualize woman's body as the site of imperial contestation (37–53). Men, patriarchal society, and male-invested women vie for custody of James's female protagonists: physically, psychologically, legally, and culturally. Within this context, various influences compete for Daisy's attention: the American expatriates, the fortune-hunting Europeans, the pull of home, and, in particular, the attraction of New York, where dinner parties were given in her honor and where she could be understood as "a fearful, frightful flirt" *and* "'a nice girl'" *at the same time* (*DM* 71). Cultural forces also pull at Daisy, as Continental norms of behavior conflict with her American-born, democratic way of taking in Europe and with her unformed but undeniable feminist spirit: "I've never allowed a gentleman to dictate to me, or to interfere with anything I do" (57). Finally and least forceful among these competing agents is Winterbourne himself. All of these entities exert claims upon Daisy's will. In response, Daisy "did what she liked," a line James added to the New York Edition, spoken by Giovanelli to Winterbourne at Daisy's grave site, to explain why the young Italian took her to the Coliseum at midnight (92). The film very ably engages 1990s viewers in the story's narrative dilemma—what forces win out over Daisy? is she a nice girl or not?—while the novella alone does not always do so.

Students bring to the film very different cultural assumptions about the story and its actors. They know nothing of the extratextual reasons why it fared so poorly in 1974. Apart from being surprised to see Cybill Shepherd so young—they know her as a television actress the age of their mothers—they generally have no predisposed opinions about the film or its cast. They are delighted by the cinematography; Vittorio Storao shoots the story in beautiful natural light and bathes the interior shots of bejeweled nineteenth-century drawing rooms, extravagantly luxurious European hotels, and magnificent Roman monuments in a "roseate" glow (Westerbeck 361). This lushness is also carried out to advantage in Tirelli's costume designs that, like the layers of hotel and drawing room decoration, tell us how complex and unbending this society is. As a single instance of the film's visual appeal, its opening scene begins with a remarkable tilt shot that begins on the ceiling of the hotel lobby. The camera works its way down, floor after polished, carpeted floor, to the lobby, which is being mopped by a lowly janitor; the shot neatly symbolizes the multilevel hierarchical society into which the uncomprehending Miller family has wandered.

The first appearance of Randolph encapsulates the boy's and, by extension, his family's anarchic response to this world of over-studied seriousness. Poking his head out of their room, he queries rhetorically, "Indians?" indicating his need for adventure and his boredom with Europe's tameness. He amuses himself by mixing up the shoes left out by hotel guests to be shined. The joke itself, the consequent confusion, and Randolph's restless refusal to be awed by any show of wealth or tradition prefigure Daisy perfectly. Bogdanovich makes clear use of Randolph's bored, restless energy as the reason that Winterbourne and Daisy's paths cross. Randolph ignores his ineffectual mother's remonstrance not to get into trouble, slides down the hotel banister, sardonically dismisses the hotel staff's greeting ("Bonjour, Monsieur." "Oh, *sure!*") and wanders outside, affording the director a splendid opportunity to contrast the American boy's rebellious isolation with the situation of some other children forced to sit politely through a monotonous, rigidly drilled language lesson. "*La* montana, *la* montana!" insists the teacher. In other words, the smallest of differences, such as the misuse of an article, can have serious consequences upon a nonnative's interactions with the Europeans, but like Daisy, Randolph doesn't allow anyone to "dictate" to him. James McMurtry is nicely cast here, a thin-as-a-slat, not particularly good-looking boy; his eyes convey the book's unnamed third person narrator's thought that Randolph wears "an aged expression" and snaps his verbal demands to Winterbourne in "a sharp, hard little voice . . . immature, and yet, not young" (*DM* 6). His phallic aggressiveness, expressed in stealing a walking stick and "thrust[ing it] into everything . . . [including] the trains of the ladies' dresses" (5–6), tells us he is small but lawless, overconfident and incredulous that any American would prefer to live in Europe. Bogdanovich adds a humorous interchange between Winterbourne and Randolph in which McMurtry capably displays true shock in hearing from Winterbourne that he chooses to live in Geneva. Randolph's surface cynicism drops completely, and he can only ask in hushed tones, "You live in Europe? Why; *what happened?*" To Randolph the Continent is nothing but a punishment.

Winterbourne's (and our) introduction to Shepherd as Daisy tells us much that we need to know about Daisy's character. In a sequence of exquisite exterior shots, Bogdanovich shows the luxurious hotel, its monied guests, and the extraordinary beauty of Vevey in its pristine mountain setting. Even in this exquisite setting, Daisy outshines every other element in the scene. Her beauty is enhanced by her excellent taste in clothes, which Mrs. Costello cannot explain, given her dismissal of the girl as "hopelessly vulgar" (*DM* 46). Barry Brown, as Winterbourne, immediately convinces us that he, like the viewer, is taken with her beautiful presence. Once Randolph performs his elliptical introduction of Daisy to Winterbourne ("How do you come to know her?" "I *don't* know her; she's *my sister*"), Shepherd, as Daisy, demonstrates the Millers' family trait of nonstop, monological "chatter[ing]" rather than conversing in dialogue (15). Like Vincent Canby, I find Shepherd's portrayal of Daisy on the mark:

> Daisy Miller, nee Annie P. Miller, back in Schenectady goes on and on, non-stop, in a voice trained to a register a little too high to sound completely natural. She chatters literally—the effect is that of a venetian blind rattling in the wind—about her mother's dyspepsia, about an English lady named Featherstone once met in a railway carriage, about European hotels, about New York society, about her dreadful little brother Randolph who doesn't care much about old castles like the Chateau de Chillon.
>
> Her pretty face framed by a white parasol, her fine figure set off by the freshly starched flounces on her white dress, Daisy Miller seems almost as harmless and innocent and desirable as she sounds, but something spoils the effect. It's the chin. There's just a bit too much of it. No wonder it's always stuck out—there's no way to keep it tucked in. It challenges fate in the form of European manners, though it hardly invites the disaster that eventually befalls Daisy in Rome. (5)

Over the years that I have taught this film, Shepherd has convinced students that she is right for the part of Daisy. She brings to the role her beauty, the complete comfort with which she conveys Daisy's lifelong experience of being an object of spectacle (no doubt similar to Shepherd's own experience), and her verbal habit of treating every subject equally, so that the Howard Hawks–like speed with which she delivers her lines becomes a linguistic equivalent of the Millers' inability in Europe to discriminate important from small matters, safe from unsafe expeditions, and proper but timid from mercenary suitors.

Separated in time from the contemporary responses that conflated her private life with this role, Shepherd enables my students to see Daisy's ignorant and stubborn but nonetheless well-defined "innocence." I believe this results from Bogdanovich's careful direction, which shows Daisy unchanging in her good-humored flirtatiousness, no matter where and with whom she demonstrates her much-debated coquettishness. Bogdanovich is careful, for example, to show several point-of-view shots from Winterbourne's perspective during his first talk with Daisy. These shots outside the hotel suggest that he (and we) wonder momentarily if she *is* innocent, as she unreflectingly chatters on to a man whom she's just met, whose name she doesn't even know, about "hav[ing] always had a great deal of gentlemen's society" (*DM* 16). Bogdanovich effectively dramatizes "poor Winterbourne's amuse[ment] and his perplex[ity]" (*DM* 16) as he struggles to identify a category into which he can mentally place and thereby know Miss Miller, a task he fails at entirely until after her death when he is given the necessary interpretive key by Giovanelli: "she was . . . the most innocent . . . young lady I ever met" (*DM* 92).

In Winterbourne's second meeting with Daisy, she teases him into rowing her "over to Chillon under the stars" (*DM* 35). Significantly, Shepherd's portrayal of Daisy is unchanged here when she is flirting with Winterbourne in front of her mother, just as she flirts with him alone at Chillon, in Rome in Mrs. Walker's crowded drawing room, and in the public gardens of the Pincio. Like her speech pattern, which doesn't vary, so she also carries on her flirtatiousness in an invariant manner in all kinds of situations with various people present. This argues for the innocence of her speech as well as her behavior, since she never attempts to hide what she is doing from anyone. Thus, Bogdanovich has directed Shepherd toward a constancy in Daisy's interactions with Winterbourne that is targeted toward her own end—trying to make him declare himself for her—but is also, to Daisy's mind, perfectly appropriate behavior for a young, unmarried American girl. This constancy also assures us of Daisy's innocence throughout the movie. She never behaves as if she were caught doing anything inappropriate when Winterbourne discovers her with Giovanelli in the family's hotel rooms in Rome, at the Palatine Gardens, or at the Coliseum.

Bogdanovich's direction, then, clarifies to a greater degree than the novella the question of Daisy's innocence. He uses the medium of film to show us Daisy more clearly than we see her in the novella. In that narrative, her story is filtered through the undramatized third person, omniscient narrator and more particularly through Winterbourne's limited, mystified central consciousness. Since James very deliberately never allows us inside Daisy's consciousness, we must infer her identity from Winterbourne's descriptions and interpretations of her. This very constrained point of view and, I would also suggest, the ungenerous prohibition against knowing her contribute to James's much later assessment of Daisy's character, in the preface to the New York Edition, as having a "certain" degree of "flatness" (*DM* vi). Noting his use of Isabel as the central consciousness of her own story in *Portrait* as well as his protective, third person narrator who interrupts that novel's action in chapter six to remind us to care for Isabel, we see how very little James gives us of his Daisy. In contrast, Bogdanovich uses the film as if it were a play, showing us Daisy and every other character through their dialogue and actions. Because we see Daisy behaving flirtatiously but always innocently, unchanging no matter who is present to witness her staged efforts to stir Winterbourne's jealousy by keeping Giovanelli close to her side, we don't truly doubt her virtue. The movie *does* ask us to reflect on the wisdom of her behavior periodically, as when we wonder—with Winterbourne—whether she is correct in chattering on to him when they have only just met. However, it is primarily the judgments of the expatriate Americans that keep us concerned about Daisy's appropriateness. What Bogdanovich *shows* us of Daisy is what keeps us on her side, as it were, against the expatriates' denunciations. We see Shepherd as Daisy: beautiful, silly, proud, and uneducated, but also generous, democratic, and quite innocent of the screeds against her. The film's control of point of view and, as a consequence, of our sympathy is deliberate on Bogdanovich's part. His *Daisy Miller* shows the expatriates as haughty and close-minded in contrast to Daisy's outgoing, completely nonhierarchical enthusiasm for life; in so doing, he more clearly makes Daisy the heroine of the tale and Winterbourne a man who has lost much in not returning her affection. It is a small change from James's novella, but one that shows Shepherd as Daisy particularly well. While the novella does not always engage students *precisely because* of the narrative distancing devices James employs, the film brings audiences closer to Daisy, and the closer the audience is to Daisy, the more they care about her dilemma.

Because what she doesn't know endangers Daisy in Europe, Bogdanovich uses Cloris Leachman's considerable acting skills to portray Daisy's mother and her appalling neurasthenic lack of will. James and Bogdanovich characterize her as "'blatantly imbecil[ic]'" (*DM* 60). Mrs. Walker's harsh but altogether accurate judgment is crucial to understanding Daisy's imperiled state in Europe due to her family's ignorance of prevailing customs, her father's absence, her mother's ceding of the role of protector, and Daisy's own stubbornness. James's first description of Mrs. Miller brilliantly symbolizes her character. While Daisy and Winterbourne are enjoying their second conversation, a "figure of a lady appeared, at a distance very indistinct in the darkness; it advanced with a slow and wavering step" (*DM* 30). Mrs. Miller's first line is an answer to Daisy's question, "What are you doing, poking round here?" The mother replies, "Well, I don't know" (32). James (and Bogdanovich in a splendid recreation of the text) encapsulate for us a mother who has never guided, protected, or formed her children, so barely able is she to figure out her other role as the wife of a *nouveau riche* American businessman. In distinct contrast to the historical and fictional female heads of wealthy households during this period who ran their estates, cared for their children, and orchestrated their social lives like field marshals, Mrs. Miller falls into another category altogether of upper-class women whose daily lives consisted of monitoring their own hypochondriacal, enfeebled mental and physical conditions. Both kinds of women may signify their husbands' wealth, the first through capable, ostentatious display of it and the second through its use as an expensive protectiveness that cushions such frail yet well-intentioned incompetence as Mrs. Miller's.

However, while Daisy may genially accept her mother's incompetence, it is not to be borne by the other Americans in Rome. As the Millers move within their social orbit, the expatriates, led by the formidable Mrs. Walker, pull up the drawbridge against vulgar countrymen in order to define themselves as the better sort of Americans. As numerous scholars have noted, the novella is carefully structured along a variety of oppositions: Vevey/Rome, Protestantism/Catholicism, summer/winter, light/dark, comedy of manners/tragedy of an innocent sacrificed.[9] Certainly, the tone of the story darkens in the second half as Mrs. Walker, empowered by her righteous sense of Daisy's social sins, excommunicates Daisy from her circle. Both she and Mrs. Costello represent expatriate American women who worship the religion of social rituals as proof of their good taste, which appears to be more valuable in their milieu than spiritual correctness.

In Vevey, Bogdanovich beautifully distinguishes the first half's lighter, more comic tone in a sequence he creates for Mildred Natwick who, as the reviewers' cliché goes, chews up the scenery conveying Mrs. Costello's "'horror'" of Daisy (*DM* 25). He shoots a lavishly mounted scene in the Vevey baths that evokes the ludicrous level of material and social refinement offered to the wealthy in Europe. Winterbourne and his aunt, more than fully dressed in their bathing costumes, standing in steaming water up to their chests, take tea on a splendid silver service floating in front of them, and in an amusing touch, a lovely vase filled with roses floats through the scene in the background. While Mrs. Costello serves her nephew tea in this watery resplendence, she verbally prohibits him from meeting with Daisy because the Millers "are horribly common; they're the sort of Americans one does one's duty by ignoring." To his inquiry whether she will "just ignore them," she responds conclusively that she "can't not" because, regardless of her own wishes, her rigorous social standards require it. And immediately after wiping her social conscience clean of the Millers, she asks Winterbourne if he wants "milk" in his tea. Her proof of the family's "horrible common[ness]" is that they "treat the courier like a familiar friend—as a gentleman and a scholar" (DM 24). She wouldn't be surprised "if he dines with them." No doubt this breech of the absolute boundaries between rungs on the European and Europeanized American social hierarchies results from the Millers' ignorance: "Very likely they've never seen a man with such good manners, such fine clothes, so like a gentleman. . . . He probably corresponds to the young lady's idea of a count" (24). As the final indication of the Millers' impossibility and, more crucially, her own vastly greater sophistication, Mrs. Costello notes with profound despair that "he sits with them in the garden and smokes in their faces." Contrary to Stanley Kauffmann's objections, screenwriter Raphael's additional dialogue blends seamlessly with James's own lines here so that Bogdanovich is able to give a new, visual dimension to James's comedy of manners while maintaining a real fidelity to James's text.

Among many other scenes that Bogdanovich added to the movie, I am particularly impressed by his additions to the scene at the Pincio gardens in which he adds two elements. First, Winterbourne and Daisy watch a simple Punch and Judy puppet show, designed for children and families to enjoy. Shepherd, as Daisy, is particularly effective in conveying a childlike enjoyment in the show. Her innocence induces a resurgence of Winterbourne's romantic feelings for her. Second, just as he is admiring Daisy's openness to innocent pleasures, he looks away from her, and his eye is caught by another woman, also dressed in white (Shepherd's costumes throughout the film are white, blue, or pastel). This woman very deliberately attracts Winterbourne's glance in a clearly suggestive manner; he does a double take, realizes the stranger is definitely not an innocent woman out here in the Pincio, and so his momentary resurgence of trust in Daisy's goodness is once more cast into doubt.

In developing the novella into screenplay length, the director creates other scenes to blend with James's story. For example, he stages a montage of Winterbourne's trips to the Millers' hotel in Rome, where he repeatedly discovers that Daisy is out (we are sure, as he is, that she is with Giovanelli). In these scenes, we see the hotel staff barely hiding their amusement, first, at this American girl's dismissal of social custom and, second, at the hapless Winterbourne's repeated, failed efforts to court Daisy. This humorous montage turns dark when Winterbourne discovers that Daisy is seriously ill. Once again, we see him repeatedly coming to the hotel, asking the hotel staff about her. Bogdanovich shoots the last of these scenes through the lace curtain of the hotel front door so that we only see Winterbourne's back and hear nothing, yet we know from his body language that he has learned of her death.

In the climactic scene at midnight where Winterbourne discovers Daisy alone with Giovanelli at the Coliseum, Bogdanovich adds a moment in which Winterbourne first hears a woman's laugh (which we expect will be Daisy's), and then he hears the unknown woman and her lover speaking in very sexually inflected tones. This couple, then, sets up Winterbourne (and modern audiences less schooled in the impropriety as well as danger in being out at that late hour in the Coliseum) to judge Daisy immediately as analogous to the scandalous lovers he has just overheard.

While Mrs. Costello's "horror" of the Millers remains comic in Vevey, James's formal requirement that the mood darken in Rome leads him to add Mrs. Walker's active voice as social arbiter of her group of expatriate friends to Mrs. Costello's more peripheral condemnation (peripheral because she's more removed from society, so exclusive is she). Eileen Brennan is powerful, haughty, and vengeful as Mrs. Walker. As Jack Kroll, among other reviewers, notes, Bogdanovich added to Walker's character an element of sexual jealousy toward Daisy (81). Brennan convincingly portrays this jealousy as a dangerous, unconscious undertone to her actions. When Mrs. Walker plays her full hand by coming to the Pincio to convince Daisy to ride with her, only to be dismissed cheerily but determinedly by Daisy, she wears a sheer black veil with an intricate pattern covering her mouth but revealing her eyes. Mary Ann Doane has forever altered our understanding of the veil as a symbol of disguise, intrigue, and deceit (44–75). When Mrs. Walker appears veiled at the Pincio, claiming to be concerned only for Daisy's reputation, her veil suggests that she has additional motives, of which she herself may not be aware. When she can't get Daisy to leave, she commands Winterbourne to get into her carriage. Her behavior suggests her unconscious sexual desire for Winterbourne, her envy of Daisy's youth, and her need to control social interaction among the Americans in Rome, motives that all converge in that final, pathetic command, as she forces one acquaintance, at least, to obey her will.

   Throughout the movie, Bogdanovich shows Mrs. Miller, Mrs. Costello, and most particularly Mrs. Walker placing the protagonists in motion and initiating the story's narrative arc, as women often do in James's stories and in nineteenth-century fiction in general. These characters create the undertow in their society that catches us unawares as it drowns Daisy. As moral and social arbiters (or as failures in this regard, as in Mrs. Miller's case), these women decree Daisy out of bounds, make one attempt to annex her undeniable life force, and, when rebuffed, turn their backs on the girl. The resulting isolation activates a more stubborn resistance on Daisy's part. She spends more time alone with Giovanelli and with her dithering mother, relying on her own untested, misguided decision-making skills. As a post hoc argument for the expatriate women's arguments against Daisy's behavior, her death is compelling. Ignore advice; end up dead. In contrast to Mrs. Miller's silence, mothers' collective voices speak to us in this novella's outcome: be safe; do what we tell you. Winterbourne seems to have learned his lesson. He has a burst of independence when initially buoyed by Daisy's charming company. However, he is cautious by nature, socially docile, and unable to risk the disapproval of his peers. He would like to help; he would prefer for Daisy to comply with the female forces who decree people's social fates, but then she would not be Daisy (either the idealized Daisy James describes in the preface, or the "real," more sexually knowing Daisys of 1878 or even 1974): she would not be the young American girl, fresh, pretty, untutored in the ways of a very complex game, overly self-confident, and destined for public disapproval, whether in Rome or in Hollywood.

   Examining the fierce contemporary reaction against Bogdanovich's fine film, primarily as a response to his ill-conceived decision to cast his mistress in the role of a virgin, is an intriguing study in the powerful consequences of publicly dismissing social norms. While opinions come and go, what remain are the texts, the book and the film. Bogdanovich's work succeeds as both a beautifully realized companion piece to the novella and an excellent film, entirely on its own merits. Now that the dust has settled on Cybill Shepherd's relationship to Peter Bogdanovich, I find that in many ways she was quite suited to her role as Daisy. Her own youthful confidence and beauty worked well with Bogdanovich's direction of the film, which rhetorically moves the viewer to sympathize with Daisy and to be shocked at her sudden demise in a strange land where no one saves her from her hazardous yet still innocent adventurousness. This film is no repetition of life, no example of life and art mirroring each other; it is not William Randolph Hearst torturing opera lovers with a dismal effort to turn Marion

Davies into a diva. Studied again twenty-five years after its release, Peter Bogdanovich's *Daisy Miller* shows him exercising considerable strengths as a director. His reverential attitude toward the earlier literary masterpiece enables him to produce a visually stimulating, entertaining period piece that gives students another, very rich vision of James's novella.

## Notes

1. While Lippincott refused to publish "Daisy Miller" because it was "an outrage on American girlhood," James went on to have the last laugh, for the novella became his single best selling work (Edel 303). Thus, the analogy between the initial negative reactions to the novelist's and the director's *Daisy Millers* ends with James's success and Bogdanovich's lack thereof.
2. Among many history texts documenting the tumult of the 1960s and 1970s, see Grun 576–78.
3. In the preface, James describes Daisy's character as "pure poetry" (*DM* vi). His description is a somewhat defensive reaction to an experience he recounts in Venice years after the story's publication in which he was pinned against a metaphorical wall by "an interesting [female] friend." She complained that James's character "falsified" the actual young American women, who, through the story's success, had come to be known as "'Daisy Millers,'" with his story's "pretty perversion" of the real thing (*DM* vii). Hence, his response that Daisy is an idealized character. James's version of the woman's criticism is worth quoting for the vitriol she directs toward the young girls (perhaps prompted by her envy of their youth) and toward James's much-noted penchant for artistic form over realistic characterization:

    you *know* you quite falsified, by the turn you gave it, the thing you had begun with . . . [through] your pretty perversion of it, or your unprincipled mystification of our sense of it, does it really too much honour— in spite of which, none the less, as anything charming or touching always to that extent justifies itself, we after a fashion forgive and understand you. But why *waste* your romance? . . . you have yielded to your incurable prejudice in favour of grace—to whatever it is in you that makes so inordinately for form and prettiness and pathos; not to say sometimes for misplaced drolling. Is it that you've after all too much imagination? Those awful young women capering at the hotel-door, *they are* the real little Daisy Millers that were; whereas yours in the tale is such a one, more's the pity, as—for pitch of the ingenuous, for quality of the artless—couldn't possibly have been at all. (*DM* vii-viii)

4. Bogdanovich's previous films were received well critically and made profits, but these profits were nothing in comparison to the acclaim generated by the early 1970s work of his two partners. *The French Connection* grossed $40 million

from its American, foreign, and video releases and won best picture, best director, best actor, best screenplay, and best editing honors at the 1971 Academy Awards. *The Exorcist* grossed $160 million and received Academy Award nominations for best picture, best director, best actress, best supporting actress, best supporting actor, best cinematography, best editing, best set direction, and won the award for best adapted screenplay. Coppola was even more successful. He made *The Godfather* which has grossed $268 million to date and won Academy Awards for best picture, best actor, and best adapted screenplay. With *The Godfather, Part II,* Coppola scored again commercially and critically; the sequel garnered eleven Academy nominations and won awards for best picture, best direction, best adapted screenplay, and best supporting actor (Biskind 212–14).

5. In particular, critics have noted that the works James published in the 1870s and 1880s convey a lack of "human feeling" (Edel 180). A friend's "notice of [Roderick Hudson] for the *North American Review*" divided itself (as do many reviews of Bogdanovich's film). He praises James's growing technical expertise, mentioning "the maturity of the prose . . . the auspicious character of Henry's emergence as a full-fledged novelist," likening "his use of language to 'the facility of a great pianist.'" Yet the reviewer goes on to note that readers "'do not identify with'" his characters: "'We are intellectually interested, but as unmoved as one may suppose the medical class of a modern school of vivisection to be. . . . All it lacks is to have been told with more human feeling'" (qtd. in Edel 180) Thus, early reviews of both the writer and the director note the artists' reliance on formalism, their knowledge of and allusions to earlier works in their own texts, and a lack of feeling in their compositions.

6. Kauffmann notes the following elements of the film as techniques derived from earlier filmmakers: "Visconti's period richness in *The Leopard* and *Death in Venice*"; "the singing lesson in *Citizen Kane;* there's even a hint, heaven help us, of Tony Richardson's *Charge of the Light Brigade*—an important moment seen through a gauzily curtained glass door . . . [and] a Wellesian ground-level shot outside the Colosseum" (20).

7. In his review, Sragow somewhat confusingly refers to Bogdanovich and Shepherd "emblazoned" on the cover of *People Magazine* "a few weeks ago" (his review appeared in the *Times* on June 30, 1974). The picture of the couple in his article is *not* the cover for the May 13, 1974, issue of *People,* which features yet another photograph of Bogdanovich and Shepherd. The picture in Sragow's article is unidentified. This unidentified picture is the one to which I refer because of the striking similarity of Cybill Shepherd's pose in it and on the movie poster for *Daisy Miller.*

8. Apropos of the possibility of Bogdanovich's reinventing himself (as well as proving detractors' inveterate criticism of his name-dropping habit) is his article in *Premiere Magazine,* November 1999, ostensibly about Audrey Hepburn. However, the piece becomes equally his own history with the note that while he was making *They All Laughed* with Hepburn in 1979, they were both starting relationships with other people and hoping to divert attention away from those

new friendships, "so neither did anything to quell press speculations, sparked by photos like the one above [Bogdanovich seated; Hepburn behind him with her hands in his hair], that they themselves might be intimate" ("Last Innocent" 129). The byline for the article states that "Bogdanovich is the director of such films as *The Last Picture Show*, *What's Up, Doc?*, *Paper Moon*, *Saint Jack*, and *Mask*. His new book of 52 film recommendations, *Movie of the Week*, will be published by Ballantine this month"; so he also does not appear to have lost his taste for making cinematic judgments (140; emphasis mine).

9. Both Fogel's fine book on "Daisy Miller" and Ohmann's excellent essay assess previous scholarship and shed new interpretive light on this tale.

## Works Cited

Alpert, Hollis. "That Was the Entertainment That Was." *Saturday Review World* 29 June 1974.

Baumbach, Jonathan. "Going to the Movies: Europe in America." *Partisan Review* 41 (1974): 450–54.

Baxter, John. "Peter Bogdanovich." *International Dictionary of Films and Filmmakers*. 3d ed. New York: St. James, 1997. 94–97.

Biskind, Peter. *Easy Riders, Raging Bulls: How the Sex-Drugs-and-Rock 'n' Roll Generation Saved Hollywood*. New York: Simon, 1998.

"Bogdanovich, Peter." *Current Biography: 1972*. New York: Wilson, 1972. 41–44.

Bogdanovich, Peter. "The Last Innocent." *Premiere: The Movie Magazine* Nov. 1999.

Canby, Vincent. "*Daisy* Is an Unexpected Triumph." Rev. of *Daisy Miller*, dir. Peter Bogdanovich. *New York Times* 16 June 1974: 11: 1: 5.

Cocks, Jay. "Culture Shock." *Time* 3 June 1974: 56–57.

Doane, Mary Ann. *Femmes Fatales: Feminism, Film Theory, Psychoanalysis*. London: Routledge, 1991.

Edel, Leon. *The Life of Henry James: The Conquest of London, 1870–1881*. New York: Lippincott, 1962.

Fogel, Daniel Mark. *"Daisy Miller": A Dark Comedy of Manners*. Boston: Hall, 1990.

Grun, Bernard. *The Timetables of History: A Historical Linkage of People and Events*. New York: Simon, 1982.

James, Henry. *Daisy Miller*. In *The Novels and Tales of Henry James*. Vol. 18. New York: Scribner's, 1909. 1–94.

Kareda, Urjo. "The Signals Movie Actors Give." *New York Times* 11 Aug. 1974: 11: 1: 1.

Kauffmann, Stanley. "*Daisy Miller*." Rev. of *Daisy Miller*, dir. Peter Bogdanovich. *New Republic* 8 June 1974.

Kroll, Jack. "Heiress of the Ages." *Newsweek* 27 May 1974.

Ohmann, Carol. "*Daisy Miller*: A Study of Changing Intentions." *Henry James's "Daisy Miller," "The Turn of the Screw," and other Tales*. Ed. Harold Bloom. New York: Chelsea, 1987. 25–34.

"Peter and Cybill: Who Needs Marriage?" *People Magazine* 13 May 1974: 19–22.

Sayre, Nora. "*Daisy Miller.*" Rev. of *Daisy Miller,* dir. Peter Bogdanovich. *New York Times* 23 May 1974: 52: 1.
Sragow, Michael. "A Sexual Battle." Rev. of *Daisy Miller,* dir. Peter Bogdanovich. *New York Times* 30 June 1974: 11: 5: 1.
"Shepherd, Cybill." *Current Biography: 1987.* New York: Wilson, 1987. 511–15.
Walton, Priscilla. "The Janus Faces of James: Gender, Transnationality, and James's Cinematic Adaptations." *Questioning the Master: Gender and Sexuality in Henry James's Writing.* Ed. Peggy McCormack. Newark: U of Delaware P, 2000. 37–53.
Westerbeck, Colin, Jr. "The Screen." *Commonweal* 28 June 1974.

## Filmography

Daisy Miller. Dir. Peter Bogdanovich. Writ. Frederic Raphael. Perf. Cybill Shepherd and Barry Brown. Directors' Company, 1974.

# "The Tie of a Common Aversion"

## Sexual Tensions in Henry James's *The Other House*

*Priscilla L. Walton*

*The Other House,* published in 1896, marks Henry James's first and only foray into the textual world of murder mysteries and suspense thrillers. More akin to a nineteenth-century sensation novel than to *The Portrait of a Lady, The Other House* concentrates on a desiring single white female and dramatizes the dangers she poses to familial social structures. The novel ostensibly details Rose Armiger's love for a man, Tony Bream, who is bound by a promise made to his dying wife (and Rose's best friend) that he will not remarry during their child's lifetime. In order to release Tony from his promise, Rose kills the child, her actions rendering her an early, if unacknowledged, precursor of characters like those played by Glenn Close in *Fatal Attraction* (1987) and Rebecca DeMornay in *The Hand That Rocks the Cradle* (1992). *The Other House,* however, did not generate the mass attention accorded to its twentieth-century offspring; it was virtually ignored in its day and has largely escaped critical notice.[1] But the novel did eventually excite cinematic interest, if at an incongruous time—the feminist-inspired 1970s—and if from an unexpected quarter—the French New Wave. Nonetheless, Jacques Rivette's assimilation of *The Other House* into his 1974 filmic tribute to female friendship, *Celine et Julie vont en bateau,* highlights an aspect of the Jamesian narrative that has gone unnoticed and opens a line of inquiry into James's anomalous and neglected thriller. In turn, another film by a French New Wave director, François Truffaut's *La Chambre verte* (1978), which incorporates "The Beast in the Jungle," also sheds light on the sexual dynamics at play in James's narratives.

The Other House may seem an odd choice for inclusion in a film that, like Rivette's, focalizes women's intimacy. But I would argue that *Celine et Julie vont en bateau* builds upon elements latent in the text, and hence offers a sort of palimpsest through which to read James's novel. *Celine et Julie* features the work of two actors, Dominique Labourier and Juliette Berto, whose improvisational performance engenders a narrative about the reconstruction of narratives. In the film, the actors play and replay scenarios from various perspectives, and their actions foreground the potential of female transgression. One of these ongoing narratives is culled from *The Other House,* and the two characters infiltrate scenes from the novel, revise them, and ultimately rescue the endangered child.

Unlike the novel on which it plays, *Celine et Julie* from its opening frames inverts expectations of linearity and gender. The film begins with Julie seated on a park bench, reading. Celine walks by her and accidentally drops a scarf, which Julie picks up. She then begins to follow Celine through the streets of Paris, and this walk, filmed with a handheld camera, invites viewers to share Celine's unease as she is literally stalked by Julie. Already thrown off balance by the filming technique, viewers are then invited to subvert gender codes (traditionally, films have taught spectators that stalking is an act performed by a man upon a woman). The same-sex dynamic at work in Rivette's film provides both for a sense of relief and for a sense of dissonance. This dissonance is magnified when Julie catches Celine's eye, lifts the scarf over her face and peers through it. Drawing on the performative aspects of masquerade, *Celine et Julie* is permeated with masks and disguises. Julie, who is a magician, practices sleight of hand, an act that parallels the cinematic structure wherein nothing is as it seems.

*Celine et Julie* is spliced with circus-style intertitles, which record the passage of time (e.g., "But the next day . . ."). Consequently, following the stalking scene, "the next day," Julie tracks down Celine at her hotel, and Celine later appears at Julie's apartment, seeking refuge for the night. While she is in the shower, Julie searches through Celine's possessions. Learning that Celine used to work as a nanny, Julie travels the ensuing morning to a deserted house and enters the door. At this point, the camera jumps back to Celine, left alone in Julie's apartment, who proceeds to search through *Julie's* possessions. Intercepting a call for her new roommate, Celine meets with Julie's lover (who does not seem to notice that he is meeting with a different woman), fights with him, and then joins her friends at a café. There, she regales the crowd with stories of an American woman who has invited her to move into her house, to be her companion. Since the viewer knows the sequence of events that has led to Celine's sojourn at Julie's (who is not American but French), Julie's duplicitous narrative anticipates the rest of the film, in which the two continue to shift and modify their identities.

In a jagged scene break, the camera records Celine's next meeting with Julie, whom she finds strangely disoriented. The two have become close friends by this time, and Celine, concerned about Julie, takes her to the club where she performs her magic act. Later, as she removes her makeup, she complains: "I hate the mask." Despite her protests, she continues to veil her activities, as does Julie. Learning that Julie has suffered a blackout and cannot recall what happened at "the other house," Celine tries to help her friend overcome her amnesia. The vague memories that she extracts comprise snippets from James's *The Other House,* which, Julie notes, are either "memory gaps or a smoky dream." She is sure, however, that the activities she has witnessed involve mysterious pacts and vows.

"But the next day," the two women again switch roles: Celine decides to go to the other house, and experiences a trauma similar to Julie's the previous morning, while Julie "becomes" Celine and peforms at the club. When they finally reunite, Julie convinces Celine that they must engage in occult rites to ferret out the story behind "the other house." Their magic ritual involves sucking stones, which enable them to "view" the Other House, of which hitherto they have only caught snippets.

Celine and Julie watch the scenario of *The Other House* as though it were a movie, continuing to suck more stones each time the "film" abruptly ends. Taking "intermissions" for cigarette breaks and commenting on the action, they become spectators-observers, replicating James's own fondness for characters in such positions. But *The Other House* narrative—the film within the film—does not proceed as Celine and Julie wish: they run out of stones before James's narrative completely unfolds. Disturbed, Celine complains, "I want a sense of conclusion," and Julie agrees that the story is "full of holes." In order to procure closure, the women break into a library to retrieve a book of magic spells, from which they concoct a "memory potion" that allows them to watch the rest of the *The Other House.* As they discuss the repetitive actions of James's scenario, the women note how the characters "do the same thing today as yesterday. The same thing every day. It's a continual showing—perpetual."

Deciding that they must intervene to rescue the child, Madlyne, whose dead body they have seen, Celine and Julie return to the other house to discover the murderer and to save Madlyne. Chanting a spell, "clever, clover," once again they enter into *The Other House* narrative. Disguised as characters within the novel, they engage with the "others," acting out their roles and sometimes forgetting their "lines." Nevertheless, their omissions do not upset the progression of the story, and even go undetected, for *The Other House* characters "didn't notice." Finally, in a comic pastiche of ballroom dancing, Celine and Julie, celebrating their fondness for each other, dance together, blundering about and kicking up their heels, while the rest of the characters float elegantly around the ballroom. Sneaking off the dance floor, the two women manage to rescue Madlyne by coaxing her out of a window—and out of the narrative.

"But the next day," Celine and Julie awake in their bed and exclaim over the previous evening's activities. At this point, they hear a cry and discover Madlyne in another room. Celine and Julie decide to take the child boating and, while on the river, pass the characters from *The Other House*. This scene appears to conclude Rivette's film; however, after a pause, an intertitle informs viewers, "But the next morning," and the plot resumes again. This time, the film circles back to the beginning, and viewers see Celine in medium-close-up, seated on a park bench. When Julie walks by, she drops a book, and Celine begins to follow her. Ending where it began, although with its characters in obverse positions, Rivette's film abruptly stops, leaving Celine and Julie to intrude on narratives already in progress, alter them, and shift their trajectories.

*Celine et Julie's* engagement with pre-scripted texts engenders a series of repetitive cinematic spirals that invite alternative inscriptions and reconstructions. Julia Lesage, inspired by the space the film opens for role-playing, defines its female-centered fantasy as "lesbian": "not because of its depiction of sexual activity (none is seen) but because of the kind of intimacy between women it depicts. . . . [*Celine et Julie*] symbolically contrasts 'childlike playfulness' with 'adult rigidity' to critique the institution of heterosexuality itself" (36). Lesage suggests that *Celine et Julie's* concentration on women's intimacy provides for an analysis of heterosexuality. And, while cinematic transformations may be problematic media through which to view literary texts, I would assert that Lesage's comments illuminate an important twist in the narrative movement of *The Other House*. Indeed, the lesbianism that Lesage finds in Rivette's film is constructed quite differently in *The Other House*, which incorporates tropes of demonized lesbianism to intensify its censure of female desire, while, contiguously, the same-sex relations that underpin the novel and unsettle its heterosexual dynamic are illuminated by Truffaut's *La Chambre verte*. Although, on one level, therefore, *The Other House* works to dramatize the dangers single women pose to familial structures, on another, it too offers a critique of heterosexuality.

Just as *The Other House's* condemnation of lesbianized women marks a point of departure from its later cinematic adaptation, so it deviates from James's earlier treatment of lesbianism in *The Bostonians* of 1886. *The Bostonians*, perhaps inspired by Alice James's relationship with her long-time companion, Katherine Loring, covertly juxtaposes the tensions between heterosexual and homosexual love.[2] While *The Bostonians* is by no means a tribute to same-sex desire, the contrast between its implicit depiction of lesbianism and that of *The Other House* points to a shift in the cultural climate that informs these two texts.

Not surprisingly, the decade that separates *The Bostonians* from *The Other House* manifests a turning point in nineteenth-century sexual reconstructions. Where the years leading up to the 1886 novel had signaled some curiosity in sexual alternatives, exemplified in the interest generated by George Sand's mid-century gender-bending and in the enthusiastic reception accorded to Oscar Wilde's 1880's heterosexual subversions, the climate of the 1890s had grown distinctly chilly. In 1895, one year before the publication of *The Other House,* the Wilde trials had incited the fury of the populace, culminating in the palpable delight that greeted the author's indictment for homosexual offenses.[3] The writings of sexologists like Carl von Westphal and Richard von Krafft-Ebing were circulating by the 1890s[4] and worked to underscore the dangers of sexual inversions. And although romantic friendships and Boston marriages among women had gone unremarked for decades, the American Mitchell trial of 1892, wherein a Tennessee woman was indicted for the murder of her female beloved, had rendered female same-sex attachments suspect. Concomitantly, the emergence of first-wave feminism, which intensified cultural anxieties about women's roles, generated an increasing hostility toward independent women. Lesbianism, which was constructed as the ultimate site of female control, became a target of public outrage. As Lillian Faderman documents, literary depictions of the lesbian were flourishing in the works of French writers like Baudelaire (*Les Fleurs du Mal* [1857]), Zola (*Nana* [1880]), Maupassant ("Paul's Mistress" [1881]), and Daudet (*Sappho* [1884]) and crossed the channel in the works of Swinburne (*Lesbia Brandon* [1877]) and George Moore (*A Drama in Muslin* [1886]). In turn, the American Mitchell case spawned writings like Mary Wilkins Freeman's "The Long Arm" (1895) and Mary Hatch's *The Strange Disappearance of Eugene Comstock* (1895). As Faderman argues, representations of lesbian "evil" had seized the imagination of the public (*Surpassing* 277–94) and contributed to a climate of cultural gay-bashing, which culminated in the Wilde trial.

While James was no friend to Oscar Wilde and even refused to sign an 1896 petition requesting Wilde's early release,[5] the 1890s was also a period in which public approval assumed an increasing importance for him. In a precarious professional position as a result of the well-publicized failure of *Guy Domville* (again in 1895), the author had decided to abandon his ill-fated theatrical ventures and to return to novel writing.[6] *The Other House* was James's first novel since *The Tragic Muse* of 1890 and might seem an anomalous choice through which to make a literary comeback, given its unusually lurid subject matter (child murder), and its idiosyncratic publication in the sensationalistic *Illustrated London News*. Leon Edel offers clues as to the novel's production, for he suggests that James thought *The Other House* to be "sufficiently melodramatic—it is his only story to contain a brutal murder—to 'capture the public of the *Illustrated News*'" (677). And James's hopes as well as his distaste for *The Other House* are apparent in a letter written to his brother, William, on May 29, 1896, wherein he confesses his belief that the novel may be "the most successful thing I have put forth for a long time. If that's what the idiots want, I can give them their bellyfull" (qtd. in Kaplan 417). *The Other House,* then, comprises James's effort to target the attention of a popular audience, an audience that had scorned his theatrical ventures and an audience that was caught in the throes of a backlash against gender disruptions.

On the surface, a novel focusing on a murderous single white female would seem likely to be well received in the backlash climate of the fin de siècle. Certainly, dangerous women proved a fruitful topic for writers like H. Rider Haggard (*She* [1887]) and Bram Stoker (*Dracula* [1897], *The Lair of the White Worm* [1911]). Within such texts, unruly women are punished and thereby "contained" and appropriately passive women saved and rewarded—generally through the efforts of a cohesive male alliance. *The Other House,* which works to sensationalize the threatening nature of a sexually assertive and lesbianized woman, is superficially in accord with the containment paradigm and with the homophobic climate of the mid-1890s. However, the novel also unsettles that paradigm—which may explain its failure to excite fin-de-siècle audiences—for it restrains its femme fatale in a male circle that is fraught with homoerotic promise. In effect, the novel takes the containment argument to its logical conclusion by hinting that the best container for insurgent women is one that is immune to female charms. Much like *Roderick Hudson,* "The Pupil," "The Author of 'Beltraffio,'" and "The Middle Years," *The Other House* speaks more to the problematics of sexual boundaries than it does to their maintenance.

*The Other House* is a curious fusion of homophobia and homoeroticism. The policing it enacts, whereby one form of sexual trespass is held in check by another, illuminates the problems in normative gender constructions. As Diana Fuss argues, homosexuality has traditionally been posited as the deviant outside of heterosexual love:

> Homosexuality is produced inside the dominant discourse of sexual difference as its necessary outside, but this is not to say that the homo exerts no pressure on the hetero nor that this outside stands in any simple relation of exteriority to the inside. Every outside is also an alongside; the distance between dis-

tance and proximity is sometimes no distance at all. It may be more accurate to say that the homo, occupying the frontier position of inside out, is neither completely outside the bounds of sexual difference nor wholly inside it either. The fear of the homo, which continually *rubs up against* the hetero (tribadic style) concentrates and codifies the very real possibility and ever-present threat of a collapse of boundaries, an effacing of limits, and a radical confusion of identities. (5–6)

James's novel provides for a literary exemplification of Fuss's argument, for its homoerotic subtexts rub up against its dominant heterotext and efface the limits of conventional sexuality. Overtly, the novel works to affirm (hetero)sexual norms, yet its covert narrative movements disrupt that process. Heterosexuality, situated as the inside center of the text, is threatened by the outside-to-inside push of the rebellious and lesbianized Rose, who is forced back outside the inside by the efforts of the male alliance. Yet through this maneuver, homoeroticism is simultaneously brought into the inside of the narrative, and it remains there—rendering same-sex desire alongside of and even as a crucial component to the heterosexual order.

The structure of *The Other House* comprises a series of layers, which bleed into and color each other, blurring the borders drawn between inside and outside. On the surface, the novel offers the chronicle of a woman gone wild with desire, but underneath its surface lies the lesbian subtext, which provides a tacit explanation for Rose's actions. The homoerotic layer comes into play when Rose is contained, inspiring a rereading of the heterotext, which motivates the initiatory action, an action informed by Truffaut's later treatment of "The Altar of the Dead" and "The Beast in the Jungle." Each layer, thus, underpins (and undermines) the others. And, like *Celine et Julie vont en bateau,* which highlights the transgressive potential of same-sex desire, *The Other House,* too, promotes the breakdown of normative sexual boundaries.

The dominant heterosexual layer of the novel is developed through the machinations of the matriarchal Mrs. Beever, who owns Eastmead, the estate that borders on Tony Breams's residence interestingly called "Bounds." Mrs. Beever presides over the textual economy, for she "has 'a distinct voice'" (*Other House* [OH] 3) in the bank her late husband and Tony's father established, and she attempts to control the sexual economy through her matchmaking. She tries to arrange a marriage between her son, Paul, and the textual ingenue, Jean Martle, who, child-loving and passive, is the embodiment of acceptable female behavior. Jean is sexually nonthreatening, since in her, "the woman peeped out of the child and the child peeped out

of the woman" (201–2). But Mrs. Beever's plans for Jean are disturbed by
the events that transpire at "the other house," of which she is a "close,
though not a cruel observer" because a "great deal more went on there,
naturally, than in the great, clean, square solitude [of Eastmead]" (3).

What goes on at Bounds is largely figured through Rose Armiger, who
performs as the antithesis of Jean Martle. Rose, who is described, at one
point, as a woman whose "mask was the mask of Medusa" (312), is demon-
strably threatening. Unlike Jean, Rose is not childlike, and her physical appeal is ambiguously striking: "In a flash of small square white teeth this second impression was produced and the ambiguity that Mrs. Beever had spoken
of lighted up—an ambiguity worth all the plain prettiness in the world. Yes,
one quite did know: Miss Armiger was strikingly handsome" (14).

Rose is not well liked by her female compatriots. Mrs. Beever is disturbed by her familiarity with Tony Bream (23) and distrustful of her ability
to "handle honest gentlemen as 'muffs'" (28). Rose also shocks Jean Martle
when she challenges the sanctity of motherhood by insisting that she likes
children "not a bit" (18) and then goes on to assert that Tony's newborn
child, Effie, is no exception: "'It would be very sweet and attractive of me to
say I adore them [children]; but I never pretend to feelings I can't keep up,
don't you know? If you'd like, all the same, to see Effie,' she obligingly
added, 'I'll so far sacrifice myself as to get her for you?'" (18–19).

Clearly, Rose is a transgressive character, but she is initially contained
and circumscribed through her engagement to Dennis Vidal. While Mrs.
Beever believes that "it ought somehow to be arranged that her [Rose's]
marriage should encounter no difficulty" (28), it does run into difficulty
when Rose ends her engagement. Mrs. Beever attributes Rose's refusal of
Dennis and her subsequent promotion of Paul's courtship of Jean to Rose's
secret love for Tony, now a widower, who is apparently captivated by the
ingenue. When Jean refuses Paul, Rose takes matters into her own hands
and concretizes Mrs. Beever's suspicions: she drowns Effie in a stream and
attempts to implicate Jean in the murder.

Rose is heterosexually contained when the other characters decide to
cover up the crime, in order to protect Tony, and send Rose off to exile in
China with Dennis Vidal. Rose is thereby contained in the colonies, which
Edward W. Said argues served as useful places "to send wayward sons,
superfluous populations of delinquents, poor people, and other undesir-
ables" (190). Her exile also leaves Tony free to marry Jean, which sustains
the dominant heterotextual trajectory of the narrative. It is not sustained
unproblematically, however, for the lesbian subtext that colors Rose's depiction foregrounds same-sex desire as an alternative explanation of her
behavior and brings homosexuality within the parameters of the text.

The lesbian subtext functions to emphasize Rose's deviance, an emphasis that is in keeping with the strictures of the containment narrative but disturbs the heterotext by moving into its inside the outside of same-sex desire. Rose's independence, in itself, is sexually suspect, for, as Elaine Showalter summarizes, at the turn of the century, representations of single unmarried women drew on the "popular image of the odd woman [which] conflated elements of the lesbian, the angular spinster, and the hysterical feminist" (23). Indeed, Rose's depiction preys on fears of female independence and conjures visions of women outside of male control, seemingly in charge of themselves and their destinies. Such imputations intensify as Rose moves out of the bounds of social "acceptability." Although she attempts to dispel Mrs. Beever's suspicions by confessing, "I may be dangerous to myself, but I'm not so to others" (166), the danger she poses to the social fabric is magnified by the lesbian tropes that ghost her characterization. Lesbian de-realization, according to Terry Castle, has a long literary history, and the scholar's argument sheds light on Rose's portrayal: "The literary history of lesbianism . . . is first of all a history of derealization. . . . Passion is excited, only to be obscured, disembodied, decarnalized. The vision is inevitably waved off. Panic seems to underwrite these obsessional spectralizing gestures: a panic over love, female pleasure, and the possibility of women breaking free—together—from their male sexual overseers. Homophobia is the order of the day, entertains itself (wryly or gothically) with phantoms, then exorcises them" (34). The lesbian, as a spectre who haunts a culture threatened by the insurgence of suffragettes and first-wave feminists, makes a (dis)appearance in James's femme fatale. While Rose is not literally spectralized, her estrangement from Dennis is described as "ghostly and ominous" (341), and her friendship with the dying (and throughout the bulk of the text, dead) Julia Bream shades her portrayal.

Rose and Jean's friendship was initiated at boarding school, a context that speaks to and informs its construction. Boarding schools had aroused public concern as early as 1810, when charges of homosexuality were laid at the doorstep of the Scottish Miss Pirie and Miss Woods's School for Young Ladies,[7] and by 1893, were cited in medical testimonials as hotbeds of lesbian desire.[8] The boarding school context, therefore, shadows the women's friendship, a friendship that is further clouded by Rose's assertion that the two share "the tie of a common aversion" (24). While, literally, this aversion refers to a dislike of Julia's stepmother, connotatively, it resonates throughout Rose's explanation that:

> "I'm the one thing of her own that dear Julia has ever had."
> Mrs. Beever threw back her head. "Don't you count her husband?"

> "I count Tony immensely; but in another way."
>     Again Mrs. Beever considered: she might have been won-
> dering in what way even so expert a young person as this could
> count Anthony Bream except as a treasure to his wife. (23)

Rose's friendship with Julia is posited as disruptive of male-female relations, a point that is reiterated when Rose contends, "Julia's the one thing I
have of my own," and Mrs. Beever stresses, "You make light of our husbands and lovers!" (27).

Underneath the heterosexual explanation of Rose's behavior, therefore, lies another. And, accordingly, although the Eastmead characters per-
ceive Rose's efforts to unite Paul with Jean as an effort to secure Tony's
affections, Rose claims that she is otherwise motivated. She insists that her
interest in the heterosexual alliance stems from her loyalty to Julia: "'I've an
idea that has become a passion with me. There's a right I must see done—
there's a wrong I must make impossible. There's a loyalty I must cherish—
there's a memory I must protect. That's all I can say.' She stood there in her
vivid meaning like the priestess of a threatened altar. 'If that girl becomes
your [Paul's] wife—why then, I'm at last at rest!'" (174–75). The priestess of
a threatened altar, an altar rendered demonic in this narrative, Rose decides to act upon her passion. Not surprisingly, the reasons she cites for
claiming Effie derive from Rose's love for the child's dead mother: "'I want
her for another reason . . . . I adored her poor mother—and she's hers. That's
*my* ground, that's *my* love, that's *my* faith.' She caught Effie up again; she
held her in two strong arms and dealt her a kiss that was a long consecra-
tion. 'It's as your dead mother's, my own, my sweet, that—if it's time—I
shall carry you to bed!'" (282–83).

The lesbianism latent in Rose's characterization provides an implicit
explanation of her deviance in that it is her perverse inclinations that induce her violent actions. As a monstrous figure whose uncontrollable passions lead her to commit murder (the murder of a four-year-old child),
Rose clearly requires restraint. She must be pushed outside of the textual
borders and contained.

Rose's overwhelming sexual powers make it difficult to contain her,
however. Even though in the conclusion Rose is confined in a locked room,
she retains the ability to attract and influence heterosexual men. This femme
fatale manages to waylay Paul Beever and is on the verge of soliciting his
assistance when Dennis Vidal arrives and circumscribes her actions. Dennis "put out a hand and seized her, and they passed quickly into the night"
(387), and Rose is excised from the text.

But, by turning to another French New Wave film, what is left in the text after Rose's removal takes on a new significance. Offering insights into homotextual readings of James's texts, long before most critics and theorists recognized the same-sex desire encoded within them, François Truffaut's 1978 *La Chambre verte* demonstrates how filmic translations can be used to open alternative possibilities in narrative movements. Contiguous with the homoerotic elements of *Celine et Julie vont en bateau*, *La Chambre verte* interweaves narratives of sexuality as it generates homotextual readings. Drawing upon "The Altar of the Dead" and to some extent "The Beast in the Jungle," *La Chambre verte* dramatizes the plight of its protagonist, Julien Davenne. Davenne works at a failing provincial magazine and is haunted both by memories of World War I and of his late wife, Julie Vallence-Davenne. When he meets a young woman, Cecilia Mandel, who also worships a dead lover, Julien is struck by her kindness. But when he discovers that the man Cecilia honors is an old friend, Paul Massigny, whom Julien believes has betrayed him, he begins to withdraw from his new admirer. Gradually fading away, Julien in effect chooses death over the life Cecilia offers. When he dies in the chapel that serves as his altar to the past, he leaves Cecilia alone in her mission of honoring the dead, among whom he now numbers. Yet, significantly, within Julien's chapel, are portraits of deceased people who have affected him deeply, and among the portraits are those of Julie, Marcel Proust, Henry James, and Oscar Wilde. The placement of Proust, James, and Wilde, here, in contrast with Julien's dead wife, invites the viewer to reassess Julien's devotions, for it suggests a homoerotic triangle, in which women perform homosocially—or as conduits for male same-sex desire—in Eve Sedgwick's definition of the term.[9]

Moreover, for those familiar with James's biography, this homosocial triangle draws attention to the author's conflicted sexual orientation, his purported devotion to his lost love, Minnie Temple, and to his many homoerotic relationships. Consequently, the pairing of Wilde, an openly gay man, with the closeted James opens the possibility that, within the film, the feelings Julien harbors toward his enemy and former friend, Massigny, are sexually oriented, since it calls to mind James's own ambivalent feelings about Wilde. As Fred Kaplan argues, James found Wilde's "sexual ambivalence and its association with art threatening to his own sexual identity and to his identity as an artist" (245). In light of the triangulation of Julie, Wilde, and James (not to mention Proust), Truffaut's film implicitly suggests that the dead Julie and the living Cecilia perform as "safe havens" for Julien's repressed desires for Massigny. Throwing Julien's sexual orientation into question, the film posits Cecilia, who serves as the lover rejected, as the passive mainstay of the ongoing memorial service. In this way, the complications of James's gender constructions are exemplified (once again, through the body of a woman), while the film concomitantly acknowledges, if obliquely, James's homosexuality.

Bearing the sexual complexities of this film in mind, that which remains present after Rose's absence, in *The Other House,* assumes a different resonance. Viewed from the perspective granted by *La Chambre verte,* the bond between Dennis and Tony Bream, which prompts Dennis's offer to act as Rose's guardian, is charged with homoeroticism. Consequently, while Rose may be pushed out of the textual inside, much like Cecilia, that inside is concurrently infiltrated by same-sex male desire. Cursorily, the primary male friendship in *The Other House* is heterosexually pre-scripted: Dennis, initially, is engaged to Rose, and Tony married to Julia. Yet, Dennis's link with the deviant Rose casts a dubious light on his character, and the affinities Tony shares with the femme fatale render him suspect. Tony's "presence" is described as similar to hers, for it "made, simply and directly, a difference in any personal question exposed to it" (166–67). And, again like Rose, Tony attracts virtually everyone with whom he comes in contact: Jean Martle seems to fall in love with him at first sight, and Julia attempts to control him through the promise that he will not remarry during their child's lifetime. Nevertheless, his masculinity remains in question, and Mrs. Beever perceives him as a charming dilettante, who expresses "a certain quality of passive excess which was the note of the whole man, and which, for an attentive eye, began with his neckties and ended with his intonations. . . . His dress was just too fine, his color just too high, his moustache just too long, his voice just too loud, his smile just too gay. His movement, his manner, his tone were respectively just too free, too easy, and too familiar; his being a very handsome, happy, clever, active, ambitiously local young man was in short just too obvious. . . . One of his "states," for Mrs. Beever, was the state of his being a boy again, and the sign of it was his talking nonsense. (35–36)

Tony's boyishness is emphasized when he first meets Dennis. For Tony, Dennis's "manliness" points up his own frivolity, and he compares himself with the visitor as he acknowledges how Dennis has intrigued him:

> "I hope indeed he's going to stay. I like his looks immensely. . . .
> I like his type. . . . It's the real thing—I wish we had him here. . . .
> Upon my honour I do—I know a man when I see him. He's just
> the sort of fellow I personally should have liked to be."
> "You mean *you're* not the real thing?" Rose asked.
> It was a question of a kind that Tony's good nature, shining
> out almost splendidly even through trouble, could always meet
> with princely extravagance. "Not a bit! I'm bolstered up with all

sorts of little appearances and accidents. Your friend there has
his feet on the rock." (96)

Tony's predilection for Rose's friend is emphasized when they meet a
second time. Expressing his disappointment that Dennis was unable to stay
at Bounds previously (and downplaying how Julia's death had made Dennis's
presence impossible), Tony urges the visitor to stay at and presses him to
accept the invitation: ["'] Mrs Beever made no scruple of removing him
bodily from under my roof. I forfeited—I was obliged to—the pleasure of a
visit to him. But that leaves me with my loss to make up and my revenge to
take—I repay Mrs. Beever in kind.' To find Rose disputing with him the
possession of their friend filled him with immediate cheer" (252).
    Tony's rivalry with Rose for Dennis's "possession," is parallelled and
inverted through Dennis's desire to "possess" Rose for Tony. Dennis, who
has returned from China and thus partakes of the forbidden homoeroticism that infused nineteenth-century constructions of the East,[10] offers to
take Rose back with him. Dennis compares Tony to Rose, in the concluding
pages, but finds his host to be more noble: "Like Rose, for Vidal, he was
deeply disfigured, but with a change more passive and tragic" (357). In a
scene fraught with urgency, Dennis appeals to Tony to accept his help:

> "For God's sake, Mr. Bream, believe in me and meet me!" he
> broke out.
>     "'Meet' you?"
>     "Make use of the hand I hold out to you." (359)

This hand is the hand that will propel Rose firmly out of Tony's presence, a
presence that is replete with "passionate perversity" (358). Promising to do
"everything but marry her" (361), Dennis sacrifices himself to Tony's comfort:

> "There's nothing, then, I shall do for *you*?"
> "It's done. We've helped each other."
> What was deepest in Tony stirred again. "I mean when your
> trouble has passed."
> "It will never pass. Think of that when you're happy yourself."
> Tony's grey face stared. "How shall I ever be____?" (363–64)

The homoerotic bond between the two men allows for the perpetuation of
the heterosexual containment narrative. Yet while heterosexual normativity
may be maintained through this homoerotic relationship, it is also complicated by it, for the movement of the narrative renders male same-sex desire

an inside-alongside of heterosexuality, which unsettles the heterotextual dynamic that the novel, on one level, attempts to establish. Concomitantly, the intensity of Tony's exchanges with Dennis pose a marked contrast to Tony's with Jean and eclipse the promise of that heterosexual union.

While Tony admires Jean Martle from the beginning of the novel, their relations are ambiguously and even ambivalently encoded. In the opening pages, Tony observes Jean seated in a "wide-backed, wide-armed Venetian chair which made a gilded cage for her flutter" (110). The cage metaphor, which in this instance describes Jean's position, continues to resonate throughout Tony's descriptions of the ingenue. Intimate relations with Jean become equated with stuffy interiors, as opposed to the breezy exteriors evoked by their friendship: "There had been no worrying question of the light this particular flash might kindle; he had never had to ask himself what his appreciation of Jean Martle might lead to. It would lead to exactly nothing—that had been settled, all round, in advance. This was a happy, lively provision that kept everything down, made sociability a cool, public, out-of-door affair, without a secret or a mystery—confined it, as one might say, to the breezy, sunny forecourt of the temple of friendship, forbidding it any dream of access to the obscure and comparatively stuffy interior" (202–3). Tony's promise to Julia, which restricts his relations with Jean, is not a liability for him, but an emancipation. He delights in the restriction because it allows him to admire the ingenue without risk of intimate involvement. He also promotes Paul's courtship, because Jean's marriage would leave him all the freer to admire her: "it was his luxurious idea—or had been up to now—that in the midst of the difference so delightfully ambiguous he was free just *not* to change, free to remain as he was and go on liking her on trivial grounds" (202).

Consequently, the heterosexual relations that climax in Tony's prospective marriage to Jean are plagued by disturbing significations of cages, limitations, and circumscriptions, which stand in marked contrast to the boundless potential embodied in Tony's friendship with Dennis. As a result, the heterotext is both supported and supplemented by the homotext, which allows for the fruition of the heterosexual relations, but which also dislocates them.

The narrative movement of *The Other House*, therefore, pushes outside the inside the aberrant female desire that threatens familial structures, yet it contains that feminine deviation in an alliance charged with homoerotic potential, an alliance that upsets the movement of the heterotextual trajectory. Demonstrating how the heterosexual inside is predicated upon the outside/alongside of same-sex desire, James's strange novel of child murder and demonized women foregrounds the problematics of containment narratives—inviting rereadings of their paradigmatic implications—at the same time that it illustrates the ways in which homosexuality in-filtrates the heterosexual center and upsets its exclusive status. While *The Other House* does not celebrate lesbian transgression, then, as does *Celine et Julie vont en bateau,* the novel, by covertly critiquing the heterosexuality it overtly works to affirm, itself transgresses conventional sexual limits. In turn, and much like Truffaut's *La Chambre verte,* James's novel also moves to collapse the sexual boundaries that have separated inside from outside and, in so doing, poses an inherent challenge to their restrictive construction.

## Notes

1. Where Wilson found the novel "dreadful" (181), and Putt (309) and Sweeney (216) claim it to be "disappointing" (216), other critics, like Barnett and Labrie, argue that the text is deserving of more attention than it has received.
2. See Fetterley (101–53) and Castle (150–85).
3. For more information, see Cohen.
4. Focalizing this interest in homosexuality is Havelock Ellis's *Studies in the Psychology of Sex: Sexual Inversion,* produced in 1897, which for years would remain one of the most influential works on homosexuality written in English.
5. Kaplan, who convincingly documents James's homoerotic proclivities, suggests that James's dislike of Wilde arose out of the threat Wilde posed to James's own sexual identity (300–301).
6. James originally conceived *The Other House* as a drama and later transformed it into a play in 1908.
7. This case is documented by Faderman in *Scotch Verdict* and dramatized in Lillian Hellman's play, *The Children's Hour,* adapted to film in 1962.
8. In 1893, Dr. Edward Mann wrote: "In one instance I have known of this morbid sexual love for a person of the same sex, starting probably, with some one girl, of a faulty nervous organization, in a young ladies seminary,—almost assume the form of an epidemic (genesis erethism),—and several young ladies were brought up before the faculty, and were told that summary dismissal would follow if this were not at once dropped. The terrible mischief which was thus arrested, and doubtless originated with an insane girl, in this case evidently assumed an hysterical tendency in others not insane, but who might have easily become so if they were neuropathically endowed, as they doubtless were" (qtd. in Faderman, *Surpassing* 291).
9. As Sedgwick describes: "the tableau of legitimation of 'modern' class and gender arrangements is something that takes place on firmly male-homosocial terms: it is a transaction of honor between men over the dead, discredited, or disempowered body of a woman" (137).
10. Said notes that "the Orient was a place where one could look for sexual experience unobtainable in Europe" (190).

## Works Cited

Barnett, Louise K. "Displacement of Kin in the Fiction of Henry James." *Criticism* 22 (1980): 140–55.

Castle, Terry. *The Apparitional Lesbian: Female Homosexuality and Modern Culture.* New York: Columbia UP , 1993.

Cohen, Ed. *Talk on the Wilde Side.* New York: Routledge, 1993.

Edel, Leon. *The Complete Plays of Henry James.* Philadelphia: Lippincott, 1949.

Faderman, Lillian. *Surpassing the Love of Men: Romantic Friendship and Love between Women from the Renaissance to the Present.* New York: Morrow, 1981.

————. *Scotch Verdict: Miss Pirie and Miss Woods v. Dame Cumming Gordon.* New York: Columbia UP, 1994.

Fetterley, Judith. *The Resisting Reader: A Feminist Approach to American Fiction.* Bloomington: Indiana UP, 1981.

Fuss, Diana. *Inside/Out: Lesbian Theories, Gay Theories.* New York: Routledge, 1991.

James, Henry. *The Other House.* New York: Arno, 1976.

Kaplan, Fred. *Henry James: The Imagination of Genius.* New York: Morrow, 1992.

Labrie, Ross. "*The Other House:* A Jamesian Thriller." *North Dakota Quarterly* 45 (1977): 23–30.

Lesage, Julia. "Celine and Julie Go Boating: Subversive Fantasy." *Jump Cut* 24–25 (1981): 36–43.

Putt, S. Gorley. *Henry James: A Reader's Guide.* Ithaca: Cornell UP, 1966.

Said, Edward W. *Orientalism.* New York: Vintage, 1979.

Sedgwick, Eve. *Between Men: English Literature and Male Homosocial Desire.* New York: Columbia UP, 1981.

Showalter, Elaine. *Sexual Anarchy: Gender and Culture at the Fin de Siècle.* New York: Penguin, 1990.

Sweeney, Gerard M. "The Curious Disappearance of Mrs. Beever: The Ending of *The Other House.*" *Journal of Narrative Technique* 11 (1981): 216–28.

Wilson, Edmund. "The Ambiguity of Henry James." *The Question of Henry James.* Ed. F.W. Dupee. New York: Octagon, 1973. 33–74.

## Filmography

*Celine et Julie vont en bateau.* Dir. Jacques Rivette. Writ. Eduardo de Gregorio, Juliet Berto, Dominique Labourier, Bulle Ogier, Marie-France Pisier, Jacques Rivette. Perf. Dominique Labourier (Julie), Juliet Berto (Celine). Les Films du Losange, Eastmancolor, 1974.

*La Chambre verte.* Dir. François Truffaut. Writ. François Truffaut and Jean Gruault. Perf. François Truffaut and Nathalie Baye. Les Films du Carosse S.A. & Les Productions Artistes Associés SA, 1978.

# Mourning, Nostalgia, and Melancholia

## Unlocking the Secrets of Truffaut's *The Green Room*

*Matthew F. Jordan*

> Mourning is regularly the reaction to the loss of a loved person, or to the loss of some abstraction which has taken the place of one, such as one's country, liberty, an ideal, and so on. In some people the same influences produce melancholia instead of mourning and we consequently suspect them of a pathological disposition.
>
> Freud

> Life in any true sense is absolutely impossible without forgetfulness.
>
> Nietzsche

Film adaptations of literary classics are notoriously tricky and often inspire as much wrath as praise. On the one hand, films can use beautiful moving images, music, flashing signs, close-ups, and the grain of the human voice to express feeling and tell a story, none of which are available to a literary text save through the power of the imagination. On the other hand, movies must often reduce parts of the literary work or expand others to make use of the visual medium. The director must choose which details will be foregrounded and which will blend into the scenery. The results of these decisions often provoke criticism from those who feel that the story is now incomplete in some way. In a sense, we face the same problem when recollecting the past. When we write history, we must always choose which particulars must be sacrificed in order to convey a general meaning. One could argue that the same poetics is at work in the faculty of memory. When we recollect the past in order to make sense of it, we often forget parts of the story, leaving out certain things in the moment of recollection. Yet if in forgetting things we lose significant parts of our pasts, what is the proper response to the loss? How can we locate the line between necessary remembrance and excessive fixation, between a healthy piety that honors the past and a pathological inability to mourn that poisons the present?

Henry James's "The Altar of the Dead" and François Truffaut's *The Green Room* dramatize this dilemma of piety, offering a warning about the dangers of an obsessive desire to keep the past alive in memory. Though derived from it, Truffaut's *The Green Room* supplements "The Altar of the Dead" in important ways. Both have protagonists who, in their relation to the past, cross the line between noble piety and obsessive fixation, but James keeps George Stransom's very private past largely closed to us, as anonymous as the foggy London streets that he and his ghosts haunt. As a result, though his story warns about morbid fixation, James leaves the causes of this attachment to the past largely mysterious. Truffaut, on the other hand, gives us a glimpse into Julien Davenne's traumatic past to see the causes of his condition. This knowledge of his past, our sharing in his memories, becomes an important component of our identification with Julien on screen, allowing us to understand both his sense of duty and how this duty becomes his undoing. Indeed, by adapting the action of James's story to 1920s rural France, Truffaut links Davenne's personal loss to a collective trauma, France's loss of a generation to the First World War. In doing so, the film serves an important function in the construction of a French national cinema and cultural consciousness: it speaks to problems of memory stemming from a shared experience.

In both stories the dilemma of having too much memory is staged through a central character or "case study," as James called it, who allows his connection to the past to drain his capacity to live in the present. And both show that problems of memory are also problems of desire. The authors want us to identify with their protagonists' desire to hold onto the past and keep it alive, but ultimately warn about what can happen when the past gets hold of us. Yet while James and Truffaut present characters who feel more at home with the dead than with the living and whose desires to remain with them are ultimately actualized, George Stransom suffers a malady of memory that corresponds to nineteenth-century conceptions of nostalgia while Julien Davenne shows an inability to mourn that makes a diagnosis of melancholia brought on by a traumatic experience more appropriate for his condition. Moreover, Truffaut's choice to link Davenne's traumatic past to a larger historical trauma allows his story to serve allegorically as a cultural lesson for France. Julien Davenne's malady of memory, his inability to mourn, becomes a problem of history. Truffaut's *The Green Room* teaches that an important part of mourning for a lost past is sharing that past with others and that for social connection to be possible in the present, one must allow for a certain reworking, a forgetting and loss of one's private memories. To look at the subtle differences between the lessons of the two versions of the story, I will first explain how James came to the problem of remembrance and how he portrays the line between noble piety and pathological nostalgia through the figure of George Stransom. Then I will examine how Truffaut compensated for certain problems of cinematic adaptation by adding visual supplements to the story. This extra material, in particular the addition of Cecilia Mandel as a counterpoint to Julien Davenne, modifies the tenor of the story. Finally, Truffaut's adaptation, despite the many alterations, ultimately remains faithful to the spirit of James's story and allows us to think with it about the meaning of piety.

In an argument about coming to terms with the past, perhaps it is best to start with how James came to think about the problems of memory and desire that are central to "The Altar of the Dead." We know that the idea for the story became clear in James's imagination in 1894, at a time when he was coming to terms with *his* dead. The weighty losses of his sister Alice, Walter Pater, Mark Pattison and others were compounded in that year by the suicide of Constance Fenimore Woolson, which left a stunned James wandering the streets of London trying to make sense of his role in her life and death (Edel 385). Save two or three intervals during the twelve years he had known Woolson, his friendship with her had been primarily epistolary. Yet in her letters, he had missed the symptoms of the melancholia that eventually led her over the balcony of her Venetian villa and plunged James into a spiral of regret. In accordance with their mutual oath, they had both destroyed their letters to one another. Now, how was he to remember her?

After traveling to Italy for Woolson's funeral, James found himself returning to and eventually moving into the house that she had once occupied at 15 Beaumont Street, Oxford. Here, he was visited by the idea for a short tale, a vision of a man whose "noble and beautiful religion is the worship of the Dead" (*Complete Notebooks* 98). For James, the idea of a story about a man who finds his refuge from the present in the worship of the dead was not tragic, but rather "happy": "He cherishes for the silent, for the patient, the un-reproaching dead, a tenderness in which all his private need of something, not of this world, to cherish, to be pious to, to make the object of a donation, finds a sacred and almost a secret expression. He is struck with the way they are forgotten, are unhallowed, unhonoured, neglected, shoved out of sight; allowed to become so much more dead, even, than the fate that has overtaken them has made them. He is struck with the rudeness, the coldness, that surrounds their memory—the want of place made for them in the life of the survivors" (98). There is good reason to read this notebook entry as an expression of James's own desire to remember the dead. He, too, was struck by the rudeness and coldness of the public announcement of Woolson's death as a suicide. He, too, felt the absence of pious fidelity toward the dead. If the world around him seemed to have no memory, perhaps the ethical response to this lack of piety was for the individual to take this responsibility upon himself. A character began to emerge who gave expression to this feeling and whose cultivated relationship to the past followed an evolution similar to James's own. James first conceived of his character's "altar" as a "merely spiritual one—an altar in his mind, in his soul, more splendid to the spiritual eye than any shrine in any actual church" (98). In order to show how this religion manifested itself as a particular type of subjectivity, to make Stransom an effective figure of consciousness, James had to "enlarge" the idea, to externalize it into a way of being that the reader could understand. He opted to show the process through which Stransom's desire to raise a spiritual altar to the past, "lighted in the gloom of his own soul" (99), manifested itself as a reality. Stransom's private sense of piety, in order to be conveyed to the reader, had to be transformed into a ritual and a way of dealing with others in the present.[1]

As Stransom came into being, what emerged was the portrait of a nostalgic. What is nostalgia, this homesickness for a lost time or place? Nostalgia first entered the medical lexicon in the seventeenth century and was used as a diagnostic category throughout eighteenth century. In the early nineteenth century, when the progress of modernity threatened traditional ways of life as never before, there was a dramatic increase in writing about nostalgia as a refusal to live in the present as the time that anticipates the future (Roth 273). By the end of the nineteenth century, however, the pervasive anxiety about cultural loss abated with the development of historical ways of knowing throughout all disciplines, and the condition began to lose its pathological connotation. Doctors began to describe nostalgia not as a morbid condition but as a normal reaction to the loss of one's past caused by modern life. This later paradigm of nostalgia as a normal, and even noble, response to loss is what we see exemplified by James, who was famously concerned about the rupture with traditional ways of life and values brought on by American modernity. One could say that James's love of England, his diet of Continental novels, and his flight from his Americanness was symptomatic of his nostalgia. Indeed, in *Terminations*, first published in 1895, there are two characters—Stransom and John Marcher in "The Beast in the Jungle"—whose resemblance to their author was a little too close, even for James: "Another poor sensitive gentleman, fit indeed to mate with Stransom of 'The Altar'—my attested predilection for poor sensitive gentlemen almost embarrasses me as I march!" (*Novels and Tales* [*NT*] ix).

George Stransom, the nostalgic, is described as a man of few passions, a man who feels little save the desire to mark the moments when he lost his dead. It was not that he had experienced more loss than others, merely that he "counted his losses more . . . he had never, never forgotten" (4); he suffers from an excess of memory. This relationship to the past is a symptom of a subjectivity constituted through a repeated withdrawal into nostalgic fantasy. Stransom's case, as James explains, is that of a man with a "cultivated habit (the cultivation is really the point) of regularly taking thought *for* them [the dead]" (vi). If problems of memory are ultimately problems of desire, then Stransom's excess of memory stems from the presence of an absence.[2] He senses that the dead cannot think for themselves and that the rest of the world, their gaze fixed on the immediate present around them, is letting the dead fade out of existence without feeling any sense of loss. Stransom, thus, feels his mnemonic duty to compensate in proportion to the amount of forgetting that he witnesses in those around him. As James wrote: "'The Altar of the Dead' then commemorates a case of what I have called the individual independent effort to keep it [the past] none the less tended and watered, to cultivate it, as I say, with an exasperated piety" (ix). This, then, is Stransom's "religion," in the sense that repeating his mnemonic ritual, following this object of his desire, becomes a faith in and of itself. Stransom's sense of piety, which is "exasperated" in reaction to the cultural tendency to forget, becomes his only way of seeing himself. His imaginary sense of himself, or his *imago* in Lacanian terms, is constituted through the endless repetition of his duty.

But how are we to understand the psychological drive behind the nostalgic subjectivity that separates Stransom from the living? What is his ontological obsession grounded in or centered around? James does not give the reader a detailed case history through which to judge Stransom's predilection, as he believed that the interior world of others is always, to some extent, secret. Instead, he gives us a picture of Stransom's condition in which the roots and causes of the "pale ghost" that rule his life are vague and obscure. We know that Stransom's excess of memory began to express itself after the death of his fiancée, Mary Antrim, who died before being able to meet the great promise of the *possibility* for happiness that she represented to him. Again, if desire is to be thought of as the presence of an absence, then he feels her absence more than any other. Never more, in fact, than on the recurrent day of her death, when he loses himself in a reverie of imaginative communion with all that she represented in his imagination. The reader does not know what this consists of, but in these mo-

ments Stransom finds peace outside of his weary body, through an "im-
mense escape from the actual" (4). The more he tends to her and to his
other dead, the more powerful they become as anchors for his subjectivity.

All Stransom's relations, at least all those in which he finds intimacy,
are safely idealized in this way. This is how he protects the definite world of
his imaginary solitary past from the intrusion of the indefinite or provisional present. The living have desires that differ from his, the dead are a
constant screen for his own desire with "their conscious absence and expressive patience" (5). They ask little from the present and, he feels, get
even less. Again, this guiding belief, his personal ideology or faith, is a
product of his nostalgia. He cannot bear to live in a world in which the
dead might soon be forgotten. Since thinking about such a future pro-
vokes anxiety, he turns from it toward the past. By living in the past and
for his dead, he might stop the forgetting. He begins to have regular communion with these "postponed pensioners" whom he calls "The Others."
Eventually, an altar arises first in his imagination, then as a material remainder, what Lacan calls the *objet petit a,* of his fantasy. Tending to this
altar, to his Others, "gave employment to his piety" (6) and brings meaning to his life.

But if the nostalgic is one who receives his enjoyment through the
reanimation of a lost past through fantasy, what is the nature of that enjoyment? Most nineteenth-century nostalgics, according to the literature, did
not want to be cured (Roth 274). They hid their disease; they found satisfaction through their sickness alone. The more the nostalgic attaches himself to the past, the sweeter his suffering for that lost past becomes, meaning
that desire for the lost object provides more pleasure than the possibilities
of finding substitutes for it. George Stransom, to be sure, does not want a
cure. He wants nothing but to be left alone to dream of the past, his only
satisfaction coming through his communion with the dead. The present is
alive to him only in so far as it offers mnemonic objects that fuel his fantasy.
Indeed, with his sympathetic portrayal of Stransom, James seems to show a
certain *nostalgia* for *nostalgia,* a certain fascination with this "sensitive gentleman," who, unlike the majority of people, feels that only he can stem the
tide of forgetting. The problem of desire means that Stransom is convinced
that *he alone* loves the past enough. Yet James, like many who describe such
nostalgic states, sees Stransom's as a condition springing from the noblest of
human sentiments. If, as I have suggested, we are to understand the constitution of nostalgic subjectivity as a circular movement focused around the
loss of a loved object—or rather as a yearning for a time when that object
was not absent—what set Stransom's circuit of desire in motion? Or to
reformulate the question in Lacanian terms, what is the kernel of loss that

became the sliding ground of his subjectivity, the "central hollow" (*NT* 28) around which his *imago* is formed?

James leaves these questions largely unanswered. He hints at "some incalculable violence or unprecedented stroke" (x), but does not elaborate. Perhaps, given the extent to which James clouds over origins, these are not helpful questions. The point is not what the *actual* betrayal was, what *the* content of the secret is,[3] but the form in which it is expressed, the way that the fantasy modifies Stransom's behavior toward others. Indeed, like the altar, which manifests itself as the *objet petite a* of his fantasy loop, all of Stransom's relations with other people are conditioned by his nostalgia. As a result, all meaningful responses and interactions with others take place in private. For instance, when Stransom meets Paul Creston's new wife, he whisks the "shock out of the way, to keep it for private consumption" (*NT* 8). The old wife is more valuable to him than this new woman, because, as one of his dead, she can serve as a screen for his desire. Paul Creston's need for change, to get on with living, serves as a buttress for Stransom's fantasy, further convincing him that his is the only noble piety and that he should stay away from the Crestons as if Paul were a murderer: "The frivolity, the indecency of it made Stransom's eyes fill, and he had that evening a sturdy sense that he alone in a world without delicacy, had a right to hold up his head" (10). Indeed, Stransom is convinced that the late Kate Creston should now be counted among his dead and be a part of that mysterious void to which he turns his gaze, the secret world of the nostalgic.

Yet in spite of his satisfaction with living in the past, there is one memory that, rather than nourish his fantasy, poisons his sense of piety. This is the memory of Acton Hague, the only human whom Stransom has ever allowed close enough for their relationship to be complicated and whose betrayal of Stransom was supremely public. Hague's death seems to threaten the "unapproachable shrine he had erected in his mind" (14). For if Stransom is to remember his former friend, how can he deal with the pain and the ambivalence? As a result of this crack in his solipsistic past, Stransom feels it necessary to preserve the "mental altar" in some concrete material act, to create some public space that will preserve his private fantasy. Indeed, as his *objet petit a* takes shape, he comes to wish that more of his friends would die so that he could "establish with them in this manner a connection more charming than, as it happened, it was possible to enjoy with them in life" (19). This externalization, however, is the greatest danger to the nostalgic's inner world. For in making a private esoteric religion public, one risks the loss of its ideal nature: it can be tainted by real ambivalency and compromise. Stransom becomes acutely aware of this as others begin to come before his altar: "To other imaginations they might

stand for other things—that they should stand for something to be hushed
before was all he desired" (19). After several years of nostalgic bliss, this
threat of change becomes real through the presence of a woman, who silently comes to the altar often enough that he begins to feel that they are the
same, that they share the same fantasy. The danger is not a material one, but
has to do with Stransom's gaze being turned from the past and onto the
present. Since his sense of being is tied to his nostalgic subjectivity, the
woman's intrusion into this space puts at risk not only the integrity of his
fantasy, but the very core of his being.

The problem with this new woman—who, importantly, remains nameless—is that she makes Stransom aware of the present. When he notices
how "pretty" and "interesting" she is, he feels his relation to the past is
compromised. Acknowledging her as a real Other coming to the altar with
desires of her own would inexorably alter the nature of his worship. Indeed, after this anamorphic moment, when Stransom starts to think more
of the woman than "The Others," he becomes aware for the first time just
how demanding his Dead are, how little they leave him. He has to resist
this change, as it means that he might be shortchanging the Dead: "He went
only for *them*—for nothing else in the world. . . . The force of this revulsion
kept him away ten days; he hated to connect the place with anything but
his offices or to give a glimpse of the curiosity that had been on the point of
moving him" (23). But the damage had already been done. Over the period
of months, "the tangle got itself woven" (23). Stransom tries to ignore the
woman, but finds himself missing her. If he is missing her, then he is
sacrificing his duty to the past. His *imago,* his imaginary sense of being, is
shifting ground through the metonymic slide of desire.

The nature of his desire for the "nameless lady" (55), his feeling of
intimacy, is crucial for understanding Stransom. It is not based on understanding her, of knowing her past and acknowledging her difference, but
on his own mis-recognition that they share a fantastic relation to the past:
"It was not their names that mattered, it was only their perfect practice and
their common need" (26). Stransom can only become intimate with the
woman insofar as she can remain a product of his imagination and he can
assume that they share the same "faith" and thus the same symbolic position of identification. In fact, as soon as she confesses that her dead are
"only one," the tangled web upholding his subjectivity and linking his
fantasy to hers begins to unravel. Stransom's growing awareness that she has
a past different from his is dramatized in the story by his visit to her home.
The moment he sees her room, he learns the secret of her past: "Its dark red
walls were articulate with memories and relics. These were simple things—
photographs and water colours, scraps of writing framed and ghosts of

flowers embalmed; but a moment sufficed to show him they had a common meaning" (34). It is to Acton Hague, the one ambivalent memory that poisons his piety, whom he can neither forgive nor forget, that the woman has dedicated her present. Their fantasies, through which their desires to honor the past were formed, are not the same: "The revelation so smote our friend in the face that he dropped into a seat and sat silent" (35).

Acton Hague had done Stransom an "unforgettable wrong" that blocked his ability to idealize their relationship. This transgression persists in Stransom's memory as a spur of resentment. Since he cannot allow ambivalence into his relation with the past, Stransom tries to ignore the man who had wronged him. At the moment when Stransom realizes that he and the woman no longer share a religion, when she turns him out and says that they will never meet again at the altar, the "spell" of his fantasy loses its charge. She makes him aware that his piety and his nostalgia, which drive the movement around the circular path through which his subjectivity is formed, are not the product of a noble sentiment, but of an ugly resentment of which he is ashamed. Unlike Stransom, the woman shows that she can take the worst wound and turn it into something sublime. His sense of duty, and his *imago* constituted through the fulfillment of that duty, become meaningless: "all the fires of his shrine seemed to him to have been quenched. A great indifference fell upon him, the weight of which was in itself a pain; and he never knew what his devotion had been for him till in that shock it ceased like a dropped watch . . . the mortal deception was that in this abandonment the whole future gave way" (45). He has entered, in psychoanalytic terms, the space between symbolic death and biological death. Stransom's decline continues for several years; he is doomed to live on, no longer having a crystalized past to save him from the future. All that can redeem his life is the hope that his life, too, might be counted as a candle on the altar: "He had given himself to his Dead, and it was good: this time his Dead would keep him" (55).

François Truffaut was fascinated by James's story for several reasons. Like his cinematic mentor Alfred Hitchcock, Truffaut was drawn to characters whose lives were formed around obsessions. In Stransom, he saw a character whose obsessive piety was not only touching, but almost justifiable. Indeed, his identification with the central character of the story is made clear by the fact that he cast himself as Julien Davenne, the George Stransom of *The Green Room*.[4] Despite the radical alteration of the details of the story, his fidelity to James's vision is poignantly dramatized in the scene from *The Green Room* when Julien first shows Cecilia the interior of the chapel he has created for his dead. Scanning the photographs of cultural heroes that line the walls, he points to a picture of Henry James (fig. 7):

Figure 7. Julien Davenne (Truffaut) explaining his fidelity to the ideas of the American gentleman (James) in *The Green Room*.

"This one is an American. He loved Europe so much that he finally became a British citizen. Unfortunately I didn't know him well, but he taught me the importance of respecting the dead." Indeed, having Truffaut, *auteur*, announce the extent to which he is beholden to James is appropriate, as it was from three stories that he drew material for *The Green Room*: "The Altar of the Dead," "The Beast in the Jungle," and "The Friends of Friends." The reasons for drawing from other James stories is that the subjective narrative of "The Altar of the Dead" presented certain problems to Truffaut, the *cinéaste* who had to tell a visual story. He discussed these problems and his suggestions for solving them in a letter to Jean Gruault, who was to help him write the screenplay: "The inconvenient thing with James is that things are never said expressly and we cannot allow ourselves to be that vague and unclear in a film. We should clarify everything and make it more precise. We should also, by a thousand inventions, expand that which I call privileged moments (like the burning of the books in *Fahrenheit 451*). Here, the privileged moments are the scenes of worship, the lighting of candles, the rites, the religious side *à la japonaise*, this is our profound reason for making the film" (Truffaut 447; translation mine). In other words, in order to dramatize the interior problems of the character and explain them to the viewer, Truffaut had to invent cinematic devices to take the place of the narrator. New characters had to be created to talk about Davenne in his absence and to explain his condition. Internal monologues had to be externalized; secret desires had to be fleshed out through relations with other characters. Specific rites, which Truffaut thought of as being analogous to Japanese tea ceremonies, had to be constructed. Film viewers had to be presented with images and plot lines through which they could recognize and understand Davenne's excess of memory and desire.

The first of these transformations, of course, was setting the drama in a French context and moving it forward in time to a moment ten years after the First World War, a period closely associated in popular consciousness with grief and loss. Instead of the gray anonymous streets of London, Truffaut brings the viewer into the dark Goya-like interior spaces of a small provincial town where people know one another and where the specter of death is everywhere. Whereas James opens his story with a discussion of Stransom's dislike of celebration, Truffaut opens *The Green Room* with a series of "time-images," as Gilles Deleuze has characterized such devices, flashbacks from the war. If Stransom's life is "ruled by a pale ghost," Julien Davenne is haunted by horrific memories of decapitated bodies, screaming soldiers caught in barbed wire, and the smell of mustard gas and filthy trenches. Davenne, dressed as a soldier, steps forward amidst a montage of superimposed black and white movies, like the newsreel footage Truffaut used in *Jules and Jim,* showing through images how Davenne's subjectivity literally emerges from these traumatic memories (fig. 8). His gaze moves back and forth, viewing the horror as if from above until he can no longer stand it and must look away. He becomes the allegorical character whose actions will speak to a collective problem: the French cultural tendency to look away and forget the past.

This is Truffaut, the comrade of the *Cahiers du Cinéma* group, using the neorealism the movement promoted in the late 1950s to construct a national cinema. Now in the late 1970s, at a time when many New Wave directors were becoming overtly deconstructive in their formalism, Truffaut's vision is, in a sense, a nostalgic one, harkening back to the high-water mark of the *Cahiers* project, when Bazin and Truffaut argued against an overt scenic formalism and promoted a national cinematic praxis that would join the ontological and psychological to provide a psychological realism.[5] True, the jumpy, quick-cut formalism used by filmmakers like Godard, which distanced the viewer from the on-screen action, created a national style that stood in contrast to the seamless montage of the increasingly dominant Hollywood cinema. However, Truffaut worried that the tendency to distance audiences from the stories on-screen also made them unable to

Figure 8. Julien Davenne (Truffaut) emerging through his memories of the French battlefields of WWI in *The Green Room*.

identify with the characters and to participate in an important collective experience.

The impulse to turn away from the real horror of war is one that Truffaut knew existed in many of his countrymen and made the provincial postwar context perfect for *The Green Room*. France lost nearly sixteen percent of its male population in World War I. In the battle of Verdun alone, over a million French, German, and British men were killed. As many as 30 million were wounded, many crippled for the rest of their lives. If the monuments erected in nearly every town in France to the fallen were not enough, there were the survivors of the war to testify to the trauma. In addition to the casualties among those mobilized, the influenza epidemic that swept Europe and America after the war killed nearly twice as many people as the war itself. In case younger viewers had no memory of these events, a text-frame in the opening of *The Green Room* tells us that the story takes place ten years after the war, "which caused millions of deaths."

Thus, unlike the vague and obscure origins of Stransom's peculiar subjectivity, Davenne's are monumental, public, and immediately revealed to the viewer: they emerge from the nation's shared traumatic loss. Knowledge of this past gives viewers something to understand and sympathize—

if not directly identify—with. True, both Stransom and Davenne suffer from an excess of memory, from an inability to forget, but their mnemonic disorders have different causes and foci. Whereas anxiety about a future that will not remember forms the circuit of Stransom's nostalgia, guilt and an inability to mourn are at the center of Davenne's turn from the present.

Truffaut uses a number of devices to dramatize the symptoms of Davenne's subjectivity. These are the "thousand inventions" that he added to the story so that it would work on film. As he wrote to Gruault, "when the heroes do bizarre things, figure out a way to expand them, to give them a good visual aspect" (Truffaut 447). Thus, there are extra situations, settings, characters and professions for the characters, each of which speaks in some way to Davenne's problematic relation to the past. Many of his symptoms are reminiscent of Freud's description of melancholia in "Mourning and Melancholia," a work that also followed the carnage of the First World War. Given the long-standing link between psychoanalysis and cinema as a source for behavioral motivation and as a shared code, this is no surprise.[6] Hitchcock's *Spellbound* and *Notorious,* two of Truffaut's favorite films, drew heavily on Freud's theories of the unconscious to stage the obsessional dilemmas of the subjects (Insdorf 63). Truffaut, though not overtly Freudian, used many of the psychoanalytic conventions that had become part of the semiotic system of cinema. For our purposes, Freud's method for understanding self-destructive melancholia by comparing it to healthy mourning provides an excellent procedure for analyzing the pathology of Davenne's condition, as Truffaut is constantly contrasting the two positions through a kind of cinematic counterpoint. Whereas James paints the picture of a nostalgic whose desire to be in the past and live amongst his dead eventually becomes an actualized fantasy, Truffaut's Julien Davenne can be best understood as a man whose traumatic past leaves him unable to mourn. The inability to mourn, to work through the loss of a loved object, determines his relation to the past. This subtle change in perspective can be seen in the "inventions" that Truffaut added to his story.

The first of these supplementary scenes comes directly after the opening credits and is based on the meeting between Stransom and the new Crestons. Instead of Paul Creston, it is Gerald Mazet who has just lost his wife and is overwhelmed by grief. Julien comes to see him and Truffaut shows us two responses to dealing with loss. Mazet is desperate to deny the reality of his wife's death and hysterically acts out his desire, trying to keep the priest and the mortician from putting the lid on the coffin. Immediately, the priest tries to console him by telling him that since his wife was baptized, she is not dead, but instead, is waiting for him in heaven, where they will be joined eternally. Resigned, Mazet attempts to take his own life, a reaction that, according to Freud, is a normal component of the work of profound mourning. Indeed, Truffaut dramatizes that in mourning, the process through which the libidinal cathexis—or ego investment in a loved object—is given up is a painful one that often involves self-reproach and self-revilings (Freud 244). To emphasize this point, Davenne screams at the priest that grieving people do not want to hear that they will be reunited with their loved ones in the future, they want them back *now.* Throwing the priest out of the house, he explains to Mazet that he should not listen to "professional consolers" and that it is *up to him* whether she lives or dies. Mazet need only dedicate his life—all his thoughts, all his actions—to the memory of his wife and she will live. He can *will* her to live on as Julien did with his wife eleven years earlier. Thus, Truffaut encapsulates Julien's character for the viewer in the first scene. Consumed by grief over his losses, Julien has dedicated all his energy, all his desire, to keeping the memory of his wife alive. In the normal mourning process, the libido withdraws its energy from the loved object and displaces it onto a new one. Julien, on the other hand, keeps reality at bay and invests all his libidinal energy into the maintenance of his fantasy. Keeping the past alive is only a matter of caring enough, of loving more than others. Julien, it seems, is able to function quite well and displays no hysterical symptoms of grief. Yet there is already a tension here in the refusal to give up the libidinal position, to give up the investment in the lost love object: is Mazet's overwhelming grief a more appropriate reaction to the loss of a loved one, or is Julien's denial of loss something noble and heroic, a way of relating to the past that should be imitated?

Truffaut visualizes this problematic by introducing a love interest who helps dramatize the question of the displacement of desire. This is important, as one of the features of the melancholic's position, distinguishing him from that of the healthy mourner, is the "loss of capacity to adopt a new object of love" (Freud 244) and the turning away from any activity that is not connected with the loved object. This psychological tendency is, of course, a dynamic in the James story. But, whereas we never learn the name of the woman who turns Stransom away from his perfect religion, the viewer is introduced to Cecilia Mandel, played by Nathalie Baye, almost immediately. She is a beautiful young secretary at an auction house where Julien has gone to search for one of the rings worn by his dead wife, Julie. This introductory scene allows Truffaut to show the viewer two things. First, we learn that Julien dislikes estate auctions, which he views as a "pillage" of the past. At such sales, objects are separated from their original owners, split up and dispersed. Again, this dramatizes a psychological aspect of the melancholic's inability to mourn, for he wants objects to remain in a fixed state. Dispersing them is like discharging their libidinal energy, and this, to Davenne, is not only unnecessary, but tragic. Cecilia understands this position, but is also more pragmatic, telling Davenne that one cannot "bring back the dead." Along with voicing this common sense counterpoint to Davenne's fantasy, Cecilia is presented to us as a desiring other and as a possible love object in the present whom Davenne is unable to see because his libidinal economy is still centered around his dead wife. Moreover, as a contrast to Davenne's melancholic tendencies, Cecilia's comment exemplifies a healthy perspective on mourning that allows for life to go on after loss.

To further visualize the nature of Davenne's peculiar subjectivity, Truffaut takes us to where he lives. If, to use a Heideggerian formula, being can be conceived of as dwelling within the house constructed through language, Davenne's household tells us much about his state of being. He lives in a dark, old two-story house with a governess, Mme Rimbaud, and a deaf orphan named Georges, a perfect companion for a man who has "lost the habit of listening." In one room, Davenne has a slide projector and a collection of images, fixed memories that he returns to again and again. He shows the young Georges some of his "very beautiful" slides one night. Whereas Mme Rimbaud is troubled by these images, Davenne and Georges gaze with ease at a picture of a decapitated soldier, followed by another of a corpse blown into a tree. The most important part of his house, however, provides the title for the story and one of the keys to understanding Davenne's dilemma. He keeps one of the rooms on the second floor locked; no one is permitted to enter. Here, in this locked-up part of himself where the candles, signs of desire, never go out, he has a private shrine to his wife, with photos, objects, and a stone hand upon which he places the ring he has recovered from the auction. He regularly spends the night with his wife in this green room, speaking to her as if she were present and losing himself in reverie. Since nothing from the present enters the room, nothing threatens its integrity; just as private memory that is kept secret and silent never evolves through the process of narration.

Julien Davenne's work is also an outgrowth of his peculiar relationship to the past. He is an obituary writer, a professional memorialist, for a little provincial journal called *Le Globe*. The first time we see his workplace, he is being offered a job in Paris by Humbert, the editor of *Le Globe*, who is relocating to a larger town and newspaper where he can cover "current events." Davenne wants no part of this. He is a provincial and is dedicated to his job and his readers. When informed that most of his "readers" are, in fact, dead, Julien's decision is only confirmed. "I want to stay for them," he explains to Humbert. Truffaut scripts a conversation between Humbert and Monique, the secretary for *Le Globe*, to explain not only Davenne's past but how he is viewed by others. Humbert asks what people in the community think of Davenne, whom he describes as a "virtuoso of obituaries." Monique explains that Davenne doesn't go out much and keeps to himself. He was not like this as a youth, but, after suffering the loss of so many friends in the war without even being wounded himself and losing his bride during their honeymoon, he had changed. Now, Monique says, Davenne feels guilty for outliving his loved ones and believes that he owes them a debt that can be paid back only by dedicating himself to them. As a result, he chooses to let life pass him by. Whereas James gives the reader little to grasp, Truffaut offers the viewer important elements of Davenne's past and an interpretive position on that past that reflects the consensual opinions of others.

Of all the additions and alterations to the story, the most significant is the relationship between Julien and Cecilia Mandel, which, according to Truffaut, was based on that between John Marcher and May Bartram in "The Beast in the Jungle": "She is amorous of him in the beginning (and she is conscious of it) whereas he is also amorous, but without knowing it, probably because he does not know that he can love two times in his life. We find there a theme which is dear to us: the definitive and the provisional" (Truffaut 447). True, Truffaut decided to follow James's lead in hinging the story on whether or not Davenne can love again. Yet Julien's love for Cecilia—and the viewer's knowledge of her—are based on more than just his imagination. Truffaut not only writes the character as a desiring woman, but gives her a past that Julien is aware of and shares. In fact, showing his pious fidelity to James, Truffaut bases the couple's shared experience on a detail drawn from "The Friends of the Friends," where the protagonist had a vision of one of her parents at the moment of death (*NT* 325). Julien and Cecilia had met fourteen years ago when she was a young girl whom he had treated with kindness and respect. As in "The Friends of the Friends," Davenne and Cecilia are people who have experienced profound loss and are perfectly suited for one another.[7] However, since Davenne's memory is entirely fixed upon the loss of his wife in Rome eleven years earlier, he has trouble remembering the details of this first meeting. The irony here, of course, is that the man who wills himself never to forget has a peculiarly selective memory. Yet, though his knowledge of Cecilia is clouded by his fantasy, she is not a blank screen for projection like Stransom's phantom lady. Indeed, whereas what Stransom and his lady say to one another is rarely revealed to the reader, the conversations between Julien and Cecilia help delineate the line between obsessional fixation on the past and healthy mourning. Moreover, if we look at their relationship as containing the possibility of reconciliation, as a kind of potential remarriage comedy,[8] Julien's inability to connect with her, to see her as she really is, dramatizes his failure to re-find a connection to the world by integrating a discharged past.

The first such dialogue between the two revolves around Julien's inability to deal with Gerald Mazet's taking a new wife. As Stransom did with Creston, Julien feels betrayed. He believes that Mazet has given up their pact to will the dead to live, merely exchanging the old for something new. Cecilia, who clearly wants Julien to do the same thing, simply asks him why the new love would necessarily replace the old. As someone suffering from the inability to mourn, whose subjectivity is constituted through the drive to keep his fantasy and hence his wife's memory unchanged, Davenne cannot comprehend this position. He says that he cannot forget for ethical reasons, for he loves the dead. She counters that it is necessary to forget and that his problem is not his desire to remember, but *the way* he loves the dead. He loves the dead *against* the living whereas she loves both the living *and* the dead.[9] Unable to give up his libidinal attachment to the dead, or his *imago* constituted through the fulfillment of his duty to them, he can see neither that she offers a possible outlet for his libidinal needs nor the reality that her common sense conveys. Instead, he brutally drives her away.

For Julien, desire seems always to be constructed in relation to the presence of an absence; only after Cecilia refuses to speak to him does he begin to be conscious of his desire for her. At this moment his fantasy, charged through his narcissistic attachment to the past, is most threatened. Again, as in "The Altar of the Dead," the action of the story hinges on the death of an old friend whom Julien is unable to forget. When Julien is asked to write an obituary for "his old friend" Paul Massigny, the virtuoso of obituaries writes a history that shows his inability to compromise his own private memories for the sake of public memory. He writes an obituary that, according to Humbert, makes it seem as though he wants "to kill Massigny a second time." This is another manifestation of his inability to mourn, to give up his libidinally charged memories and discharge them by reworking those memories into new ones that can be successfully integrated. For to give up his ontological certainty about the past would be to give up his sense of duty to that past, an act that would threaten to bring the whole edifice down.

Yet with the conflict between his recollection of Massigny and the public memory of him and his vague desire for Cecilia, the ideological support for Davenne's subjectivity is dangerously threatened. His secret past, kept apart from reality and alive in fantasy, begins to lose its crystalline purity. As in James, we can understand the protagonist's fantastic duty as a repeated circuit constructed through *drive*. Slavoj Žižek points out that the real purpose of *drive* for the subject is not reaching the final goal, which in this case would be bringing back the dead, but its *aim*. The ultimate aim of the fantasy is simply to reproduce itself, to return to its circular path, to continue its path ad infinitum (5). For Davenne, the man who is unable to give up his libidinal attachment to his lost dead, the real source of enjoyment, and hence the basis for his peculiar subjectivity, is the repetitive movement through this closed circuit. But once Davenne loses his certainty about the past and his libidinal energy begins to direct itself toward a new goal, the fantasy through which he denies the reality of the present loses its consistency. Truffaut visualizes this psychological deterioration with the figure of the house, showing a breeze blowing into Julien's locked green room, knocking over the candles and setting it ablaze from within. Once the damage is done, the ritual can no longer remain the same. Davenne is desperate to find a new way to maintain his heroic imaginary identity as a man who can will the past to live. The remainder of the film shows the various ways that he tries, and ultimately fails, to keep reality at bay.

According to Freud, the person who is unable to perform the healthy work of mourning and refuses to give up his libidinal attachment to a fixed past must maintain his belief through a deflection of libidinal energy or risk the deterioration of his sense of self. Whereas healthy mourning involves separating onself from the lost object by looking at the good and the bad of the lost love, the melancholic turns this criticism back against himself as a form of narcissism, insofar as the narcissistic identification with the object becomes a substitute for the erotic cathexis (Freud 249). Davenne has been able to occupy a position between these two poles by keeping his psychic investment in Julie, the lost love object, alive through ritual. However, once this dutiful circuit loses its consistency and its ideological support, his usual calm slides toward melancholia. He is aware of the onset of forgetting and desperately tries to think of Julie more and more to keep her alive. Truffaut is, in a sense, testing Pascal's proposition that if you submit to ideological ritual, act *as if* you already believe, the belief will come by itself. The external custom or habit will condition an internal belief. "I don't know where I got the will not to forget, but I have invented a ritual," Davenne tells Cecilia. But this Pascalian position goes beyond a mere behavioralist wisdom. Not just any ritual will do, it must be adequate to the libidinal charge being deflected onto it. Truffaut visualizes this dilemma through another supplement, sending Davenne to pick up a wax replica of Julie that he has commissioned in the hope that this icon will help anchor his memory. Upon seeing the eerie figure, Davenne immediately orders the artist to destroy the figure. The externalized replica threatens to further erase the inner ideal, the secret memory that he kept locked away from the world. Davenne's reaction dramatizes not only the point that there is no adequate representation of the past that does not alter a private memory, but that belief is also contingent upon love, not mere ritual.

Davenne feels lost after this failure, unable to allow himself fulfillment in anything but the past. Truffaut visualizes this symbolic position by locking Davenne in the graveyard, where he finds a chapel that will serve as his new altar. Setting up this new temple, with its "forest of flame" gives him a way to sublimate his anxiety and deflect his libidinal energy. Yet, whom is this work dedicated to? Who is its addressee? Is the altar for the dead, as he believes, or is it, unbeknownst to him, really for Cecilia? If the shrine is for Cecilia, his connection to her is conditioned by his fantasy, and, hence, a mis-recognition of her.

Truffaut devises a situation through which to dramatize the nature of Davenne's mis-recognition of Cecilia. As in the James story, where Stransom's intimacy depends upon the woman serving as a screen for the projection of his desire, Julien can only relate to Cecilia when she enters the field of his fantasy. Thus, Truffaut has Davenne bring her to the temple and place her before the altar. Here, he dictates what is essentially a marriage vow, asking her if she will take his dead as her own and, in return, promising to add hers to the altar as well. Rather than being a mutual exchange, this "marriage" depends upon the woman's willingness to submit to the man's fantasy. One can hear the tension in Davenne's voice when he responds to her statement that she would rather that their dead all blend together into one candle for which they could have one ceremony. In this way, the dead could lose their particularity and transform into a general sense of loss with which the survivors could live. Along with this example of a potentially normal mourning process, Truffaut shows the extent to which Davenne's love for Cecilia, though he wants to dress it up as merely a shared dedication to the dead, is what is protecting him from the profound effects of melancholia. For the moment, Davenne is happy with the possibility of their union inside the iron cage of the altar. He believes that he has found someone who holds the same beliefs as he, who shares his sense of duty to the past.

When she does agree to be the guardian of the temple with him, Cecilia still wants it to be a place of healthy piety rather than morbid fixation. They are walking together, as lovers would, and are talking about pressing present engagements. Cecilia tells Julien how much he has helped her get over her loss, saying that she feels as if she is "finally coming out of a long illness." Though Julien is blind to it, she is telling him that it is he, not the temple, that has helped her emerge. Whereas for Julien, the temple reconciles him to the future, for Cecilia, the temple reconciles her with the past, making life in the present possible. Yet trapped in his habitual solipsism, he does not hear what she is saying and through this *méconnaissance* attributes their mutual feeling of contentment to a shared relationship to the dead. As he prepares to leave on a lecture tour, Julien gives Cecilia the key and charges her with the maintenance of the chapel in his absence.

Upon his return the action comes to a head. Davenne goes to where Cecilia lives, symbolizing an attempt to get to know her, and sees that, for her, reconciliation with the past means mourning for Paul Massigny. As in the James story, the introduction of the Girardian third leads to a rupture between the couple. Before the altar, Davenne had promised to admit her dead into the temple, but now he will not admit Paul Massigny, the stain on his idealized past. Since the public memory of Massigny conflicts with his private one, he belongs to others, not to this temple for "the people who belonged to him in life." "Our past doesn't belong to us," she pleads with him, but he will not compromise the certainty of his. Upset by his brutal denial of what makes her past meaningful, and by his hatred and inability to forgive, she breaks with him: "The spell is broken." Without Cecilia, Julien's temple loses its meaning. Now, all the libidinal energy that he had displaced onto her and the possibility for happiness that she represented are turned back upon his ego in self-reproach. With his fantasy broken and without any possibility for love, he loses the will to live and immediately falls ill. Davenne locks himself in that burned-out shell of a green room, sending the doctor away. Fixed in the past, his subjectivity no longer supported by ritual or fantasy, his narcissistic sense of guilt and regret eats him up. He too, dreams of the candles becoming one, of the past melding into one giant flame, but locked in his burned-out subjectivity, he cannot act. His obsessive fixation on his private past, his inability to give any of it up to forgetting, keeps him from being able to love Cecilia and the present world of healthy mourning that she represents.

When Cecilia, now aware that she indeed loves Davenne and misses him, comes to his aid it is too late. "Forget it! Forget it!" she pleads. Before the altar, with one candle yet to be lit—his—, he admits to her that the tragedy was that "nothing ever happened" between the two of them. In the end, the lesson of *The Green Room* is that noble piety, no matter how "exasperated," is not enough. For the person who experiences its loss, love cannot be replaced by ritual and religion, no matter how regular or profound. This is the message that Truffaut leaves us with: only love can heal the wound caused by the loss of love.

Of all the inventions that Truffaut added to James's story to overcome the problems of a vague subjective narrator, supplementing the love story and giving both Cecilia and Davenne a knowable past is probably the most significant. Truffaut makes Davenne's recovery from traumatic memories contingent upon his ability to connect with Cecilia, a woman with a past and with a worldview of her own that the viewer is given access to. In doing so, his story places two opposing symbolic positions toward the past into dialogue and conflict. In Davenne, Truffaut gives us a man whose inability to mourn for a certain past, to give up his investment in it and forget, leaves him anxious for the future and unable to live in the present save through his ritualized animation of that past. In Cecilia, Truffaut shows healthy mourning, an approach to loss that involves grieving, forgetting, and integration of a discharged past into a living present. Both characters display a sense of piety toward the past, but Davenne's inability to forget the particulars, forsake certainty, and accept ambivalency turns his piety into an obsession that blinds him to the present.

Truffaut, too, though he radically altered the details of "The Altar of the Dead," setting it in post–World War I France and linking it to a collective experience for which the healthy work of mourning was supremely important, remains true to James's story. Though the ontological obsessions around which Stransom and Davenne organize their subjectivity are slightly different, the fact that both versions allow us to identify with characters whose relationship to the past crosses over into the realm of the pathological shows that they serve the same cause and teach the same lesson. From James, Truffaut learned the "importance of respecting the dead" and showed that such piety was a collective problem of history. Like James, Truffaut demonstrates that this respect can become an obsession that can poison the present. Both authors wanted to create characters whose concern for the past would provoke an empathic and mimetic response. They wanted audiences to connect with the noble piety dramatized in their stories.[10] Yet Truffaut, more than James, shows that part of connecting with Others is giving up one's attachment to a fixed and private past. In the end, Truffaut's adaptation of "The Altar of the Dead" shows that a story, or a history, that is altered for the cinema can remain faithful if its sense is retained through a healthy piety. This kind of piety, allowing for an adequate remembrance that would both honor the past and allow its hold on the present to be loosened through healthy mourning, can be located somewhere between the examples presented through Julien and Cecilia. Truffaut shows us that he has it.

## Notes

1. James wrote: "All life comes back to the question of our relations with each other" (*Lesson of Balzac* 10). On the importance and paradoxical absurdity of relations with others within the Jamesian phenomenological economy, see Armstrong (137). James saw that relations with others *could* bring joy by expanding our experience of the world and by enriching our understanding of ourselves. However, relations with others could also lead to despair because the Other must ultimately remain a mystery, making misunderstanding and conflict more probable than harmony. Stransom dramatizes the latter, and his response to this problem is to resign from life, making him a figure of consciousness similar to Hegel's "Beautiful Soul."
2. Bell, among others, has noted that many of James's ghost stories concern themselves with characters whose act of perception is turned toward an absence. Bell argues that this turns them into quest stories that are about the pursuit of some phantasmal object present only to the perceiver (66).
3. As with Marcher's secret in "The Beast in the Jungle," these shrouded pasts have been a screen for critical projection as well. For instance, many critics follow Sedgwick into an epistemology of the closet and use such cloudy secrets to "out" James and his characters. Positing that previous readings of such situations were guided by the projection of assumed male norms, Sedgwick argues that "to the extent that Marcher's secret has *a* content, that content is homosexual" (169).
4. Truffaut stated in an interview: "It seemed to me that if I played Julien Davenne myself, it would be like writing a letter by hand rather than typing it" (Insdorf 220).
5. For an analysis of this position and this period, see Hayward.
6. On this relation, see Bergstrom and Greenberg.
7. On the failure ever to meet of two perfectly matched persons, see Bell's *Meaning in Henry James* (27). Bell argues that the ghostly persistence of the one represents the "might-have-been." She sees James's ghosts as doubles who tempt or warn or represent a possibility no longer available to the living.
8. I am alluding to this genre as established by Cavell in *Pursuits of Happiness.* Cavell reads particular members of the comedy genre to establish the subgenre of the "remarriage comedy," which, he argues, helps illuminate Freud's early vision that "the finding of an object is in fact the re-finding of it" (Cavell 68). Though Cavell uses films whose narrative is structured around the threat of divorce and the obstacles in the way of a couple's getting back together, the concept is also helpful for reading films whose characters' potential for happiness depends on their ability to give up something of themselves, to give up their ideal, in order to acknowledge the individuality and difference of their companion.
9. As with Cecilia, Truffaut gives depth to the flat female characters in "The Altar of the Dead," having the new Mme Mazet explain how content she was to find someone during an era when good men are scarce. Thus, he gives the audience a past through which to understand and identify with the Mazets.
10. The extent to which they were successful is another question. As Truffaut worried, audiences who were predisposed to turning away from the past and

forgetting did not connect with a story about the importance of remembering the dead. In a letter to François Porcile, he wrote: "As you know, *The Green Room* (*La Chambre Verte*) has a good reputation, but from a distributor's point of view, the real title should be *The Empty Room* (*La Chambre Vide*)" (Truffaut 539). Audiences did turn out in record numbers to see Truffaut act during the summer of 1978. However, it was not to see him as Julien Davenne, but in his role as a French scientist in *Close Encounters of the Third Kind*.

## Works Cited

Armstrong, Paul B. *The Phenomenology of Henry James.* Chapel Hill: U of North Carolina P, 1983.

Bell, Millicent. *Meaning in Henry James.* Cambridge: Harvard UP, 1991.

Bergstrom, Janet, ed. *Endless Night: Cinema and Psychoanalysis, Parallel Histories.* Berkeley: U of California P, 1999.

Cavell, Stanley. *Pursuits of Happiness: The Hollywood Comedy of Remarriage.* Cambridge: Harvard UP, 1981.

Deleuze, Gilles. *Cinema 2: The Time Image.* Trans. Hugh Tomlinson and Robert Galeta. Minneapolis: U of Minnesota, P 1989.

Edel, Leon. *Henry James: The Middle Years.* New York: Lippincott, 1962.

Freud, Sigmund. *The Standard Edition of the Complete Psychological Works of Sigmund Freud.* Trans. James Strachey. Vol. 14. London: Hogarth, 1957.

Greenberg, Harvey. *Screen Memories: Hollywood Cinema on the Psychoanalytic Couch.* New York: Columbia UP, 1994.

Hayward, Susan. *French National Cinema.* London: Routledge, 1993.

Insdorf, Annette. *François Truffaut.* Cambridge: Cambridge UP, 1995.

James, Henry. *The Complete Notebooks of Henry James.* Ed. Leon Edel and Lyall H. Powers. Oxford: Oxford UP, 1987.

———. *The Lesson of Balzac.* Boston: Houghton, 1905.

———. *The Novels and Tales of Henry James.* Vol. 17. New York: Scribner's, 1922.

Roth, Michael S. "The Time of Nostalgia: Medicine, History and Normality in 19th Century France." *Time and Society* 1.2 (1992): 271–86.

Sedgwick, Eve Kosofsky. "The Beast in the Closet: James and the Writing of Homosexual Panic." *Sex, Politics, and the Nineteenth Century.* Ed. Ruth Bernard Yeazell. Baltimore: Johns Hopkins UP, 1986. 148–86.

Truffaut, François *Correspondance.* Recueillies par Gilles Jacob et Claude de Givray. Renens: 5 Continents/Hatier, 1988.

Žižek, Slavoj. *Looking Awry: An Introduction to Jacques Lacan through Popular Culture.* Cambridge: MIT UP, 1991.

## Filmography

*The Green Room.* Dir. François Truffaut. Writ. François Truffaut and Jean Gruault. Perf. François Truffaut and Nathalie Baye. Les Films du Carosse S.A. & Les Productions Artistes Associés SA, 1978.

# Still Me(n): Superman Meets *The Bostonians*

*Leland S. Person*

James Ivory was "one of the directors who cast me *because* he had liked my work in *Superman*," Christopher Reeve acknowledges in his recent autobiography, *Still Me* (1998), but most reviewers have done little more than note Ivory's decision to cast "Superman" as Basil Ransom in the 1984 film adaptation of James's 1886 novel. David Sterritt observes Reeve "trading his Superman cape for a 19th-century model" (23). Robert Emmet Long notes that "Mr. Reeve retains some of the qualities of his Superman impersonation" (77). Millicent Bell says that Reeve "looks as healthily handsome as if he were drawn in cartoon outline (as befits Superman)" (109–10). And Vincent Canby comments that Reeve goes "way beyond Superman with charm and guts" (266). Taking a cue from Bell, who notes that "every film version of a novel is an instructive mistaking" and considers *The Bostonians* "one of those works that seems to change shape as the times change" (109), I would like to explore the implications of Christopher Reeve's casting as Basil Ransom, to compare the representation and role of masculinity in both novel and film, especially in the political and social context in which the film first appeared.

Reviews of the Merchant Ivory *Bostonians* were generally favorable. Barnaby Conrad called the film "one of the finest cinematic adaptations of James ever made" (36), while Vincent Canby went even further, terming the film "one of the best adaptations of a major literary work ever to come onto the screen" (265). I want to explore the film in the context of its 1984 release—its insertion into ongoing debates during the first Reagan Presidency about women's rights, the Equal Rights Amendment, homosexuality, and gay and lesbian rights.[1] Uncannily, the "envelope of circumstances" (to borrow a wonderful phrase from *The Portrait of a Lady*) in which James's novel and the Merchant Ivory film appeared have many similarities. *The Bostonians* premiered at a moment when the conservative movement, especially its social and moral reform wing, was beginning to assert itself. The decade-long struggle to ratify the Equal Rights Amendment (passed by Congress in 1972) had ended unsuccessfully, despite the extension of the Constitutionally mandated seven-year deadline. Reagan won the 1984 Presidential election against Walter Mondale by one of the largest margins in United States history. He carried forty-nine states, losing only Minnesota (narrowly) and the District of Columbia, and won nearly 60% of the popular vote. Mondale, of course, had chosen Geraldine Ferraro to be his running mate—the first woman to run for vice president in United States history. Two years after the Equal Rights Amendment failed to win ratification by three-fifths of the states, the election of 1984, among other things, represented a new referendum on equal rights for women—and women lost.

Reagan had won the 1980 election by a narrower margin, barely garnering half of the popular vote against incumbent Jimmy Carter (and Independent John Anderson). While Carter supported the Equal Rights Amendment, the Republican Party removed ERA support from its platform, and Reagan obviously opposed the amendment. The 1980 election, it can be argued, turned at least in part on gender issues—not only Reagan's opposition to the Equal Rights Amendment, but his apparently superior masculinity, his leading-man qualities of appearance and self-representation. Susan Jeffords has gone furthest in linking Reagan's presidency with American films of the 1980s, and she too considers the 1980 election as imaginatively pivotal for many Americans. The Carter presidency had been plagued by double digit inflation, the Middle Eastern oil embargo (that led to lines at U.S. gas stations), and especially the Iranian hostage crisis. Carter seemed stymied and weak—even "feminine" (Jeffords 10–11)—as the hostage drama dragged on, and the crisis ended very shortly before Reagan took office in January of 1981. To some perceptions, Super*man* had saved the day. Reagan's most recent biographer, Edmund Morris, credits Reagan with the "moral regeneration" of America. When Reagan took office, Morris recently told Leslie Stahl on *60 Minutes,* the country was suffering from "self-doubt," but "overnight there was a mysterious change which can only be attributed to him" (Morris).

Basil Ransom's most famous characterization of his own times provides an exaggerated anticipation of Morris's complaint about the late 1970s. Ransom tells Verena that he wants to save the country from the "most damnable feminization":

> The whole generation is womanized; the masculine tone is passing out of the world; it's a feminine, a nervous, hysterical, chattering, canting age, an age of hollow phrases and false delicacy and exaggerated solicitudes and coddled sensibilities, which, if we

> don't soon look out, will usher in the reign of mediocrity, of the
> feeblest and flattest and the most pretentious that has ever been.
> The masculine character, the ability to dare and endure, to know
> and yet not fear reality, to look the world in the face and take it
> for what it is—a very queer and partly very base mixture—that
> is what I want to preserve, or rather, as I may say, to recover; and
> I must tell you that I don't in the least care what becomes of you
> ladies while I make the attempt. (*Bostonians* 327)

Interestingly, this speech does not appear in the film, even though the
scene in which it appears in the novel—the scene in Central Park that ends
chapter 34 in book 2—is filmed in some detail. It certainly can be argued
that Ivory's elision of this hysterical speech reflects a determination to
downplay an antifeminist or antiwoman ideology. Since Ransom's speech
reflects rather badly on him, however—he really does sound hysterical—
toning down his character and his language actually gives him and his
reactionary plans more credibility. The film, in short, enacts what it does
not explicitly state—the remasculinization of American society in 1984.

By the time Christopher Reeve performed in *The Bostonians,* he had
played Superman in three films (in 1978, 1980, 1983), and in attributing
his casting as Basil Ransom to Ivory's appreciation for his work in that
earlier role, Reeve encourages us to consider parallels between the Superman films and the James adaptation. What exactly was it about Reeve's
portrayal of Superman that brought him to Ivory's mind as he considered
whom to cast as Basil Ransom? What is there about his portrayal of Superman that fit Ivory's interpretation of James's novel? James himself had certainly experimented with strong male characters inclined to cast themselves
in the role of saviors for women. Christopher Newman in *The American* and
Caspar Goodwood in *The Portrait of a Lady* come immediately to mind. Not
a role that James himself would be likely to play, this traditional male type
nonetheless attracted him at some level, and Basil Ransom represents his
most sustained treatment of that hypermasculine figure. As Stanley
Kauffmann remarks about Christopher Reeve's portrayal of the character,
"With his columnar neck—almost as big around as [Madeline] Potter's
waist—and his gigantic chest, he demonstrates his costumes rather than
wearing them. It's difficult to understand how the Confederacy lost the war
with him in its army" (27). Projecting backward, Kauffmann illustrates
how *The Bostonians* registers some of the same male fantasies as *Superman.* In
both scenarios a powerful male character emerges phoenix-like out of the
ruins of an old civilization (the South, Krypton), heads for the American
Metropolis (New York City), and sets about saving, or attempting to save,

Figure 9. Superman (Christopher Reeve) restores dome and American Flag to the White House in *Superman II.*

civilization from various threats. Civilization in both cases is embodied in a young woman—Verena Tarrant, Lois Lane—whose "rescue" by the work's super male assumes a Prince Charming and Cinderella form. (Lois Lane even refers to herself as Cinderella in the first *Superman* movie.) Lest anyone think that the self-reliant Lois Lane is a secret feminist, Margot Kidder simply melts when she touches Christopher Reeve's Superman. When he takes her flying on their first "date," she feels as if she is "holding hands with a god" and describes herself as "quivering."

    *Superman II* (1980) and *Superman III* (1983) explore different sides of Superman's character, but both films return him to "normal" before their conclusions. Superman decides to become an "ordinary man" in *Superman II* in order to marry Lois Lane, but then must reverse that metamorphosis in order to save the world from the three Kryptonian villains whom his father Jor-El (Marlon Brando) had exiled in the first film. Without going too far, the film fulfills certain male fantasies of self-reliant manhood. In its final scene, Clark Kent beats up Rocky, the bully who had bested him in front of

Lois during his brief stint as an "ordinary" man. Just before that, he has given Lois Lane a kiss that makes her faint—a kiss that may remind James's readers of the remarkable "white lightning" kiss Caspar Goodwood gives Isabel Archer in *The Portrait of a Lady*. Released in Europe in 1980 but not in the United States until the summer of 1981, and thus after Reagan's presidential victory and the rescue of the Iranian hostages, *Superman II* plays out a hostage drama of its own, even depicting the president of the United States (E.G. Marshall) kneeling before General Zod (Terence Stamp) in a futile attempt to appease the power-hungry villain. Zod actually walks on water when he first lands on Earth—flaunting his otherworldly power and giving it an anti-Christian edge that helps to associate him with anticonservative demonism and to ally Superman by default with conservative activism. Superman eventually wins the day, of course, and in a final, painfully phallocentric gesture, he restores the American flag to the roof of the White House (fig 9).

 *Superman II* also takes a stab at gender issues, it seems to me, through the character of the evil Ursa (Sarah Douglas). In a startling line in the first *Superman* film, Jor-El passes sentence on Ursa by labeling her a woman "whose perversions and unreasoning hatred of all mankind have threatened even the children of the planet Krypton." In *Superman II* Jor-El does not repeat that accusation, which conjures up the worst right-wing fears about feminists, but Ursa does seem to exemplify what happens when a woman seeks and exercises power equal to men's. Refusing to play any stereotypical feminine role, she kills as many men as her male counterparts, arm wrestles a man in a cafe, and destroys a snake that has bitten her by sizzling it with her X-ray vision (fig. 10). As a Kryptonian Eve in an earthly garden, Ursa treats serpents with contempt. She kills men for the pleasure of it until she meets her match, so to speak, in Superman, who kills her and her two male partners in crime.

 Otherwise a hodgepodge of a film, *Superman III* played interestingly with Superman's dark side, splitting off an evil alter ego from his character before restoring him to his former, super-manly self. Indulging obvious male fantasies before returning to "normal," the dark Superman has a fling with the enchanting Lorelei Ambrosia (Pamela Stephenson) that begins on—of all places—the top of the Statue of Liberty. He also gets drunk in the middle of the day, trashing a bar before stumbling out the door just in time to disillusion a young boy who idolizes him. After a knockdown, crush-'em-up fight with Clark Kent in an auto junk yard, the real Superman emerges intact in time to save the world (arguably, like Ronald Reagan in 1980) from an oil and gasoline crisis illustrated by long lines at America's gas pumps and fights between frustrated customers. Disguised as Clark

Figure 10. Ursa (Sarah Douglas) kills a serpent with her X-ray vision (*Superman II*).

Kent when the film ends, he seems on the verge of engagement to an old high school sweetheart who loves to cook—the divorced Lana Lang (Annette O'Toole), who has come all the way from Smallville with her son Ricky to be near Clark and to work as Perry White's secretary at the *Daily Planet*.

The gap between James's *Bostonians* and the Superman films may be wide, yet James's melodramatic imagination, as Peter Brooks terms it, is clearly at work behind the structure and characterization of the novel, and James certainly experiments with some of the same features of super manhood that we see illustrated in the films. Brought to the screen as a film, arguably in a context established through Christopher Reeve's casting by the three Superman movies, the Merchant Ivory *Bostonians* further exploits the melodramatic aspects of James's text within the context formed by 1980s politics.

The Merchant Ivory *The Bostonians*, of course, brings issues of gender and sexuality—feminism *and* lesbianism—to the big screen and thus has the potential to counter the conservative backlash that the early 1980s elections confirmed. *The Bostonians* represents an interesting decision by Ismail

Merchant and James Ivory, especially in the political environment I have described. The choice is an inspired one, I think, precisely because *The Bostonians* represents a clash between James's nineteenth-century versions of "super-manhood" *and* feminism, as well as between heterosexuality and homosexuality. I want to emphasize this intersection of gender and sexuality, especially as James uses it to complicate the character of his hypermasculine male protagonist and as it challenges Christopher Reeve's portrayal of Ransom. As a Southerner, James's Ransom embodies patriarchal power exerted most palpably upon the "othered" bodies of women and slaves, and he imports that power to Boston and New York, bringing it to bear upon the post–Civil War battle he wages with Olive Chancellor for the embodied subjectivity of Verena Tarrant. Without the aid of a phone booth, Ransom changes identities, metamorphosing from gentlemanhood to hypermanhood. Josephine Hendin calls this the "paradox of a Southern character—its surface amiability and charm, its hidden ruthlessness" (27)—but the paradox of Ransom's character is not essentially Southern, even though it does reflect, as Hendin claims, the "distortions of masculine authority by plantation culture" (28). I have argued elsewhere, however, that James persistently undercuts Ransom's enjoyment of phallocentric power by casting him into subject positions (involving race, gender, and sexual orientation) that reverse lines of power. While the novel seems to "normalize" sexual desire by switching it into a heterosexual track, I believe that James subverts that intention by transgendering Ransom's subject position. Although Ivory repeats the language of the novel rather faithfully, having Ransom tell Olive Chancellor (Vanessa Redgrave) in their opening scene together that he would change his position for hers any day, he does not play with this idea as much as James does in the novel. James's novel represents a more complex and unstable model of masculine identity than the Merchant Ivory film—in part, because of Christopher Reeve's casting in the male lead. Whereas the novel explores homoerotic desire by transgendering male identity, Reeve's portrayal of Ransom stabilizes and normalizes male identity for viewers who would be hard-pressed not to see Ransom through his super-manly filter. The film reserves same-sex desire for women and more simplistically than James's novel reduces the central conflict to a battle between Basil Ransom and Olive Chancellor—between a normalizing heterosexuality and a deviant, lesbian feminism.

Coincidentally, 1978 (the year that Christopher Reeve appeared in the first Superman film) marked a turning point in literary criticism of *The Bostonians,* as Judith Fetterley, Lillian Faderman, and Nina Auerbach published landmark studies of the novel that changed the way subsequent scholars have approached it. Faderman and Fetterley both attacked male critics of the 1950s, 1960s, and early 1970s for their simplistic, essentially homophobic view of the novel: "Olive, a lesbian, has entrapped Verena, who is basically a normal woman, in an unnatural relationship" from which Basil Ransom rescues her (Faderman 325). In *The Resisting Reader* Fetterley catalogues and criticizes many of the same "phallic critics" who, with "relentless sameness" (107), construed the novel as a post–Civil War battle between good men and evil women, as if an "embattled phallic principle" were making a "desperate stand" against James's version of the "castrating bitch" (109). Both cite Louis Auchincloss, for instance, who figures the conflict in the novel in almost super-manly terms—"Ransom against Boston, a real man against a city of paper men," the story of a "real man, a warrior who has killed other men in combat and who desires [Verena]" (78). The novel "scares the phallic critic" (108) for this very reason, Fetterley argues; it threatens what one critic calls the "heterosexual basis of existence" (McMurray 341). Charles Anderson, for example, considers Ransom the "embodiment of the sentiment of sex," by which he clearly means heterosexuality, and thereby determined to "snatch" Verena from the "clutches" of Olive's "incipient Lesbianism" (310). Robert McLean terms the "tears Verena is to shed in the future" a "small price to pay for achieving a normal relationship in a society so sick" (381). Lionel Trilling, who considers Ransom the "only man in Boston" and the "only man in the book," credits James with "daring to seize on the qualities of the women's movement which were 'unnatural' and morbid" (114). Along with the studies by Faderman and Auerbach, *The Resisting Reader* inaugurated a new way of approaching the novel that the Merchant Ivory film could have pursued. Fetterley claims that the critical commentary on *The Bostonians* provides "irrefutable documentation of the fact that literary criticism is a political act" (101), and while her own resistant reading of the novel is equally political, the film's representation of male-female relationships—with the help of Superman in the hero's role—aligns it ideologically with the conservative political movement of its time. As literary interpretation, the Merchant Ivory version of *The Bostonians,* while remarkably faithful to the novel, is more reactionary than progressive.

James's portrait of Ransom gains all the more significance because he plays his part not only within the context of the nineteenth-century women's movement but within the veiled context of the same-sex relationships whose dynamics James was confronting in his own life and in his sister Alice's relationship with Katharine Loring. When James finally met Katharine Loring in 1881, Jean Strouse notes, Katharine's "presence altered the connection between brother and sister" (199). James felt "troubled" by the intensity of the relationship and expressed his "unease" in *The Bostonians* (200). Reviewers have not always acknowledged the film's representation of homo-sexuality—surprising in view of Ivory's emphasizing the lesbian relation-ship between Olive and Verena. Vincent Canby writes that Olive "has no inkling of the possible sexual aspects of her love"—indeed, that the idea of "any kind of sex" would be "appalling to her" (266). Stanley Kauffmann observes that "even more difficult to handle on film is the subtext, the invisible drama, which James couldn't make explicit: the basic struggle in Verena, conscious or not, between homosexuality and heterosexuality" (26). But Ivory includes several scenes of physical intimacy between Olive and Verena—more certainly than James included in the novel. *The Bostonians* can certainly be read as a protolesbian novel, but its depiction of a so-called "Boston friendship" only rarely blossoms into physical intimacy. From Verena's point of view James had described it as a "very peculiar thing" and "probably as complete as any (between women) that had ever existed"—although "more on Olive's side than on hers" (*Bostonians* 376). James's brief descriptions of hugs and kisses between Olive and Verena are overshad-owed by the language that surrounds them, but on the screen moments of physical intimacy leap out at the viewer—and Ivory includes more such scenes than James's text "authorizes." Intentional or not, the effect is to sexualize the work's political message and, I think, to play into the hands of early 1980s conservatism. By representing progressive intimacy between Olive and Verena—nearly always initiated by Olive—the Merchant Ivory film al-lies itself with apocalyptic narratives about man-hating lesbians bent upon seducing America's daughters. Fortunately, audiences were assured, Super-man will come to the rescue and restore "normal" relations between the sexes.[2]

James had complicated Ransom's response to Verena's first speech by placing him in a vexed, triangulated relationship with both Verena and her father. Ransom's immediate reaction to his first sight of Selah Tarrant—"Ransom simply loathed him, from the moment he opened his mouth" (*Bostonians* 81)—conjures up complex memories of his post–Civil War ex-periences. "He had seen Tarrant, or his equivalent, often before," James writes; "he had 'whipped' him, as he believed, controversially, again and again, at political meetings in blighted Southern towns, during the horrible period of reconstruction" (82). More important, however, as Selah places his hands on Verena, stroking and smoothing her, Ransom begins to resent Tarrant's "grotesque manipulations" as much as "if he himself had felt their touch" (83). "They made him nervous, they made him angry," James notes, "and it was only afterwards that he asked himself wherein they concerned him, and whether even a carpet-bagger hadn't a right to do what he pleased with his daughter" (83). Claire Kahane rightly notes that "James points to Ransom's identification with Verena and flirts with the pleasure as well as the fear of being handled" (293), but Ransom also resists identification with Verena and, to prevent such repositioning, imagines taking Selah's place with her. His nervousness and anger register ambivalence, an identification with both Verena and her father. The film represents none of this complex identification. As Selah (Wesley Addy) labors over Verena's bowed head—to "start her up," as he says—the camera focuses on Selah. There is no cut to Ransom or the sort of close-up—whether of Selah or Verena—that might replicate the conflicted subject position that James represented. Indeed, Ransom and Dr. Prance (Linda Hunt) talk over much of Verena's speech, neither of them paying attention to her words. Ivory does show Ransom looking at Verena—finally, with his head resting on his hand, his eyes converging in obvious longing upon their object—and he also shows Olive watching in rapt fascination. Whereas James had suggested a transgendered, triangulated identification, Ivory emphasizes a more conventional triangle: Basil and Olive both gaze desiringly at Verena.

Ivory highlights this conventional triangle by subtly altering the scene that follows—Olive's and Basil's first meeting with Verena. In the novel Basil and Olive approach Verena together after her speech. Olive makes the first move and Basil, saying to himself that "now, perhaps, was his chance," follows her (90). Olive wastes no time in inviting Verena to come and see her, while Ransom stands silently beside her, feeling tongue-tied and even wishing at one point that he were a "Boston lady, so that he might extend to her such an invitation" (91). Ransom's position in the novel version of this scene might be described as dependent and conflicted—dependent upon Olive's initiative, conflicted over his lack of stature and power. In the film, however, Ransom interrupts Olive's tête-à-tête with Verena, emphasizing his aggressive and intrusive purpose. To underscore Ransom's intentions and his focus upon Verena, Ivory positions the camera behind Verena's head, which appears fuzzy in the left foreground. With Olive's teary-eyed face filling the right side of the screen, Ransom appears to fully occupy the space—the very center of the frame—between the two women. He announces himself with only a subtle nod to Verena and never speaks, but his look—the scopophiliac power of the male gaze at its most intent—dominates the scene from the center of the frame. While Ransom's gaze does not rival the Man of Steel's, his steely-eyed stare acts powerfully on Verena. Reeve's Superman sees through Margot Kidder's dress to tell her she is wearing pink underwear in the first *Superman* film—reassuring the 1978 viewing audience that Kidder's workaholic Lois Lane is feminine at heart. In this introductory scene in the Merchant Ivory *Bostonians*, the apparently feminist Verena initially greets Ransom with an innocent smile, but, ominously, that smile slowly fades under the power of his gaze.[3]

Figure 11. Basil Ransom (Christopher Reeve) interrupts Verena Tarrant (Madeleine Potter) and Olive Chancellor (Vanessa Redgrave) (*The Bostonians*).

When the scene shifts to the private space of Olive's parlor, where Olive has just proposed to Verena (the speech is the same in novel and film) that she be her "friend," her "friend of friends . . . forever and ever," Ransom appears even more aggressively. In the novel he is simply "ushered in by Miss Chancellor's little parlour-maid" (107). In the film, he charges the Chancellor stronghold like a Confederate soldier. As Olive's sister Adeline Luna (Nancy New) spies Ransom striding up the walk, martial music and an ominous drum roll get louder as Ransom approaches the door. Verena had called the room a "regular dream-like place" as she moved slowly from object to object, but Ransom's entrance immediately dispels whatever dreamy atmosphere the scene possessed. Ransom enters aggressively, moving across the room and the screen toward Verena and Olive. Olive retreats to a marginal place at screen left, where Ransom greets her and shakes her hand—while he turns his head to his right and looks directly at Verena. Olive moves across the room from left to right, hoping to entice Verena to move past Ransom to the door and a passageway to the safety of the special friend-

ship she has just offered the young woman. Ransom prevents easy escape
with his bulk and his voice, using Olive's distance to challenge Verena.
Although he had hardly paid attention to Verena's speech the night before,
he addresses Verena confidently, even impertinently. "Miss Tarrant," he says,
"I know what your ideas are. You expressed them last night in such beautiful language. I am duly ashamed to be a man." Ransom means none of it, of
course, but his words do suggest his redirection of attention and value from
ideas to the style of their expression—and thus from Verena as a speaking
subject to Verena as a beautiful object. In the earlier triangulated scene
Ransom had been positioned behind Olive, looming over her shoulder and
forcing Verena to split or alternate her attention between the two of them
(fig. 11). Now, Olive is barely visible over Ransom's shoulder as his imposing torso eclipses her presence at the doorway through which she desperately wishes to usher Verena. In effect, this scene is hardly triangulated at
all (fig. 12). Olive circles Verena and Ransom as she moves stage right, but
the effect of this movement is to take herself out of the triangle and leave
Verena all for Ransom. When Verena joins Olive outside, Olive immediately seeks to restore the intimacy that was developing before Ransom's
interruption. "He's an enemy," Olive insists, "an enemy of our movement
and our sex. You must fear him." Olive then caresses Verena's shoulder and
takes her hand—the first of many physically intimate gestures on Olive's
part and an indication that she, too, confuses the political and the personal. Ivory, I think, has clearly upstaged the political with the personal,
emphasizing the lines of desire—homoerotic and heterosexual—that are
converging upon Verena. While personal desire does not eclipse political
purpose, personal relationships relegate politics to the background.

    While Olive certainly responds initially to Verena's words and never
loses sight of Verena's importance for the women's movement, she also quickly
tries to forge a personally intimate relationship. Gilbert Adair perceptively
notes that "the central conflict arises from the imposition of a choice on the
protagonist, a choice between two cultures, two ideologies or two individuals. What gives Verena's choice its particular poignant resonance is the
rigorous, almost algebraic interdependence of the individual and the ideological: she can have Olive and the clubby solidarity of the feminist cause,
or Basil and a presumably lopsided, male-dominated marriage, she cannot
have both; nor can the equation be re-set in different terms" (295). Adair
does reset the equation, albeit with a gauzy filter, by attributing to Ivory a
"malicious pleasure in juxtaposing a conventionally binary, tête-à-tête (or
sexe-à-sexe) relationship with a more diffracted, more even diffused form of
sexuality: what might be described as an eroticised camaraderie" (296).
Adair in fact pointedly closets homoerotic desire, remarking that the film

Figure 12. Basil eclipses Olive (*The Bostonians*).

"ascribes to the suffragettes an amorous dimension of their own, a Courbet-like physicality, which divests Olive's love for Verena of any 'taint' of lesbianism in the narrow sense" (296). It is hard to know, of course, what he means by "lesbianism in the narrow sense." *The Bostonians* represents lesbianism in many "senses."

Ruth Jhabvala and Ivory emphasize the "amorous dimension" of the women's relationship, as well as its increasing "physicality," by inventing a montage of scenes to illustrate Olive and Verena's increasing intimacy. Ivory shows the two women reading together in Olive's parlor. He shows Olive touring Verena around Boston and then examining a photo album titled "The Revolution." Olive asks Verena if she is ready to "renounce everything"—to give up her self and her life to the women's movement. In response Verena embraces Olive, leaning against her breast and smiling while she keeps her eyes focused on the picture they have just been discussing. When Ivory cuts to the seashore, he depicts Olive and Verena (both dressed in white) standing arm in arm, gazing out at the water. Here, too, Olive asks Verena to give up everything for the movement, and in response Verena puts her arms around Olive and softly sings the ballad "Annabel Lee." The two women sway together, dancing in place (fig. 13). Verena tilts her head up and to the side in the conventional movie pose, suggesting the possibility of a kiss that doesn't come, as the two women embrace each other tenderly. Sue Sorensen notes that Olive and Verena embrace as if they were "trying to coin a new language of embrace," because they "approach each other delicately, almost diagonally," rather than "conventionally, straight-on," as Basil and Verena do (234). Within the context of 1984 politics, however, I think the increasing physical intimacy between Olive and Verena would resonate in a different key—as evidence that the women's movement posed a threat, as one critic of the novel had characterized it, to the "heterosexual basis of existence" (McMurray 341). Whatever new "language of embrace" Redgrave and Potter develop in their relationship, the film resorts to a conventional grammar of jealousy and desperation as Potter's Verena redirects her feelings toward Basil Ransom.

Vanessa Redgrave emphasizes Olive's increasing desperation—her increasing hysteria—as Verena's relationship with Ransom develops. James had certainly represented this, too, describing Olive as "stricken as she had never been before" (*Bostonians* 366), as she recognizes the full danger of Ransom's intentions. When Verena seems flattered by Ransom's lovemaking, James describes Olive flinging herself on the couch, "burying her face in the cushions, which she tumbled in her despair, and moaning out that he didn't love Verena" (369). But James also describes Olive as matching her despair with combative energy. "She took hold," he says, "with passion, with fury; after the shock of Ransom's arrival had passed away she determined that he should not find her chilled into dumb submission" (366). Ransom himself thinks of her as a "fighting woman" who would "fight him to the death, giving him not an inch of odds" (381). As directed by James Ivory, however, Vanessa Redgrave gives far more emphasis to Olive's "dumb submission" and hand-wringing desperation—suggesting, as Alan Nadel observes about her portrayal in another scene, that she is a "tortured pre-Raphaelite subject" (281). Interestingly, Ivory has acknowledged the tension between his conception of Olive's (and Verena's) behavior and Redgrave's. When Redgrave finally agreed to play the part, he notes, she quickly began to "bear down ideologically" on the novel, on James, and also on Jhabvala's conception of the characters. "Was not the reactionary Basil Ransom a 'nigger-beater,'" Ivory quotes her as asking. "Was he not deeply evil, and should he not therefore be made to seem more satanic?" Redgrave thought that Jhabvala had made Ransom too sympathetic. "Shouldn't he be shown in his true colours so that she, Olive, by contrast could shine forth—not be seen just as a hysterical eccentric, but as a figure of righteousness?" (Ivory 97).

Figure 13. Olive and Verena embrace (*The Bostonians*).

Redgrave's interpretation of Olive's character seems to diverge significantly from Jhabvala's conception, from Ivory's direction, as well as from
Christopher Reeve's more conventional expectations of female characterization, and Ivory suggests that her alternative vision affected the film. Redgrave
coached Madeleine Potter to underplay her feelings for Basil Ransom, Ivory
remembers, and while Christopher Reeve "knew nothing of these discussions," he did feel that "Verena, the character, wasn't having as much fun in
his company as she should be" (97). More important, Jhabvala and Ivory
deviate significantly from the novel by showing Olive's desperation expressing itself in a steady escalation of physical intimacy with Verena. Intentional or not, the effect is to uncover the lesbianism beneath Olive's feminism—to reveal feminism *as a cover* for homoerotic desire—and thus, I
think, to reinforce the conservative stereotypes of 1984 politics. During the
episode in the middle of the film where Henry Burrage and his mother
court Verena, Ivory includes a scene in Verena's bedroom in which she and
Olive talk over their commitment to women in light of Burrage's personal
interest in her. Ivory uses dialogue from the novel in this scene, but his

decision to set it in Verena's bedroom—with Verena lying in her bed—gives it an erotic edge that it does not have in the book. When Verena expresses some doubts about her commitment to women, Olive kisses her hand while affirming her own constant feelings of dedication. Verena responds by hugging Olive and promises to "take any vow" her friend wants. The two women embrace, touching foreheads, an embrace that, like the earlier one, starts out looking like a kiss.

Ivory also uses Mrs. Burrage, played brilliantly by Nancy Marchand, to "out" Olive's desire for Verena. James devotes chapter 32 of the novel to a meeting between Olive and Mrs. Burrage—a negotiation over Verena's future. Mrs. Burrage wishes to bribe Olive to "exert herself" in encouraging Verena to accept Henry Burrage's marriage proposal (*Bostonians* 301). She offers to support the women's movement in extravagant fashion, and she also tries to persuade Olive to work on Henry's behalf on the grounds that Verena would be "safer" with her son than as a "possible prey" to "adventurers" and "exploiters" (308). More important in view of what Ivory takes from this scene, James writes the following: "'I dare say you don't like the idea of her marrying at all; it would break up a friendship which is so full of interest (Olive wondered for a moment whether she had been going to say "so full of profit") for you'" (301). As spoken by Nancy Marchand in the film, this line acquires a very significant edge. "I dare say you don't like the idea of her marrying at all. It would break up a friendship that has . . . so much . . . *interest* for you." While the words are virtually identical, Marchand speaks them sardonically, with a knowing look and the pauses I have indicated with ellipses. Olive looks flustered, scarcely making eye contact throughout the conversation—as if speaking from an official script, while the older woman penetrates her mask to reveal the hidden motives underneath. Olive defends herself, claiming that Mrs. Burrage's attitude reflects the way women's relations are still "misunderstood," but I think the scene powerfully undercuts Olive's claims that her friendship is a pure function and example of the women's movement. While part of the underlying motive, as James himself suggests, may be financial profit, the larger part is clearly personal and erotic, and I think the Merchant Ivory film emphasizes that part of Olive's motives in her scenes with Verena.

In a scene following Verena's ride with Henry Burrage through Central Park, Ivory again places Verena in her room, this time at her toilet. Olive enters and begs her to help her remove her clothes. Both women now appear in their undergarments. "Did he try to make love to you?" Olive wants to know. "I suppose it was meant for love," Verena replies. "He says he likes me for the same reason he likes old enamels and old altar cloths." The women, sharing a towel, sit on Verena's bed. Verena shows Olive a

Figure 14. Olive helps Verena get dressed in *The Bostonians.*

letter from Ransom and says that she wants to see him again because she is curious and wants to make him give in on one or two points. This straightforward discussion about women's business is not matched by the two women's actions, however, for while Verena is speaking, Olive is dressing her and kneeling in front of her (fig. 14). Expressing her anxiety about Verena's seeing Ransom, Olive evokes an offer from Verena to "go home tomorrow." She reaffirms her dedication to the women's movement and asks Olive to trust her. In response, Olive kisses her on the cheek. By itself, this scene hardly suggests a developing lesbian relationship between Olive and Verena. Placed beside other scenes and also compared to the original scene in the novel, however, the scene becomes part of a larger pattern designed to emphasize the women's growing physical intimacy. James stages this same scene in Olive's room, and the only clothing that he describes being removed is Verena's hat (285). In the novel Verena touches Olive's hand at one point to reassure her, and as the two women descend the staircase for lunch, she slips her arm through Olive's (288).[4]

In the film it is Olive's desperation that leads to the increasing physicality with Verena. Olive appears more stricken with every scene. She claims that Verena is killing her by seeing Ransom, and Vanessa Redgrave plays Olive as if she were dying. "Don't leave me," she begs Verena at one point, embracing her at the same time. "It would kill me." In the scene between the two women that Ivory stages on the beach Olive lectures Verena breathlessly that Basil doesn't love her; he simply "hates" their cause and wants to prove that a man "only has to whistle for a woman—for you—to come running." Verena insists that she wants Olive to make her "hate—not him, but what I feel for him"—and in response Olive draws her near so that Verena can rest her head on Olive's hip. Such appeals to melodrama—to exaggerated versions of love and hate—suggest a growing perversity in the film's emotional register. A little later Verena herself announces to Ransom that she can't see him that day: "Olive will die. It will kill her." Ransom's insistence that she spend "one hour" with him and Verena's assent (she takes his arm and begins walking away from the camera with him) reinforces the idea that "killing" Olive—vampirishly draining her of energy—is part of the film's purpose. After Verena sees her parents off in their carriage (following Miss Birdseye's funeral), Olive joins her outside, coming up behind her, reaching around her waist, kissing her neck. Verena turns and cuddles into the taller woman's breast. Olive kisses her passionately, several times on the cheek, cupping her face in her hands. And after the critical scene in which Verena's ten minutes with Ransom turns into an all-day affair, the scene in which the frantic Olive looks all over for Verena and even has a vision of her dead body washing up on the shore, Olive nuzzles and then cups Verena's head, kissing her all over, including on the lips. Olive's hand brushes Verena's breast before she takes off her shoes, rubs her feet, and hugs her. Interrupted by the maid, Olive frantically motions her away with her hand. While this reunion scene occurs in the novel, James indicates only that Olive and Verena sit together silently in the darkness, holding hands: "that was all she could do; they were beyond each other's help in any other way now" (400).

Although Jhabvala and Ivory do less to undercut Ransom's masculinity than James did in the novel, they do include several scenes that reveal Ransom's difficulties in making a living. When the action shifts from Boston to New York early in the film, the scene opens in Ransom's law office. Ransom is having lunch delivered, but when asked to pay the ten-cent cost, he must ask for time from the delivery boy. That vignette brings to life James's observation that "Ransom sat for hours in his office, waiting for clients who either did not come, or, if they did come, did not seem to find him encouraging" (197). Later, when Verena only half facetiously informs Ransom that she presumes he wishes to be president of the United States, he acknowledges the fantasy (in both novel and film). In the novel, however, Verena actually taunts Ransom with the question, "Do you consider that you have advanced far in that direction, as yet?" (323). The question causes Ransom to blush and to feel his "beggarly condition" with special acuteness (323), but in the film he seems good-humored in describing his lack of success as a writer. He acknowledges that, as one editor put it (also in the novel), his ideas are "300 years out of date," at least on the "rights of minorities." He goes on to claim that in fact he has "come too soon," and he says somewhat angrily that he is "tired of always hearing about women and their freedom and their education and their liberty." Here, too, the film follows the novel in most respects, but the exchange between Ransom and Verena in the film enables Ransom to appear more confident and thus give his reactionary views more credibility. Throughout this scene, in fact, Ransom is on the offensive. When Verena suggests, "Woe to American women when you get going," Ransom insists that he loves American women. What he doesn't like, he says, in a speech that does not appear in the novel but does codify 1980s conservative attitudes toward feminists, are women who say, "Down with men. Down with the love between women and men." James describes Verena responding to Ransom's "narrow notions" by realizing that the "ugliness of her companion's profession of faith made her shiver; it would have been difficult for her to imagine anything more crudely profane" (*Bostonians* 328). But in the film Verena simply hangs her head, while Ransom moves closer to her, insisting that she doesn't mean what she "preaches" and is "meant for something different." "You're meant for privacy," he tells her. "You're meant for love—for me." Verena runs away at this point in the film, demanding that Olive take her away from New York, but she does not combat Ransom's ideas as she does in the novel (at least in the responses James attributes to her). Ransom wins the argument on film, it seems to me, because he gets to speak far more than Verena. His rhetorical advantage in the film emphasizes the national political implications of his project—for a 1984 audience as much as for an 1886 audience—and enables him to express a good-humored, "aw shucks" humility that might remind some 1984 viewers of Ronald Reagan.

Another complication that James creates for Ransom's character—Adeline Luna—also gets changed significantly in the film. Although Jhabvala and Ivory do include several scenes in which Adeline Luna pursues Ransom, they do not show him considering her suit as seriously as James did. Acutely feeling financial pressures, Ransom actually contemplates becoming Mrs. Luna's literary protégé in the novel, writing and publishing at her expense. "Images of leisure played before him," James observes, "leisure in which he saw himself covering foolscap paper with his views on several sub-

jects, and with favourable illustrations of Southern eloquence" (*Bostonians* 205).
Ransom almost persuades himself "that the moral law commanded him to
marry Mrs. Luna" (206), but doing so would put him in a paradoxical
position as a kept man. In the film, however, Ransom doesn't respond
when Mrs. Luna, speaking lines that do not appear in the novel, tells him,
"You're not to belong to any Verena; you're to belong to me." And in the
scene where Mrs. Burrage hosts Verena's first New York speech, Ransom
appears merely irritated when Mrs. Luna plays upon his gentlemanly impulses and coerces him into listening to Verena's talk with her in the study.
Whereas James had depicted Ransom on the verge, at least imaginatively, of
prostituting himself, the screenplay allows him to preserve more dignity
and, I think, escape any threat to his masculinity.

The scene with Mrs. Luna plays a more pivotal role in the novel precisely because it represents an imaginative low point for Ransom. When
Mrs. Luna teases him that Verena will run off with "some lion-tamer" and
speculates that Verena will thereby "give Olive the greatest cut she has ever
had in her life" (*Bostonians* 213), she gives Ransom new terms for reconstructing his embattled masculinity. Repositioning himself imaginatively
within a new triangle—rewriting "lion-tamer" as "woman-tamer"—Ransom
"chuckled" at the "idea that he should be avenged (for it would avenge him
to know it) upon the wanton young woman [Olive] who had invited him
to come and see her in order simply to slap his face" (*Bostonians* 213). As he
leaves Mrs. Luna's apartment, escaping marriage and the patronized position it portended, Ransom exhales an "involuntary expression of relief,
such as a man might utter who had seen himself on the point of being run
over and yet felt that he was whole." By the time he reaches his lodgings,
James notes, "his ambition, his resolution, had rekindled" (*Bostonians* 216),
and the next scene (in both novel and film) finds him back in Boston and
calling on Verena.

Although James certainly used Dr. Mary Prance to exemplify women's
self-reliance and to cast some doubt upon the need for an equal rights
movement, Ivory gives her role greater emphasis and uses her more directly
to undermine the women's movement. Ransom sits with Dr. Prance during
Verena's first speech, for example, and neither character listens to what
Verena says. Dr. Prance leaves before Verena finishes, in fact, explaining
dismissively, "I've heard it all before." This allows Ransom to rejoin, "But
she looks so pretty when she says it." Ransom and Dr. Prance will have
similar conversations periodically during the film. In each of them Ransom
feels free to voice his negative attitudes toward the women's movement and
his conservative plans for Verena. Not only does Dr. Prance not contradict
him, she usually adds her own disparaging remarks. When the scene shifts

to Cape Cod (book 3 of the novel), the two characters spend a lot of time together—much of it fishing. In the one fishing scene included in the film, Dr. Prance speaks sardonically about Olive's "big plans" for Verena's speech at the Music Hall, and she assures Ransom that she "stands" where he stands on the women's movement. In her last scene, invented for the film, she stops to talk with Ransom in the cemetery, where they have come for Miss Birdseye's interment. She gives him a message from Verena—that she wants to "think things over" for three or four days. When Ransom says that he understands, she replies that she doesn't and then wishes him good luck.

The Merchant Ivory *Bostonians* stages Verena Tarrant's eroticization as one of its primary effects. The climax of Verena's evolving relationship with Ransom—a moment that makes the Boston Music Hall scene almost anticlimactic—occurs after their stolen afternoon on Cape Cod. Framed by Olive's frantic search for the missing Verena, the scene on the beach ends in a passionate embrace and kisses. Similarly, when Olive finally discovers Verena, as I have noted above, she too covers her face with passionate kisses. Dueling kisses: the advantage, obviously, is Basil Ransom's—even though Verena goes into hiding to prepare for her speech on "A Woman's Reason." Reason, the film makes clear, will have very little to do with Verena's future. The angry Ransom tears down several posters announcing Verena's speech from the walls and posts around the Music Hall. He need not have bothered with such melodramatic gestures, for despite her temporizing (she begs him at one point to let her speak to the crowd while agreeing to meet him the next day) Verena ultimately resists every entreaty to speak, finding energy only when Ransom bursts through the door of her dressing room— and then only to demand that they be given a moment alone. That moment, of course, turns into a lifetime according to the film's and the novel's implication. Although Verena pleads weakly to be allowed to go out and address the crowd, Ransom kisses her and, like Olive in the earlier scene, pulls a cloak around her, covering her head, and spirits her away. Without a will of her own, Verena can only ask him where they will go and what they will do. "We shall take the night train for New York," Ransom replies. "In the morning we'll be married." Not exactly Superman's cape, but the cloak in which Ransom envelops Verena (in both novel and film) suggests a similar power to mask her identity as spokeswoman for the women's movement and to initiate her into the invisibility and anonymity that are in store for her as Mrs. Ransom. In statements that recall Trilling's judgment that Basil Ransom represents the "only normal male in the novel" or Anderson's view of Ransom as "the natural representative of the sentiment of sex" (321) and thereby "the opposition to this unnatural friendship between the two young

women" (310), Molly Haskell judges that, with his "honey dipped" South-
ern accent (76), Reeve's Basil Ransom is "just the sort to make a girl loosen
her tenuous grip on the feminist cause for a good romantic euphoria" (80).
To Haskell, as to earlier male critics of James's novel, Ransom "normalizes"
Verena's desire, redirecting it from politics to the personal. Christopher
Reeve's voice coach for *The Bostonians* was Haley Barbour III, the Mississippi
lawyer who later served as chairman of the Republican National Committee
(Reeve 209), and Ransom's reeducation plan for Verena seems compatible
with 1980s conservatism. "Can't I make you see," Ransom tells Verena in the
film, "how much more natural it is, not to say agreeable, to give yourself to
a man instead of to a movement or some morbid old maid?" Verena breaks
into tears at these words, but she lends them credence by burying her face
in Ransom's chest. Ransom comforts and holds her, cupping her face in his
hands and kissing her. Verena drops her eyes and doesn't speak. "Come on
now," Ransom says, and he leads her away.

In the most stunning departure from the novel, Jhabvala and Ivory
add a scene to the end of the narrative. Their *Bostonians* ends not with
Ransom's kidnapping of Verena but with Olive Chancellor addressing the
initially dwindling and then slowly returning crowd in the Boston Music
Hall. As Olive discovers her voice and oratorical power, the film encourages
us to identify with the feminist movement, but also to feel that gender
identities and roles have been reconfigured in a more normal way. Verena,
the implication is, was not really the appropriate spokeswoman for the
movement. Like Cinderella, she was a princess in disguise awaiting the
strong identifying presence of Prince Charming to claim the place in society
she deserved. The feminist movement is left with Olive.

And what of the homoerotic desire that Olive brings with her?
Christopher Reeve has been quoted as saying the film presents a "'clas-
sically structured story with a very satisfying, though open-ended, finish'" (Conrad 36). Richard Grenier says that, in a "twist," at least morally
considered, Olive wins this "second battle of *The Bostonians*," but he also
believes that this turning of the novel "on its head" (64) represents one of
the "most singularly perverse adaptations of a classic" he has ever encountered (60)—largely because he likes the antifeminism he sees in the novel.
Grenier recalls that when he saw the movie in New York, "feminist rowdies
in the audience booed Basil Ransom when he carried off Verena, and
cheered Olive Chancellor at the end of her tub-thumper, as the credits
rolled" (65). In Grenier's view, it seems, Ivory and Jhabvala have adapted
the ending for contemporary profeminist viewers by balancing Ransom's
aggressive actions with Olive's speech. Jhabvala and Ivory's addition of this
scene to the narrative seems more vexed, however, when viewed within the

cultural and political context surrounding the film's release in 1984. To save Lois Lane, who has died in an earthquake, at the end of the first *Superman* film, Superman fulfills a reactionary fantasy; he makes time go backwards. "This country is safe again—thanks to you," the prison warden tells him, as he takes delivery on the evil Lex Luthor and his henchman, and this "Save America" ending is repeated in each of the next two Superman films. The Merchant Ivory *Bostonians* can also be read as reinforcing a reactionary political agenda. While Olive's accession to the pulpit in *The Bostonians* might be construed as a promise that the women's movement that had foundered with the defeat of the Equal Rights Amendment just two years before would go on, it seems to me that the mood of this final scene is more elegiac, perhaps even dismissive.[5] The current women's movement, this scene seems to say, is losing its audience. Women, even its spokeswomen, are leaving the movement for marriage, and the film thereby magnifies the "divide" between women's rights and gay/lesbian rights. Whatever may happen to the feminist movement, Verena has been rescued for heterosexuality and the domestic conventionality of the nuclear family, while the feminist movement is left to an aging lesbian. "We will be heard," Olive insists, in the film's closing moment, but the audience to whom she speaks, the film suggests, is small.

As I noted at the beginning, Christopher Reeve won the part of Basil Ransom because James Ivory liked his "work" in *Superman*. In this essay I have tried to expand the sense of "work" to include the cultural work that Reeve's portrayal of Ransom performs at a particular cultural moment. Reeve himself has characterized that moment as one of change. "By the late 1970s the masculine image had changed," he explains, in reviewing his performance as Superman: "People expected marriage to be a genuine partnership. Now it was acceptable for a man to show gentleness and vulnerability. It was even admirable for him to cook dinner, change diapers, and stay home with the kids. I felt that the new Superman ought to reflect that contemporary male image" (192–93). Reeve's iconographic appeal as Superman shadows his characterization of Ransom and the plot of the Merchant Ivory *Bostonians,* but the Ransom he performs seems more an old than a new "super" man in the terms that Reeve uses. Whisking Verena away from the meeting that would climax her commitment to the feminist movement, Ransom wraps her in a "cape" and heads for New York—to Metropolis—where their wedding ceremony will take place. Christopher Reeve's Basil Ransom may not have X-ray vision, but his actions similarly reassure the viewing audience that, for all of her feminist pretensions, Verena Tarrant, like Lois Lane, wears pink underwear. It is hard to imagine Ransom, furthermore, cooking dinner, changing diapers, or staying home with the kids.

Appearing as it did in 1984, the Merchant Ivory *Bostonians* unavoidably entered a debate within the American imaginary about equal rights for women and the situation of homosexuality, gay and lesbian identities. Even though the Merchant Ivory film elides Basil Ransom's famous speech, in the context of early 1980s politics their version of *The Bostonians* helps to fulfill the wish, expressed in other films of the period, that some "super" man would save America from the "most damnable feminization" and restore the "masculine tone" to a "womanized" generation.

## Notes

1. Jeffords lists *Superman* with other successful films of the Reagan era. "Certainly the election of Ronald Reagan in 1980 and his reelection in 1984 by the largest electoral margin in U.S. history," she observes, "offered Hollywood some insight into 'what audiences wanted to see': spectacular narratives about characters who stand for individualism, liberty, militarism, and a mythic heroism" (16).
2. Interestingly, Ivory notes that he gave Christopher Reeve "consultation rights in the casting of Olive and Verena." Reeve's first choice for Olive was Glenn Close, who had just played a "virulent man-hater" in *The World According to Garp,* and the risk (for Close), according to Ivory, "was in doing another castrator" and thereby getting "type-cast" (96). Regardless of the acknowledged risk to Close, both Reeve and Ivory, it would seem, originally conceived of Ransom's character as "virulently" opposed by Olive's—Superman vs. Man-Hating Lesbian Feminist.
3. James's novel certainly authorizes such representation of Ransom's powerful male gaze. In chapter 34, for example, Verena feels Ransom's "eyes on her face—ever so close and fixed there" (331)—and her feelings at a later point register the phallocentric, penetrating power of Ransom's gaze, making him seem almost possessed of X-ray vision: "she felt that his tall, watching figure, with the low horizon behind, represented well the importance, the towering eminence he had in her mind—the fact that he was just now, to her vision, the most definite and upright, the most incomparable, object in the world. If he had not been at his post when she expected him she would have had to stop and lean against something, for weakness; her whole being would have throbbed more painfully than it throbbed at present, though finding him there made her nervous enough" (375).
4. In a later scene from which Jhabvala and Ivory have borrowed to stage this one, Olive takes Verena in her arms and gives her a "silent kiss" (*Bostonians* 298). I am not claiming that James's text does not authorize Olive's physical intimacy with Verena, but I am intrigued by Jhabvala and Ivory's decisions to portray more intimacy than James writes into the novel. The most important question, however, involves viewer responses to these scenes in 1984 America.
5. Sorensen has argued, for example, that "in allowing the film to climax so dramatically on her quivering and moving public address, the filmmakers ultimately affirm a feminist message" (234).

## Works Cited

Adair, Gilbert. "The Ivory Tower: *The Bostonians*." *Sight and Sound* 53 (1984): 295–96.
Anderson, Charles R. "James's Portrait of the Southerner." *American Literature* 27 (1955): 309–31.
Auchincloss, Louis. *Reading Henry James*. Minneapolis: U of Minnesota P, 1975.
Auerbach, Nina. *Communities of Women: An Idea in Fiction*. Cambridge: Harvard UP, 1978.
Bell, Millicent. "The Bostonian Story." *Partisan Review* 52 (1985): 109–19.
Brooks, Peter. *The Melodramatic Imagination: Balzac, Henry James, Melodrama, and the Mode of Excess*. New Haven: Yale UP, 1995.
Canby, Vincent. "*Bostonians*: A Proper Jamesian Adaptation." *New York Times Film Reviews* 5 Aug. 1984: 265–66.
Conrad, Barnaby, III. "Bombay to Boston." *Horizon* May 1984.
Faderman, Lillian. "Female Same-Sex Relationships in Novels by Longfellow, Holmes, and James." *New England Quarterly* 51 (1978): 309–32.
Fetterley, Judith. *The Resisting Reader: A Feminist Approach to American Fiction*. Bloomington: Indiana UP, 1978.
Grenier, Richard. "*The Bostonians* Inside Out." *Commentary* Oct. 1984.
Haskell, Molly. "Brought to Life." *Vogue* Oct. 1984.
Hendin, Josephine. "What Verena Knew." *New Republic* 16 July and 23 July 1984.
Ivory, James. "The Trouble with Olive: Divine Madness in Massachusetts." *Sight and Sound* 54 (Spring 1985): 94–100.
James, Henry. *The Bostonians*. Ed. Charles R. Anderson. New York: Penguin, 1984.
Jeffords, Susan. *Hard Bodies: Hollywood Masculinity in the Reagan Era*. New Brunswick: Rutgers UP, 1993.
Kahane, Claire. "Hysteria, Feminism, and the Case of *The Bostonians*." *Feminism and sychoanalysis*. Ed. Richard Feldstein and Judith Roof. Ithaca: Cornell UP, 1989. 280–97.
Kauffmann, Stanley. "A Civil War." *New Republic* 6 Aug. 1984.
Long, Robert Emmet. "Dramatizing James: *The Bostonians* as a Film." *Henry James Review* 6 (1984): 75–78.
McLean, Robert C. "*The Bostonians*: New England Pastoral." *Papers on Language and Literature* 7 (1971): 374–81.
McMurray, William. "Pragmatic Realism in *The Bostonians*." *Nineteenth-Century Fiction* 16 (1962): 339–44.
Morris, Edmund. Interview with Leslie Stahl. *60 Minutes*. CBS. New York City. 26 Sept. 1999.
Nadel, Alan. "Ambassadors from an Imaginary 'Elsewhere': Cinematic Convention and the Jamesian Sensibility." *Henry James Review* 19 (1998): 279–85.
Person, Leland S. "In the Closet with Frederick Douglass: Reconstructing Masculinity in *The Bostonians*." *Henry James Review* 16 (1995): 292–98.
Reeve, Christopher. *Still Me*. New York: Ballantine, 1998.
Sorenson, Sue. "'Damnable Feminization'? The Merchant Ivory Film Adaptation of Henry James's *The Bostonians*." *Literature/Film Quarterly* 25 (1997): 231–35.

Sterritt, David. "*The Bostonians:* So Far, the Best Movie of the Year." *Christian Science Monitor* 2 Aug. 1984.

Strouse, Jean. *Alice James: A Biography.* Boston: Houghton, 1980.

Trilling, Lionel. *The Opposing Self: Nine Essays in Criticism.* New York: Viking, 1955.

## *Filmography*

*The Bostonians.* Dir. James Ivory. Writ. Ruth Prawer Jhabvala. Perf. Christopher Reeve, Vanessa Redgrave, Jessica Tandy, Madeleine Potter. Merchant Ivory Productions, 1984.

*Superman.* Dir. Richard Donner. Writ. Mario Puzo, David Newman, Leslie Newman, Robert Benton. Perf. Marlon Brando, Gene Hackman, Christopher Reeve, Margot Kidder. Warner Studios, 1978.

*Superman II.* Dir. Richard Lester. Writ. Mario Puzo. Perf. Gene Hackman, Christopher Reeve, Margot Kidder. Warner Studios, 1980.

*Superman III.* Dir. Richard Lester. Writ. David Newman and Leslie Newman. Perf. Christopher Reeve, Richard Pryor, Robert Vaughn, Margot Kidder. Warner Studios, 1983.

Watching Isabel, Listening to Catherine

# Conscious Observation: Jane Campion's *Portrait of a Lady*

*Nancy Bentley*

In Henry James's 1881 novel, *The Portrait of a Lady*, Ralph Touchett decides that observing his cousin, Isabel Archer, henceforth will be the primary occupation of his life. The "conscious observation of a lovely woman," the narrator tells us, "struck him as the finest entertainment that the world now had to offer" (231). Today, in an age when watching lovely women has become a mainstay of mass entertainment, James's sentence carries an unexpected resonance, a note of literalism he could not have anticipated. Moviegoers, whether partial to art films or horror flicks, know that the observation of a beautiful woman is a central preoccupation of the celluloid world: voyeurs do it, worshipful suitors do it, star-struck fans and demented slashers do it—above all, film directors do it, as prelude to the woman-watching their audiences will do in theaters. This skewed continuity between James's novel and contemporary film makes for a provocative anachronism: James's *Portrait of a Lady* was published more than a decade before the invention of cinema, yet, strikingly, the themes of James's novel offered director Jane Campion an opportunity to explore film as a medium for the conscious observation of women.

These cinematic aims make Campion's *Portrait of a Lady* an unusual sort of movie adaptation. Critic Robert Sklar observes that Campion used James's novel as "a pretext for intervention, rather than a text to be translated directly to the screen." Campion's disregard for strict textual fidelity is particularly notable, moreover, for the way in which her boldest innovations can all be said to point self-reflexively to matters of cinema. There is a sense, then, in which Campion has made a movie about movies, recreating James's nuanced study of the "sweet-tasting property of observation" (*Portrait of a Lady* [*PL*] 231) as her own proleptic history of women in film.

Yet Campion's cinematic "intervention" in the story, I wish to argue, still deserves to be called a faithful adaptation of James's novel, though to do so may require us to suspend our assumptions about what it means to translate novels into films. Campion's focus on her medium, I contend, allows her film to sidestep a species of nostalgia frequently generated by movie versions of nineteenth-century novels of manners. In that sense, Campion has avoided importing something foreign—contemporary nostalgia—to the world of James's novel. But there is no question that the style of Campion's adaptation also alters the story's narrative substance: her film recasts Isabel Archer's crisis as sexual, a predicament of the body and of bodily desire, much more than the crisis of consciousness and social agency that Isabel suffers in James's novel. This shift toward the problem of Isabel's sexual repression and agency has struck some critics as a regrettable distortion, an evasion of the moral and social questions that are James's primary concerns.[1] But it is also possible to read Campion's focus on sexuality as the logical result of rendering Isabel's plight in the medium of film, a medium in which female agency is finally inseparable from the questions of the body and its visual image. In this cinematic context, the sexual, technological, and commercial aspects of the female film image become the very ground for exploring women's power as social actors. By reworking James's narrative thematics of sight, consciousness, and the sometimes coercive force of manners, Campion's film contains a historical specificity that is not erased but rather transposed into the distinctive terms of its own medium.

A self-conscious attention to medium is an original feature of James's novel. His title, *The Portrait of a Lady*, announces the story's subject matter—Victorian womanhood—but also directs attention to questions of genre. By calling his work of fiction a portrait, James presents his readers with an implicit analogy, a sort of titular riddle: how is a novel—*this* novel, anyway—like a painted portrait? One clue comes in chapter 37, when James's narrator imagines Isabel Archer "framed" in a "gilded doorway," the very "picture of a gracious lady" (570). The image conveys the fact that nineteenth-century portraits of woman featured, almost exclusively, a certain kind of woman: wealthy, socially ascendant, belonging to an indoor world of beautiful rooms and objects. Like Isabel pictured inside the geometric border of a golden-toned doorway, such women were understood as worthy of individual representation. Fiction *framed* this sort of woman as an absorbing, singular subject and offered her story to a greatly expanded reading public.

Read in this way, James's painterly title reflects, somewhat ironically, his understanding that the close observation of women was an important provenance of the realist novel. James's plot, no less than his title, places Isabel at the center of others' scrutiny. In Isabel's life there are "plenty of spectators" (344), the narrator tells us, observers who form a circle of family, friends, suitors and predators all intensely interested in Isabel's fate. We might ask, though: If those who surround her are "spectators," in what sense is Isabel a spectacle? Ralph's intention to give himself over to the "entertainment" of observing Isabel is secured by arranging her unexpected inheritance, and with that event, Isabel's life, like all good spectacles, offers a high degree of novelty and suspense. Ralph describes it as the "entertainment of seeing what a young lady does who has refused" an English lord in marriage (344). The pleasure of watching Isabel springs from the novel sight of a Victorian woman who is newly, unexpectedly released from the imperative to marry. Isabel is free from any financial compulsion to choose a husband, if not from the emotions and desires that compel her in other ways. Unforeseen and untested, Isabel's windfall gives a concrete shape to what was an emergent possibility of independent agency for women of her station and era.

Isabel is in this sense the spectacle that intrigued and in many quarters, riled an age: the figure of a woman actively trying to redefine the terms of her own womanhood. Although what James called "the situation of women" had been a social issue for decades, by the 1880s the topic had acquired a new visibility. Observers of the world of work noted that there was "scarcely an occupation once confined almost exclusively to men in which women are not now conspicuous" (qtd. in Shi 91). Many scientists possessed an urgent and sometimes alarmed sense that women, as social and biological creatures, required special scrutiny. As Paul Broca put it, any change in the social status of women "necessarily induces a perturbation in the evolution of the races, and hence it follows that the condition of women in society must be most carefully studied by the anthropologist" (qtd. in Bentley 163–64). And the multiplication of forms of media in this period helped to make women and the female image a far more pervasive feature of public life. "We see forms and phases of [women's] degeneration thickly scattered throughout all circles of society," lamented the Rev. James Weir, "in the plays which we see performed in our theatres, and in the books and papers published daily throughout the land" (825).

As a spectacle of narrative realism, then, James's Isabel brought question of women's uncertain agency to the pages of fiction. James would later describe this process as the precarious birth of a realist "subject" or protagonist, a moment when a "mere slim shade of an intelligent but presumptuous girl" (standing in, he writes, for "millions of girls") was "endowed with the high attributes of a Subject," imagined with new powers to see and act in the world. For James, though, the elevation of young woman to active agent also opened up the possibility that she might become a tragic subject—that she might (to use James's ominous word) be "vitiated" (*French Writers* 1077). In James's terms, a novelistic portrait of a woman must represent the unfixed consequences of her attempt to "affront" her destiny, counterpoising a new recognition of a woman's independent will and desire with a heightened awareness of forces that might thwart her. Similarly, Isabel's watchers expose motives and interests that are divided, never pure. The entertainment Ralph finds in watching Isabel, though not "immoral" (as his father fears), still colors his good will toward Isabel with traces of recklessness and erotic enchantment, and his complex sentiments anticipate the mixed responses of Isabel's other spectators, from Henrietta Stackpole's flat, unhelpful sympathy to Osmond's insidious pursuit. In the diversity and intensity of their interest, James's characters were much like James's contemporaries: in the 1880s, the entertainment of watching women was a provocative and timely affair, animated by a new urgency regarding the puzzle of women's freedoms and social constraints, and capable of triggering strong, even volatile, emotions.[2]

A film adaptation of *Portrait* could not help but recast the spectacle of Isabel in significant ways. Could the "high attributes" of the Jamesian realist subject be successfully transferred to the screen? And should precisely those attributes define a successful adaptation of the novel? In any movie version, of course, Isabel's social visibility, her role as a realist type or case, would be transformed into the most literal visual terms, a "spectacle" on the screen. And within this filmic context, the entertainment of watching Isabel on the screen becomes enmeshed in a set of historical and commercial pressures, not always consistent with each other but impossible to banish or escape. Perhaps the most obvious of these forces is economic. Brought to the screen, any James novel would be a candidate for what has become a fairly lucrative niche market in "highbrow" literary films. The last decades of our century have brought a flourishing cottage industry in film versions of nineteenth-century novels of manners. The trend is represented most notably by the films of Merchant and Ivory, as well as by high-profile adaptations of novels by Jane Austen, Edith Wharton, and E.M. Forster. This market for movies, observers have noted, has proven to have links to other kinds of commodities, from clothing and magazines to interior design.[3] But to consider the meaning of this proven economic drawing power is also to consider the aesthetic appeal for our age of a certain kind of literacy, an appeal that is partly at odds with contemporary markets and commercial culture.

Even without Ralph's pronouncement that Isabel offered the "finest entertainment," it is easy to imagine why any number of late-twentieth-century filmmakers would be drawn to her story. For a certain segment of present-day audiences, Isabel Archer's species of womanhood—the nineteenth-century "lady"—remains an object of interest, her enduring appeal evident in everything from the look of traditional wedding gowns to ad campaigns for diamonds and perfume. Yet the allure of her beauty, it seems clear, is inevitably tinged with a certain wishfulness. While Isabel's type was disquietingly new to James's contemporaries, for us her beauty is historical, somehow displaced from its proper time, like the term "lady" itself. A whole aesthetic of graciousness we associate with that type is focused retrospectively; even in objects or scenes not expressly historical (Impressionist-style posters, Ralph Lauren photo shoots), an attraction to certain kinds of well-mannered beauty seems partly a hunger for a lost moment in the past or more precisely, for a set of meanings that have been attached to that past—high civility, leisure, wealth without vulgarity, a relatively tranquil sexuality, at least as compared to the often fraught and bewildering sexual mores of the late twentieth century.

Movies have fed this longing and refined its visual look. Projected onto the screen, the desire for a lost civility is fed by the immediacy of a present vision. As Craig Cairns has said of these period films, "The audience is invited to understand the plot of the film as though we are contemporary with the characters, while at the same time indulging our pleasure in a world which is visually compelling precisely because of its pastness" (12). In 1996, Campion's *Portrait of Lady* joined this company of movies, helping to prompt talk of a "James revival" in cinema and bringing the novel within the orbit of the established market for literary films. But Campion's film also stands apart. Her interpretation of James's *Portrait,* from its opening frame, evinces a pointed suspicion of our millennial absorption in the beauty of the nineteenth-century lady and her world.

Calling the recent Jane Austen films "too soft" (qtd. in Sklar B7), Campion would seem to share the view of disapproving critics who have interpreted recent novel adaptations as a form of cinematic salve for postmodern fatigue, a "comforting antidote to contemporary disconnections" (Hutchings 217). Campion's skepticism about these period films, I shall argue, gives her own movie some of its most arresting features. At the same time, though, the real and often complex pleasures of the genre are significant indicators of our own social conditions. Immersed as we are in the unstable ironies and jumpy technological rhythms of our time, movies about gracious living and the lives of beautiful women offer the increasingly rare experiences of slow, languorous contemplation, the sound of sustained conversation, and charming intimations of the sort of uncorseted sex possible only in an age of corsets. Similarly, the costumes and sets in these movies might be said to raise consumption beguilingly to the order of art. It is as if these film versions of nineteenth-century novels conjure an

Figure 15. Two contemporary young women meet the viewer's gaze in the opening sequence of Jane Campion's *Portrait of a Lady*.

imaginary plenitude of human experience that somehow disappeared exactly at the moment when the invention of cinema—the art wed to technology, the visual image, and ever increasing mechanical speed—inaugurated a new phase of modernity. These film adaptations of novels, in other words, can be said to belie their own medium. They aim not just to retell a story, but to imitate the absorbing seamlessness of novel-reading, the slow, transporting entertainment of a world without movies. In this sense recent period films heighten an effect already built into the nature of cinema. As Walter Benjamin points out, film elides from its viewer the conditions of its own production, creating an "equipment-free aspect of reality" that has "become the height of artifice" (233).

Campion, though, refuses her viewers any such forgetting. The opening moments of her *Portrait* insist on a conscious acknowledgment of the movie's own modern medium; it is an introduction that blocks any illusory return to an idyllic bourgeois world before film. Campion greets the viewer with blackness; the film and soundtrack are running but the screen re-

Figure 16. Another young woman from Campion's opening sequence.

mains dark. This blindman's bluff has at least two effects. During the several minutes of the blackout, disembodied voices of women, speaking in
modern idioms and cadences, describe their ideas about love and desire.
The result is a kind of framing of female subjectivity, an isolation of interior
experience. At the same time, the absence of any image actually serves to
heighten our awareness that film is a medium of pictures, its vocabulary
chiefly visual. Where is the portrait? we ask of the dark screen. Where, for
that matter, is the expected "lady"?

When the movie's first images appear on the screen, it is clear that the
look and meaning of a "lady" in this film is in some doubt. Instead of the
rich period costume and pale (always pale) skin of an actress from central
casting, the viewer sees modern-day young women posed in a series of outdoor tableaux—some of the women moving or dancing, some motionless,
but all of them silent and looking at the camera that is filming them (figs. 15
and 16). Casually dressed, with a range of different skin tones, the women
are all beautiful; Campion has not changed that aspect of the novel's womanhood. But by withholding for a time the expected movie look of the gracious

Victorian lady, Campion's sequence shifts attention to our cinematic looking. We are made to notice our own gaze at the faces, clothing, and bodies
of the unnamed women, as if Campion means to begin the adaptation of
James's novel with a kind of basic grammar for observing women in film.

A "portrait" in film, Campion seems to insist, is not a novel. Brought
to the screen, even this famous nineteenth-century text by a famous lan-
guage-obsessed novelist will be fashioned out of elemental acts of looking at
women on a screen. (Campion seems to underscore this by transforming
one of the few conventional places for any written words in a movie, the
title shot, into a handwritten inscription on a woman's finger.) The film's
opening sequence announces that the themes of love and womanhood,
unmoored here from both James's nineteenth-century text and from the
visual style of recent highbrow film, will be located in relation to female
film image. If the sequence can call to mind the glossiness of a Benetton
advertisement (Bousquet 198), the resemblance may only bolster the point
that imagining conflicts about social agency in the medium of film may not
be able to stand wholly apart from conventions of modern visual media,
any more than James's Isabel could have been imagined in isolation from
the generic pressures of the marriage novel.

By calling such stark attention to the act of looking at women, Campion's
concerns with agency seem to dovetail with those of much recent film theory.
Scholars of the visual arts have argued for the importance of implicit gender differences—distinct male and female viewing positions—built into
the structuring conventions of much Western painting and film. Traditional art, the argument goes, presumes male habits of sight that are active
and self-contained. And while men's looking asserts a possession and mastery of visual objects, a woman's gaze is always occluded, circumscribed in
some fashion by her subordinate position in society. Because she has internalized her role as an ornamental object, women rarely look at the world—
hence at art—from the same active position as do men. In John Berger's oft-
cited formulation, "Men look at women. Women watch themselves being
looked at" (47).[4]

Campion clearly shares with such scholars a keen interest in women
as objects of vision. Her introductory sequence in *Portrait* heightens—almost parodies—women's familiar role in film as the object of pleasurable
looking; the women here are "isolated, glamorous, on display, sexualised"
(Mulvey 21). But the display function is so curiously overstated in this
sequence that Campion seems interested less in unveiling this role than in
exploiting it, using women's default position as object of others' gaze for
her own ends. This opening sequence recontextualizes the novel's efforts at
social sight, at understanding the spectacle of Isabel as a modern young

woman, in overt terms of cinematic vision. Like the extreme close-up shot of Nicole Kidman's eyes that follows the sequence (our first sighting of Campion's Isabel), the most literal kind of looking bears the weight of interpreting James's concern with sight as narrative understanding (fig. 17).

In the body of James's writing, the effort at social seeing at the heart of realist fiction is intensified but also highly ironized, made subject to failures and unexpected insights. *The Portrait of a Lady* marked one of James's major advances in his ironic realism. The novel, I have suggested, uses Isabel's position before the eyes of social "spectators" to try to reimagine the limits of female agency. As Ralph puts it to Isabel, "You want to see life, as the young men say." "I do want to look about me," she replies (*PL* 345). But the central irony of James's novel is that Isabel's attempts to see the world leads her into a devastating blindness, her misapprehension of Osmond. The celebrated chapter 42 in the novel, a tour de force of psychological revelation, renders the remarkable "motionless seeing" through which Isabel acquires a consciousness of her blindness and thwarted agency. Jamesian consciousness of this sort is usually a compensation for but never a resolution of the ironies uncovered by realism.[5] Disconnections remain, though they are transformed by being known—by being *seen* and recognized within the scope of the narrative.

In Campion's film, the same disjunctions between sight, agency, and consciousness are articulated most strongly in the cinematic language of vision and vantage. In Campion, as in James, when you closely observe young women, you will see their own desire for (male) sight, for an outward-looking reach in the world. The women who greet us in the first frames of Campion's film are visual objects who *look back*. They eye the camera with an equanimity suggesting equal parts confidence and inexperience. We might be tempted to see them as having already acquired the autonomy that James's Isabel longs for but never secures. But it's more likely these women are not Isabel's triumphant modern daughters but her sisters, screen versions of James's "millions of girls" whose evident powers of free imagination are a sign of their vulnerability as well as their strength of will. Though serene-looking, the women in this threshold sequence are also mute, detached from the expressions of intimacy and feeling we can no longer hear.

Are there meanings to their silence? For anyone who has seen Campion's previous movies, it will be difficult to count this muteness as mere style.[6] The self-reflexive introduction seems designed to challenge any expectations for Merchant and Ivory realism, but it also ends up staging a kind of dumb show, an allegory of modern womanhood in which female desire and subjectivity are seen as somehow displaced from women themselves, cut off or detached from the bodies under our gaze. This introduc-

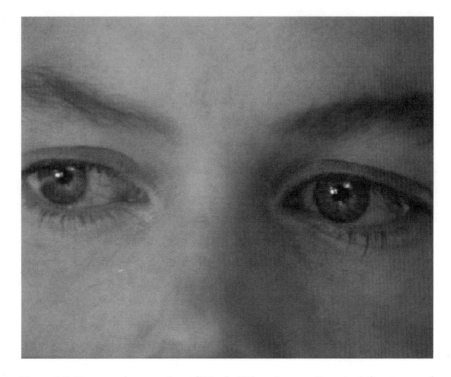

Figure 17. Extreme close-up shot of Nicole Kidman's eyes, Campion's first image of
Isabel Archer.

tory sequence—emphatically postmodern, transcultural, and cinematic—
does not insist on the universality of Isabel's story so much as its openness
to creative transfiguration. Through it Campion expresses a conviction that
film, never simply an imitation of narrative, will express anew the disjunctions and ironies of Isabel's life, the silences in what she speaks, the blindness in her seeing.

   When the film turns to Isabel's story proper, Campion preserves an
emphasis on character disjunction through cinematography and a manipulation of plot. According to *Portrait's* cinematographer, Stuart Dryburgh,
Campion "sees this as quite a modern story and therefore felt that it should
be quite modern in its treatment" (qtd. in Gentry 52). Whereas period films
tend to create an illusion of looking in on a polished world that existed
before the advent of cinema, Campion's *Portrait* heightens the formal disjunctions of her medium. Constant camera movement was used "to
contemporize the film," Dryburgh recounts. Quite deliberately, Campion
and Dryburgh avoided the integrating conventions of period films. There

are few wide shots—either for outdoor scenes or for sequences in rooms and corridors—and the use of long lenses and unusual modes of backlighting frequently reduces the movie's depth of field. "There is no sense of 'portrait photography' in the illustrative sense," Dryburgh observes (52). And techniques such as shooting through beveled glass even introduce outright visual distortion, intended to convey "a displacement of the spirit" (57).

Anachronisms, motifs of formal "cinematic aberration," unusual camera choreography: these and other techniques show Campion's unwillingness to subordinate her medium to James's. For Campion's viewers, "conscious observation" is consciously cinematic, and this feature may well be part of the reason why the movie has been largely applauded by film scholars.[7] For precisely the same reason, however, it is not surprising that a number of literary critics have expressed dissatisfaction with the film. To these critics, Campion's enchantment with her own medium tempted her into violating the spirit as well as the letter of James's novel. Campion imports film's lower (or at least more limited) tastes and habits, her critics charge, when she substitutes blunt visual sensation, especially the obviousness of screen sex and violence, for James's signature indirection, making Isabel's dilemma an erotic rather than social predicament. The substance of this complaint seems to me wholly accurate; Campion's adaptation reshapes Isabel's story to fit the bias of its own medium. Yet it remains to be asked whether Campion's way of representing the sexual and coercive forces in Isabel's life may not in fact convey in other terms the same disjunctions that were for James the basis of Isabel's hard-won consciousness.

Of her fidelity to James's text, Campion has confessed this much: "I felt invited to be free" (qtd. in Sklar). Perhaps nowhere is Campion freer than in the way she has made *Portrait* a story about kissing. The sexual tension James conveys through verbal irony and silence Campion makes into a complex series of fully visualized kisses. In James's account, for instance, the first scene between Madame Merle and Osmond contains only the charged air of "something indirect and circumspect" (*PL* 437). Campion, in contrast, signifies their past love affair through a kind of hollow pantomime of overt sexual embraces, as Malkovich's Osmond reenacts his former passion for Madame Merle (Barbara Hershey) in a manner that is at once mocking and seductive. Taken together, the kisses Campion has added to James's story probably mark all of the major plot developments.

Campion's frequent use of on-screen kissing can quite rightly be attributed to her medium. A movie may have declared "a kiss is just a kiss," but as a credo movies have never believed it; the celluloid kiss and the whole continuum of expressive sexual touch that eventually followed it to the screen remain a primary vocabulary for cinema, its most freighted imagery. Yet even in the matter of sex, Campion could still be said to have taken a cue from James, who was aware of the distinctions and meaning that can be signified in a kiss (in his narrator's words, "there are kisses and kisses" [*PL* 400]). After all, one of the first people to take liberty with James's literary kissing was James himself, when he made a significant revision in the New York Edition of *Portrait* that quite radically redescribed the kiss in the crucial last scene between Isabel and Caspar Goodwood.

In James's revised ending, the kiss inaugurates a metaphorical flourish in which the interior landscape of Isabel's desire is mapped onto larger plot conflicts. The boldest innovation of Campion's *Portrait,* a scene presumably issuing from Isabel's imagination, resembles just this Jamesian revision, in its effect if not its content. In Campion's imaginary scene, Isabel is caressed and kissed by both Caspar Goodwood and Lord Warburton. Coming as it does immediately after Isabel has dismissed Caspar and his entreaties to marry, the fantasy suggests not only that Isabel sexually desires both men, but that her ability to refuse them in marriage brings on its own eroticized excitement. There are no hints of any imaginary ménage à trois in James's novel, to be sure, yet the idea of Isabel's pleasure in refusal is surely James's: he describes her rejection of Caspar as something charged with a "throbbing" from the "enjoyment she found in the exercise of her power" (*PL* 359). Campion's scene employs a Freudianism James never knew or else ignored, but the fantasy offers a vivid interpretation of some of the contingent powers and pleasures that motivate James's Isabel.[8]

The fantasy scene incorporates another dimension of the story, this one possibly less psychological than self-referential about Isabel's status as a portrait in film. In the midst of Isabel's increasing sexual transport, the figure of Ralph Touchett appears in the scene, not as a third lover but as a spectator to the others' lovemaking. The scene thus enacts a strange literalizing of the "entertainment" Ralph finds in his "conscious observation" of Isabel and her relationship with the other two men (fig. 18). Merged as part of Isabel's fantasy, Ralph's watching is presented as part of the makeup of her own desire. They see each other and pause, exchanging a look: his voyeurism and her exhibitionism are for a moment perfectly matched. At that moment, too, our own pleasure as onlookers seems to be allegorized in the undetected way Ralph has been drawn from the ranks of invisible watchers to his place as an on-screen spectator. As soon as these previously unacknowledged motives (Ralph's and our pleasure in watching, Isabel's pleasure in being watched) find their way to the screen, however, the fantasy swiftly breaks down. As Isabel begins to become fully aware of Ralph's watching, his presence seems to terminate or transform the lovemaking as a scene of desire and becomes instead something she wishes to escape.

Movies have traditionally presented female sexuality as something transparent, open to view, and thus easily converted to an object the viewer can imaginatively possess. Campion's fantasy scene seems to recognize this fact by letting us see Isabel's otherwise hidden or suppressed desire. At the same time, though, the scene complicates any simple idea of the viewer's power of possession when it makes Ralph's intense observation a distinct part of Isabel's own desires. To be seen and observed, to have her desire exposed, is stimulating for Isabel, but it is also disturbing, as if to recognize her pleasure and its source is simultaneously to recognize its danger—the threat of possession. This sense of threat may be a neurosis: Isabel's fear of sex. It may also be prudence, Isabel's fear of possession. In either case, the projection of Isabel's fantasy, its exposure on-screen, has moved quite beyond any idea that her desire is simply there for the taking. The notion of "conscious observation" can be said to accrue here an additional density of meaning: made vivid on the screen, Isabel's consciousness of Ralph's observation—and her awareness of its place *in* her own consciousness—these projections realize some of the complex and precarious circuits of Isabel's sexuality, as they hint, too, at her struggle toward a fuller self-consciousness.

This fraught desublimation, it must be allowed, is an inexact analogue for the growth of consciousness at the heart of James's novel. The film largely does elide the novel's attention to social conditions and moral crisis in favor of Isabel's erotic travails. And yet by presenting Isabel's awakening as a source of disjunction rather than liberation, as a failure to match desire and understanding to social sight, Campion makes Isabel's ironic story an apt template for what is finally not a retreat to the banalities of romantic angst but a hard-nosed social insight: that sexual desublimation may actually heighten the social disjunctions between desire, agency, and consciousness. Such an insight, issuing from our own age of greater sexual license, may be part of what prompts Campion to call Isabel's story a distinctly "modern" one (qtd. in Gentry 52).

If it is true that Campion's shift from Isabel's moral consciousness to her sexual awareness is a logical transposition for her medium, then it shouldn't surprise us that one of the film's most striking and controversial innovations is a sequence that is also Campion's most overt meditation on the place of women in film. The scene in which Osmond first declares his love concludes with—what else?—a kiss. A kiss, though, that Osmond protects from the camera's eye, blocking our view with Isabel's parasol, as if to block his motives from scrutiny. But where Osmond attempts to hide his seduction, Campion reveals its effects by cutting to a succession of wildly anachronistic allusions to twentieth-century film styles, all of which express Isabel's erotic confusion and fears. What begins as a crude home

Figure 18. Isabel's sexual fantasy, a departure from Henry James's novel.

movie purporting to record Isabel's world travels, turns into a rapid series
of signature cinematic styles, from the look of a Valentino-era silent film
(recalling the exoticism of *The Sheik*), to the bold visual patterns and odd
framing made popular by Hitchcock, followed by the bizarre effects of surrealist film (a plate of beans that echo Osmond's professions of love), and
recalling finally the isolated, stripped look of the female nude in exploitation films. As different as they are, these brief snippets convey a similar
idea. All present female desire as troubled, fraught, even pathological. But
by presenting such disparate film styles in such quick succession, the sequence also breaks up any easy sense that we are seeing that desire as it is,
as a simple and knowable object. We become conscious of the fact that
female sexuality is, quite literally, mediated, visible only through time-bound
conventions of representation. We become conscious, in other words, that
we are seeing not a woman but a portrait.

     If Isabel is erotically troubled then, the trouble seems to come as much
from outside her—from an anterior source of vision—as from her own
inherent sexuality, or perhaps from the way internal desire and external

vision are mutually shaping. The effect is to make female sexuality appear as something disjointed, dispersed, but also something dynamic and open to change. A woman's complex desires may hold the melodramatic peril portrayed in silent film, or the menace in Hitchcock, or the anxiety in surrealism; but if it holds such different meanings, might not her sexuality also mean something else? Might not it *look* otherwise—look, for instance, like the recovered self-possession of an Ada McGrath (from Campion's *The Piano*)? Campion's portrait manipulates its own medium to try to sustain conflicting possibilities about the imagination, desires, and fate of a woman placed before our observation.

Though these self-consciously cinematic manipulations make Campion's *Portrait* a significant departure from James's, still Isabel's dilemma in the film shares with the novel a structuring tension, almost an impasse, between the possibilities of agency and the forces of social coercion. The screen portrait, I want to suggest, mimics formally the paradoxes that are a hallmark of James's brand of fiction, the tension between characters' freedom and their social entrapment. One of the most notable things about the complex entertainment of watching Isabel in James's novel is the fact that we do not end up seeing her dead. This is saying quite a lot: as a genre, the nineteenth-century realist novel features a remarkable number of dead women. Because realism developed by supplying an increasingly dense background of social causes for human action, realist works often resolve vexing questions about a woman's subjectivity (what does she want? is she free to act?) by locating a social explanation—or at least a social closure—in her death. The world's cruelty killed her. Or (as another novel might contend) the world's guile and illusions. Or its indifference to a woman's need for love. Or her inability to read social signs, to distinguish them from her own enchanted wishes. Even a woman's suicide, oftentimes, is less an act of will in this fiction than, as one critic puts it, "a virtually involuntary surrender to social forces" (Higgonet 78). In realism there is an aesthetic logic, hence a beauty, in the death of the heroine; Anna Karenina, Emma Bovary, Edna Pontellier, Lily Bart, Tess D'Urbervilles, and James's own Daisy Miller and Milly Theale are among the finest examples of realism's "cult of the beautiful corpse" (Higgonet 78).

In *Portrait,* James considers the possibility of Isabel's death and gives it a striking aesthetic resonance. By the time Isabel recognizes her mistake in marrying Osmond, death has become something darkly alluring: "To cease utterly, to give it all up and not know anything more—this idea was as sweet as the vision of a cool bath in a marble tank, in a darkened chamber, in a hot land" (*PL* 769). When Caspar Goodwood appears before her in their final confrontation, "she believed that to let him take her in his arms would be the next best thing to dying" (*PL* 798). But while death is an enticement, point-ing toward an alternative ending that would offer a certain "sweet" closure, the novel keeps Isabel alive and living with the problem of her agency.

Agency is a problem in this novel because it remains to the end a force incommensurate with what the novel shows to be the cunning power of external social forces. Isabel's sudden wealth gives her a field for indepen-dent action that is rare for a woman, but it is precisely her status as a woman of means that brings on her unforeseen fate. "If ever a girl was a free agent, she had been," the narrator says of Isabel's own sentiments. "She had looked, and considered, and chosen" (*PL* 609). This assertion might stand, as well as any single line could, for the plot of the novel. And yet the weight of the novel's most dramatic elements—its suspense, its irony and psycho-logical insight—give a greater force to doubts about Isabel's agency, doubts that lurk in the very grammar of the conditional sentence ("*if ever* a girl was a free agent . . ."). The grammatical tension in that sentence distills the force and counterforce that structures the novel as a whole. That same tension, however, gives the idea of her agency enough life in the novel (even if, like Isabel's, it is a damaged and suspended life) to supply plau-sible "proof that she should some day be happy again" (*PL* 769) and to hold off the fatality that Isabel and her narrative both consider. The novel *enter-tains* the beauty—the aesthetic rightness—of Isabel's death, but in the end the novel remains poised in an aesthetic of uncertainty.

Campion, too, keeps her Isabel alive, though not without flirting with death, dismemberment, and even masochism as the touchstones of Isabel's predicament. In stark, sometimes startling, visual effects, the film conveys James's aesthetic of an uncertain fate for Isabel as a would-be "free agent." Campion has taken the psychological coercion used against Isabel in James's novel (Madame Merle asserts that Isabel "is not to be subjected to force," which only prompts the Countess Gemini to exclaim "you are capable of anything, you and Osmond" [*PL* 466]) and converted it into Osmond's overt acts of force. Osmond strikes her, trips her, thrusts her on a sofa. Campion's Isabel is strangely responsive to his violence, as when in the wake of one instance of Osmond's abuse, she appears to lean toward him for an expected (desired?) kiss or embrace.

Osmond's manhandling in these scenes is a form of aggression that James had quite pointedly excluded. James's Osmond is vicious, to be sure, a man of "morbid passion" (*PL* 688), who inflicts some of his worst harm by unwittingly drawing from Isabel a sadism that mirrors his own: she discov-ers she is capable of a "horrible delight in having wounded him" (680). But in James these hostilities are terrible precisely for their civility. They derive their force from the fact that they can coexist with the best manners, with the most exacting requirements of genteel taste and decorum.[9] In James, the ability to harm comes from the web of custom that can protect and intensify certain acts of will. Caspar Goodwood uses this kind of aggression, albeit with far less malevolence than does Osmond, when he presses on Isabel his claims: he "had not been violent," James writes, "but there had been a violence in that" (691).

The civilized aggression so finely calibrated and traced in James's fiction, because invisible by nature, may resist any direct depiction on the screen. Nevertheless, this kind of unseen wounding filters into Campion's film in oblique ways. The nearly monochromatic blue tones of some of the movie's scenes in Rome, for instance, register the coldness and hostility that suffuse Isabel's marriage to Osmond. And even the acts of physical force that flare into view, I would argue, can be said to express a Jamesian understanding of the way bourgeois gentility can generate its own strains of violence. The scenes in which Malkovich's Osmond assaults Kidman's Isabel are among the few in the film that include a great deal of visible background. While much of the film, as Dryburgh notes, was shot to "isolate the characters and put the background out of focus" (qtd. in Gentry 52), these scenes in Osmond and Isabel's villa create an uncharacteristic integration of character and period setting. When the sumptuous interiors are unveiled in these villa scenes, we finally see the gorgeous rooms only to find that the burnished furniture and objets d'art are ornaments that adorn startling acts of hostility. As a result, visual signs we associate with high civilization— opulent interiors and collected works of art—are framed as icons of cruelty.

But while Campion's color tones and interior shots can effect a Jamesian sense of intangible aggression, these remain diffuse forces. An anthropomorphic medium, film finds its greatest fascination in the human body— in "the relationship between the human form and its surroundings, the visible presence of the person in the world" (Mulvey 17). The social traps and the masochism that James intimates in metaphor and dialogue Campion represents through the sight of physical force or its threat. The actors' bodies, giving and receiving violent force, supply the ultimate visual proof of the cruelty that is tolerated, even nourished, by this world. In one of Campion's most arresting visual effects, she uses a broken statuary of gigantic, isolated body parts as the backdrop for the scene in which Madame Merle first obliquely acknowledges to Isabel her machinations. For Campion, the social is always potentially violent: every elegant room or city stroll may harbor some trace of coercive force. Campion sees the world of the nineteenth-century bourgeoisie as a world at once beautiful and sadistic. (When I screened the film in a theater, more than one viewer in the audience, no doubt remembering Campion's film *The Piano,* gasped when

Isabel declares "I would have given my little finger to say yes," though the line in fact comes from James.)[10]

But despite the film's rich vision of coercive social relations, Campion also seems to resist the pull of this vision and even the beauty of what James called its "exquisite, far-reaching sadness" (*PL* 755), in order to sustain the possibility of a stronger female agency. She rejects the smooth perfection of the period film genre, roughening the surface of her own portrait. The movie's anachronisms and self-reflexiveness keep female desire alive as a problem rather than a point of termination. Uncertainty and hesitation have to supply whatever repose of beauty Isabel's story has to offer. The film's final sequence, the portrait of Isabel that endures, perceptively slows and then freezes her in a wintry threshold, halfway between the promise of shelter and a bare, white desolation.

For Campion's viewers, as for James's readers, the uncertain resolution to Isabel's plight offers a curious form of entertainment, one that strains the very concept of what it means to entertain. Probably the more familiar understanding of the term, "to hold attention with something diverting," best fits the entertainment Osmond finds in Isabel. Osmond's watching of Isabel is an obsessive diversion; indeed, we might say he aims to *divert* Isabel's "pretty appearance" from her "ideas," feeling, and judgment (*PL* 632) and therefore anticipates the more exploitative tendency in a good many mass media portraits of women. But Campion's movie, like James's novel, aspires to offer us entertainment in a more archaic sense, one in which "to entertain" means "to hold in mind." Campion attempts a far-reaching idea of what it means to observe a woman in film, an idea that would hold in mind the confluence of a conscious watching with a complex visual portrait of a woman's desire and feeling.

## Notes

1. See for instance Nadel, Ozick, and Bousquet.
2. On the emergence of the "woman question" and its relevance for fiction see Banta, Montgomery, and Shi.
3. Hipsky and Hutchings discuss some of the economic and political implications of this lucrative if limited market, including its connections to other media and industries.
4. For examples of theoretical discussions of gender and looking in art, see Mulvey and Kaplan, as well as Berger.
5. For a provocative argument that Isabel's growth in consciousness is actually an indicator of James's evasion of the social situation of women, see Daugherty.
6. Campion's best-known film, *The Piano* (1993), features a female protagonist, Ada McGrath, who refuses to speak. Ada's desire and feeling is expressed instead through her piano playing. Another Campion film, *Angel at My Table*

(1990), could also be described as a movie about a woman who attempts to claim powers of expression.

7. Examples of highly appreciative analyses by film critics include Francke, Gentry, and Murphy.

8. While James's narrative contains nothing resembling Campion's bedroom scene, the novel does include a "reverie" in which Isabel pictures Caspar and Warburton together. During an interlude at San Remo, Isabel is visited by a vision of "two figures which, in spite of increasing distance, were still sufficiently salient; they were recognisable without difficulty as those of Caspar Goodwood and Lord Warburton." In the imagined scene, which has the "supernatural aspect of a resurrection," Isabel seems concerned primarily to affirm her decision to reject their offers of marriage. ("She had so definitely undertaken to forget him, as a lover," the narrator says of Isabel's sentiments toward Warburton, "that a corresponding effort on his own part would be eminently proper.") So, while Campion's fantasy scene presumes Isabel's continuing desire for the suitors, Isabel's reverie in the novel asserts that she has relegated the two men to her past: "It was strange how quickly these gentlemen had fallen into the background of our young lady's life." At the same time, though, the memory itself is James's hint to the reader that, contrary to Isabel's confident assumptions, the men still have a significant place in her life and her consciousness. And though James doesn't attempt to uncover or describe any suppressed feeling, he does make readers aware of Isabel's habit of active suppression: "It was in her disposition at all times to lose faith in the reality of absent things. . . . She was capable of being wounded by the discovery that she had been forgotten; and yet, of all liberties, the one she herself found sweetest was the liberty to forget" (420–21).

9. For a full discussion of this dimension of James and its connections to late-nineteenth-century social thought see Bentley.

10. In *The Piano,* Ada McGrath's finger is cut off by her husband. James actually uses three different versions of the idiom. When Warburton presses Isabel regarding his proposal, the narrator notes that his "tender eagerness" moved her, "and she would have given her little finger at that moment, to feel, strongly and simply, the impulse to answer" (*PL* 302). Osmond uses a variant of the phrase when he tells Isabel that he "would give [his] little finger to go to Japan" (*PL* 507). And Madame Merle, in a moment of remorse or self-disgust, tells Osmond that she "would give [her] right hand to be able to weep" (*PL* 28). The repetition gives the light-hearted expression a weight it would not otherwise have. Each idiomatic reference to self-mutilation comes at the height of a charged marital or sexual negotiation, as if to mark verbally the risks and potential powers of the bodily self within marriage.

## Works Cited

Banta, Martha. *Imaging American Women: Idea and Ideals in Cultural History.* New York: Columbia UP, 1987.

Benjamin, Walter. *Illuminations.* Ed. Hannah Arendt. New York: Schocken, 1986.

Bentley, Nancy. *The Ethnography of Manners: Hawthorne, James, Wharton.* Cambridge: Cambridge UP, 1995.

Berger, John. *Ways of Seeing.* London: Penguin, 1972.

Bousquet, Marc. "I Don't Like Isabel Archer." *Henry James Review* 18 (1997): 197–99.

Cairns, Craig. "Rooms with a View." *Sight and Sound* 1.2 (1991): 11–14.

Daugherty, Sarah B. "James and the Ethics of Control: Aspiring Architects and Their Floating Creatures." *Enacting History in Henry James: Narrative, Power, and Ethics.* Ed. Gert Buelens. Cambridge: Cambridge UP, 1997. 61–74.

Francke, Lizzie. "On the Brink." *Sight and Sound* 6.11 (1996): 6–9.

Gentry, Ric. "Painterly Touches." *American Cinematographer* Jan. 1997: 50–57.

Higgonet, Margaret. "Speaking Silences: Women's Suicide." *The Female Body in Western Culture.* Ed. Susan Rubin Suleiman. Cambridge: Harvard UP, 1986.

Hipsky, Martin A. "Anglophil(m)ia: Why Does America Watch Merchant Ivory Movies?" *Journal of Popular Film and Television* 22.3 (1994): 98–107.

Hutchings, Peter J. "A Disconnected View: Forster, Modernity and Film." *E.M. Forster.* Ed. Jeremy Tambling. New York: St. Martin's, 1995. 98–107.

James, Henry. *French Writers, Other European Writers, the Prefaces to the New York Edition.* Vol. 2 of *Literary Criticism.* Ed. Leon Edel. New York: Library of America, 1984.

———. *The Portrait of a Lady.* Ed. William T. Stafford. New York: Library of America, 1985.

Kaplan, E. Ann. *Women and Film: Both Sides of the Camera.* New York: Methuen, 1983.

Montgomery, Maureen E. *Displaying Women: Spectacles of Leisure in Edith Wharton's New York.* New York: Routledge, 1998.

Mulvey, Laura. *Visual and Other Pleasures.* Bloomington: Indiana UP, 1989.

Murphy, Kathleen. "*Portrait of a Lady.*" *Film Comment* 32.6 (1996): 28–33.

Nadel, Alan. "The Search for Cinematic Identity and a Good Man: Jane Campion's Appropriation of James's *Portrait.*" *Henry James Review* 18 (1997): 180–83.

Ozick, Cynthia. "What Only Words, Not a Film, Can Portray." *New York Times* 5 Jan. 1997.

Shi, David E. *Facing Facts: Realism in American Thought and Culture, 1850–1920.* New York: Oxford UP, 1995.

Sklar, Robert. "A Novel Approach to Movie Making: Reinventing *The Portrait of a Lady.*" *Chronicle of Higher Education* 14 Feb. 1997: B7.

Weir, James, Jr. "The Effect of Female Suffrage on Posterity." *American Naturalist* 29 (1895): 818–25.

*Filmography*

*Angel at My Table.* Dir. Jane Campion. Writ. Laura Jones. Perf. Kerry Fox and Alexia Keogh. Fine Line Features, 1990.

*The Piano.* Dir. Jane Campion. Writ. Jan Campion. Perf. Holly Hunter, Harvey Keitel, Sam Neill. Miramax, 1993.

*The Portrait of a Lady.* Dir. Jane Campion. Writ. Laura Jones. Perf. Nicole Kidman and John Malkovich. Polygram, 1996.

# "Prospects of Entertainment"

Film Adaptations of *Washington Square*

*Julie Rivkin*

Unlike other James novels recently adapted to the screen, *Washington Square* poses what would seem like an immediate impediment to cinematic translation in the person of its protagonist—a young woman characterized as neither beautiful nor clever. A mobile and engaging Isabel Archer, a Kate Croy who remains always in the line of one's vision, even a Milly Theale with a resemblance to a Bronzino (or is it Klimt?) portrait are easily imagined on screen. But Catherine Sloper—placid, dutiful, and above all undemonstrative—seems an unlikely prospect for cinematic adaptation. If there is, as Nancy Bentley argues, an element of "girl watching" in James's novels that makes them translatable to the conventions of cinematic entertainment, then we don't have much of a girl to watch here (174). But it's not just that Catherine is plain; it's also that she remains so resolutely opaque and uncommunicative to those who surround her. The extreme privacy of her drama is its signature; surrounded by people she learns she cannot trust, she comes to keep her knowledge and emotions to herself. While such hermeticism might be a boon to a narrator who can "go behind" and tell us what she would never express, it would seem to offer little to the cinematographer. Yet these apparent difficulties appear not to have troubled Hollywood, since *Washington Square* has come in for not one but two cinematic adaptations, first the 1949 William Wyler film *The Heiress* and more recently the 1997 Agnieszka Holland *Washington Square*. What do producers and directors see in *Washington Square* that makes it such a popular choice? Alternatively, what do they do to *Washington Square* to make it work on screen?

While the physically plain heroine and the uncommunicated nature of her life's drama might make *Washington Square* difficult to film, other elements of the novel offer intriguing resources. The novel's tight plot, small cast of characters, and intense focus on a single setting come close to following the dramatic unities. The play *The Heiress,* adapted by Ruth Goetz and Augustus Goetz from the novel and itself the basis for Wyler's script, does not need to make many changes to acheive dramatic economy. Yet the novel also offers a wide historical reference. Written in 1879 about New York of the 1830s–1840s, it pursues its almost archetypally simple story of a daughter torn between the demands of her father and the promises of her suitor with a sense of how intricately engaged such a story is in the commercial development of New York (Bell 8ff.). The novel has been called Balzacian in its depiction of human relationships as embedded in issues of money, social class, and power. The historical imbrication of this drama, first visible in the opening analysis of the medical profession, makes it clear that Catherine Sloper's story can only be told as of a piece with the social and economic history of New York. Moreover, the temporal separation between narration (1870s) and story (1840s) invites us to see "the historical" as a matter of re-coding; the narrative registers the way in which the 1870s makes its impress upon the 1840s. Such a process acquires further historical layering when the films of the 1940s and 1990s reengage this story.

    In analyzing these two films, then, we might consider both the ways in which they respond to or compensate for *Washington Square's* private or uncommunicated drama and the ways in which they re-code the material according to the assumptions and values of their own historical moments. Neither filmmaker can leave Catherine's experience of her life as sealed off to other characters as does Henry James. *The Heiress,* which turns the plot into a one of revenge, makes visible the degree to which revenge is really about communication—that is, the communication of one's meanings to those who have done one wrong. What Wyler's film seems to find most unacceptable about the novel—upon which it is only loosely based—is a protagonist whom no one understands, who keeps her own counsel, who grows and acquires quite extraordinary perceptions, but shares that understanding with nobody. If in James's novel ultimately no one knows what Catherine knows, in Wyler's film Catherine makes it perfectly clear in the extravagant lessons of melodrama exactly what she knows and what impact her knowledge has upon those who have attempted to keep her in the dark. When she refuses her father the love he once denied her and lets him dies alone or when she pretends to accept Morris's belated proposal and then bolts the door against him, she not only copies the cruel behaviors of her father and suitor but also finds the exact actions to convey to them her understanding of what they have done to her. The symmetrical acts of the revenge plot register a transfer of both knowledge and power; Catherine's knowledge operates as power precisely because it is communicated, and the act of communication assumes a sadistic dimension that compensates for earlier suffering even as it inflicts pain of its own.

One effect of empowering Catherine in this way, however, is that the film's plot acquires the melodramatic elements that the novel satirizes in the figure of Mrs. Penniman and renders suspect in the smooth performances of Morris Townsend. In considering the 1949 version of this tale, then, it is important to make sense of the reclaimed value of melodrama, as it provides a medium of female agency. Catherine's transformation from the perfectly domesticated daughter and future wife to the figure of female vengeance can be read in relation to the changing expectations for women in the post–World War II years, when they were being asked to return to the home, even as films of the era depicted (and punished) strong women characters who did not follow that social injunction. Wyler's Catherine might be compared with the heroines of late 40s film noir: like them, she wields a vindictive "masculine power" that repels the spectator even as it answers to a certain sense of justice. When Catherine assumes the hard edges of her father's authority, she does so without his mitigating wit. The film becomes increasingly sympathetic to the father as his power is assumed by his daughter. The spectator is thus steered to view the patriarchal figure as appropriate in his domestic role, and when the once submissive girl shows herself as an independent woman beyond the will of her father and the need for a husband, the moment occasions a certain social vertigo. The melodramatic genre of the revenge plot becomes the medium for exploring these gendered transfers of power in the postwar years, in directions both with and against the social tide.

If Wyler (via the Goetzes) finds in the revenge plot an adaptation of *Washington Square* that speaks to issues of gender and power in the late 1940s, Holland finds different generic resources for the late 1990s. Nominally more faithful to the original, Holland's *Washington Square* turns James's novel into a kind of a love story and an awakening of Catherine's "inner child." Such changes record a different kind of unease with Catherine's hermeticism even as they convey a 1990s blend of feminism and psychological realism in the depiction of "relationships." The largest change that Holland makes is in the characterization of Morris Townsend, who ceases to be the fortune hunter of Henry James's novel (and Wyler's film) and instead becomes a genuine if forgivably inadequate suitor to Catherine. Changing Morris in this way necessarily involves altering both Doctor Sloper and Catherine herself. Doctor Sloper simply becomes a brutal patriarch, his opposition to Catherine's engagement no longer the product of his scientifically accurate vision but instead a matter of paternal jealousy and pique. The notion of the father who can be wrong while being right—right about Morris's character, wrong in the way he imposes his vision upon his daughter—disappears. The impact of this change upon Catherine may be more subtle but is no less consequential. Because Morris genuinely loves her, even if he loves her with her money, Catherine's own development registers the impact of that emotional connection rather than the discovery of its absence. Moreover, with a very late-twentieth-century sense of the psychology of relationships, Morris is shown not simply to love Catherine but to understand and value the qualities of her character that make her a psychologically appropriate mate for someone like himself. No longer an isolate, this Catherine does not need revenge to manifest her being. Instead, Morris has found her out. Even if he deserts her, the self he helped her to discover is one she retains for herself at the end. In the closing chapters of the novel, James's Catherine is distinguished by "something dead in her life," killed by a suitor who "trifled with her affection" and a father who had "broken its spring" (173). Holland's Catherine, by contrast, is vital and childlike, surrounded by children whom she herself resembles.

This transformation can again be seen in historical terms. In the late 1990s there is little sympathy for the patriarch; several decades of feminist critique have exposed his familial tyranny as the product of unacknowl-edged incestuous desires and his so-called professional authority as dis-gruntled narcissism. The suitor, however, is redeemable if he has the qualities of feeling and fallibility and beauty—all somewhat androgynous—possessed by this version of Morris. Holland's understanding of how material condi-tions affect emotions is also very different from either James's or Wyler's. In both James's novel and Wyler's film, Morris's interest in Catherine's money is evidence of his inauthentic emotions, while in Holland's film, material circumstances are assumed to be intimately connected to all forms of feel-ing. Catherine's naive "goodness" is a product of her great financial ease. Because Morris recognizes that his attraction to her is an attraction to her whole privileged setting, he is simply more realistic about love than any of the other characters. He knows the limitations of his own poverty, just as he knows how the liberating effect of a small inheritance permitted his own fabled quest for experience in Europe. Moreover, if valuing Catherine with her money is a form of commodifying her, he also performs this act upon himself. He sees his beauty and charm as negotiable attributes much like her wealth, and to say that his feeling for her depends on her money is no different from noting that hers for him is conditioned by his own attributes. That there is a gender reversal in this commodification only makes Morris more sympathetic; after all, it is more familiarly female beauty up for sale in a male marketplace. This acceptance of the centrality of commodification may be the most telling signature of the late twentieth century in this film; it works along with the feminist devaluation of the patriarch and the focus on feelings to define Holland's version of *Washington Square.*

## Irony, Sadomasochism, and Entertainment

In considering these adaptations of the novel into a story of revenge or a love story/discovery of one's "inner child," cinematic genres that suit certain social attitudes of their respective eras, we might place those genres in relation to the novel's own analysis of its sources of entertainment. For like so many of James's novels, this one contains reflections on what constitutes "entertainment" in a set of events and circumstances. What may be surprising is that there is a connection between Catherine's least cinematic attribute—her impassive or undramatic quality—and the novel's dynamics of pleasure. The difficulty of knowing Catherine relates to the whole management of knowledge in the novel. If Catherine is associated with the withholding of knowledge, this behavior might well derive from and certainly responds to her father's reliance upon irony. The novel's analysis of entertainment points out that this handling of knowledge is the source of the novel's pleasure. Whether that pleasure derives from Doctor Sloper's witty ironic tone with his daughter or his daughter's reticent responses has been a subject of some critical debate.

The character who reflects on the sources of his spectatorial pleasure is Doctor Sloper. Although he is a participant in the drama, he views his role as sufficiently undemanding to allow him the leisure to be a spectator as well. The narrator comments on how he views his daughter's struggles mainly in terms of the amusement he derives from them: "I know not whether he had hoped for a little more resistance for the sake of a little more entertainment; but he said to himself, as he had said before, that though it might have its momentary alarms, paternity was, after all, not an exciting vocation" (79). His bemused view of his own position in the drama does not forsake him even when Catherine offers "a little more resistance"; again, the doctor thinks mainly of the "prospect of entertainment" such resistance offers: "'By Jove,' he said to himself, 'I believe she will stick—I believe she will stick!' And this idea of Catherine 'sticking' appeared to have a comical side, and to offer a prospect of entertainment. He determined, as he said to himself, to see it out" (99). Even as Doctor Sloper muses about the sources of his entertainment, his anguished daughter stands outside his study door, having been turned away by her "grimly consistent parent" in spite of her "pitiful cry" and "[h]er hands . . . raised in supplication" (99). Refusing to "let her sob out her misery on his shoulder," instead he "took her arm and directed her course across the threshold," only to find himself "listening" for her presence on the other side of the door (*WS* 99). What he calls her "resistance," her "sticking," is this overwhelmingly painful experience for the girl. Doctor Sloper's "prospects of entertainment" are explicitly sadistic.

But Doctor Sloper's pleasure is not the only one that might provide a paradigm for the reader or spectator. Catherine, as the product of her father's care, displays an early masochism that rhymes with his sadism:

> The poor girl found her account so completely in the exercise of her affections that the little tremor of fear that mixed itself with her filial passion gave the thing an extra relish rather than blunted its edge. Her deepest desire was to please him, and her conception of happiness was to know that she had succeeded in pleasing him. She had never succeeded beyond a certain point. Though, on the whole, he was very kind to her, she was perfectly aware of this, and to go beyond the point in question seemed to her really something to live for. (10)

This sadomasochistic relation between father and daughter can also be seen as a relationship of knowledge. The father's power is in withholding knowledge, and thus the main feature of her father's cruel treatment of her is his irony. Catherine's sense of her father is of meanings that escape her, an expanse of significance to which she generously grants great value. The narrator comments:

> You would have surprised him if you had told him so, but it is a literal fact that he almost never addressed his daughter save in the ironical form. Whenever he addressed her he gave her pleasure; but she had to cut her pleasure out of the pieces, as it were. There were portions left over, light remnants and snippets of irony, which she never know what to do with, which seemed too delicate for her own use; and yet Catherine, lamenting the limitations of her understanding, felt that they were too valuable to waste, and had a belief that if they passed over her head they contributed to the general sum of human wisdom. (22)

The sewing metaphor indicates Catherine's mind at work, since embroidery is the medium of her creation. Her pleasure comes from taking his words more literally than they are spoken, taking her father's compliments, for example, as if they were genuine rather than mocking. But if Catherine's pleasure is produced by editing, the "light remnants and snippets" of irony are too precious to waste, and ultimately her own sense of thrift will lead her to make use of them to stitch a different garment. One might say this is the garment in which she learns to clothe herself, the garment of inaccessibility.

In developing the sewing metaphor into a sartorial one, I am simply picking up on the context in which this observation about Doctor Sloper's irony is provided. His daughter has just appeared in a dress of the kind that she favors: "she sought to be eloquent in her garments, and to make up for her diffidence of speech by a fine frankness of costume" (13). Looking at his daughter's "crimson gown," he comments, "And is it possible that this magnificent creature is my child?" Catherine cannot cut away enough irony to take pleasure in this attention; denying her "magnificence," she find herself "wishing that she had put on another dress" (22). Her father insists on the point, his cruelty becoming more overt as he makes the connection between the way she looks and the only thing he considers worthy about her, his money: "You are sumptuous, opulent, expensive. . . . You look as if you had eighty thousand a year" (22). Catherine denies the connection between her dress and such a fortune, and then extends the act of conceal-ment to her words. Pretending a "tiredness" that she does not feel, she begins to costume herself not in "frankness" but in "dissimulation." This act of dissimulation occurs at an "entertainment"—the party at which she meets Morris—that is described here as "the beginning of something important for Catherine" (22).

Catherine develops by learning how to hide things. She first protects her interest in Morris by concealing his name. "And, with all his irony, her father believed her" (24). This dissimulation is followed by other acts of concealment. The ultimate opacity comes with her father's request at the end, when she is simply able to say, in response to her father's demand that she promise never to marry Morris, "I can't explain. . . . And I can't prom-ise" (176). Her father remarks on her "obstinacy," but she is now able to take satisfaction in the fact: "She knew herself that she was obstinate, and it gave her a certain joy. She was now a middle-aged woman" (176).

This sadomasochistic treatment of knowledge and opacity, irony and resistance, gets translated from the characters to the readers and spectators. Critics have differed precisely on the degree to which they find their plea-sure identified with that of Doctor Sloper. Richard Poirier's reading of the novel in *The Comic Sense of Henry James* goes a good distance with Doctor Sloper, sharing his perspective up to the scene in the Alps when Sloper's sadism becomes even too overt for him to tolerate. Thus in Poirier's view: "The scene marks the point in the novel where Sloper's way of expressing himself about Catherine begins to diverge most radically from James's. By tracing the progress of that divergence we see how James's identification with Sloper's ironic manner in the first half of the novel gives way to a criticism of it" (Poirier 172). Other critics, like James Gargano, part company with Sloper at an earlier point: "[Poirier] ignores Catherine's very early stirrings of life and fails to respond to James's almost clinical precision in recording the order of her awakening sensibility" (129). The reader must find the location of his or her own entertainment, a task connected with working out the relation between Doctor Sloper's irony and Catherine's privacy.

The filmmakers too must locate their own entertainment in relation to the perspectives of these two characters. Yet the externality of the film medium alters the balance. The doctor's irony might be just as representable, but how visible will Catherine's growth be, charted only by a narrator who notes its invisibility? In the alterations these two films make, we can follow how the filmmakers shape the spectators' sympathy around changing dynamics of power and knowledge, enacting in some way a response to the sadomasochistic dimensions of pleasure that appear in the novel.

### The Heiress: Revenge as Communication

What does The Heiress do with these issues? Both play and movie, tell a tale of revenge. Catherine learns how she is viewed by her father and her suitor, and when they are in situations of need, she subjects them to exactly the treatment to which they have subjected her. The title suggests the source of the revenge: she is the inheritor not only of a fine house and magnificent fortune, but also of the cold intelligence and emotional manipulativeness possessed respectively by the two men she loved. When her cruelty is questioned by her companion Aunt Penniman, Catherine acknowledges that inheritance: "I was taught by masters." In the novel, of course, she does not inherit her father's fortune any more than she inherits the emotional attributes that make for revenge. But that change only works to emphasize the exact needs that the revenge plot serves. The tight symmetries of the revenge plot, so well suited to the dramatic form, convert the novel's narrative irony into dramatic irony and provide a tight closure to the action. When Catherine snips the thread of her embroidery, slides the bolt on her door, and ascends the stair, she gets the last word.

In emphasizing that Catherine gets the last word, I want to draw attention to the *communicative* dimension of revenge. In the novel, Catherine comes to understand her father, her suitor, and her aunt, but none of them knows what she knows. In Wyler's film Catherine not only learns of her father's scorn, her lover's dishonesty, and her aunt's collusion, but also communicates her knowledge. By the conclusion of the film, Doctor Sloper and Morris Townsend in particular are forced both to recognize all that Catherine has learned and to feel the full force of what she has suffered.

She gets to design the lesson for their exact instruction, symmetrical to their treatment of her but condensed and metaphoric.

However, as Catherine acquires the power of her former oppressors, the director's shaping of the spectator's sympathy changes, so that it takes a direction very different from that experienced by the reader of the novel. The film invites a new kind of sympathy for the displaced father and rejected suitor, even as it acknowledges a kind of cold respect and even horror for the triumphant Catherine. As Catherine acquires the powers of her father and her suitor, she gains admiration but loses spectatorial sympathy. The sadomasochistic elements of pleasure that work in the novel also appear in the film but associated with different characters. With the inversions of the revenge plot, Catherine becomes linked to the sadistic entertainment values produced by Doctor Sloper in the novel, while Doctor Sloper and Morris Townsend acquire the sympathy invited only through the masochistic sufferings of Catherine in the novel.

William Wyler's compositional technique is ideal for registering these shifts in power and spectatorial sympathy. His highly staged symmetrical compositions and his deliberate use of camera angles and of the deep-focus lens (which keeps both foreground and background in focus) serve to register the dynamics of power and shape spectatorial sympathy among the characters. All of these cinematic resources come into play in the opening scenes of the film, which work to establish the hierarchy between Catherine and her father, even as they create certain thematic associations that might make for its reversal. In particular the relationship between Catherine and her father is partially thematized as an opposition between natural spontaneity and formal conventions, with Catherine linked to the former and her father to the latter. The film opens with a shot of Catherine's embroidery fading into an exterior shot of the park and the trees of Washington Square, thus associating Catherine with the natural world. By contrast, Doctor Sloper first appears as a name on a nameplate, shot from a low angle with the residence at 21 Washington Square looming above. Catherine's subordinate position is established by her association with a servant upon her first appearance. In the opening scene, a servant opens the door to receive Catherine's new dress. As the servant ascends the stair with her package, the descending Catherine is reflected in the landing mirror on the other half of the screen. The stair draws attention to relations of hierarchy, and the fact that Catherine and the servant meet at the landing places them literally on the same level, thereby marking the subordinate role of the daughter in the household. If Catherine is linked to a servant, her father first appears as master to a servant, dictating instructions to another woman employee of the household. Shortly after, Catherine is seen performing a servant-like role in purchasing a fish from a fishmonger to provide something to please her father's appetite. Her father's response is to criticize her for performing such an undignified task; he instructs her, next time, to "let the man carry it in for you."

But that same set of interests in the domestic realm of costume and table, linked to servitude when seen through the eyes of Catherine's father, acquire different meanings in a private bedroom conversation between Catherine and her Aunt Penniman. In this intimate space, natural spontaneity takes over. Mrs. Penniman celebrates the pleasures of "huswifery"; Catherine, in a state of semi-undress, is witty and mischievous; a small spirit of carnival rules between these less powerful members of the household. But the mere mention of paternal expectations puts Catherine back in her place, subordinate and inadequate to the public role he requires her to perform. When she descends the stair in that dress provided by the servant, she is again subject to her father's domination, daughter-domestic costumed in a failed magnificence, denigrated by her father and condemned anew to servitude providing "punch cups" for her cousin's engagement party.

Much of the thematic opposition between formal convention and natural spontaneity, as well as between masters and servants, is conveyed through the film's settings, settings that make direct use of certain characteristic architectural features. If the stairway draws attention to issues of hierarchy and power, the doors and windows emphasize the antithesis between freedom and restriction. The opening door at the outset, for example, is contrasted with the bolted door at the conclusion of the film, an indication that all possibilities have been closed off forever. Like doors, windows also mark a potential freedom, an opening to the outside world. The doctor, on his first appearance, appears in what looks like a sunroom surrounded by windows; when he discovers his fatal illness he is in the same room but all the curtains have been drawn ("curtains" might almost operate as a kind of visual pun for his self-diagnosis). If windows signify an opening, they still mark a separation from an external world of greater freedom. For example, on the night of her intended elopement, Catherine looks out the open window and says with great poignancy that she "may never stand in the window again . . . may never see Washington Square again on a windy April night." Catherine's exclamation suggests how little the window has been a release for her, how much it has still meant looking at the world from the perspective of her father's house, the house of his will, the house of convention. The scene of her impending escape from her father's house contrasts with the scene of her falsified elopement at the end of the film, when the house is her own and she has no intention of leaving it. Here again, windows are as crucial as doors. The bolted door is of course the most dramatic symbol, conveying the finality of Catherine's intention. But no less significant is Catherine's gesture of closing the drapes at the end, thereby signaling that there are no more openings or possibilities in her life. Like the completed embroidery ("Be careful not to make it your life's work," her father had warned), the closed-up house is Catherine's life; both are contained and complete. When she ascends the stair at the film's end, she rises in serene triumph, an ascent that contrasts not only with her initial descent, but also with the long climb that follows the scene of her jilting by Morris. In each of these scenes, architectural features—especially doors, windows, and stairways—locate characters in a field of thematic significance. Wyler's use of architecture as metaphoric resembles James's own.

Another architectural feature that Wyler's film relies on heavily for its visual composition is the interior column. The columns work to divide the screen into segments, marking out the changing separations and alliances among the characters. Perhaps the most remarkable scene in which columns, along with doors, figure importantly takes place on the night of Catherine's intended elopement. After Morris fails to come for Catherine, she sits in profile next to an interior column, her bowed figure exactly parallel to that of her Aunt Lavinia (fig. 19). Although Catherine is dressed for her wedding night, she is clothed in black; Mrs. Penniman, dressed in her nightclothes, appears in white. The parallel postures emphasize the inversion: the would-be bride dressed in mourning, the widow dressed in bridal white. The two still figures possess a kind of statue-like rigidity: Mrs. Penniman is bowed by the weight of her knowledge; Catherine sits on the verge of discovering what her aunt knows full well. For a moment the figures are still, waiting, before the knowledge is transferred and the figures are propelled into motion. The composition of the frame, however, tells the truth that Catherine has yet to discover. Lavinia, for all her high spirits and comedy, knows about masculine power and money and ambition; she has learned to survive by compromise and collaboration. For she too is a dependent in the house of the powerful Austin Sloper; she differs from Catherine only in knowing and accepting the constricted space of feminine agency. She is the appropriate mentor for Catherine's lesson this terrible night. When Catherine breaks down with grief at the recognition of her lover's desertion, Mrs. Penniman closes the great parlor doors, shielding Catherine from discovery and providing a private space for her suffering. Catherine is also shielded from the spectator's view when the doors close, and the effect is to give her a saving privacy to absorb this terrible knowledge. When she emerges from these doors in the morning, she is a changed

Figure 19. On the night of her intended elopement, Catherine sits in profile next to an interior column, her bowed figure exactly parallel to that of her Aunt Lavinia.

person. She is now the Catherine who will enact vengeance in the final portion of the film.

In the scene that follows, Catherine's changed status is indicated by her striking climb up the long stairway. Now the camera is on the landing, and it focuses on Catherine as she emerges from the great doors of the parlor, moving up toward and then past the camera at the turn of the stair. Weighted down by the baggage of an elopement that will never occur, her face aged and graven with lines of knowledge, she approaches and then passes beyond us. Her climb conveys a rise in power; her face shows the cost of the terrible truths she now contains. And when her back turns and she continues her ascent, we feel how she moves beyond sympathy and identification. Now she is ready to become the merciless figure of unrelenting truth who will command 21 Washington Square for the duration of the film.

Catherine's ascent is exactly balanced by her father's decline. And as Doctor Sloper descends from the position of household tyrant, Wyler uses camera angles and the composition of frames to evoke spectators' sympathy.

Figure 20. The change in power relations in the final portion of the film involves altering the alignment between daughterly concern for the gravely ill Doctor Sloper; Catherine's posture and cold expression emphasize her refusal of sympathy.

In the scene following Catherine's climb, the doctor descends the same stair, moving toward the room in which he will perform his self-diagnosis and discover his fatal illness. We see Doctor Sloper's face in close-up as he listens to his lungs and hears his condition; the effect is to create a bond with this now frail but soldierly man. When he tells the truth of his condition to Maria and Catherine, only Maria sheds tears. Catherine's response is to deliver a message as fatal as any he takes in through his stethoscope. Learning that Catherine will not be leaving Washington Square, her father briefly lights up with the hope that she has dismissed her unworthy lover. Behind him at this moment is the light from an uncurtained window. Catherine's response destroys his illusion (fig. 20). She uses Morris's abandonment as a weapon to hurt her father in the same way that she has been hurt: "Morris deserted me. Now do you admire me, Father?"

If Catherine tries to put her father in her own place, the scene works just as much by putting Catherine in her father's place. In other words, the inversions of power and sympathy that follow from the revenge plot are complete. Because Catherine's newfound power manifests itself in her ability to speak, dialogue becomes particularly important. The wit and point that once characterized her father's utterances now become Catherine's. When he argues that he only tried to stop her engagement to protect her, she comes back at him with her full accusation; he has done so not out of love but out of contempt: "I lived with you for twenty years before I found out you didn't love me. I don't know that Morris would have hurt me or starved me for affection more than you did. Since you couldn't love me you should have let someone else try." Her father is stunned and can only respond: "You have found your tongue at last and it is only to say such terrible things to me." When he proposes to change his will to prevent her from pursuing Morris, she seizes pen and paper and assumes his name and person: "I, Austin Sloper . . . ," she reads and dictates, having taken on the patriarchal will, voice, and power. When he protests that he doesn't want to disinherit her, she assumes his knowledge as well. Forced to admit that he no longer knows what she will do, he receives from her the final blow: "You'll never know." These are the last words spoken in the scene. He departs without knowledge or will or voice, opening the great doors of the parlor but lacking the strength to close them. However, if he leaves in complete and fatal defeat, he also carries with him a level of the spectator's sympathy that will never return to Catherine.

Conveying this change in power relations in the final portion of the film involves not only changing the relative positions of Catherine and her father but also altering the alignment between Catherine and the servant Maria. For example, when Doctor Sloper descends the stairs, he passes these two female figures, but the parallel between daughter and servant is no longer sustained. Maria expresses sympathy for the suffering man; Catherine's turned back as she sits at her embroidery gives no indication of any feeling. Although the two figures are aligned in visual parallel in several frames, the parallels serve to underscore their differences, as Maria acts in daughterly ways exactly unlike Catherine. In the final scene that treats of Doctor Sloper, Maria comes to Catherine who is seated on a bench outside in the square. Delivering the doctor's request that Catherine come in and see her dying father, Maria is simply told, "It's too late." Catherine remains seated; Maria performs the filial/servant-like role of returning to the doctor's bedside alone.

In the scenes involving Morris's return, the parallels and distinctions between Catherine and Maria are again important. On the night of his arrival, Maria requests permission to take the night off and walk in the square. Maria's request was preceded by a compliment to Catherine's costume, an elegant white dress that formed part of her Paris trousseau. Repelling the compliment as manipulative, Catherine coldly responds that Maria doesn't need to praise her to gain a privilege: "You are as free as I am," she tells Maria. But this assurance does not work to align Catherine with a domestic servant any longer. If anything, the parallel indicates how far Catherine is from the servant-daughter she once was. Maria is like a trace of the young Catherine, particularly in her willingness to open the door to the returning Morris. Catherine's command to bolt the door might be one her father would issue, Maria is compelled to obey Catherine as she once would have obeyed Doctor Sloper, and the effect is to show how far Catherine has moved from the servant she once resembled.

The revenge plot is well suited to Wyler's compositional practices, since the symmetries and inversions of the plot match the symmetries and inversions of his visual compositions. These patterns predict the migration of sympathy James's critics describe in their readings of Washington Square, though The Heiress would scarcely elicit the range of critical response exhibited by Poirier and Gargano, for example. In the early scenes of the film, the viewer might experience the mingled sadomasochistic pleasures of the doctor's acerbic wit and Catherine's mildly comic mortification. But once the film reaches the nadir of Catherine's humiliation and turns toward revenge, the spectator's responses are more singular. Sympathy is reserved for those like Doctor Sloper who suffer, and it becomes harder to find "entertainment" in the pain that Catherine inflicts. Such clarity can be seen to correspond to social categories of the immediate postwar era: a woman might seek masculine authority, but the consequences of her doing so are more chilling than just. Doctor Sloper becomes like Lear, a man more sinned against than sinning, and that judgment is endorsed in an era that essentially seeks to restore the power of the patriarch, even while acknowledging his fallibility.

## Holland's Washington Square: Love's Alchemy

In Holland's version, Washington Square ceases to follow the elegant symmetries of plot and composition that govern The Heiress and focuses instead on Catherine's growth through love. Doctor Sloper and Morris Townsend are no longer balanced rivals competing for control over Catherine: Morris has become quite a genuine if limited suitor of Catherine, while Doctor Sloper seems less the dispassionate scientist than a fallible and jealous father. Not exactly Romeo and Juliet, but there is a "course of true love" running through this film, and the film attends to the ways in which emotions and material needs shape relationships. Recognizing the impact of material needs in relationships is not deemed a moral flaw. Mrs. Almond, for example, comments about her future son-in-law, "He's a stockbroker. He'll make a fine husband. . . . I ofttimes think it's easier to be basic." The diction ("basic"), more 1990s than 1870s or 1840s, is only part of the modernizing of James that this version performs; Marian says, "Okay, Alice," handing a piece of wedding cake to her sister in a distinctly late-twentieth-century way. In keeping with the contemporary ethos, Morris's recognition that Catherine's money makes a difference to him does not prove him a cad but a self-aware person cognizant of his own limitations.

The alterations that Holland makes in two scenes may be the best indication of this change. The first of these is Doctor Sloper's visit to Mrs. Montgomery's, undertaken as part of his "scientific research" about Morris's character. In the novel, the scene operates with a complex irony; while the doctor is able to "work" Mrs. Montgomery to uncover her brother's selfishness and then to oppose the engagement, the older man's manipulations simultaneously expose the defects of his own character. In Holland's film, only Doctor Sloper comes off badly; Mrs. Montgomery and her brother look like heroes. Mrs. Montgomery repels the doctor's attempt to buy her off and delivers a high-minded speech:

> Mrs. M: People talk greatly about it: a plain stupid girl with a large fortune marrying a handsome worldly man without a penny, don't they, Doctor? Imagine the indignity. Why people might even think that *you* had been taken for a fool. It's more than a man in your position should ever have to bear.
> Doctor S: You do me a grave injustice.
> Mrs. M: Do I? Time will tell the truth of it.

Mrs. Montgomery, who in this film markedly resembles her handsome and distinctive brother, puts her finger on the motive behind Doctor Sloper's opposition to the match. His own dignity is at stake: *he* will have been tricked, even figuratively cuckolded, by a man he disdains. Mrs. Montgomery holds her own daughter in her arms as she delivers this judgment, implying that her parenthood is of a higher order than his, conducted perhaps on a modest budget but with a wealth of emotional wisdom and generosity that the doctor, for all his claims to parental feeling, clearly lacks. Her conviction in the accuracy of her perception—"Time will tell the truth of it"—grants her the full moral authority in this scene.

The scene that immediately follows develops our sense of Morris's and Dr. Sloper's' relative stature. Morris asks for Catherine's hand in the doctor's clinic. (In the novel, Catherine speaks to her father first, a deviation from custom that Doctor Sloper reads as a sign of Morris's cowardice.) The scene begins with a body on a stretcher being wheeled out after some procedure—dead or alive the spectator cannot tell. Morris finds the doctor behind a screen cleaning up after this procedure. All we seen of the doctor is his shadow as we hear his voice. This dialogue is new:

> Morris: Dr. Sloper, I don't pretend to know what alchemy is at work here. But the fact is, that I've never been happier than these last ten weeks.
> Doctor S: To introduce magic to a man of science in the course of a dialogue signals that common ground has long departed.
> Morris: Well then let me speak a language you'll understand. I've lived long enough to learn certain truths about myself. One is that my vanity requires an audience. Now this is not the most attractive of traits, and women are quick to acknowledge this. Not so, Catherine. I tire of myself before she tires of me, which is saying a great deal. What you see, and my stories, are all I bring to this union. And she makes me feel like the most important being ever to roam the planet. Do you know what it's like to be the most important person in the world to someone? Perhaps you do. Perhaps that is—Perhaps that is what brings us to this place.

This scene establishes an opposition between two value systems: one, the doctor's professional code, and the other, the quest for happiness embarked on by Morris. From the beginning, the opposition between the two is signaled by the mutual exclusivity of their pursuits. Morris does not know what it is like to practice a profession; Doctor Sloper does not know what it is like to "scale an Alp or ride in a gondola." This opposition develops into that between "science" and "alchemy," the second of these the term Morris uses to describe the emotional transformation that has presumably turned the straw of his life into gold. The balance between these two opposed views is reinforced visually with a shot of the two men in profile facing one another, at the same height, with the same degree of force and conviction (fig. 21). Sloper dominates only because the exchange takes place on his turf; Morris's position is actually made more persuasive than that of his opponent.

Let us consider Morris's case. First, his devotion to Catherine is convincing in the contemporary language of psychology. His self-knowledge is the hallmark of his declaration. He knows himself to be a narcissist, and he recognizes that Catherine offers the perfect mirror to his performances. This realism about psychological needs, including unattractive ones, extends to material needs. He recognizes that Catherine's extraordinary good-

Figure 21. The balanced rivalry between Morris and Doctor Sloper is reinforced visually with a shot of the two men in profile facing one another, at the same height, with the same degree of force and conviction.

ness is a product of privilege: "Catherine is so good and honest and true. She—she lives in a place where everything is shining and clean and where everyone has the best of intentions. I never imagined such a world. And now I want to live there with her." The connection between material privilege and moral virtue is only suggested here in the notion of "a place where everything is shining and clean and everyone has the best of intentions." Morris "never imagined such a world" because he lives in a very different place. The contrast between the poor garret in which Catherine later finds him and the gracious and well-appointed parlors of 21 Washington Square work to create sympathy for Morris in his desire to live in a world of material and presumably moral ease.

Such an exploration of the relations between material and moral conditions is not alien to the James novel, which begins, after all, with an analysis of the profession of doctor and establishes at great length the social codes of New York. But in recognizing the force of economic and social forces, James does not excuse Morris for seeking Catherine's money. He is

characterized as a fortune hunter in a way that precludes a genuine love for
Catherine. Holland's film makes an entirely different argument, and the
contemporaneity of this analysis of "love"—that unattractive psychological
traits like vanity and uncompromising material needs play a role in the
otherwise mystified "alchemy" of love—is signaled in the diction that Morris uses to describe the effects of Catherine's devotion: "She makes me feel
like the most important being ever to roam the planet." Henry James's characters do not "roam the planet" any more than they say "okay," but the
diction accords with this contemporary analysis that love is an effect of
psychological and material needs.

Further, Morris refers to himself in a manner that suggests yet another
dimension of this contemporary conception of love: "What you see, and my
stories, are all I bring to this union." His reference to his physical beauty as
part of his value will become more explicit in a later scene with Catherine
in which he refers to his good looks as equivalent to her money, attributes
without which neither is lovable. When Morris treats his physical appearance and charm as equivalent to her money, he shows how commodified is
his view of their relationship. But this commodification is not rejected or
criticized; instead, it is presented as a honest appraisal of how attraction
works in the real world. Material circumstances and physical beauty are
part of the "alchemy" of love—no alchemy after all once one considers the
elements. Further, there is an interesting gender reversal in this
commodification, for the common pattern is that female beauty is valued by
men using their purchasing power in the marriage market. Morris is feminized by his beauty and abnegation of professional authority, a gender bend-
ing that actually works to create further sympathy for him.

Morris also realizes another reason for rivalry between the two men:
"Do you know what it's like to be the most important person in the world to
someone? Perhaps you do. Perhaps that is—Perhaps that is what bring us to
this place." Morris recognizes that the way in which Catherine gratifies his
ego must be similar to what she has done for her father; indeed, he may
guess that her upbringing has trained her to serve a narcissistic ego. But
that very recognition must mean that he glimpses what he is taking away
from Doctor Sloper: he will no longer "be the most important person in the
world" to Catherine because Morris has usurped that position.

Doctor Sloper's treatment of Morris as a rival for Catherine's affections
is underlined in this film, an additional element that works to demonize
him and elevate Morris. One particular scene makes this point most clearly.
Doctor Sloper is returning home through the square from work. In earlier
scenes we have witnessed Catherine's extraordinary and effusive welcomes
for her father, clumsy services rebuffed and gruffly endured. Now his eyes

catch the sight of a glowing and expectant Catherine standing by a tree under a scarlet parasol. Even as she seems to be waiting for her father, the figure of Morris Townsend appears at her side. He bends to kiss Catherine, and the two young lovers walk off together out of the screen, unaware of having been observed by the vigilant father. The scene emphasizes the way in which Morris has displaced Austin Sloper in Catherine's life—just as the scene discussed above emphasized Morris's recognition of how Catherine's father has experienced (and undoubtedly trained) the narcissistic gratification in which her suitor now revels.

While the doctor is not the master of scientific truth in this film, but a vain and jealous rival, even these failings are seen more in the light of the psychological than the moral. The primacy of the family romance is signaled in the opening scene, which concludes with the doctor getting into bed with his dead wife, her body bloodied from childbirth, after having failed to respond to the nurse's presentation of his new daughter. That this body will later echo visually with the body wheeled out of the clinic when Morris makes his proposal suggests a connection between his wife's mortality and the practice of his profession. It also suggests that the doctor may be killing his daughter's prospective marriage in some kind of retaliation for the way she, in being born, killed his. Such is what he literally says in the scene in the Alps, with a brutality more extreme than anything in the novel: "How obscene that your mother gave her life that you might walk the earth." The link between the doctor's profession and the death of his wife is emphasized in the film, and the effect is to suggest how much even his so-called science is distorted by the emotional violence of the family romance.

What this condemnation of Doctor Sloper and redemption of Morris Townsend permit is a genuine love between Catherine and her suitor. The film uses music as the metaphor for their shared emotions, and the duet Catherine and Morris perform at the piano is very different from Morris's self-serving solo performances in both the novel and the Wyler film. Music fills the house after Morris's arrival; the ways in which characters respond to that music are the ways they respond to this young love (fig. 22). The servants—no longer linked to Catherine in any way as a metaphor for her subservience—hear the music of love downstairs in the kitchen and smile. Lavinia joins in the refrain when Morris and Catherine perform their duet; only the doctor sits unpersuaded. This duet contrasts with a failed childhood performance in which Catherine opens her mouth to sing and, instead of a voice, what comes from her is an embarrassing trickle of urine. Catherine finds a voice with Morris.

Further evidence of their love is the scene in which Morris declares his infatuation. He speaks of his obsession, and they slide down to the

Figure 22. Music is a metaphor for emotion, and the piano duet that Catherine and Morris perform together signifies the genuine and mutual love that exists between them. Aunt Lavinia in the background is the charmed audience and arranger for their romantic harmonies.

floor. His last words, "I find myself overcome," are like a signal for her strength, and she now rises in her embrace as the camera pulls back, showing a Catherine confident in her passion and sustaining the "overcome" figure of Morris. When Catherine returns from Europe, the bared shoulders and decolletage of her new European elegance arouse the passion of her deferred lover, and again Catherine meets his desire with an equal passion. Their love is more rather than less "true" or authentic because the film acknowledges how money and beauty and social status all play a role in romantic desire.

The representation of love as music which gives Catherine a voice connects with a major motif in the novel: Catherine's undemonstrative or quiet nature. Of course, nature might not be the best term for this quality, since she seems more a silenced than a silent figure, muted in all her demonstrations by her father's admonitions and the cultural codes for proper female behavior. The film signals Catherine's preoccupation with failed expression by giving her physical mannerisms that draw attention to her mouth. Rather than being undemonstrative, she is twitchy, gulping with explosive, nervous laughter, covering her face and mouth with her hand or her fan, blinking her eyes closed, ducking her shoulders as if to escape notice. These tics convey her enormous unease about her visible, audible appearance in the world.

Another striking filmic alteration is in the final scene, the scene of Morris's return, a change even more notable after viewing the ending of *The Heiress*. Catherine sits at the piano with a parlor full of children, and all are singing. The lyrics of the song tell Catherine's story—in the concluding line: "A plain little piece of string / Makes the prettiest music of all." Catherine, the plain little piece of string, has learned to make music. The music comes not from Morris but from Catherine, who is a child among children, making up for the childhood she was denied by her father, finding the voice that she had felt come only from Morris. When Morris comes, the dialogue is almost identical to that in the novel. But when he leaves, she does not pick up her embroidery "for life, as it were," but instead finds her eyes met in the eyes of a young girl. Catherine is mirrored in the child, whose gap-toothed grin suggests a source of joy that Catherine retains. The music is the operatic aria of her duet with Morris and her European journey, but now it is hers, the song of her spirit.

In some ways the two films part company so absolutely that it is hard to bring them back to a single point of comparison. But returning to our initial focus on the "uncinematic" Catherine, the Catherine so contained in her knowledge, so undemonstrative as she lives through emotional cataclysms, we can arrive at a certain common observation. By making Catherine demonstrative, either in revenge or in love, the two films offer a kind of implicit tribute to the power of James's silent figure. It has always seemed ironic to me that *Washington Square* is celebrated as a comic novel, since Catherine endures a kind of pain that has few affinities with comedy. Dianne Sadoff, in a persuasive essay about the three recent James adaptations, does suggest, however, that such pain may be connected to the source of the novels' appeal to Hollywood; as she puts it, "Full of eroticised perversity, innocent female victimage, and familial or marital distress, the stories seem culturally and historically transportable and relevant to postmodern audiences" (288). James's *Washington Square* actually features a level of sadism toward women that exceeds even the taste for such in Hollywood. The films could each be said to offer palliatives—the anger of a woman scorned, the joys of romantic love—to counter the less dramatically satisfying but in some sense more potent figure of a woman who simply endures.

## Works Cited

Bell, Ian F. A. "Washington Square": Styles of Money. New York: Twayne, 1993.

Bentley, Nancy. "'Conscious Observation of a Lovely Woman': Jane Campion's *Portrait* in Film." *Henry James Review* 18.2 (1997): 174–79.

Gargano, James. *Critical Essays on Henry James: The Early Novels.* Boston: Hall, 1987.

James, Henry. *Novels, 1881–1886: "Washington Square," "The Portrait of a Lady," "The Bostonians."* New York: Library of America, 1985.

Poirier, Richard. *The Comic Sense of Henry James: A Study of the Early Novels.* New York: Oxford UP, 1967.

Sadoff, Dianne F. "'Intimate Disarray': The Henry James Movies." *Henry James Review* 19.3 (1998): 286–95.

## Filmography

*The Heiress.* Dir. William Wyler. Writ. Ruth Goetz and Augustus Goetz. Perf. Olivia de Havilland, Ralph Richardson, Montgomery Clift, Miriam Hopkins. Paramount, 1949

*Washington Square.* Dir. Agnieszka Holland. Writ. Carol Doyle. Perf. Jennifer Jason Leigh, Ben Chaplin, Albert Finney, Maggie Smith. Hollywood Pictures/Caravan Pictures, 1997.

# "Her Ancient Faculty of Silence"

Catherine Sloper's Ways of Being in James's *Washington Square* and Two Film Adaptations

*Karen Michele Chandler*

Agnieszka Holland and Carol Doyle's cinematic adaptation of *Washington Square* (1997), like Jane Campion's *The Portrait of a Lady* (1996), opened to mixed reviews and mediocre box office. Many reviewers bemoaned the movie's allegedly vulgarized treatment of Henry James's nuanced psychological narrative. Hostile reviewers objected, for instance, to the preadolescent protagonist Catherine Sloper's urinating before a group joined to hear her sing and to the adult Catherine's falling prone on a rain-drenched street as her lover forsakes her. Neither scene appears in James's novel. In addition, Catherine is portrayed by Jennifer Jason Leigh, an actress better known for playing brazen twentieth-century writers, drug addicts, and prostitutes. Such scenes and casting seemed to signal the filmmakers' unfortunate, unjustified departure from their staid nineteenth-century source. Many reviewers also compared the recent *Washington Square* unfavorably to a prior film adaptation, William Wyler's *The Heiress* (1949), which one critic asserted had captured "the book's soapy essence" without its "verbal heavy lifting" (Keough 1). Holland and Doyle's film, by contrast, seemed to simplify and modernize characters' difficulties, presumably to attract an audience interested in seeing broadly or anachronistically played scenes of female victimization and triumph.[1]

While it is certainly true that Holland's *Washington Square* differs from both *The Heiress* and James's novel, both film adaptations use key elements of the novel to re-envision his representation of the limits and possibilities of female power in nineteenth-century American society. Each film focuses on how a young woman can emerge from a self-protective silence to use her voice and control her fate. In effect, each of the texts foregrounds a female protagonist's struggle for a language through which she can understand herself, as well as identify and express her desires to others in her world. In translating James's novel to film, Holland, Doyle, and Wyler have retained many aspects of his plot, whose fairy tale elements easily intersect with popular Hollywood formulas for love stories (Poirier 58). The films, like the novel, treat a love affair between the rich, awkward Catherine and the charming, handsome, unemployed Morris Townsend. During the course of the affair, Catherine, a loving daughter, must endure her father's disapproval of her suitor, and she comes to understand how her father, aunt, and lover use her as an object in their own machinations. The films render James's psychological narrative into melodramas in which the triumphs of Catherine's reserve and resilience ultimately enable her to escape the social categories in which her oppressive father, her scheming aunt, and her mercenary lover would confine her.

Like other successful film adaptations of complicated novels, *The Heiress* and *Washington Square* do not faithfully reproduce their fictional source, but transform some of its thematic concerns for a different medium, film, and for different audiences, twentieth-century moviegoers rather than readers (though obviously these groups can overlap). For example, James's novel uses Catherine's love affair as a means of comparing the main characters' differing ways of understanding and valuing her identity and her experience. The novel gives almost equal weight to detailing Dr. Sloper's vision and Catherine's maturation. As in much of James's work, revealing how minds work is imperative, with his finely nuanced prose uncovering the weaknesses and strengths, absurdities and revelations possible in various characters' processes of thought. Although film can suggest cognitive tendencies (such as Aunt Lavinia's tendency to convert prosaic events of her life into romantic intrigues from popular fiction), it cannot portray consciousness as effectively as fiction. In addition, James's novels often reveal the power of language to describe psychological realities. Hollywood films, by contrast, more adeptly portray action (even passive action such as waiting) and change. Accordingly, Wyler and Holland both reshape James's detailed, often bleak appraisal of how family members observe and interpret Catherine's experience. The films shift focus to Catherine's transformation into a woman who acts and speaks to challenge her family members' and lover's narrow perceptions of her. Whereas the novel is as much Dr. Sloper's story as Catherine's, the films focus on her, delineating her oppression by others and privileging her desire and growing independence.

Despite the films' dramatic similarities, they diverge in their representations of Catherine's power and the means of achieving that power. *The Heiress* presents a woman's power as largely negative, showing that Catherine achieves social authority only by denying herself to the men who have tried to control her. The film is comparable to another Wyler adaptation, *The Little*

*Foxes* (1941), which also upholds women's ability to achieve power in a male-dominated world as an ability to act as men do, which, according to the films, means acting without respect for others' feelings or needs. These two Wyler films, made in the 1940s, an era in which many women were newly entering the labor market, offer stark appraisals of women's capacity to function in male-dominated societies. The films indicate that women can become integrated into patriarchal social systems by imitating aggressive, destructive men. In the process, however, such women lose touch with those who love them and slough off their own capacity to love. Holland's *Washington Square* provides a more optimistic interpretation of woman's power, befitting the romantic idealism of the director's other films (such as *Europa, Europa* and *Total Eclipse*) and reflecting New Age assumptions about healing, individual self-development, and nurturing community. Holland's film suggests that even a damaged self can emerge whole from oppressive, self-denying social conditions. It shows how a woman who has been slighted and silenced by aspects of patriarchy, such as male presumption and competition, can triumph over these negating powers to fashion a rich life of her own.

Although neither of the film adaptations foregrounds a woman's silence as consistently and completely as Campion's esteemed *The Piano* (1993), they both draw on James's book's silences and on conventions of melodramatic narrative to test the possible manner and extent of woman's agency. Of course, melodrama can be both a noisy theatrical genre and a wordy mode of expression found in fiction, journalism, and other media. Yet it also depends on silence as a register of oppression and as a state in which the disempowered operate as they confront and withstand their oppressors. Silence often figures importantly in melodrama when common speech proves inadequate to the meanings characters need to convey. As Peter Brooks has commented about the silences in eighteenth-century theatrical melodrama, "Implicit in this proposition of a dramaturgy of inarticulate cry and gesture is no doubt a deep suspicion of the existing sociolinguistic code" (66). Rather than equating silence with passivity, then, Wyler's and Holland's films make it a means of expression distinct from the linguistic conventions that have proved incompatible with Catherine's needs. The films' treatment of silence grows out of the book's ambiguous portrait of its protagonist, a portrait whose silences hint at a more complex individual than the narrator's reasoned, dismissive analysis reveals.

### *"Her Ancient Faculty of Silence": Catherine's Oppression and Power*

As Lauren Berlant has commented, James's *Washington Square* "painstakingly represents both the public and private conditions of cultural negation within which even the most privileged female subject knew herself and the world in pre-Civil War America" (440). The "cultural negation" to which Berlant refers is the widespread suppression or narrowing of women's abilities, a suppression that stunted their intellectual and physical powers and limited their participation in the public sphere. Nineteenth-century feminists such as Sarah Grimké, Margaret Fuller, Elizabeth Cady Stanton, and Charlotte Perkins Gilman targeted social customs that silenced and disempowered women; they attacked patterns of women's socialization that discouraged independent thought and eliminated the likelihood of their finding or creating alternatives to socially prescribed roles. In *Washington Square* cultural negation manifests itself most clearly as Catherine's silence and the responses it draws from others, namely, attempts to control her. In the novel and in the film adaptations, the household and the larger society to which Catherine Sloper belongs circumscribe her sense of self and possibility. These environments long render her unambitious, compliant with her father's will, and silent. In each text silence is, at some level, a condition of restriction and lack, a sign of Catherine's powerlessness. Morever, Catherine's silence is not only rooted in her particular personality and expressive of a social condition common to women but also central to the novel's structure, to its disclosures about character, motivation, and action. Because the films draw on many of the book's uses of silence, turning to it first makes sense.

The novel's portrayal of Catherine's silence and social awkwardness serves as a starting point for her personal and social evolution, an evolution that culminates in purposeful self-expression. The novel opens to Catherine's silence and invisibility in the midst of her father's and the narrator's calculation of her significance. Catherine is merely present as a topic of consideration for her father, other associates, and the novel's readers, not as a speaker and actor in her own right. The opening chapters inform us, for instance, that Catherine lacks the accomplishments of many women in her social position, that "she was not ugly; she had simply a plain, dull, gentle countenance" (*Washington Square* [WS] 34). Not surprisingly, given the expectation that upper-class young women use their beauty and vivacity to attract notice and ensure a good marriage, the quiet, shy Catherine "occupied a secondary place" in society. Indeed, "on most social occasions, as they are called, you would have found her lurking in the background" (34). Although "Catherine displayed a certain talent" on the piano (33), we see little evidence or discussion of this distinction, a possible means of creativity, self-development, and social connection. Instead, emphasis lies on her status as a social disappointment: her father "would have liked to be proud of his daughter; but there was nothing to be proud of in poor Catherine.

There was nothing, of course, to be ashamed of; but this was not enough for the Doctor" (35). In effect, the novel delays presenting a direct view of Catherine, underscoring her shyness in the realms of family and the larger society. Among the many narrative problems the first chapters set up, then, is the question of whether Catherine can find a way of representing herself and expressing her desires.

Related to this question is how we as readers are to credit Catherine's associates' assessments of her. For Dr. Sloper, Catherine's silence signifies a lack of substance, for he takes the ability to use words precisely and sparely as a sign of intellect and sophistication. (He also views his sister Lavinia's flamboyant use of language as sign of her intellectual deficiency.) For Dr. Sloper, Catherine is an empty vessel, a "simpleton" (68). Even after Catherine has stood up for herself with her father to try to secure her relationship with Morris, her father comments, "She hasn't much to say; but when had she anything to say?" (201). For her Aunt Lavinia, Catherine's silence about her feelings for Morris signals an absence of the passion necessary in romance, as well as a failure to trust her friends. In effect, the aunt suspects her of a lack of proper sentiment. Late in the novel, for instance, in objecting to her aunt's intrusions into her relationship with Morris, Catherine asks her, "Why do you push me so?" (119), to which Aunt Lavinia replies, "I am afraid it is necessary. . . . I am afraid you don't feel the importance of not disappointing that gallant young heart!" (119). Later, after Morris has distanced himself from Catherine, Aunt Lavinia tries to get information about the relationship from her, even though Catherine complains, "I don't want to converse" (190). In addition, Morris, who usually engages Catherine with charming talk and an assumption of intimacy, late in the novel cruelly tries to force upon her an identity that does not fit: "'But don't you think,' he went on, presently, 'that if you were to try to be very clever, and to set rightly about it [getting Sloper to approve of their match], you might in the end conjure it away? Don't you think,' he continued further, in a tone of sympathetic speculation, 'that a really clever woman, in your place, might bring him round at last?'" (135). For her loved ones, Catherine's silence would seem to evidence ignorance and thus to justify others' guidance and manipulation of her. As readers have pointed out, James's narrator at least initially endorses such an assessment, especially supporting Dr. Sloper's view of Catherine (Poirier 64–65). Although this view is later challenged by signs of Catherine's emotional depth and capacity for independent action (65), critics tend to emphasize her grave limitation (Griffin 133).

Much recent debate about James's *Washington Square* has centered on whether Catherine achieves agency given the deprivations of her family life, deprivations that have left her with a weak identity.[2] Catherine does manage to overcome her shyness to assert herself with her aunt, her father, and Morris. Yet the novel ends with her alone, silent, and arguably still misunderstood by her associates. Like Dr. Sloper, critics have seen Catherine's inability or unwillingness to use language as a sign of her failure to achieve independence. In comparing Catherine's dilemma to that of the hero of one of James's favorite fairy tales, for instance, Susan Griffin has asserted that "Catherine differs from Hop [O' My Thumb] in that, rather than mastering language, she is mastered by it" (132). Where Griffin does see Catherine expressing her independent spirit in very limited ways through her body (133), Elizabeth Allen sees Catherine as a complete failure at conveying meaning and presenting an identity within the public sphere. According to Allen, "the structures of signification are supplied by those around Catherine, but she does not fit them. She is condemned to a trivial and meaningless existence because she does not appear to suggest any signified at all. There are meanings in plenty but she obstinately, yet passively, refuses to signify any of them adequately. She is neither the romantic heroine nor the sensible, obedient, practical girl who will accept the suitable offer for her hand" (44). The novel offers much evidence to support these negative assessments. After Morris leaves Catherine and she understands he has betrayed her, she settles into a life of routine that looks to the past rather than the future: "her opinions, on all moral and social matters, were extremely conservative; and before she was forty she was regarded as an old-fashioned person, and an authority on customs that had passed away" (204). Catherine realizes that both her father and her lover have devalued her and thus failed her, and she feels that "there was something dead in her life" (203). As Berlant remarks, "she fills the void by making a vocation out of old maidhood, doing the good deeds unmarried women traditionally do, including being a confidante for younger women." Berlant adds, however, that "to speak of her 'private' life, the life lived within her domestic space, is to witness a studied and practiced set of negations: she refuses all marriage offers, choosing to move through the world instead with 'an even and noiseless step'" (456).

This sense of Catherine's lack partly results from James's refusal to analyze her processes of thought as objectively and appreciatively as he has Dr. Sloper's. Catherine is negated not only by American society and by her intimate associates but also by the narrator who presents and interprets her. The narrator both describes and reveals Dr. Sloper's many cognitive strengths, referring to him as "a clever man" (27) and "so intelligent" (72). Even after the doctor has obviously been untactful and abusive in his dealings with Catherine and Morris's sister, Mrs. Montgomery, the narrator avers, "he had never been wrong in his life" (207). The narrator does suggest Sloper's limitations: his self-assurance does not allow compromise; he obsesses about Morris's possible attraction to the Sloper money.[3] The result is a clear, well-rounded, sometimes critical, portrait of a man's reason and rigidity that outweighs the narrator's more obscure and dismissive presentation of Catherine's cognitive and sentimental features. In describing Catherine's healthy, glowing look after a night awake crying about her father's disapproval of Morris, for instance, the narrator explains, "She was really too modest for consistent pathos" (129). Although this statement can be taken in numerous ways, it, like many others the narrator makes, points to Catherine's deficiency: she is lacking the self-respect that might inspire more sustained sorrow. Other explanations might be more viable and less condescending, such as "Catherine's practicality or self-respect prevents her from wallowing in her sadness" or "Catherine's hopes for the future help her overcome her present unhappiness" or "she hides her feelings well." Instead, the narrator has Catherine appear shallow. The narrator does not carefully trace Catherine's development from a person who misses the meaning of much of her father's ironic speech to one who apprehends his disdain (46, 156). Neither does he trace her growth from one who expects little or nothing to one who can tell her father that he should not malign her lover (155) and reprimands Morris, "When persons are going to be married they oughtn't to think so much about business. You shouldn't think about cotton; you should think about me" (182). Indeed, the narrator's approach to Catherine inspires some resistant readers' efforts to look beyond or between the lines of his assessments for meanings that are more substantial and respectful than those he usually confers.[4] Berlant, for instance, writes of gaining a fuller sense of character by "modify[ing] what the narrator, the Doctor, and the other characters think about Catherine's ordinary and unexceptional behavior" (448). Apparently, filmmakers who have adapted the novel agree, building on the novel's images of Catherine's silence as a condition of strength, not just lack. They seek ways Catherine may resist the various forces of negation that impede her self-development and self-assertion.

## "You Have Found a Tongue at Last": Silence and Speech as Weapons in The Heiress

In the novel Catherine does overcome some of the confining aspects of James's narration. Her silence functions not simply as a result of others' abuse or neglect but also as a process of reflection, growth, and expression. According to Berlant, Catherine's silence in the novel not only marks her marginality but also her defiance of a social system that subordinates her. Silence

functions "as a strategic reaction to her experience of delegitimation" and as
"the only remaining 'positive' act available to Catherine, seeking clean revenge
on the world of rhetoric and a rest from interpretation altogether" (442). As
Berlant asserts, Catherine's silences challenge a familial order dominated by
Dr. Sloper's lucid, judgmental speech and by Aunt Lavinia's high-flown
fantasies about romantic adventure, which constitute rhetoric and interpretations incongruent with Catherine's needs and desires. The films of
*Washington Square* expand on the book's ambiguous treatment of silence,
more adamantly stressing the virtues of Catherine's silence, celebrating it as
a means of expressing personal power. Consequently, *The Heiress* and
Holland's *Washington Square* both explore the effects of "cultural negation"
on Catherine and portray silence as one of the principal tools she uses to
overcome them. In doing so, the films challenge James's more pessimistic
portrait of Catherine's experience, pointing to ways in which she might
triumph over those who would suppress her spirit and her voice.

　　Although *The Heiress* obviously empowers Catherine (Olivia de
Havilland) in ways James's novel does not, it comes out of a tradition of
woman's film that, according to Mary Ann Doane, "insistently and sometimes obsessively attempts to trace the contours of female subjectivity and
desire within the traditional forms and conventions of Hollywood narrative—forms which cannot sustain such an exploration" (13). Produced for
women moviegoers and starring such actresses as Bette Davis, Joan Crawford,
Joan Fontaine, Barbara Stanwyck, and de Havilland, woman's films thrived
in the 1940s and have influenced later films written and produced by
women. Although many of these films celebrate women's power and versa-
tility, they usually undercut this obvious message and ultimately end by
severely limiting women's options. They put women in line, in subordinate
social positions, to ensure the continuance of patriarchy (Penley 50). According to feminist theorists such as Doane and Constance Penley, the
woman's film presents women's experience through story structures that
have been designed to tell men's stories and privilege men's agency. As a
woman's film, *The Heiress* translates many of the narrative constraints surrounding the novel's Catherine to the screen, even as it presents a more
assertive character who openly defies her father and triumphs over him. In
many respects, Catherine becomes a female reflection of her father, with
her speech and her silence mirroring his. Although the film presents
Catherine as ultimately powerful, she suffers a fate similar to that of her
father, a kind of spiritual death that prevents her continued growth and
her embrace of life's riches.

　　Wyler's *The Heiress* opens with an adult Catherine who lacks confidence in social situations but who has a clear head and voice in speaking

privately with her aunt. Early in the film Catherine not only jokes easily with Aunt Lavinia (Miriam Hopkins) about the latter's tendency to live on romance but also shows skill as an actress who can conceal her real intent. For instance, Aunt Lavinia refers to her skill at cooking for her late husband. Catherine shows a serious face and accuses her aunt of having deceived her: "You led me to believe that you and the Reverend Penniman lived on love alone." Later, when Lavinia wonders aloud if her husband is looking down on her, Catherine coyly remarks, "That depends on where he is." Her sense of humor and penchant for performance signal her distance from the book's Catherine and indicate a critical detachment and willingness to interpret human behavior and social phenomena that parallels her father's. She even smiles at some of the ironic barbs her father launches at Aunt Lavinia's expense. While Catherine's own jokes are gentle, she has a critical mind that can be condemnatory, as when she complains of members of a charitable organization who do not share her interest in cooking and other kitchen duties. In scenes with her father she is shy, deferential, and accepting of his criticism, and in public scenes she clearly is insecure. Yet she has an integrity and sense of her own rectitude that prepare her for her battle of wills with her father.

The grounds for such a battle are not initially evident in the film, however, because Dr. Sloper (Ralph Richardson) seems to be a loving, concerned, if stiff, father, with Catherine an obedient daughter. Unlike the Sloper in the book, he urges Catherine to socialize with her peers and worries about her prospects for marriage. Yet in discussing her with his sister Elizabeth Almond, Sloper refers to her lack of "social adeptness" and calls her "an entirely mediocre and defenseless creature without a shred of poise." He makes her the target of his irony as well, offering extravagant praise of her party dress and capping his remarks with a comparison to her mother's that hurts Catherine deeply. Such spoken slights and the thoughts that inspire them have apparently contributed to Catherine's isolation and lack of confidence. She is not, as Dr. Sloper claims, "defenseless," for she protects herself from her peers' lack of appreciation through her shyness, quietness, and absence. Rather than risking rejection and discomfort from interacting with peers, she avoids their company and finds solace in her needlework.

Morris Townsend (Montgomery Clift) gains her confidence by emphasizing his commonality with Catherine. And Wyler's camera supports this equation by capturing the pair together repeatedly either in profile or frontal medium two-shots. At the party at which they meet, Morris reveals his own empty dance card after seeing Catherine's (fig. 23). When they dance clumsily, he admits he is as responsible as she and counts out their

Figure 23. Director Wyler emphasizes openness and easy friendliness.

steps to facilitate their movement. Catherine, who, according to Dr. Sloper, has failed at her dancing lessons, becomes less self-conscious and begins to enjoy the rhythm and camaraderie of the dance, rather than obsessing about her body's awkwardness. And later, Morris makes a confession about his shyness that parallels Catherine's to her aunt. Before the party Catherine tells Lavinia, "I have sat here in my room and made notes of the things I should say and how I should say them. But when I am in company it seems that no one could want to listen to me." After their first meeting, Morris admits that he has trouble finding the right words to use with Catherine, even though he can be quite eloquent alone in his room or in conversation with Aunt Lavinia, who adores him. Although Morris's evident devotion to Catherine may result in part from his interest in her fortune, Wyler's spatial arrangement of the couple's meetings helps define the relationship as a haven that contrasts with Catherine's hierarchical relationship with her father.

Wyler's deep-focus photography also stresses the distance between Catherine and her father and suggests their unequal balance of power, with the father usually having a clear visual, verbal, and social advantage. In an important scene that does not appear in the novel, Dr. Sloper tells Catherine that she holds only one attraction for a man, her money. The scene occurs after the pair returns from Europe and Catherine proves unwilling to forsake her plan to marry Morris. For most of the scene Sloper remains in the foreground, while Catherine either stands or sits in the background. The exaggerated distances of deep focus render him very large and Catherine small, even though the actors are not physically far apart (fig. 24). Dr. Sloper expounds on his opinions at length, where Catherine is succinct in presenting her point of view. Dr. Sloper ironically lists the attributes that might attract Morris—"your grace, your charm, your quick tongue and subtle wit"—attributes he does not see Catherine possessing. When she tries to affirm her value for Morris ("He finds me pleasing"), Sloper exclaims, "A hundred women are prettier; a thousand more clever. You have one virtue that outshines them all—your money. You have nothing else." Although Catherine replies, "What a terrible thing to say to me," Sloper's words have effectively silenced and stilled her. Yet this scene is a turning point for Catherine: in the future she will not be submissive to her father, and her silence will register her anger and coldness toward him rather than her fear.

As she says in a later scene with him, his efforts to control and protect her stem from his contempt, not his love, and she never forgives his betrayal. Catherine is reborn through learning her father's poor estimation of her and through enduring Morris's desertion, which comes after he discovers her alienation from Dr. Sloper. The film subsequently represents her rebirth into an angry, vengeful, stingy woman. The film registers the force of her anger and denials by upsetting the pattern of spatial organization Wyler has previously established. Scenes late in the movie overturn the power dynamics of Wyler's deep-focus shots and undercut the apparent balance of the earlier two-shots with Catherine and Morris. Whatever Catherine's position in the film frame, she retains power over the men, through her

Figure 24. This image registers the imbalance of power within Catherine and Dr. Sloper's relationship.

Figure 25. Wyler here shows a dominant Catherine and an almost pleading Morris.

ability to see their vulnerability and to deny their desire for her attention, love, and respect (fig. 25).

Indeed, by the end of the film Catherine is powerful enough to drive the men out of the film frame, through her silence and deception. Although Sloper's death is imminent and a deathbed scene might fit nicely in a family melodrama, Wyler's camera focuses instead on a still, silent Catherine sitting in the park across from her house waiting for her father to die. In refusing her presence, Catherine marginalizes and silences her father at a time when he seems to have grown, to have discovered a love and appreciation for her. Similarly, she victimizes Morris, banishing him from her presence, her house, and, to a great extent, the screen. In their final scene together, she replays the earlier scene in which he promises to elope with her, even though it has become clear to film viewers, if not to Catherine herself, that he has become set on deserting her. Desperate to believe in their reunion after years of poverty and loneliness, Morris accepts her performance as reality. He leaves the house with the plan to return with his belongings, but once he does, he is not admitted.

Catherine's vengeance may be crowd-pleasing as a rare woman's victory over an unreliable, selfish man, perhaps evoking the rush of a favored underdog team's triumph in a sports melodrama. Yet the victory comes at the price of Catherine's integrity. When her aunt, who sees through Catherine's ruse of promising and then denying herself to Morris, asks, "Can you be so cruel?" Catherine asserts, "Yes, I can be very cruel. I have been taught by masters." And indeed, she shows no sign of having learned a new language or having developed a new way of life. Although she has grown in confidence and beauty, she remains locked in a struggle with Morris and her dead father, perpetuating the contest long after the men are too weak to keep it up. One result of her obsession with the men's betrayal is Catherine's incapacity to give credence to any kind words others offer. She is always suspicious and ready to fight to protect herself. But just what she is protecting has become unclear. At the beginning of the film, she has been much more than the social blank her father saw, but by the end, her identity has shrunk to the repeated gesture of denying others access to her. In effect, she has come to enact a kind of negation that unconsciously internalizes others' past dismissal of her. In denying others, she denies herself new experiences. At the end of the film, she nobly ascends the stairs as Morris desperately knocks on the door to enter the house, but her ascent is ironic, for she has simply become what she has previously resisted—a dignified, unlovable rich woman safe from the world. Her final constructive act is finishing her last piece of needlework. The work's content, which features an alphabet, suggests that Catherine has stopped at the beginning of her education and has not even begun to put together her own words.

### "You Call on a Life": Silence, Song, and Self-Development in Holland's Feminist Refashioning of Catherine Sloper

The Heiress certainly privileges womanly desire in showing Catherine enacting her revenge. Yet Catherine ends the film having regressed from the promise she shows at the film's start. In their updating of Catherine's dilemma, Holland and Doyle have sought to privilege a woman's power to

more constructive ends. The sweeping romantic music of The Heiress constitutes a suggestion of what that film's Catherine might have become had she
asserted herself differently. The music of the recent Washington Square figures its Catherine's transcendence of the powers aimed to suppress her.

In translating James's narrative to the screen, Holland and Doyle have
recreated James's protagonist and the events that shape her life to underscore the virtues of silence and song. Their Catherine achieves fullness of
character and emerges from the margins of a world dominated by languages
that work to exclude and diminish her. Holland and Doyle's film restruc-
tures James's narrative, subordinating the tragedy of Dr. Sloper's failed modes
of seeing, which is central to the novel, and emphasizing Catherine's evolution as a woman. Through her romance and then through her changing
relations with Morris (Ben Chaplin), Sloper (Albert Finney), and Aunt
Lavinia (Maggie Smith), Catherine attains a form of self-reliance and self-
respect that films about women seldom portray. In effect, the film responds
not only to James's novel and The Heiress, but also to countless woman's
films that seek to portray women's desire and power but ultimately undercut them. Holland and Doyle create a feminist fantasy inspired by nineteenth-century romanticism and contemporary optimism about the possibility of perfecting the self. Their Catherine develops herself fully and
nurtures others rather than using her power to avenge past wrongs. The
film draws on the novel's suggestion of Catherine's self-reliance and its
signs of her inner life.

Holland's Washington Square differs dramatically from the other texts
in offering little or no credence to the doctor's views of Catherine. Instead
the film early hints at his inability to love and nurture his daughter because
she has not been able to take the place of his beloved wife, who has died in
childbirth. After establishing shots of the affluent Washington Square neighborhood and interior shots of one well-appointed home, a long scream
precipitates the camera's hasty ascent to an upstairs bedroom. A woman's
dead body lies on a bloodied bed. The young, stricken Dr. Sloper stands in
a corner looking toward the bed. Catherine, who has just been born, lies
swaddled in the arms of a servant, who tries to show her to the doctor. He
ignores the baby, moving to the bed, and sinks down on it to embrace the
corpse. The final shots of the scene are of the full-cheeked baby in a bassi-
net in an adjacent room. The scene sets up Catherine's isolation and suggests that she will have to draw on reserves of inner strength to survive
because her father will not give her the love she needs. This opening evokes
sympathy for Catherine, rather than presenting her through her father's
judgmental eyes. Where James's narrative gradually reveals a discordance
between the narrator's appraisal of Catherine and the doctor's, the film

begins with a suggestion that the doctor's view will always be impaired by the loss of his wife.

The Catherine who emerges early in the film, both as a preteen and a young woman, has clearly been influenced by her father's rejection, but she nevertheless has more expectations of herself and others than her counterparts in the other texts. Clearly insecure, she is searching for ways to express her love of life, her desire to please others, and her great stores of physical energy and power. Unlike the novel's protagonist, she is not a blank. She is experimenting with her identity, even faced with her father's obvious disgust. To convey Catherine's spirit and the constraining forces she faces in her home, the film presents a pair of scenes that define her as isolated, emotionally deep and wanting, and potentially artistic. The scenes feature the child and the adult Catherine sitting at her bedroom window waiting for the father's return, her only company a caged bird. These scenes allude to the book's characterization of Catherine as a promising musician, a characterization that the novel introduces early but promptly drops. The novel presents Catherine as a woman of moral goodness lacking any frills, such as artistic talent. Although it may be argued that James's narrator is simply presenting the way her family has failed to appreciate (to make something of) her talent, I see this de-emphasis as a reflection of the family's neglect. Either way, Catherine's individuality is barely admitted, and it is not encouraged. The movie makes much of this deprivation, equating Catherine, somewhat tritely, with her caged bird. Neither is free to develop her inner resources by exploring the world, but each can learn to sing within her particular cage.

Holland's film early emphasizes how Catherine's inability to manipulate language and other signs of gentility properly alienates her father and increases her isolation. After the first bedroom scene she noisily descends from her room to greet her father, for whom she has been waiting. He comments to his sister Lavinia, "I see your instruction of behavior befitting a young lady goes on, business as usual." To which the young Catherine replies, "Oh, please do not be angry at Aunt Lavinia, Father. She tried to stop me, but my heart beat in my breast with such a voluptuous swell." She proceeds to prepare her father's port, placing a berry in his glass. The doctor brands these efforts to please as "overdone." Catherine has clearly modeled herself after her aunt, whose taste for the extravagant is comically absurd. Yet the girl's most embarrassing moment comes at a more public occasion, a party for Sloper at which she is supposed to sing "The Tale of the String." As her audience gathers and her aunt plays an introduction on the piano, Catherine is paralyzed and speechless. Like the young protagonist in Maya Angelou's *I Know Why the Caged Bird Sings,* she urinates profusely and obviously, losing control of her body only to have it express her fear and self-denial. That she cannot sing the chosen song suggests that she does not accept herself, that she accepts, instead, her father's negative appraisals of her. "The Tale of the String" tracks the path "a plain, little piece of string" takes to become a maker of "the prettiest music of all" and creates a frame of reference through which the young Catherine might assert her acceptance of her social difference—her awkwardness, girth, and plainness. Yet Catherine is not ready to represent herself through song. On the contrary, her mode of expression, her urinating, makes her feel more different and more isolated from the genteel, self-restrained people who sit in the parlor.

Like her counterpart in the novel, the movie's Catherine seeks a language through which she might express herself honestly, and finds it in her relationship with the handsome, gentle Morris Townsend. Though she is initially speechless on meeting him, she quickly manifests the mode of expression she will use with him in all their encounters—speech that lacks artifice, that conveys what she feels or understands. This Catherine (Jennifer Jason Leigh) often speaks hesitantly, as if she has to work for her thoughts to settle and for the right words to come, but she is committed to representing herself without embellishment or distortion. Hence she distances herself from her aunt's artifice and differentiates herself from her father in her interest in expressing her feelings rather than the products of rational thought.

Like the female protagonist of Campion's *The Piano*, Catherine embraces romantic music as a means of expression. Early in her relationship with Morris, she discovers that he is an amateur musician, who also lacks the technique to express himself effectively through music. During this second meeting, on a street near Catherine's home, they nervously speak with each other as they twice set her sheet music flying into the air. The shy Catherine invites him to visit to use her piano, and the practice sessions, which are not shown, become a pretext for meeting regularly and developing their friendship. After the dinner at which Dr. Sloper interrogates Morris about his prospects for employment, Catherine and Morris sing and play the piece they have been practicing. The song, "Tu chiami una vita," is one of the film's anachronisms that has drawn criticism (Simon 2). The Puccini-like music seems at least fifty years ahead of the couple's time, and the lyrics are a setting of a famous poem by 1959 Nobel Laureate, Salvatore Quasimodo.[5] Yet the late romantic swell of the music suits Quasimodo's words, which assert the power of love to: "call on a life / that inside, deep, has names / of skies and gardens" (Quasimodo 38). More openly sensual than respectable poetry and music from Catherine's era, the song points to the gifts that only love uncovers. It asserts the need to look beyond Catherine's plain, clumsy surface to her inner riches, which are akin to the beauties of nature. In singing the song with Morris, Catherine is indicating that his love has given her new insights into herself and a means of expressing her gifts. Through love she has discovered both language and the inner gifts it can convey. When the song recurs after Catherine and Morris's final parting at the end of the film, it signifies her discovery that simply loving herself yields this awareness of depth and beauty.

The film indicates that alternative ways of knowing the self, such as the doctor's empirical studies as a physician and social observer and Lavinia's escapist, romantic scheming, yield far less knowledge of experience. During an interview between the doctor and Morris in which the latter asks to marry Catherine, the deficiency of Sloper's methods are clear. The interview occurs in an operating theater, from which a corpse is being removed as Morris enters. (Interestingly, the two patients we see of the celebrated Dr. Sloper are dead—his wife and the corpse in this scene.) In a shot late in the scene, Morris stands between a diagram showing part of a human skeleton and a jar containing a preserved organ. Among the meanings the shot conveys is the disjunction between the analysis in which Sloper specializes (e.g., cutting up bodies to heal or understand them) and the idealistic description Morris offers of Catherine and his relationship with her: "Catherine is so good and honest and true. She lives in a place where everything is shiny and clear and where everyone has the best of intentions. I never imagined such a world and now I want to live there with her." Where the doctor searches for flaws to root them out, Morris and Catherine are concerned with the wholeness of life. Sloper's approach obviously has its merits, but the scene suggests it may not be applicable to his daughter's situation. In turn, Morris's interview with Lavinia at a working-class restaurant deflates her fanciful view of love. As she encourages Morris to elope with Catherine first and have her father come around to accept the marriage later, a couple loudly have sex in the compartment behind Lavinia. This juxtaposition suggests Lavinia's narrow conception of romance, which omits any material concerns, from physical passion to economic sustenance.

Although Morris's motives seemed mixed, his support and appreciation of Catherine help her accept herself. And Catherine's newfound self-acceptance steels her against her father's abuse and her lover's betrayal. A number of scenes emphasize Catherine's commendable self-reliance and prepare for the film's ultimate, celebratory portrayal of her independence. After she discovers her father has rejected Morris's proposal, she apparently hears the latter's call and sees him from the window. The camera setup recalls the earlier window scenes with the caged bird, which reappears in this scene. It also recalls countless images from woman's films that figure women waiting passively by windows for the objects of their desire to reach them. The scene initially seems no more than this, but then Catherine moves from the window to a full-length mirror where she kisses and tries to embrace her image. Although the gesture suggests she may be playing the role of Morris kissing her, it also suggests her love of self. Her growing self-respect is also apparent in her scenes with Morris, in which she asserts her plans for their relationship and discourages Morris from looking beyond it for social security. Unlike her counterpart in Wyler's film, this Catherine's withdrawal from her father is not spiteful but a logical move away from unnecessary constraints on self-discovery and growth.

Catherine's independence is nowhere more apparent, than in the scene in which she leads children in song. After her father's death, Catherine has not isolated herself from the world and become an old maid. She has continued to grow and made efforts to ameliorate the world outside of her house on Washington Square. A long shot of the parlor shows more than a dozen children sitting on the floor playing with toys. Catherine sits at the piano in the background accompanying the children singing a rendition of "The Tale of the String," the song she could not perform for her father and his party guests. In this scene, even with a few mothers watching, the children sing with ease and delight, and Catherine plays the piano with no sign of nervousness. She has created an atmosphere that encourages play and self-expression and that permits largely democratic exchanges between persons of different ages and social classes. This utopian scene recalls the fictional schools Louisa May Alcott characters run and the social work done by Jane Addams and other independent women who became social reformers. Holland and Doyle have crafted a denouement that enacts Margaret Fuller's theory, which posits a woman's self-development as a prior condition of social progress. Fuller envisions a woman "not 'needing to care that she may please a husband' . . . Her thoughts may turn to the centre, and she may, by steadfast contemplation entering into the secret of truth and love, use it for the use of all men, instead of a chosen few, and interpret through it all the forms of life" (63). Holland and Doyle have remade James's Catherine to realize this feminist ideal through her embrace of play, song, and self-acceptance.

This recent revision of James lacks the formal innovations of alternative films that challenge Hollywood conventions of portraying women. It relies, for instance, on the shot-reverse-shot pattern that some theorists argue objectifies women and undercuts attempts to portray female subjectivity (Penley 53). Yet the film does manipulate the formulas of popular melodramatic narrative to present a powerful, self-possessed woman. That some viewers feel this effort to be forced signals a continuing need to explore the possibilities of narrative for tracing woman's experience. The recent *Washington Square* presents a woman who has detached herself from men's negating power to create a community that accepts social difference. If *The Heiress* and James's narrative offer less radical images of women's agency, they nevertheless cater to our culture's curiosity about the sources of women's power within lives of convention and constraint.

## Notes

1. For reviews that fault the recent film for coarseness or anachronisms, see Miller, Schickel, and Simon.
2. See, for instance, Griffin, Berlant, Veeder, and Allen.
3. See Poirier for a discussion of Sloper's sentimental limitation, a result of his overdeveloped reason. Also, note Sloper's crude apprehension of Catherine's condition after Morris deserts her: "She is perfectly comfortable and blooming; she eats and sleeps, takes her usual exercise, and overloads herself, as usual, with finery. She is always knitting some purse or embroidering some handkerchief, and it seems to me she turns these articles out about as fast as ever" (201).
4. I witnessed many examples of such resistant reading during a discussion of the novel in Professor Sarah Wider's senior seminar on James and Edith Wharton at Colgate University during the 1991–1992 academic year. A majority of the students who spoke about *Washington Square* distrusted the narrator's evaluations of Catherine. These students criticized him for being unable to present her adequately, because of a condescension that mirrored Dr. Sloper's.
5. The composer, Jan Kaczmarek, has commented that he "grew up in a school that believes music must convey strong emotions in a spiritual context. Music that doesn't communicate important emotions to me is worthless" (Kaczmarek website).

## Works Cited

Allen, Elizabeth. *A Woman's Place in the Novels of Henry James*. New York: St. Martin's, 1984.

Angelou, Maya. *I Know Why the Caged Bird Sings*. New York: Random, 1969.

Berlant, Lauren. "Fancy-Work and Fancy Foot-Work: Motives for Silence in *Washington Square*." *Criticism* 29 (1987): 439–58.

Brooks, Peter. *The Melodramatic Imagination: Balzac, Henry James, Melodrama, and the Mode of Excess*. New York: Columbia UP, 1976.

Doane, Mary Ann. *The Desire to Desire: The Woman's Film of the 1940s*. Bloomington: Indiana UP, 1987.

Fuller, Margaret. "Woman in the Nineteenth Century." *Woman in the Nineteenth Century and Other Writings*. Ed. Donna Dickenson. New York: Oxford UP, 1994. 3–149.

Griffin, Susan M. "The Jamesian Body: Two Oral Tales." *Victorians Institute Journal* 17 (1989): 125–39.

James, Henry. *Washington Square.* London: Penguin, 1984.

Jan Kaczmarek website. Online. Internet. 28 Sept. 1999. Available: www.geocities.com/~kaczmarek/Pages/biopage.html.

Keough, Peter. Rev. of *Washington Square,* by Dir. Agnieszka Holland. *Boston Phoenix* 13 Oct. 1997:3 pp. <http://www.imdb.com>. Accessed 8 Sept. 1999.

Miller, Laura. "'Washington' Monument." *Salon* 10 Oct. 1997: 4 pp. <http://www.imdb.com>. Accessed 8 Sept. 1999.

Penley, Constance. *The Future of an Illusion: Film, Feminism, and Psychoanalysis.* Minneapolis: U of Minnesota P, 1989.

Poirier, Richard. "*The American* and *Washington Square:* The Comic Sense." *Modern Critical Views: Henry James.* Ed. Harold Bloom. New York: Chelsea, 1987. 27–72.

Quasimodo, Salvatore. *Complete Poems.* Trans. Jack Bevan. New York: Schocken, 1984.

Schickel, Richard. "Misplaced Affections." *Time* 20 Oct. 1997: 2 pp. <http://www.imdb.com>. Accessed 8 Sept. 1999.

Simon, John. "Climbing, Social and Mountain." *National Review* 10 Nov. 1997: 3 pp. <http://www.nationalreview.com>. Accessed 27 Sept. 1999.

Veeder, William. *Henry James: The Lessons of the Master.* Chicago: U of Chicago P, 1975.

## Filmography

*The Heiress.* Dir. William Wyler. Writ. Ruth Goetz and Augustus Goetz. Perf. Olivia de Havilland, Ralph Richardson, Montgomery Clift, Miriam Hopkins. Paramount, 1948.

*Washington Square.* Dir. Agnieszka Holland. Writ. Carol Doyle. Perf. Jennifer Jason Leigh, Albert Finney, Ben Chaplin, Maggie Smith. Hollywood Pictures/Caravan Pictures, 1997.

Getting James in the Nineties

# Ambassadors from an Imaginary "Elsewhere"

## Cinematic Convention and the Jamesian Sensibility

*Alan Nadel*

Terry Southern's *The Magic Christian* contains an episode in which Guy Grand, the billionaire whose practical jokes comprise the bulk of the novel, purchases a movie theater in the 1940s so that he may show altered versions of first-run films:

> In one scene in *Mrs. Miniver,* Walter Pidgeon was sitting . . . in his firelit study and writing in his journal. He had just that afternoon made the acquaintance of Mrs. Miniver and was no doubt thinking of her as he paused reflectively and looked toward the open fire. In the original version of the film he took out a pen knife from the desk drawer and meditatively sharpened the pencil he had been writing with. During this scene the camera remained on his *face,* which was filled with quiet reflection and modest hopefulness. . . .
>
> The insert Grand made into this film . . . introduced just at the moment where Pidgeon opened the knife . . . a three-second close shot of the fire-glint blade [which] seemed to portend dire evil, and occurring as it did early in the story, simply "spoiled" the film. (48–49)

As un-Jamesian as such an episode may be, it evokes succinctly, I think, some of James's concerns. Like so many moments in James's novels, Guy Grand's intervention in the narrative of *Mrs. Miniver* illustrates how an inadvertent glimpse, creating the smallest degree of alteration, inflects everything. If James can be seen as conducting experiments testing the threshold of cognition, experiments from which his best characters must (like Guy Grand) gain nothing for themselves, cinema can be viewed as the ideal medium. The "moving picture" arose not out of a quest for a new narrative form but rather out of time/motion studies that sought to use a series of photographs to break motion into discrete units. Reversing this process yielded an experiment in perception: what degree of difference in the sequencing of the photos constituted the threshold of apparent animation? Under what conditions could the figure in the carpet appear to move or two discrete postures oxymoronically appear to disappear into one coherent gesture. The coherence of the social gesture or quotidian act, broken down to its minimum thresholds of significance and then reconstituted as the illusion of itself, as an imaginary plenitude, describes equally well, I think, the fundamental trick of cinema and the sensibility of James's fiction.

Cinema's illusion of coherence, moreover, contains the potential for brutal rupture. Because human perception usually blurs—that is, cannot shake off the ghost of its last impression—in less than one sixth of a second, the conventional film speed of 24 frames-per-second, in safely obscuring even the flicker of difference, also permits abrupt change of images, with a simple cut, in a twenty-fourth of a second. Complex syntactical codes, in turn, restore the cut's disruption to an imaginary coherence of time and space. The rich syntax of cinematic representation thus usually engages the viewer in a chain of modifying clauses that, like the late James prose, continuously recontextualize speech and motion within psychological frameworks that give the visual and aural action resonant significance.

In film and fiction, this syntactic relationship allows exactly what theater precludes: control of the gaze. To put it another way, theater is all presence; everything of it stands before the spectator. While the spectator may thus choose *where* to look, she has little choice about *how* to look, for neither the playwright, the director, nor the spectator can manipulate, as cinema does, the frame, distance, angle, and focus that construct theater's "window" on reality. Cinema acquires its variegated gaze by implying limitless absence, in that the cinematic world, unlike the stage set, is incomplete. The spectator sees fragments—potentially unlimited fragments, but fragments, nonetheless—of an always partial world. In this way, film suffers many of the same limitations and thus many of the same freedoms as does the novel, especially those freedoms and limitations cogent to James's form of realism, a point suggested in a famous passage from the preface to *The Portrait of a Lady*:

> The house of fiction has in short not one window, but a million—a number of possible windows not to be reckoned, rather; every one of which has been pierced, or is still pierceable, in its vast front, by the need of the individual vision and by the pres-

sure of the individual will. These apertures, of dissimilar shape and size, hang so, all together, over the human scene that we might have expected of them a greater sameness of report than we find. They are but windows at the best, mere holes in a dead wall, disconnected, perched aloft; they are not hinged doors opening straight on life. But they have this mark of their own that at each of them stands a figure with a pair of eyes, or at least with a fieldglass, which forms, again and again, for observation, a unique instrument. (*Art of the Novel* 46)

James's description here uncannily glosses the fundamentals of narrative cinema: the fragmentation and reassembly of unique perceptions, acquired through an optical mechanics and creating the illusion of multiple—potentially infinite—windows on an imaginary reality.

Consider, in this regard, the segment midway through the 1984 Merchant Ivory film, *The Bostonians,* in which Basil Ransom (Christopher Reeves), standing in the doorway at the rear of a room, hears Verena Tarrant (Madeleine Potter) speak at a private reception. While the continuity of Verena's voice and speech unifies the scene, the camera cuts among shots of Verena speaking, expressions on the faces in portions of the audience, and Basil looking on. Thus as the sound track organizes the sequence temporally, Basil's cognizance organizes it spatially and conceptually, so that the themes of Verena's speech are subordinated to Basil's gaze, and Verena's topic—the public politics of women's rights—becomes one aspect of the complex social politics implicating all the people in the crowded room, the politics surrounding the meaning, value, acquisition, and control of Verena. Because this series of cuts creates a metonymic rendering of the room, it reflects the way in which all the characters are, in two senses of the word, partial: aligned with specific points of view, they are partial to their own viewpoints; incompletely seen, they are partially clear to the viewer.

At the reception after Verena's talk, Basil tells Olive Chancellor (Vanessa Redgrave), his cousin and his chief rival for Verena's affection, that he intends to visit Verena. When Basil leaves, the scene concludes with a close-up of Olive's face in profile, her head tilted back, her eyes closed, and her chin pointed up. The lighting and makeup give her face a glossy shine that sets her blondness and whiteness in sharp contrast with the dark, roughly unfocused background. The contrast and stylized physical posture, especially the extended line of Olive's neck, suggest that Olive is a tortured pre-Raphaelite subject. From our point of view the shot, framed and lighted this way, indicates Olive's apprehension, suffering, and sacrifice. Perhaps Basil left with similar assumptions about Olive's state of mind, but only a gaze unique to the viewer confirms them, for in this segment, unlike the one in which Verena is speaking, neither Basil nor any other character in the story anchors the final view of Olive.

Although this technique—concluding a scene with a privileged close-up—is a common element of cinematic phrasing, it is nonetheless very Jamesian. Specific adaptations of James, therefore, regardless of their differences, share a generic affinity between James's techniques and those of mainstream narrative cinema, both techniques dependent on a specific psychology of perception that exploits the tension between infinite possibility and necessarily partial representation, a tension that understands realism as the construction of windows and narrative as the integration of the privileged gazes that those windows provide. The general point I am making is that cinema is Jamesian and James is cinematic. James's fiction and mainstream narrative film both exploit an imaginary "elsewhere," never fully revealed but rendered with implicitly infinite complexity.

Mainstream cinema—which refined most of its current narrative conventions during the time James was preparing the New York Edition and the bulk of its production and narrative conventions during the last decade of his life—has accompanied this multilayered complexity of perception with a commensurate simplification of motivation. These two contradictory characteristics inform, in different and significant ways, two of three recent adaptations of James's novels, *The Portrait of the Lady* (1996) and *The Wings of the Dove* (1997). Only the third, *Washington Square* (1997), comes close to reflecting the Jamesian potential of cinematic narrative.

## The Portrait of a Lady

Jane Campion's *The Portrait of a Lady* sets itself at odds, intentionally, I think, with some of the most Jamesian characteristics of cinematic representation. If earlier Merchant Ivory productions (*The Bostonians* and *The Europeans* [1979]) emphasized James's control of the gaze, Campion seems to find that aspect of his work intrusive *because* it typifies mainstream cinema. Ever since Laura Mulvey's provocative and influential essay on visual pleasure in narrative film, much attention has been given to film's role as a masculine discourse producing pleasure by representing women either as desired image or image of desire. In this light, Campion has worked to undermine cogent aspects of cinematic syntax while providing a palate of images that ground meaning in the textured (feminized) body of experience rather than the (masculine) symbolic order. Campion's style thus attempts to situate the power of cinematic representation not in the male gaze but in the traditional object of that gaze, the potentially threatening and subversive woman's body. In *The Piano* (1993), for example, when Stewart (Sam Neill) occupies the role of voyeur, becoming, as Mulvey sees it, surrogate for the audience, his observing the naked body of his mail-order wife, Ada (Holly Hunter), provides not contained pleasure but uncontainable humiliation. Although imprisoned linguistically, geographically, economically, at one point even physically, Ada uses her indomitable will, outside the regime of language, to subordinate male desires to the orchestrations of her body, playing those desires as though they were extensions of her keyboard and hence of her hands.

The rustic, rainy, nineteenth-century New Zealand, a verdant and mud-ridden sensual world, mixed with the film's imported Victorian clothing and sensibilities, creates an exotic unreality that allows the narrative to unfold in such a way that the fairy-tale of Ada's adventure to the nether world complements the very real disempowerment of women that circumscribe her bodily resistance. Because Campion's setting thus seems so graphically ill-suited for her heroine, *The Piano* takes place in a world that, for all its distance, seems intended to be uncomfortably like our own, in all the worst ways.

Campion's *Portrait,* too, ostensibly takes place in a temporally distant location, the nominal nineteenth century, and in both films, female desire exists in a play of silence and autoerotic fantasy, punished by symbolic (female) castration at the hands of aggressive boy-men. Campion thus very much shares James's interest in how one represents an imaginary elsewhere and his concern with people as representatives, as well as representations, of specific groups, places, and times. Numerous James characters delimited by their sense of place (social, economic, national, sexual, geographic) find themselves ambassadors engaged in negotiations, reconciling themselves to their place or speaking on its behalf, misunderstanding their place and/or trying or failing to escape it. The characters are Americans, for example, or ambassadors from America, or Europeans, or Bostonians, or as he says in *The Wings of the Dove* of Kate Croy's father, Lionel, "so particularly the English gentleman. . . . Seen at a foreign *table d'hote,* he suggested but one thing: 'In what perfection England produces them!'" (12–13). James's work is informed, I am suggesting, by that place whence the other emanates, representing his or her background in ways that are necessarily imprecise and partial, that are, in other words, cinematic. Any film set in the past, moreover, presents ambassadors from a temporal elsewhere in order to hone in some way our perception of loss and thus negotiate a more refined sense of our own place, although it is hard to say, in that regard, whether James would have appreciated the fact that he was to Jane Campion what Edith Wharton's *The Age of Innocence* was to the maker of *Raging Bull* (and the good ship *Titanic* to James Cameron).

Campion also foregrounds temporal and spatial dissonance in ways not typically Jamesian. In the middle of *Portrait,* for example, Isabel Archer takes a trip—through Egypt, the Mediterranean, some other unspecified places—that is supposed to mark the first full expression of her new freedom to realize the potential of her imagination. Just prior to this trip, however, Osmond, somewhat against her will, has kissed her and told her that he loves her. This act is part of a conspiracy against her, an attempt to seduce her into marriage despite the fact that she has other more ambitious plans and the ostensive (i.e., financial) means to accomplish them. Osmond thus corrupts Isabel's journey by tainting it with erotic desire so that Isabel finds herself looking back instead of ahead, displaced not as the foreigner of her own making but as the subject of Osmond's uninvited narrative.

Isabel's voyage is represented visually as an extreme fissure in the diegesis (the representation of the world constructed by the narrative), disrupting the coherent cinematic gaze that creates a film's visual self-containment. The film shifts from a color to a black and white format, one that alludes alternately, and sometimes simultaneously, to home movies and to early silent films. Both of these media, of course, are jarringly anachronistic. Silent commercial films are, for all intents and purposes, a twentieth-century phenomenon, and home movies would not become a common practice for more than half a century after Isabel's voyage in the 1870s. In some shots, nevertheless, Isabel mugs as though she were posing for a fellow tourist creating a memento of the trip. In parts of this segment, however, the camera records the scene with the same conventional invisibility that characterizes the rest of the film or for that matter, most classic Hollywood cinema. Those portions nonetheless contain the flickering, graininess, and unevenly paced movements that typify early silent films, or they bear kinship to the surreal films of the 1920s, taking as their implied referent the dreamlike aspects of Isabel's subjective perception. At one point, for instance, she looks at a plate and sees the beans (of Egypt) speak to her, echoing incessantly Osmond's "I love you."

Campion clearly wants to disrupt the complacency with which we assume a coherent site of identification, dislodging us from the tacit coherence produced by traditional Hollywood-style continuity editing. This is consistent with other strategies in the film. The film begins, for example, with another black and white scene in which we view a circle of young women from above, lying on the ground or posing for outdoor portrait shots. Although the sequence provides few temporal references, the hairstyles, makeup, and clothing indicate that the setting is roughly contemporary. The models in this opening segment, moreover, often stare directly into the camera, a pose typical of TV commercials and print ads but rare in

mainstream narrative cinema because direct eye contact disrupts the pre-
sumed invisibility of the camera by placing the spectator in a fixed position
vis-à-vis the spectacle. The voice-over too is very contemporary: A series of
women's voices talk in distinctly Australian accents about the erotics of
being kissed, the problems and joys of finding oneself in the gaze and
touch of an other. The opening segment thus resembles the black and white
segment in the middle of the film in that it disrupts not only the visual
construction of the cinematic space but also its temporal referents.

Foregrounding the film's anachronism at the midpoint is very apt in
that Osmond has indeed reoriented the narrative. Until this point, all of
the conditions and decisions have focused us on the unfolding future of a
remarkable woman with wind in her sails, on course, full speed ahead. But
now, while Isabel is supposed to be going forward, Osmond is pulling her
back. Osmond's interventions have put her hopelessly at sea, the shaky
seaboard shots serving as a metaphor for her halted progress. More significant, the anachronistic styles of the insert represent the disruption of Isabel's
progress as cinematic figure by changing the genre. As Isabel is about to
become the articulate star of her own life, Osmond is beckoning her to a
role in a home movie or a silent film. Campion's adaptation of James's
"portrait" thus substitutes film for painting, delimiting Isabel's metaphoric
portrait by the perspectives of the celluloid rather than the oil medium.

But a celluloid portrait emerges not from nuanced strokes carefully
overlaying opaque and blendable matter. Rather it functions through trans-
lucency and motion, depending upon the illusional substitution of one
frame for another. The progress of Isabel Archer in a cinematic "portrait" is
thus the progress of a woman whose protean transformations attempt to
make her central to a narrative and to a gaze. To this end, Campion has
given us the lush Victorian decor, the intense chiaroscuro lighting, and the
sweeping camera movements that capture the catholic texture of Isabel's
world, in contrast to which the black and white insert seems all the more
disconcerting, emphasizing dramatically the way in which Osmond's pronouncement of "love" has made it impossible for Isabel's cinematic portrait
to realize its informed plenitude.

But this cinematic portrait, we should remember, implies not only
visual but also narrative plenitude, and the generic disruption of the insert
thus makes clear how much Isabel's success or failure relies on cinematic
ideals. Because these ideals determine not only Isabel's half-formulated goals
for herself but also everyone else's best hopes for her, she has dual problems: she must structure the narrative of her life and also control the genre
in which that narrative operates.

These problems evoke comparisons with another nineties film, Francis

Ford Coppola's *Bram Stoker's Dracula* (1992), which is also self-consciously aware of the power of movies. Like Campion's *Portrait,* that film uses the Victorian setting to examine restrictions on female sexuality and is self-consciously aware of the way in which cinematic technology has replaced Victorian manners as the mechanism that delimits and informs desire. In *Dracula,* Mina and Lucy select among potential lovers in much the same way that Isabel does in Campion's *Portrait,* that is, as characters identified with movie genres. In both films, the Victorian world becomes the gothic elsewhere of female sexuality from which movies promise freedom. Dracula first meets Mina by asking her for directions to the "cinematograph," telling her that he hears it is the most wondrous invention of the modern world, and at the cinematograph he begins his seduction. Coppola's *Dracula* thus represents the love-hate relationship with a vampire as synonymous with the seductive potentials of the cinematic apparatus. To the extent that Count Dracula, as transcendent and transmorphic presence, represents the power of cinema itself, the other generic heroes of the film pale as boyish, immature, incapable of satisfying Mina's or Lucy's desires. Isabel has comparable desires, we see early in Campion's *Portrait,* when she has the vivid fantasy, lying on her bed, of being sexually groped simultaneously by Caspar Goodwood and Lord Warburton, while Ralph Touchett looks on. Like the would-be heroes of *Dracula,* these men are mere boys, but in Campion's *Portrait,* so is the bloodsucking Osmond. When we first see him, in fact, he is tossing something—a sugar cube perhaps (surely it can't be a jelly bean)— up in the air and catching it in his mouth while having tea with Madame Merle. Throughout, his behavior contrasts him with the young men not in terms of man to boys but in terms of bad boy to good boys.

If, by the standards of the Victorian world, these "boys" all behave improperly, their improprieties seem to fall under the rubric of (benign or malicious) adolescent behavior, for Campion seems intent on showing how hard it is for an attractive woman to find a good "man" (in the sense that that topic has been covered by *Cosmo,* not by James). With its violation of physical space and personal decorum, Campion's *Portrait* reminds us, therefore, that despite the sets and costumes this is not nineteenth-century England or nineteenth-century Italy but that contemporary place where people who are coming of age learn to reconcile their normative (i.e., cinematic) reality to life as they know it: a college dorm. Thus Isabel has no compunction about munching on a snack while leaning on the staircase banister of the Touchett mansion. Thus when men visit her bedroom she is more embarrassed about her carelessly strewn underwear than about manners and propriety. Thus Ralph Touchett, played by Martin Donovan with a surfeit of Brad Pittiful grunge, is perfectly comfortable smoking cigarettes nonstop while loafing around in Isabel's private quarters, or touching her face and pulling her head within inches of his when they speak. Thus the American accent that Nicole Kidman has learned for the role seems appropriately modeled not on that of Grace Kelly or Sigourney Weaver but on that of Melanie Griffith.

The characters in this film, therefore, do not visit or call so much as hang out, with the chief topic of conversation being who is cute and who isn't, who should or should not date whom, who said or did what to whom. Implicit in this undergraduate milieu is the idea that each of the participants wants to be a star in the motion picture of her or his life, or if not in a motion picture then at least in an episode (or two?) of the television show *Friends*. Part of the popular appeal of *Friends*, it seems to me, is that it not only valorizes dormitory-cafeteria life but also promises it need not end with graduation. Some place, perhaps in the big city, people can continue to discuss in small domestic-like groups their mundane couplings, or near couplings, or would-be couplings, or breakups, as though these events were the stuff of movies, as though they were people of enormous potential—Isabel Archers in the rough—on the verge of achieving not wind in their sails but their names in the credits.

If Coppola's *Dracula* glosses the understanding of success in Campion's *Portrait*, therefore, *Friends* glosses the cultural narrative that determined the adaptation choices. Excerpted as fragments for an ur-episode of *Friends*, James's novel seems most ludicrous when it is quoted verbatim, because the lines are being spoken by characters who find irrelevant everything James held important. Reduced to dorm talk, the only thing that Campion's *Portrait* leaves out is reminders about safe sex, something that Coppola's *Dracula* dwells upon. Dracula and Mina are players at risk, seduced beyond the safe limits of medical technology by a cinematic understanding of transcendent love. But the proximity of love to death that lingers in the air of dorm talk and at the fringes of late-adolescent cuddling in this age of disease is not completely escaped in Campion's *Portrait*. Like Mina with Dracula, Isabel too embraces death, confessing her love for the dying Ralph, climbing into bed with him, and kissing him passionately.

So Campion's *Portrait* is not so much an adaptation of James's novel as it is an appropriation of it. The garb, the setting, the script, the manners, even the Roman statue with its penis knocked off, that shares the frame with Madame Merle (Barbara Hershey) late in the film, are appropriated to tell a very non-Jamesian story. This material, like that Roman statue, appears denuded of its historical specificity and political potency. If that Roman statue resulted from art and politics in collision and/or collusion, here it suggests a very different story, some possible explanation—albeit not as complex as the one offered by Flannery O'Connor—of why a good man is hard to find.

## The Wings of the Dove

If the elsewhere under scrutiny in Campion's *Portrait* ultimately turns out to be the college dorm, in Iain Softley's *The Wings of the Dove*, it is the twenty-first century, that is, the perspective from which the contraptions of modern living and the pragmatic materialism that goes with them, in short, the values of the American century, will quaintly dissolve into a form of sentimentality, like the American heiress, Milly Theale (Allison Elliott). The decision, therefore, to remove the film from the cusp of the nineteenth century by setting it in 1910 makes the moment of the film's action a bookend to the moment of its production. Sandwiched between is all the technological, political, and moral "progress" that characterizes the century from which we now depart. If it could be called, in addition to the "American" century, the century of working-class vulgarity, mass culture, kitsch, it could also be called the "cinematic" century (to the extent that all those terms are not redundant).

The doomed love affair of Kate Croy (Helena Bonham Carter) and Merton Densher (Linus Roache)—manifest in such post-Jamesian courtship rituals as making out in elevators and fornicating in shadowy Venetian alleyways—requires, both as its necessary middle term and unremovable obstacle, a self-deluding enchantment with the representative of everything America has to offer. Exactly what America does have to offer remains unsaid, but it is certainly much more or much less than money, although without its wealth it might well have gone unnoticed. In any case, whatever "it" may be, it is already becoming a memory. If much of James's exploration of human psychology is about not getting it, to ask what "it" is would surely miss the point and, in any case, be unpardonably vulgar. Is Milly Theale's unfathomable disease the result of a minute vulnerability in the recesses of her DNA, or is it the condition of perception that allows one's own best qualities to be reflected in the fragile and ephemeral cognizance of the other? Is it something to be captured through a more perfect system of biomedical pathology, or is it the trace of uncapturable otherness and unattainable desire?

The film hints its answer to these questions by showing Lionel Croy in an opium den to signify his serpentine depravity, as if to update Marx by indicating that in the twentieth century the opiate of the people is opium. In other words, instead of exploiting the play of absence endemic to film narrative, this film opts to stabilize and literalize. Hence we see Sir Luke examining (or is he treating?) Milly with the aid of carbon arcs, circular tubes, green glows, and sound effects, so simultaneously antiquated and bizarre as to evoke, not without some nostalgia, connotations of a mad scientist—that gentleman whose primary residence is the "B" movie, even if he sometimes leases a London flat. The tragedy of Milly's circumstance, in this context, results from antiquated knowledge, in other words, from specific historical conditions under which an unwarranted and naive faith in wealth and science seemed appropriate, just as it did for the designers of the *Titanic.*

From our millennial perspective, we can say simply that they were all wet. In the film *The Wings of the Dove,* in fact, they were continuously pelted by rain, whether on assignations in the park, or in the streets of Venice, or traveling through London at night. Milly visits the museum, in fact, to get out of the rain rather than, as in the novel, because she is interested in art, which nowadays isn't really that cool. Thus the film represents the characters' problems, like the weather, as the product of their temporal rather than their ethical, psychological, or spiritual conditions. At this end of the century, we know that drugged-up fathers should get a dose of tough love; people should marry whomever they please; diseases should be treated by the Mayo Clinic, not by a mad scientist or a Venetian restaurant; and now that we have the "Make a Wish Foundation," a dying young person need not be rich to ride at least once in a gondola (albeit preferably at Disney World).

If I am accusing this film of making things too clear, I believe I am taking the same attitude toward the film that it takes toward its characters, in that a number of scenes seem intentionally overlit as if to suggest that the characters suffer a surfeit of clarity, a failure to recognize the shady aspects of their behavior. The orchestration of shots and camera angles also privileges the spectator's superior perspective. The self-conscious array of God's view shots (i.e., from directly overhead) and ground's view shots, for example, imply a contrast between particular and general perspectives on the story. The shot selection, in other words, helps foreground the (somewhat condescending) illusion of omniscience that mainstream cinema shares with James's fiction. James, however, understands that that illusion works to cloud truth, that truth, to the extent that it resides anywhere, resides like Milly's disease in the inaccessible absence that the cleverness of mainstream cinematic representation obscures.

Recognizing that James almost always uses the term "clever" as a pejorative, we can easily see how cleverly Softley reduces the problem of Milly Theale to simple melodrama: Kate, a desperate and somewhat weak woman, hatches a plot to acquire the wealth of a dying American heiress, Milly, by leading her boyfriend, Merton, into an affair with the heiress. Struck by the immanent success of her plot, Kate succumbs to unanticipated jealousy and intentionally sabotages the plot, destroying not only her relationship (marked by lesbian overtones) with Milly but also her relationship with Merton. Regretfully, hopelessly, Kate wants to undo the consequences, but Merton makes clear that they cannot. He is, after all, a crusading journalist, one who understands the plight of the oppressed and what it means to work for a living. He can comprehend, therefore, the moral consequences of Kate's naive scheme.

With this scenario, Softley removes James's murkiness, giving the plot the crispness of a 1930s melodrama or a 1950s soap opera. In this context, the film appropriately concludes with Merton paying final respects to Milly's memory, thus becoming the "new man," literally of the twentieth century and figuratively of the twenty-first, one who can extract in memoriam the best of the American experiment, no longer blinded by its economic power. Merton Densher, not Kate Croy, thus realizes that they shall never be again as they were. In diametrically reversing the final dynamic of the novel, the film invests a great deal of integrity in a person named "Merton Densher." Ought the weight of names have been so completely lost on Softley? Hardly. But clarifying the motivation (in keeping with traditional cinematic conventions) demands a narrative that leaves Densher to chew on the story's moral implications.

For Jamesians, ceding Densher alone this moral authority may seem hard to swallow, but from the perspective of mainstream cinema it is exceedingly apt. The film succeeds on its own terms by helping the spectator overcome the murky and partial elements that comprise its diegesis and thus by obscuring our knowledge of the inaccessible elsewhere from which cinematic experience emerges. To this end, Softley substitutes historical opacity for psychological or ethical ones so that he can then reduce causality to explicit acts, which the movie spectator can observe with security from a privileged position. Helena Bonham Carter's stunningly lit nudity in the final scene thus returns the triangulated relationship of the film's three principals to the reductive norm of mainstream cinema's fetishistic gaze, reasserting the masculine authority that Densher consolidates. Softley makes a concise and successful film out of James's novel by rotating the sexual triangle constructed by Kate, to restore the traditional hierarchy, so that Densher ends up on top. No matter how cinematic James's sensibility, this almost certainly is not how he would have converted The Wings of the Dove into A Turn of the Screw.

### Washington Square

Instead of exploiting the complex codes of cinematic representation to reveal the moral and psychological complexity of The Wings of the Dove, Softley used the formidable power of the cinematic apparatus to obscure that complexity, employing the techniques perfected in the first half of this century aimed at creating the illusion that a motion picture provides the spectator a single, coherent window on reality, a transparent and unified perspective. In adapting *Washington Square*, Agnieszka Holland does exactly the opposite, as is evident from the opening shot, which manifests vividly James's concern with individual perception and the multiple windows that they create.

The credits open against a solid black background and continue to appear as that background changes from black to light blue; as the camera pans further down we see that light blue is the sky. The camera moves slowly from the blue sky to what appears to be an orange-tinted shot of the low early nineteenth-century sky-line at the edge of Washington Square Park. As the camera—positioned just above the level of the roofs of the three-story, brick townhouses—starts to tilt downward, the colors become more vivid, and we see that the orange tint was caused by the angle of the afternoon sun on the camera lens. Without cutting, the camera rotates to provide an overview of the park; it is verdant and populated by ladies at leisure and well-dressed children at play. Gradually the camera descends as it moves slowly across the park, so that by the time it reaches the far end of the park it is five or six feet off the ground. It then crosses the street and moves along the row of houses opposite the park until it reaches the residence of Dr. Sloper, at this point, providing a view from about shoulder height. Without cutting, in other words, the viewer has shifted perspective from omniscient to pedestrian. The shot nevertheless has retained its objectivity and seems, despite the shift in angle, to represent the anonymous gaze that typifies most cinematic narrative.

At this point, however, the two-and-one-half-minute shot, which is barely half over, undergoes a remarkable change. The camera draws too close to the Sloper home for the shot to retain its objectivity, and then it tilts up toward the roof at a very sharp angle and back down to the first floor window, as though it were replicating the head motion of someone surveying the façade. Then the camera takes us through the parlor window, moving slowly toward the dining room, looking around at the décor as it goes. We can tell now that our view is being guided by a handheld camera, indicating that we have assumed the perspective of some subjective, although ostensibly invisible, presence. As our view enters the dining room, we see a cat sitting complacently on the table. And then, remarkably, *the cat sees us*. Within a single shot, in other words, Holland has changed our perspective from omniscient to subjective to visible. She has taken us from the film credits that exist outside the world of the story, to an omniscient perspective of that world, to an objective human-level perspective, to a subjective point of view, and, finally, to a visible presence in that world.

Then we hear a scream, and the camera moves rapidly, as if uncertain where to go. It turns and rushes to the staircase; as it races up the stairs, all we see is the baseboard molding where the wall meets the steps. At the top of the stairs, the camera moves left and right with great confusion until it identifies the correct door: the bedroom of Mrs. Sloper, distinguished by the foot of her bed where her feet lie stiffly on blood-drenched sheets. The servant racing by makes it clear that the camera has returned to a state of invisibility, if not objectivity, from which perspective it examines the corpse of Mrs. Sloper. Then we get the film's first cut—to a shot of Dr. Sloper (Albert Finney) standing in a corner, clearly in a state of numbing emotional anguish. Since nothing we have seen in the long opening shot tells us where this corner is in relation to the spectator whose perspective has brought us to the second floor of the Sloper home, or to any of the objects we have thus far seen, we can assume that the camera has reassumed its objective perspective. That assumption is qualified, however, when the maid shows Dr. Sloper his newborn daughter; after glancing at her, he proceeds to the bed of the dead Mrs. Sloper while the maid takes the infant into the next room. The camera, instead of following Sloper or the maid, retreats into the hallway, moving as a person would, and finds a doorway from which to watch the maid place the infant in her crib. Then we cut in objective fashion to Dr. Sloper climbing into bed beside his deceased wife. The segment ends with a cut to the camera moving in on a close-up of the baby in the crib, one that could be associated—especially given the camera motion—with the subjective gaze that watched the maid place her there or with the objective gaze that watched Dr. Sloper.

The oscillations between objective and subjective perspective in this remarkable opening sequence illustrate the perfect synergy possible between cinematic technique and James's understanding of fiction as the integration of privileged windows, a point underscored when the close-up of Catherine in her crib dissolves into a close-up of the preadolescent Catherine looking out of her window. This leads to a short segment in which Catherine tries desperately to please her father in several ways and fails in all. The segment concludes, as it began, with Catherine, now dressed for bed, looking despairingly out of her window. This dissolves into the grown up Catherine (Jennifer Jason Leigh), looking out the same window. But the transition takes place with an intermediary step, a dissolve between the dissolves in which we see the young Catherine, dressed in the same night clothes, with her posture and gaze slightly altered. This intermediary shot dissolves in less than a second, and so, although the sequence of shots informs us that we are seeing the same Catherine through this window, the keen observer can also see, nonetheless, that she changed even before she has reached adolescence.

These shifts prepare us for the story to follow. Morris Townsend (Ben Chaplin) a handsome, charming, but unemployed young man will, despite

Catherine's extreme awkwardness, become her suitor, and Dr. Sloper, suspicious of Morris's motives, will forbid marriage and threaten to disinherit Catherine. In his attempts to dissuade her from marrying Morris, Dr. Sloper will also convince Catherine that he does not like her, and Morris in the face of the threatened disinheritance will abandon Catherine. She will never marry, although her father will die thinking that she intends to marry Morris after his death. Years later Morris will return to Catherine only to be rejected by her.

The tension of the story thus comes not from the twists of plot but from the nuances of character and the multiplicity of perspectives from which those nuances are apprehended. Understanding Catherine's character and Morris's motives proves a much more complicated task than Dr. Sloper imagines it to be, and thus the subtle shifts in visual perspective, established at the outset and manifest throughout the film, and the careful attention to revelatory details (the significance of which can, like the cat on the table, be easily overlooked), all place the viewer in the same realm of uncertainty and redefinition that the novel *Washington Square* and James's fiction in general do.

In denying his daughter her lover, Dr. Sloper is testing Catherine's loyalty and employing his superior "scientific" reason to ascertain in advance the proper outcome of his test and the best means to achieve that outcome. Such determinations, of course, reflect bad scientific method. To determine the best outcome of an experiment in advance is to introduce an intervening variable, giving science, which is supposed to be neutral, an ethical dimension. The limitations of Dr. Sloper's position are revealed by the technology of the cinematic apparatus, capable, as we have seen, of always adding a new dimension to the issue by reframing our privileged window and directing our gaze to details unnoticed by the principals of the fictional world we have entered. Thus we see, even if Dr. Sloper does not, that his test of Catherine's loyalty has blinded him to Catherine's test of ethics. She wishes to find a way of being both a good daughter and a good wife. It is not that she is too simple for Dr. Sloper's experiment but too complex in ways that fall outside the frame of his perception.

In a confrontation with Dr. Sloper, Morris points out how Catherine's character makes her appealing to him: "Catherine is good and honest and true. She lives in a place where everything is shining and clean, where everyone has the best of intentions. I never imagined such a world, and now I want to live there with her." Reasoning from the premise that Morris has no profession or position, Dr. Sloper rejects this argument, explaining what Morris perceives as virtues as the attributes of "a weak-minded woman." At stake again are competing perspectives, a point emphasized by a series of metaphors about vision: The doctor assures Morris "you need not be concerned with my vision." When Morris responds, "that is not what Catherine sees," Dr. Sloper offers to buy her spectacles.

Holland, reaching beyond the specifics of the novel, makes this disagreement resonate with one of James's central themes: what it means to be an "American." Is the American the pragmatic man of science, governed by visible facts rather than Old World prejudices, or is he the man of vision, dedicated to the proposition that all men are created equal and endowed by their creator with certain unalienable rights, among them life, liberty, and the pursuit of happiness? Morris, in rejecting Dr. Sloper's authority, cogently identifies himself with the latter definition of "American," asserting his unalienable right to the pursuit of happiness: "A man who spends his life—you call it idling, I call it searching—seeks something. For me it was happiness. Now having gone to the ends of the Earth in pursuit of it, what do you suppose are the chances of giving it up, having discovered it on his doorstep?"

The chances, as it turns out, are better than Morris imagined, but the happiness he gives up pales in comparison to that which Catherine and Dr. Sloper each sacrifice. They lose one another's love, or rather they lose the perception of love that comprised their binding familial illusion. James knew that no windows on reality could define explicitly how people deal with the loss of those illusions or reveal what replaces them. Holland concludes, therefore, with a long close-up of Catherine in which our view of her consolidates hints of the unrepresentable. Although Catherine is playing the piano during that final close-up, we can only see her face, bordered at first by faint surroundings tinted in an orange hue and then by darkness. She is playing "Tu chiami un vita," the tune that she and Morris had performed in duet for her father at that time when they thought there would be no obstacle to their marriage. As the background darkens, the actual piano playing is replaced by an orchestrated version of the tune and then a soprano (April Armstrong) joins in. Clearly, we are no longer hearing the sounds from the parlor on Washington Square, but music that comes from elsewhere, as do the unspoken referents of the protean expressions on Catherine's face, which dissolve into the darkness of the credits, as the opening shot of *Washington Square* emerged out of that darkness at the moment of Catherine's birth.

## The American Century

Morris has left, thinking that Catherine has banished him from that world he had described to Dr. Sloper—the one where everything is shining and clean and everyone has the best of intentions—but she could not have banished him from that world, because he and Dr. Sloper had destroyed it years earlier. Since, as Holland represents it, that (formerly) clean well-intentioned world is America, this film, too, participates in a millennial inquiry into the parameters of the American century. But Catherine Sloper is *not* Milly Theale, and especially not Iain Softley's version of Milly, so that our conclusion is neither condescending nor elegiac. *Washington Square* does not tie up lose ends by inviting us to share a position superior in its morality or complexity to Catherine's. Her ambiguous smile, just before the final dissolve, suggests unnamed possibilities for future pursuit of happiness. Perhaps Henry James, watching a D.W. Griffith film in London, everything he would say about his former country already written, would have had a similarly ambiguous smile on his face, watching this new medium's crude representation of America and contemplating its unimagined potential.

## Works Cited

James, Henry. *The Art of the Novel.* New York: Scribner's, 1962.
———. *The Wings of the Dove.* New York: Signet, 1964.
Mulvey, Laura. "Visual Pleasure and Narrative Cinema." *Film Theory and Criticism.* Ed. Gerald Mast, Marshal Cohen, and Leo Braudy. 4th ed. New York: Oxford UP, 1992. 746–57.
Southern, Terry. *The Magic Christian.* New York: Bantam, 1964.

## Filmography

*The Bostonians.* Dir. James Ivory. Writ. Ruth Prawer Jhabvala. Perf. Christopher Reeve, Vanessa Redgrave, Jessica Tandy, Madeleine Potter. Merchant Ivory Productions, 1984.
*Bram Stoker's Dracula.* Dir. Francis Ford Coppola. Writ. James V. Hart. Perf. Anthony Hopkins, Gary Oldman, Winona Ryder. Columbia Pictures, 1992.
*The Europeans.* Dir. James Ivory. Writ. Ruth Prawer Jhabvala and James Ivory. Perf. Lee Remick, Robin Ellis, Wesley Addy, Tim Choate, Lisa Eichhorn, Kristin Griffith, Nancy New, Norman Snow, Helen Stenborg, Tim Woodward. Merchant Ivory Productions, 1979.
*The Piano.* Dir. Jane Campion. Writ. Jane Campion. Perf. Holly Hunter, Harvey Keitel, Sam Neill. Miramax, 1993.
*The Portrait of a Lady.* Dir. Jane Campion. Writ. Laura Jones. Perf. Nicole Kidman and John Malkovich. Polygram, 1996.
*Washington Square.* Dir. Agnieszka Holland. Writ. Carol Doyle. Perf. Jennifer Jason Leigh, Albert Finney, Ben Chaplin, and Maggie Smith. Hollywood Pictures/Caravan Pictures, 1997.
*The Wings of the Dove.* Dir. Iain Softley. Writ. Hossein Amini. Perf. Helena Bonham Carter, Linus Roache, Alison Elliott. Miramax, 1997.

# Cultural Capitalism and the "James Formation"

*Marc Bousquet*

I have always thought of Henry James as presiding over the house of culture as a kind of queenly Tudor monarch, stern and virginal and long-winded, but benign and briskly competent in the matter of cultural work—reliable, professional, fair-minded, timely, and thoughtful. Like the liberalism that this image continuously labors to help constitute, "Henry James" is not really given to failure—except at the drama. There seems to be no such thing as disappointing prose by Henry James (so long as we spot him *Watch and Ward* and possibly *The Reverberator*). The short stories and criticism, each of the ten thousand letters, the novellas, journals, and, especially, the major fiction—all of it, rather brilliant if you like that sort of thing. James, like a good merchant—more like a Venetian merchant prince, perhaps, not really like our own Merchant Ivory—always delivers the goods. Even Shakespeare, who entertained Tudor monarchs but never aspired to be one, doesn't enjoy quite the same reputation for reliability. If we are bored by *Titus Andronicus,* the Bard fails us, not we him. *Coriolanus*? A peculiar play. *The Henriad*? Not bad when the adaptation is short and bloody. I don't mean to ignore the long tradition of fashionable James-bashing by intellectuals, writers, and the media alike, but with the exception of the three late masterpieces, this tradition doesn't differentiate its experience of James: nobody bashing James's prose criticizes an individual work as unsuccessfully Jamesian. Unlike Melville, Dickinson, Twain, even Whitman, Milton, and Shakespeare, James, it's agreed, consistently, successfully, produced James-quality work.

Considered as "cultural capital," this unusual reliability of the Jamesian product initially appears to operate rather simply as an unmediated good thing. We believe in the usefulness of culture as an antidote to class disadvantage, and we give that faith powerful reality through a complex system of social arrangements, practices, and values that makes possible the everyday transubstantiation of cultural competencies into other advantages, including material advantages. In this process, which we might fairly name "cultural capitalism," individuals capitalize on their engagement with certain kinds of culture—so that acquisition of a socially valued familiarity with Shakespeare's tragedies, for example, can (and generally does) lead to material advancement.[1] Of course, not all cultural encounters are equally valued—Shakespeare's comedies have less currency than the tragedies, and acquaintance with the histories can generally be converted into economic advantage only in the most academic of circumstances. These valuations change over time. In the social world of artisans and clerks in the antebellum United States, for example, the history plays represented a quite significant cultural capital. From a perspective that shares the values of cultural capitalism, the unusual consistency of the Jamesian product is unproblematic: with several recent and forthcoming film adaptations, including two of the three famously difficult late masterpieces, the stock of "Henry James" has been on the rise. Like Internet stocks, all things Jamesian figure as a good investment. With pluck and with luck, and a copy of *The Golden Bowl*, any young Ragged Dick should be able to rise into the stratosphere. Young advertising executives are at this very moment playing golf with the partners in their firm, conversing knowledgeably about James, converting their "investment of time" in viewing Campion's *Portrait* and Softley's *Dove* into material advantage. Possibly they've joined a book club and are tackling *The Golden Bowl* in preparation for the Merchant Ivory production. Who could complain? Most especially: how could a Jamesian complain?

From a more critical perspective, the special relationship between Henry James and cultural capitalism does have a few disadvantages, at least for some people. The tautology of cultural capital, through which the Jamesian product always seems to meet Jamesian standards, works in tandem with the related tautology of economic capital, through which wealth always seems to land in the right hands. This perfect fit between "Henry James" and the general tautology of cultural capitalism concerns this essay. How is it that "Henry James" cannot fail but readers can? The startling consistency and reliability of the Jamesian product relies in part on its continuous and apparently effortless relocation to the reader of all fluctuations in value. Readers vary in worthiness, but James's merit remains the same or even enlarges over time. The sense that any failure of the circuit between Jamesian prose and the reader seems inevitably to lie in the reader is a sense created by the logic of a cultural capital that presents itself as accumulating inevitably, even naturally, in the hands of the most worthy.

The accumulation of cultural capital closely follows the accumulative logic of economic capital, which requires the everyday reinvention of necessity itself, the continual introduction of new goods and services without which everyday life would be actually impossible. Importantly, not imaginarily impossible, actually impossible—the life one leads without invented necessities as various as telephones, chemotherapy, or new sneakers on the playground does not count as "everyday life" but some other, radically diminished order of existence. The culture industry's continuous reinvention of the Jamesian product can be understood not merely as a simple production process—enabling the worthy to acquire, secure, and enlarge cultural capital—but much further, as also a continuous reinstallation of James in the sphere of necessity. Insofar as the culture industry works to produce the sense that "Henry James" ought to figure in a properly lived everyday life, it simultaneously labors to install the corollary proposition that life without James is a radically diminished order of existence—too alien for the James-rich to quite imagine. The process by which Jamesian prose produces cultural capital for the most "worthy" is inextricable from the process through which it produces failure in the resisting reader. That is, so long as "Henry James" cannot fail, readers inevitably will.

Talking about a "Henry James" that produces the failure of a readership is ultimately not talking about the historical James, who lived and wrote for a living audience now dead. It is talking about a contemporary site of cultural production named "Henry James" that locates the work, money, and experience of millions of people, some of whom only participate by watching television or buying movie tickets—or even by declining to buy them. Within this productive complex, references to the historical Henry do have tactical value, especially in struggles for legitimacy. Certain other kinds of value are sustained by claims about what the historical Henry actually intended or how the historical Henry's experiences help us to find what a text "really means." But the concern of this essay is to try to resist the quick cash value of appealing to the historical James and stick with certain questions raised by the contemporary formation that involves so many people. My interest is in this large, rich, always changing "Henry James" formation and the phenomenon of cultural capitalism, the social process through which certain kinds of cultural engagement are translated into material advantage. Specifically, does the James formation have a necessary relationship to cultural capitalism or can it be made to support some other cultural materialism?

Addressing this last question requires a response to Richard Salmon's recent skeptical meditation on cultural-studies approaches to Henry James. Urging that we view James as a kind of precursor-collaborator of the Frankfurt School, Salmon writes that critical reassessments leading to a "Henry James" more friendly to popular culture help to perpetuate what he views as an unhealthy academic populism that in turn obscures the ideological work of the "capitalist culture industry," which is to conceal real social inequalities that can be addressed only by "radical transformation of the relations of production and consumption" (217). This essay is directly concerned with at least one of the general urgencies that Salmon invokes, which I take in its largest sense to be that of how to frame a materialism after poststructuralism and specifically how cultural practices retain the possibility of socially transformative politics. Nonetheless, I wish to consider his remarks with some care, for two reasons. First, Salmon writes as if only cultural-studies theorists are "updating James merely to suit current concerns" (215), while he—by contrast—has hold of a reality anchored by a historical James who cleverly anticipates Adorno. It's obvious, at least to me, that cultural studies approaches are useful even if they accomplish nothing more than the dissemination of a larger self-consciousness about appeals to history for positive authority. Cultural studies usefully distinguishes between a historical Henry about whom we're all inevitably going to tell conflicting stories and "Henry James," the cultural-material (signifying, economic, and experiential) field. (One doesn't have to employ a cultural-studies perspective to see that Salmon's essay is primarily a skirmish with his contemporaries—the academic enthusiasts of mass culture—and to this extent opportunistically located in the James formation.) Second, Salmon too quickly locates only popular and mass culture (which he virtually conflates) in the realm of "capitalist industry." Deploying assumptions that are widespread in an academy markedly unwilling to see its own complicities with capital, he writes as if high culture were not only free of but somehow inherently antagonistic to the logic of economic capital. One might address this assumption with ideology critique, describing the complicities of liberal education, high culture, and economic domination; a more direct materialism might point out the profound capitalization of high culture in the academy and other state-supported institutions, such as the opera. But in this essay, I'd like to respond to Salmon's notions as emblematic of a phenomenon remarked by Lawrence Grossberg: "Reading the literature on popular culture, one would never guess that the various fractions of the middle and upper classes have a popular culture of their own" (75). When British culture studies began distinguishing between popular culture and mass culture, the consequences vastly exceeded the early opposition between massification and resistant formations of the folk (or resistant formations of the elite). In talking about culture as media in a mass society, it has become increasingly impossible (or at least inaccurate) to equate mass media formations exclusively with middle- or working-class experience.

In western mass democracies, cultural elites form a rather large group and do, I think, have a popular culture of their own. (Who else buys all of those Jimmy Buffett recordings?) The ideas of the dominant class don't only appear in mass-media formations designed to be consumed by the dominated; the culture of the dominant classes is also a popular, frequently a mass-mediated, culture for itself, articulated in every dimension of the massified media: paperback books, compact discs, network television, cable channels, and cinema. One might fairly describe the James formation generally as belonging to this popular culture of the dominant class—quantifiable, if one wished, by surveys of title recognition, ownership of paperback books, and so forth, correlated with such factors as net worth, income, and status markers.[2] And it is probably useful to look at the recent film adaptations as belonging largely to the mass-mediated popular culture of elites in particular, rather than as the popular culture of some other group. One might distinguish between the adaptations according to their appeal to different class fractions within (and across) the dominant class: Holland's *Washington Square* (1997), for instance, is in this way perhaps fairly characterized as appealing largely to the intellectual adherents to "legitimate" culture for whom the impression of fidelity to the novel is an important criterion. With a larger market share and slightly more interpretive approach, Campion's *Portrait* (1996) alienates a small number of the intellectual fraction (for whom the impression of fidelity overrides other concerns) but appeals to the sizable proportion of the dominant class hospitable to the ethos and aims of a specifically bourgeois feminism (who in all likelihood encountered the textual practices of ludic feminism in higher education between 1975 and the present). Only Softley's *Wings* has so far appealed to an audience outside of the dominant class, while alienating members of the intellectual fraction and other liberal elites.[3] I'll go on to argue that the liberal reservations regarding Softley's work and its larger appeal beyond the dominant class are interrelated and that this relationship says a few interesting things about the way that different classes and groups experience the James formation.

Rather than pursuing the question of how the historical Henry James encountered popular culture, cultural studies is more interested in the way that contemporary popular culture encounters "Henry James." This doesn't mean that we can't make assertions about the historical Henry—I'm going to conclude by arguing that the structures of class, youth, and ideology crossing the contemporary James formation probably do lead to interesting speculations about the relationship of prose written by the historical James to structures of feeling informing youth and class experience at the time of composition. This means of speculating about an historical Henry James by way of contemporary experience is a kind of earnestness—an honesty in recognition of contingency, an unwillingness to pretend that one is the true apostle of the historical and only other people are constructing a usable Henry from the remnants of the past. A less friendly view of this approach might describe it as cynical and not earnest—pragmatic, willful, and self-aggrandizing rather than (as I see it) as evincing a kind of delicacy, precision, and respect for difference. Certainly the disparaging view is more likely to have appeal if our goal is to say more things with greater positivity about an historical Henry. But if our goal is to say more things with greater precision about the operation of "Henry James" within the actually existing social reality (i.e., at the present time), we might do worse than begin by seeing the James formation as experienced differently by different social groups. Seen properly, the cultural-studies approach invokes new responsibilities and not wild new liberties. When Grossberg remarks that "cultural studies argues that much of what one requires to study culture is not cultural" (21), he is invoking the problematics of materialism against the excesses of textualism—de-emphasizing academic consideration of "free play" on the plane of meaning and, instead, highlighting culture as a lived reality crossed by social determinants such as age, race, and class.

For literary scholars, the most understandably disturbing consequence of a presentist cultural-studies approach to the James formation is a multiplication of the texts under consideration, with a consequent shift in the relative value of one's investment in book culture. Certainly novels and stories by the historical James can tell us things about the James formation, as can academic and journalistic writing, interviews, ethnography and data regarding sales figures, course enrollments, and legislation regarding the teaching of great books. There will inevitably be many circumstances when cinematic adaptations of the prose have more utility (scholarly capital) than one's Norton edition. Even more disturbing is the real likelihood that much can be learned about the James formation when the text itself has gone missing, as in the 1999 film *Notting Hill*, where the character played by Julia Roberts is briefly shown filming an adaptation of an unnamed Henry James novel. On the one hand, the film's short sequence featuring the actress at work is vividly intelligible—in the intertextuality provided by the recent series of James adaptations featuring star actresses whose professional personae cue us to the evolution of Roberts's character. But this vivid new intelligibility is conspicuously (and perhaps for professional Jamesians, alarmingly) detached from any specific re-presentation of the historical James's writing. In this film, "Henry James" appears *as* "Henry James," not as a marker of the historical Henry but as a register of the culturally capital-ized location "Henry James" itself, as crossed by such contingencies as the professional image of Helena Bonham Carter.

Given that the appearance in question transpires in a film with a market share exponentially larger than all of the recent adaptations taken together, it seems likely that we're learning something about the James for-mation as encountered by a large audience with a marginal relation to the culture of elites. Like the television show "Friends," *Notting Hill* is about a group of what passes for bohemians, young college-educated artists and intellectuals. This "bohemian" ensemble experiences domination as "the dominated fraction of the dominant class," in Bourdieu's description of the intelligentsia. By contrast, the mostly youthful audience of the film have probably less than a fifty-fifty chance of holding a degree.[4] For the most part, the audience experiences domination as members of the dominated class—a group very likely to have some experience of college but to have "failed" at that encounter by not earning the degree or to have earned it "too slowly," or at the wrong institution, or with insufficient distinction, etc. This group experiences "Henry James" as a name redolent of cultural capi-tal, but mostly just a name, encountered in college lectures (more rarely, acquired for an assignment, perhaps partially read and more fragmentarily recalled), movie advertising, entertainment news programming, or news-paper reviews. In all likelihood, the vast majority of the audience group has a slight but continuing acquaintance with "Henry James" that unfolds with-out an engagement with literary fiction of any kind. That is, the audience of *Notting Hill* is largely composed of persons who have "failed" to read James, who lead a life radically diminished by the standards of cultural capital, but who presently consent to acknowledge "Henry James" as a marker of the popular culture of an other, more intellectual class. It is at least in part through their encounter with James that this audience acknowledges itself as culturally inferior.

Not incidentally, *Notting Hill* is at least putatively a film about failures. Like our James films, it is also an adaptation, a rather loose one, of *La Boheme* and is inescapably a meditation on the relationship between cul-tural capital and material conditions. Despite the apparent looseness of the adaptation, *Notting Hill* preserves the skepticism of previous accounts of bohemian life toward the claims of cultural capitalism. My reading focuses on the film's encounter with the James formation: toward the end of the story, it sets up the audience to think that its star-crossed lovers, separated by cinematic markers of class, will be united on the set of the James film. This expectation, that the material differences between the characters can be healed in the house of culture, is strongly supported within and without the film by the processes of cultural capitalism. But this movie, having addressed and activated that assumption, stunningly frustrates it: a shared taste for James is not enough to unite this film's lovers (as shared cultural competency was, indeed, not enough for Puccini's lovers, whose opera ends in death and separation for lack of cash, not culture). By contrast to more faithful adaptations of the story (such as *Rent*), the film produces a happy ending. Yet it does so by a startling device that spotlights the unexpected failure of culture to remediate class experience.

In this film, only a massive redistribution of wealth resolves class conflict. After repeated romantic failures over long cinematic time (the story unfolds over a period longer than a year) and the decisive failure to connect under the sign of James, Roberts's character ultimately gives her bohemian lover Grant a Chagall painting that they've both admired in mechanical reproduction. His realization that she's given him the actual painting, not a copy—a cash transfer of twenty million dollars or more—does bear a sentimental load (it testifies to her sincerity, etc.).[5] But more important for our reading is the film's insistent rematerialization of the cultural. There is no way to interpret the scene that enables us to believe that some more sentimental and less costly substitute (such as a Chagall picture postcard) would have united the lovers. The audience is compelled to recognize the transfer of the painting as an economic exchange. Indeed, throughout the film there is a kind of casual insistence on the economic reality of culture, especially but not exclusively the film form, in a manner perfectly consistent with a popular awareness suggested by the newspaper publication of the box office gross of studio films, the auction prices of impressionist paintings, and so on. Perhaps it is only elites who experience psychic dislocation when faced with evidence of the material basis of taste, whereas nonelites know that self-culture costs money. In any event, having addressed the cardinal faith of cultural capitalism that culture conquers all, the film deploys a gesture of breathtaking materialism that simultaneously introduces new confusion into the old clarities (money isn't important to persons of culture) and pushes toward a new intelligibility that millions of dollars can do things that "Henry James" cannot.

There are many ways to take the reading of the materialist structure of feeling in *Notting Hill*. For instance, one might explore the crossing of this materialism with gender, since it's Roberts's character who enjoys all the agencies of cultural capitalism. Another reading would press hard at the juncture with race—the London neighborhood after which the film is titled enjoys a specifically multiethnic identity of ludic tolerance and sponsors London's most famous annual ethnic carnival. A race-conscious reading might make two moves, one that looks into the erasure of that multiethnic identity in the all-white bohemianism of the production; the subsequent move might suggest the peculiar honesty of that erasure, given that Notting Hill's "ethnic" reputation and its carnival is by now a kind of Benetton commercial construct in a neighborhood filled with three-million-pound flats occupied by liberals who flatter themselves that they spend with tolerance. Another reading would pursue the question of class and "the folk": at the moment of pivotal decision for Hugh Grant's character, the film locates ultimate value in the romantic opinion of his visibly working-class roommate, a head-scratching, pants-drooping, masturbating Welshman, who simultaneously represents "some other" folk culture from the viewership and the common sense of a large fraction of the viewership itself. And any of these paths, I think, would provide useful grounds for reexamination of the prose produced by the historical Henry James and the relationship of that prose to structures of feeling contemporary with its creation and associated with the relevant social determinants of race, gender, and working-class ethos.

In what remains of this effort, however, I propose to concentrate on the way that young people encounter the James formation, both in *Notting Hill* and the most popular of the James adaptations, Softley's *Wings of the Dove*. Both films stage an encounter between young bohemians and capital, and both thematize the economic experience of youth in terms of desperation, self-betrayal, and failure. I think that the popular materialism of Notting Hill can be read in connection with the materialism ascribed to "Generation X," though not in the usual symptomatic fashion, as evidence of some collective moral collapse. The fact that the materialism of Gen X is a quality attributed to them by the members of the baby boom highlights the relationality of the concept of generation: the baby boomers constitute themselves as a generation in part negatively, i.e., by naming the distinguishing qualities of other cohorts.[6] It's not really incidental that Gen X bears a reputation for a consumerist materialism at the same time that it bears the apparently contradictory reputation for economic failure. The paradoxical image of Gen X makes perfect sense as the obverse of the baby boom's self-congratulatory peace medallion, a generation that sees itself as both idealist and economically successful, indeed successful in consequence of its idealism (rather than in consequence of its pro-peace enjoyment of a perpetual war economy).[7] The peculiar lived contradiction of the materialist "slacker" is inextricable from the lived contradictions of the baby boomer, for whom theories of cultural capitalization serve to obscure the material basis of that generation's accumulation of wealth in military production financed by public debt.

Viewed as a cinematic event addressing a feeling that is both common to youthful viewers and evocative of their relation to another generation, the failure of "Henry James" to unite the lovers in Notting Hill expresses a powerful suspicion of the enormous claims made for the social agency of culture by the baby boom. In the experience of Generation X, cultural competence does not lead to any particular material advantage, and the film seems to cast doubt on at least some of the claims supported by the system of practices that we've called cultural capitalism. The question is whether these doubts extend to culturalism generally—a rejection of the belief that culture shapes material reality and a return to some variation of economic determinism—or, on the other hand, whether they simply indicate a desire for a different kind of culturalism, a desire for a specifically noncapitalist cultural-material practice. Gen Xers will not necessarily oppose cultural capitalism just because it's in their interest to do so. There are clearly many Gen X formations that figure as hypercapitalist materialism (Roberts's character is in fact an example of a mass-mediated meditation on a culturally hypercapitalized Gen Xer). Nonetheless, I think that the generation has produced alternatives, many of which are compatible with the broad hint provided by the redistribution of wealth in Notting Hill. The special importance of Notting Hill for us is, in part, its representation of the failure of "Henry James" to remediate class antagonism. If the support of cultural capitalism prevents James from failing, an unexpected slide in his performance possibly signals the emergence of an alternative to the system backing his stock.

The film's representation of the failure of the James formation is therefore something more than a carnivalesque inversion through which the failed readers of James applaud a pie in the master's face. Unlike the James-bashing discourse, Notting Hill's response to the James formation exceeds a "simple" expression of class resentment. As Bourdieu notes, the dominated classes generally approach cultural icons with exaggerated respect (318). Instead the mass-cultural or oafish bashing of figures like James by class-specific characters usually represents a ventriloquized expression of hostility by cultural elites to the untouchable icons of its own popular culture.[8] Taken as members of a generation or taken as members of a dominated class, the audience constituted by Notting Hill shows no desire to bash "Henry James." Rather, the film represents the temperate, nuanced, and earnest desire to make the house of culture—as represented by the James and Chagall formations—do different cultural work. That is, if the materialism signified by the transfer of the painting signifies something more than a wish to sell off the contents of museums and redistribute the proceeds, it might be the film's Gen X audience's desire to update James to suit what Salmon pejoratively calls "current concerns." The baby boom has had their James and

Chagall; succeeding generations will insist on a James and a Chagall to call their own.

In what follows, we'll look at some of the different cultural work that people under thirty-five might expect from the James formation, and specifically at the way that Merton Densher in Softley's *Wings* represents the desire of a generation of cultural workers for a radical transformation in the relations of cultural production.

## The "Actually Existing" Cultural Materialism

When I was first imagining this essay in August 1999, I heard a story on National Public Radio that is fairly typical of the fare produced for that venue. This was one of the human-interest narratives, written and narrated by a listener, that gives NPR its flavor of an ongoing dialogue among those who do the cultural work of the nation. This segment featured the voice of "a writer living in Cleveland," whose aim was to remind the audience of the "power of stories to change our lives." The exemplar for this homily was a kind of reading clinic for the homeless, through which the most disenfranchised were organized into great-books reading groups. The fact that eleven of the thirty-seven homeless readers were subsequently enrolled in a community college was directly attributed to the powerful prose of Anne Tyler and Toni Morrison. I will not belabor the point, but this literary sermon obviously flings its pieties in the face of enormous evidence that homelessness is produced primarily by domestic abuse and the absence of beds in mental-health and rehabilitation facilities, not by the absence of good literature. A more temperate view of the reading program would see it as the heir to and contemporary analogue of nineteenth-century tract distribution: a moral-reform society that provides material assistance but subsequently attributes the material results of that assistance to the moral consequences of the tract. In this case, of course, the idealism being disseminated with tracts of Morrison and Tyler is not Christian self-help but cultural-capitalist self-help. Despite its wildly counterfactual claims for the social agency of literature, the program figures as profound human truth on NPR because it recirculates the common sense of the dominant class. It presents a false-yet-intelligible, specifically cultural-capitalist series of propositions: some persons who read succeed; therefore, reading produces success; unsuccessful persons must be unsuccessful in rough proportion to their failure to read; homelessness is therefore the consequence of economic failure; so homeless persons must be those who've read least of all, and evidently need it most. Sentimental reiterations of these cherished propositions explode in the consciousness like flashbulbs, producing the photographic certainties of witnessed truth.

The problem with these luminous intelligibilities of cultural capitalism is that they figure as inevitable as well as true. Cultural capitalism
shoulders aside any other practice of culture as a social agency, seeming to
fully occupy the space of the real. All other culturalisms are relegated to the
realm of "theory," because they are more or less unintelligible in proportion
to their antagonism to dominant practice.[9] Only the most intelligible tales
(told in clear, strong, accessible prose) get told on National Public Radio;
unintelligible tales (told in dense, convoluted, unconvincing jargon) get
told in journals of theory. This means that when Generation X is described
on NPR, for instance, the tale is told with perfect clarity: Xers figure as
cheery devotees of leisure who "prefer" the system of flexible labor to the
unfreedom of "settling down" into any one career, live with their parents
because they'd rather buy clothes than pay rent on an apartment, and take
college really slowly because it's just one of many neat interests taking up
their slack time.[10] Cool! This intelligible knowledge—that youth today is
different and cares more about "lots of free time" to go snowboarding than
health care or a living wage—is a tale produced by a kind of cultural
hypercapitalism: youth today, we dimly recognize, is being shortchanged in
terms of economic capital, but hey, look at all the cultural capital they
enjoy. Those kids are slackin' big time, living off of their parents, buying
CDs, hitting the slopes, piercing themselves.

The historical James professed a lifelong suspicion of intelligible tales.
And like most intelligible tales, this cheery account of a generation is bogus
by any measurement: this generation works harder for less. They spend
more time in school because they're working their way through. They live
at home because they can't simultaneously afford rent, car payments, and
health care. They're not enjoying leisure; they're waiting on the tables of
the baby boom, selling them computers, real estate, and stock, educating
and diapering their children. Paradoxically identified with leisure, student
living is a lifeway of labor. Nearly all students between the ages of 16 and 24
work; most of those who aren't working "are looking for work, but can't
find jobs" (Mitchell 50). Thirty to forty percent of students between the
ages of 20 and 24 work full time. All of this work dramatically lengthens
time to degree. Student enrollment grows ever larger and older (more than
40 percent of all college students are 26 or older [MacManus 119]). The
many years of student life no longer serve merely to "warehouse" the labor
of youth. Higher education is in large part a sentence to a term of flexible
labor, and expansions in the time to degree unsurprisingly correlate to
expansions in the availability of flexible Gen X labor to serve the historically unprecedented accumulation of capital by baby boomers and seniors.

Well into "maturity," members of Gen X work longer hours with fewer benefits, and at age 25 to 34 are substantially less likely than boomers were at the same age to have professional-managerial employment; Gen Xers of that age fraction in 1998 are more likely to work in sales/service or manufacturing than were their boomer counterparts in 1979 (Maguire 19). Gen Xers aged 25–34 earn a lot less than boomers of that age did in 1979. The average weekly pretax paycheck for Gen Xers aged 25–34 in 1996 was 15 percent lower than their 1979 counterparts. Indeed, the actual generational disparity in incomes for persons under 35 is much larger when factors of race, class, and gender are considered. For one thing, the median income for the category "all women" has actually *risen* 33 percent between 1980 and 1995, as through affirmative action women's wages move closer to parity with male earnings. But that movement is toward an enormously reduced benchmark: by 1998, the average earnings of young men aged 20– 34 had dropped 32 percent since 1972 (Rhodes). These gains for the category "all women" are at a closer look enormously differentiated by cohort. Women in the baby boom profited much more from gender-equity initiatives than have Gen X women. While the median income of women of all ages rose 33 percent between 1980 and 1995 (with most of the gains happening before 1990), the median income of women aged 25–34 only rose 21 percent, and that of women under 25 actually *fell* 8 percent (Mitchell 98). Once you factor in 5 or 10 percent for lost health benefits, reduced vacation time and other losses, the true magnitude of the generational chasm in economic experience becomes partially apprehensible. During these "economic good times," men under 35 work longer hours and earn perhaps 40 percent less than their boomer counterparts during the 1970s (a period, oddly, of "economic crisis"). Women now under 30 similarly work more than their boomer counterparts and are likely to share notably less or not at all in the enormous economic gains enjoyed by women of preceding cohorts. Yet this lived experience of youth is barely intelligible, while the cheery propaganda is so persistent that Xers try to believe it themselves, living in a state of partial awareness of their own experience. Gen X experience recedes from visibility precisely because it contradicts the claims of cultural capitalism during years which figure as "good times" for the baby boom and the elderly.[11]

The emerging theories of Gen X cultural hypercapitalism serve to mystify the generational register of the economic order, in which young persons are generally constrained to a decade or even two decades of flexible labor before they reach the securities of a job. The "hypercapitalist" image of young people serves to suggest that youth have made this economic reality for themselves: by valuing these hypothetical rich lives of leisure, youth has "chosen" flexible working hours and the accompanying consequences. From this perspective, an older form of cultural capitalism is envisioned as peacefully and naturally giving ground to a newer form through a series of personal choices made by individual members of generational groups. The older form of cultural capitalism I've been describing, invested in the liberal-democratic values of political modernism (and which the baby boomers like to believe they "chose" for themselves). The new form that we can call cultural hypercapitalism is by contrast a postmodernism, more flexible, more global, characterized by the crossing of the borders sustained by the grand narratives of authenticity, nationality, gender, and so forth. Theories of this cultural hypercapitalism relate to what Teresa Ebert and Mas'ud Zavarzadeh have named a "ludic" postmodernism, through which ludic theories of subjectivity and resistance largely reinstall the regimes they seemingly resist (see Zavarzadeh 31–89). These explanations succeed because they present the contemporary economic regime in a positive light and because they present as natural, painless, and even desirable the transition from one form of capitalism to another.

Theories of hypercapitalism protect the accumulation of economic capital by introducing new flexibility into the older forms of the cultural-capitalist project. Essays such as this one are an example of flexibility in the James formation. It wouldn't be unfair to look at this effort as professing a cultural hypercapitalism by way of its investment in the mass media, yet in a manner largely compatible with the accumulation of already-existing cultural capital. Just as we increasingly recognize the coexistence and even collusion of postmodern with deeply institutionalized modern forms, cultural hypercapitalism proliferates alongside older cultural-capital formations. As a general rule, the older forms of the culture industry work to accumulate capital in the James formation by making claims about the social good of encounters with Jamesian prose. To the extent that any given social good interfered with capital accumulation, it was useful to maintain the idea that cultural capital was a special form of capital that could be mobilized against economic capital. To this end, political modernism preserved the "obvious" conflict between money and art that emerged under romanticism, sustaining a vision of a kind of Wordsworthian country-city opposition through which the "house of culture" naturally opposed the "culture industry." This vision plays out, for instance, in the perception of a "struggle" between the film producers raising millions of dollars to create adaptations as popular as possible and professional Jamesians, who consistently argue that those adaptations fail James in rough proportion to their popularity. This "obvious truth" of a putative opposition between capital and the academy provides continuing support for a view still current in the popular culture of higher education that the logic of capital can be turned against itself.

By contrast to the older cultural capitalists, theorists of hypercapitalism are more inclined to see a collusive complexity in the "conflict" between sectors of the culture industry producing scholarship and sectors producing film. Part of this new vision springs from a greater willingness to recognize the material basis of the professoriate, whose scholarship in tenured lines is capitalized at between one and two million dollars per position—a vision consistent with the ever growing role of tenured faculty in the management of flexible labor in the academic workplace. One view of the postmodern culture industry takes the position that there is no exterior to the logic of capital accumulation, that all resistances are perpetually contained. That is, through flexibility, the culture industry uses these apparent conflicts to sustain itself by generating new goods and services. From the hypercapitalist perspective, filmmakers and scholars work together in service of capital accumulation precisely because they take different views. In their disagreement they create different James products for as many different market fractions as possible: a university James, a postfeminist James, a class-conscious James. The James formation creates products for these markets, but it also splendidly produces the markets themselves! Once we understand that these markets (and the demand for James products through which they are constituted) don't preexist the work of the James formation, we can recognize that this collusive complexity of apparent conflict generates new desires, without which the steady accumulation of capital within the James formation would eventually slow and even stop.

From this view, even left-theoretical critique appears complicit with the logic of capital accumulation, insofar as its resistances seem perpetually harnessed to the invention of new Jamesian product and new Jamesian desire. Paradoxically, the observable shift toward hypercultural practice, representing a significant rupture with cultural capitalism, is the agency through which cultural capitalism continues. The capitalist and hypercapitalist culturalisms labor together to represent a system without an outside: critiques of the one set of practices seem naturally to fall into the space of the other set. It is, in fact, very difficult to frame a criticism of the older forms of cultural capitalism without appearing to celebrate hypercapitalism (i.e., by opposing elitist forms of the Leavisite discourse, one seems inevitably to figure as a fan of a hip-hop Henry James). And it's equally difficult to develop a standpoint at a distance from hypercapitalism that doesn't invoke charges of elitism (i.e., from elites practicing ludic postmodernism).

From this standpoint, it's easy to see how conservatives portray theory itself as the instrument of Gen X cultural hypercapitalism. The survival of older cultural forms under hypercapitalism is to a visible extent a survival of those forms for a particular group. Obviously, the film adaptations of Shakespeare, Forster, Austen, and James have large audiences—even a failed major-studio film is eventually seen by millions of people—but most of these large audiences are composed of older members of the elite classes. Younger elites can acceptably profess ignorance of Shakespeare and hostility to Henry James—exactly as cultural conservatives among the antitheory crowd lament, because hypercapitalist theory allows them to do so. Now that professionals and managers understand culture to include mass culture nonpejoratively, they increasingly "capitalize" on mass culture, valuing engagements with baseball and football over wrestling and ice hockey, "Ally MacBeal" and "Xena, the Warrior Princess" over "Baywatch," and films featuring Arnold Schwarzenegger over films featuring Sylvester Stallone. With the assistance of the Campion film, even the name "Isabel Archer" no longer belongs to the language of mutual recognition employed by young elites. Indeed, a more reliable measure of contemporary professional-managerial acculturation might be the willingness to use the verb "deconstruct" or the prefix "post-"; in this sense, "theory" really has been the engine of the hypercapitalist triumph over "major authors," in exactly the way that the right wing of cultural capitalism has been decrying for years.

The fact that certain theoretical knowledges springing out of anticapitalist critique can be converted to cultural capital does indeed attest to the flexibility of professional-managerial hypercapitalism. But just as the practices of cultural elites under political modernism did not necessarily testify to the practices of dominated persons, the cultural hypercapitalism of postmodern elites does not necessarily speak to the experience of the working persons of a generation. Rather than take the cynical view of theoretical knowledges suggested by ludic postmodernism—that they inevitably reproduce cultural (hyper)capitalism—I propose instead to take theoretical knowledges earnestly, as the emergent intelligence of nonelite youth.

Describing theoretical knowledge as the intelligence of nonelites might sound outlandish since I've just described the display of familiarity with theoretical knowledge as a marker of elite status. After all, wasn't "theory" composed by baby boomers and Parisian intellectuals? But these objections are only reasonable if we persist in viewing the discourse of "theory" as a different order of cultural production from film or literature. We regard film and literature as radically open to the social, so that texts rarely encountered by the working class are nonetheless intelligible as addressing the experience of work. Unless theory has some special positive responsibility, or some special privilege, its texts are themselves radically open and it must be possible to read the experience of the other in the voicings of the same. Indeed, insofar as theory belongs to the popular culture of education professionals, we might view it as having a particular openness to young-adult structures of feeling, its claims perpetually circulating through the institutions of education, framing and being framed by the common sense of youth. While the most visible work of the university is the reproduction of playfully hypercultural elites (i.e., those who know the cash value of modernist irony and postmodernist parody), the whole apparatus of higher and secondary education supports less-visible but nevertheless larger social groups fairly characterized by tendencies toward earnestness that are only incompletely repressed. I think there is a relationship between the invisibility of these nonelites in higher education and the vulnerability of their earnestness to parody by elite hypercapitalism on the cultural front. The theoretical discourse of "postmodernism" serves as the cultural agent of late capitalism, perpetually striving to secure the unintelligibility of alternatives: they are "only theory," whereas "postmodernism" is fully visible as a coherent set of practices, fleshed out with an actually existing "postmodern condition," of which it figures as the natural and necessary consequence.[12] If there is a relationship between the visible elites and intelligible postmodernism, why shouldn't there be a relationship between the invisible and unintelligible, between nonelites and theoretical alternatives?

## The Importance of Being Earnest

From the perspective of cultural studies, the "theory wars" can be seen as a struggle to bring into intelligibility some noncapitalist cultural materialism, one part of the recurrent contest that continually decides the real relationship of cultural practice to social formations. Cultural-capitalist formations tend to conflate "theory" and "cultural studies" into one large "postmodernism." This erroneous conflation is the perhaps unwitting consequence of the collaboration between capitalist and hypercapitalist culturalism, part of the strategy through which anticapitalist alternatives are obscured and incorporated. This is essentially a collusion between a newly dominant postmodernism and a residual-yet-vigorous, deeply institutionalized modernism. But if we are to fully pursue Raymond Williams's note that any given social formation contains not only dominant and residual but also emergent practices, "theory" can be usefully taken as representing the always repressed, always emerging field of the alternative.

I think that there's an actual and productive articulation between popular-materialist formations and the resurgent "theoretical" attempt to frame a materialism after poststructuralism. In response to Derrida's *Spectres of Marx* (1994), Jameson hypothesizes that materialism—long stigmatized by the playful and performative dominant lines of theory—is making a comeback, in a kind of return of the repressed ("Marx's Purloined Letter" 36). At the epicenter of the performative, Judith Butler is at pains to suggest the centrality of queer theory "to the project of materialism" (271). And Slavoj Žižek pursues the possibility of a materialist psychoanalysis by insisting that a political subjectivity can only emerge by confronting the materiality of globalization, through which the "logic of capital remains the real which lurks in the background" ("Ticklish Subject" 222).[13] In a world radically textual ("culturalized," in Jameson's term), theorists as unlike one another as Žižek and Grossberg insist that theory must attempt "radical repoliticization" ("Ticklish Subject" 353), must strive to get at textual effects beyond the "plane of meaning" (Grossberg 43).[14] The pressure on Butler and Derrida to declare a materialism seems to offer compelling evidence of the resurgence of a structure of feeling that is left cold by a politics of evasion rather than commitment.

## Is Youth the New North American Working Class?

In Softley's *Wings* we have a product of the James formation that appealed to a Gen X audience more successfully than Campion's glossier, better-promoted, more celebrated and politically more straightforward tale of erotic liberation. Campion's work is essentially a nostalgia film though not, as I have argued elsewhere, a nostalgia film for the 1870s but one for the 1970s, and a less complicated feminism.[15] Despite the historical costumes, I think Softley's film repeatedly deploys strategic interventions in the James formation to call attention to itself as an artifact contemporary with its audience. Like her core audience of baby-boom liberals, Campion evades the materialism of the James formation, giving us upwardly mobile Americans, bohemians grown suddenly rich whose wealth has no origin besides consciousness of their own worthiness and who are destined to spend the rest of their days mourning a lost idealism. Softley captures and extends the materialism of the James formation, giving us a Merton Densher who begins the film as a knowledge worker considering his relationship to labor, not at all unlike the position of graduate students today, who increasingly choose to form unions affiliated with the United Auto Workers. The film directly indexes the Gen X sense of a generational struggle and generation-specific exploitation: in Softley's film, Kate's Aunt Maud hosts a party in which a well-capitalized older generation visibly trades in the flesh and affections of the young and economically disadvantaged.

Softley's Kate Croy and Merton Densher are not bohemians; they're the children of bohemians, as emphasized by the scenes of Lionel Croy in the opium den. They belong to a generation whose parents have consumed their future and expect to be supported in self-gratifying profligacy by their children. The parents have not only consumed the youth of the children with economic demands; they've colonized the idea of youth itself. In this film only the parental generation and the super-rich enjoy the pleasures and perquisites of youth. There's a remarkable absence, in films produced by the baby boom for Generation X, of a strong sense of a distinctive youth subculture—at least not in the way that films like *The Wild One, Rebel without a Cause,* or even *West Side Story* publicly acknowledged the distinctiveness of youth culture and its differences with the parent culture (and the culture of parents). Films produced by the baby boom instead display a youth culture that is markedly continuous with the parent culture (occasionally this continuity is thematized, as in *Cruel Intentions,* the recent adaptation of *Les Liaisons dangereuses*). This continuity renders youth culture seemingly transparent to parents who themselves still make a claim on youth; this sense of transparency fosters the illusion that youth is performative—that anyone can do it, that youth is constituted by the pleasures and perquisites associated with it. The felt colonizability of youth accounts for the special repugnance and sense of violation that the Gen X audience feels when the aging bohemian Lionel Croy suggests to his daughter, "we're the same, you and I."

For this reason, I don't think that the film's representation of the parental Croy's "materialism" is primarily the sort of sentimental rejection of materialist practice that Alan Nadel describes in his largely unfavorable reaction to the film ("Ambassadors" 283–85), but rather an indictment of a generationally marked hypocrisy and greed. It's perfectly reasonable to view the film as "antimaterialist" and see the separation between Kate and Merton as the consequence of a moral disgust on his part. While I'd guess from the reviews that a number of viewers did see the film as this kind of morality tale, most of the favorable reviews seem to feel that Softley and Bonham Carter treated Kate with as much ambiguity as James, or more.[16] I'm inclined, however, to view the separation between Kate and Merton as the consequence of a more horrible materialism, even what might be called an economic determination: Milly Theale's wealth does, indeed, make her lovable. A conventional reading of the film as antimaterialist tract would in any event have to reduce Softley's Kate to a villainess or femme fatale, giving credence to her father's claim of moral identity with her, and I'm unwilling to see the film's representation of her in this light. Nadel's reading of Softley's Croy as a naive schemer, while not inconsistent with his interpretation of the film's participation in the consolidation of an oppression based in gender and not "economic power" (284), ignores the generational register of her actions. In his account of Softley's film, Kate, though "a desperate and somewhat weak woman" is also rather inconsistently the sole agent of the plot; to me the film insists on the role of the parental generation in creating the bind in which Kate and Merton find themselves. A reading that concentrates on Kate as a moral failure reproduces a profound erasure of generational difference, rests on the implausible suggestion that she has indeed become her father, and ultimately holds her responsible for his sins—even while he continues in his enjoyment of her stolen youth.

The film succeeds, in part, because it addresses Gen X structures of feeling that are rather less sentimental, utopian, and nostalgic than the other James adaptations. Newspaper reviewers generally concurred with the judgment expressed by one of them that *Wings* was the best of the adaptations because of its distance from Masterpiece Theater: "the closest you'll see to a Henry James noir" (Millar). The noir comparison that occurred to many of the reviewers was apt, because 1998 saw a second adaptation of the James novel—this one quite explicitly a piece of 1990s noir. Premiering at Sundance during the Softley film's first run, Meg Richman's *Under Heaven* also saw national distribution during the summer of 1998, opening shortly after *Wings* closed: this film featured a young waitress and her shoplifting boyfriend in the roles of Densher and Croy and was widely reviewed as the "Gen X version" of the story. Changing jobs to become the caretaker of a wealthy young cancer patient, the former waitress eventually arranges to have her substance-abusing lover hired as the gardener, and the patient's crush on "Buck" leads to a sexual affair. One of the virtues of the Richardson version is that her threesome doesn't balk at the possibility of complex affection. For me, the only wrong note in Softley's film was Densher's assertion that he "never was in love" with Milly Theale. At this point, Amini's screenplay is quite similar to the prose version and includes Kate's reply that she believes Merton's assertion that he didn't love Milly until after she was dead.[17] Regardless of what one feels about the idealism of this moment in the novel, the film jarred with my previous sense of a compact with its contemporary audience.

That is, if the film is really addressing a generation that grew up in the erotic aftermath of the 1960s, the zero-sum view of affective relations that this moment proposes is unlikely. From the post-Woodstock point of view, or even from a post-*Waiting to Exhale* point of view: of course Densher loved Milly Theale; how could he not love her, enjoy her and her money, and also go on, splendidly, to continue loving Kate? The film's creators made a vigorous effort early on—that is, in preproduction—to provide support for Densher's eventual claim that he never loved Milly by casting an actress whose looks are eclipsed by Bonham Carter in the role of Kate. But this casting decision produces what may have been the unintended consequence of encouraging the audience to feast on the corpse of Milly Theale along with the pretty Helena Bonham Carter to take the enjoyment that the quaint historical Densher so nostalgically declines. This reading would support Nadel's view of Kate Croy as a vivacious postmodern hypercapitalist—indeed her father's daughter—and give us Densher as a nineteenth-century idealist, the very enemy of pleasure, a kind of Victorian-for-our-own-time, who ends up "on top," as Nadel observes, by consolidating "masculine" and "moral" authority ("Ambassadors" 285). The problem with this reading despite its utilities for the proliferation of hypercapitalist pleasure is that, in disciplining a Gen X Densher (now imagined as the enemy of feminine enjoyment) it also passes over and even partly apologizes for the excessive enjoyments of the boomer, Lionel Croy. A Žižekian reading would identify the boomer father passed over in this gendered indictment of Densher with the totalitarian mode of paternal authority: the father whose injunction to "enjoy" actually produces the state terror of excessive discipline.

My own reading focuses on the film's reinvention of Densher and the significance of that reinvention for his relationship with Milly Theale, rather than on the virtues or failings of Croy's character. In casting Densher as a labor-conscious knowledge worker, Softley invites us to consider his relationship to Milly Theale as one of labor to capital. Indeed, as Densher and Croy are both reinvented by Softley as docents to Theale—as a type of character very common within the James formation, the European cultural informant—we might consider them both emblematically, as cultural workers. Indeed, the creepiness of their failed lovemaking at the end of the film has in my mind less to do with the emptiness of their love than the character of it—their intimacy with capital has made them aware of themselves as working "for" it (under its direction but also in order to possess it) and made them conscious of a new fraternal character to their relationship, inappropriate to a specifically erotic passion.

The film emphasizes Kate and Merton's status as paid cultural informants in order to address a contradiction specific to cultural capitalism. Cultural workers like Merton Densher produce distinction in all of its senses (beauty, categorical knowledge, social differentiation), but members of the dominant class, like Milly Theale, enjoy the product of their labor. This is exactly the problem that *Notting Hill* addresses: Hugh Grant's character is unable to realize his "cultural capital" until it is first enjoyed by Julia Roberts's character. This suspicion that cultural capital and economic capital are not fully equivalent contradicts the elite idealism that cultural capital can always be "cashed in" for more than its face value (as if economic capital were

Canadian dollars trading at 70 cents to the American Standard). The problem is a very Jamesian one, and one way of developing this reading would be to seek support in the prose for this nonelite skepticism. One wouldn't have to look far: James repeatedly observes that his European culture workers can't capitalize on European culture until American capital arrives to create the opportunity for them to exploit themselves. Performing European culture work and enjoying American capital, a good case could be made for the historical James as an authority in this connection. But it is not really necessary to minutely adjudicate the fantasies of cultural capitalism in some final debunking in order to go as far as Frederic Jameson in observing that materialism might be best (re)conceived not as a fully fledged alternate "systematic philosophy," but as a location "designed to organize various anti-idealist campaigns" ("Marx's Purloined Letter" 36).

By illuminating heretofore obscured contradictions in cultural capitalism and providing a location for a materialist structure of feeling, both *Notting Hill* and Softley's *Wings* help to sustain the resurgence of at least a mediated consciousness of class experience in nonelite youth. One sociologist describes the Gen X identity as belonging properly to "the lower middle class [which is really] the working class in middle-class clothing" (Ortner 423).[18] From this point of view it might be argued that generational consciousness dilutes and divides class consciousness. There is real merit to this view. On the other hand, the increasingly organized affect of generational struggle cannot be dismissed so easily. The collective will to eradicate class as a category of analysis has meant that, as Paul Gilroy and Stuart Hall have argued, race is one modality through which class can be lived. I think the same has to be said of the concept of Generation X, that youth is one modality through which class can be lived.

But the film pushes at this substitution of generational friction for class antagonism even as it replicates it: in Merton Densher's relation to "the world's richest orphan," working youth is visibly in relation to dominant youth. Theale never figures as just another young person; she always figures as a fabulously wealthy person, an ultimately unbridgeable difference that her illness underlines. In this film Theale's attempts to claim the fraternity of youth are always frustrated and painfully pathetic, and Kate Croy's largely undisturbed confidence in Densher's affections represent her sense of a primary solidarity based on class. For the most part, however, any realization of the class relation is not "inside" the film but outside it, in the intertextuality with the generational anger of a vast cohort of young knowledge workers. Densher's not aware of it, but at least a fraction of the audience is willing to view him as sleeping with the enemy. The knowledge worker used to be viewed as "in bed" with capital in the sense that intellectuals helped secure the hegemony of the bourgeoisie; in the strongest formulation of this thesis, they are capitalist tools, serving as the "comprador to the capitalist class" (Kelsh 10–11). But more recent understandings of class as "multidimensional" have argued for knowledge workers as emerging historically into a class of their own: "If they are able to constitute a community that shares a common discursive space that leads them to identify with each other independently of their subordination to capital, the designation 'intellectual' connotes a collective that is in the process of 'class' formation." (Aronowitz and DiFazio 179). Because the knowledge worker has increasingly experienced proletarianization—that is, her expectations of material return on her cultural capital have been disappointed—the knowledge worker can no longer be viewed as in bed with capital in the old way.

Kate and Merton end the film in consciousness of the impossibility of getting satisfaction out of sleeping with the enemy and also in consciousness of their enforced mutual alienation produced by the relations of cultural production, through which Milly Theale enjoys what they should enjoy between themselves. Softley's *Wings* succeeds with a youth audience because it renders visible an actually existing class antagonism in contemporary youth, an antagonism that is generally masked in culture produced by boomers. Both *Wings* and *Notting Hill* are remarkable for the degree to which they represent *intra*-generational class conflict not seen in youth culture since the John Hughes films. As this essay was going to press, a remarkable adaptation by Anthony Minghella of Patricia High Smith's *The Talented Mister Ripley* also painfully catalogued the unbridgeability of the class injury except through an inevitably violent interaction of the performative. All three of these films document a real movement in the contemporary youth formation toward vigorous differentiation into class-specific fractions.

The way in which "Generation X" is a way for youth to understand its economic experience helps to explain the reluctance of most members of the X cohorts to identify with it. That is, members of the generation don't identify with it until they become conscious of economic exploitation—fail to get a job appropriate to their "cultural capital," find that they have to seek health care as an indigent in a hospital emergency room, etc.[19] Gen X is the formation through which the new knowledge workers begin to understand that they cannot be cultural capitalists even if they were willing (the boomers' brief refusals to "sell out" were based on the confidence that somebody was always buying), and the nostalgic note on which Merton Densher acknowledges his alienation from Kate Croy is a nostalgia for a time when the knowledge worker could so easily have played gigolo to capital. But with this nostalgia there is also a dawning realization that some new arrangement is necessary. The film thematizes the failure of cultural capital to produce justice or even happiness, and the rejection of Theale's bequest symbolizes a rejection of the hypercapitalist "alternative." The no-exit feeling of the existential bind in which youth finds itself in Softley's film represents the collective desire to find the outside of the capitalist-hypercapitalist system.

It is inevitable but not sufficient that we'll read hypercapitalism into any Gen X formation. Given the cultural dominance of postmodernism, we'll find all the nasty whining greedy materialist youth we want: under postmodernism, hypercapitalism has become the new transcendental signifier, so inevitably we'll find that, indeed, many young people want either to be Julia Roberts or have her. The question is, though, why do "we" want to find them? I think it's far from sufficient to perpetually rediscover the cultural dominant, and far more urgent to lend our efforts to delineating emergences and alternatives. Similarly, it's inevitable but not sufficient for the James formation to have "discovered" liberalism in the prose by the historical James. Perhaps we do not need to work so hard at uncovering the logic of capital accumulation dominant in that prose or apologizing for it. We might instead reserve some of our energy for the task of learning how thoroughly the James formation has worked to erase the traces of other logics visible in that prose—emergencences and alternatives represented by the historical struggle of illiberal social movements such as revolutionary Marxism, trade unionism, artisanal utopianism, and radical separatisms (race nationalism, gendered communitarianism, ethnic antiassimilationism). It seems reasonable to expect to find traces of these struggles vibrant in the prose, and it is the work of cultural studies to render them legible, and make the James formation sufficient to the purposes of a different generation—and less inevitably complicit in their "failure."

## Notes

1. Bourdieu discusses the social construction of the relationship between what he describes as economic and educational capital within the dominant class in chapter 5, "The Sense of Distinction" (260–317). It is quite common in educational circles to assume, as Bourdieu argues in this chapter, that there is a "symmetrical" and "chiastic" structural distribution of economic and educational capital in the dominant class—that those with more wealth tend to enjoy proportionately less cultural capital, and vice versa, "whereby the first in one order are likely to be the last in another" (317). Regardless of the validity of this assertion, the staying power of this idea in academic circles testifies to a will to view cultural capital as exchangeable for wealth (though because cultural capi-

tal is believed in these circles as always "more important" than wealth, this putative equivalence is rarely tested). By contrast to this folk-academic view, Bourdieu recognizes the nonequivalence of cultural and economic capital ("they are unequally powerful in real terms") and describes those with high cultural capital as the "temporally dominated" fraction of the dominant class: the "inner-worldly" value of cultural capital "and their sense of 'mission,' are the true opium of the intellectuals" (316–17). While he recognizes that professional spending on the symbolic capital of luxury goods to enhance respectability represents one location where "the accumulation of economic capital merges with the accumulation of symbolic capital" (291), he argues that amongst intellectuals the acquisition of cultural capital tends toward "further such accumulation" rather than the accumulation of economic capital: teachers, for instance, become "systematically oriented" toward "the least expensive and most austere [high-cultural] leisure activities" (286).

2. This approach to the James adaptations responds in part to Sadoff's remarks on the increasing inutility of such terms as "middlebrow," which she terms "a problematic cultural category whose industry functions are unstable" (287). My view of the films as belonging quite identifiably to the popular culture of particular fractions of the dominant class is an attempt to start seeing the question of "popularization" as not primarily one of degree on a spectrum with a largely intellectual valence (i.e., highbrow, middlebrow, mass), but really one of many other specificities—so that when we say something is "popularized," we should also feel compelled to ask: popularized for whom, exactly?

3. At $13.7 million, the U.S. box office of *Wings* nearly quadrupled the domestic ticket revenue of *Portrait* ($3.7 million) and exceeded *Washington Square*'s $1.7 million by a multiple of seven. In the U.S., it was seen on as many as 700 screens, and remained in first release for five months (9 Nov. 1997 to 12 Apr. 1998) by comparison to *Portrait*'s U.S. run of less than two months (29 Dec. 1996 to 17 Feb. 1997). It enjoyed comparable success overseas ("Business Data"). There are other measures of a film's popularity, including other revenue, such as video and other subsidiary rights, but box office sales probably say most about a film's relationship to young adults.

4. Moviegoers in general tend to be better educated and younger than the population at large—so they are likely to have some college education or be preparing for it—but only one-fourth of men and women between the ages of 25 and 34 have actually earned a bachelor's degree (Mitchell 38–45).

5. It is possible to give the film's encounter with the Chagall painting a kind of reflexive Benjaminian reading. That is, the painting appears with its ritual value or aura seemingly intact by contrast to the degraded film form represented by the abject film actress in possession of it, so that the painting figures as having a special unmediated reality—that of "an orchid in the land of technology"— only paradoxically. Only through the pervasion of reality by the technologies of reproduction (such as cinema) does presentation of an unmediated reality become possible. Such a reading might go in several directions, the most useful of which would describe the relation between the actress's capitalized gesture

and the tactical abjections of the realist film form. Just as we can only understand the "real thing" of the painting by way of the film form that by confessing itself false installs its own reality, so does the actress's gesture of unconcern for the painting's worth testify to the primary reality of her sentiments. In the end, only the pervasion of her reality by capital makes it possible for her to declare a zone of sentiment unmediated by it. However, this reading seems to me to go rather a long way around to get to a materialist critical posture toward what is already an actively materialist circuit between the film and its spectatorship.

6. That is, I take the concept of "generation" to be a term deployed in large part by the baby boom to name and frame its developing historical relationship to other groups, by analogy to the Marxian emphasis on class as an active relation between groups in history, not a description of a group's essential nature. The marked lack of enthusiasm of Generation X and its successor ("Y") for deploying generational heuristics (preferring instead subcultural self-descriptions) strongly suggests a felt absence of agency in this relationship.

7. Following several observers, Ortner remarks that "today's 'middle class' is not aware of, or does not seem to recognize, the degree to which it was created by what would now be seen as 'government handouts'" (436 n. 11).

8. As when the *Boston Globe* book section led off its review of the "best fiction" of the season with the remark that 1997 had been "the year everyone pretended to like Henry James" by going to the movies "instead of trying to befriend the prose" (qtd. in Caldwell).

9. On the relationship between theory, ideology, popular culture and the "class politics of intelligibility" and on the language of "luminosity" as a description of the operation of ideology's power to represent itself as the nonideological real, see Zavarzadeh (1–29).

10. Even where the attack on Gen X consciousness is direct, as in Kinsley's assault on young people as "whiners" from the pulpit of the *New Republic,* it takes the form of insinuations regarding a notional leisure. Kinsley's "evidence" for "debunking the notion that x-ers are suffering compared with their predecessors" is the stray datum that 30 percent of teenagers own cars, up from 7 percent in 1968. The point connotes, exactly as Kinsley intends, a blithe "American Graffiti" affluence, of working- and middle-class kids tooling about the strip and getting laid. It's of course much more likely that his loose factoid simply reflects the transportation demand generated by the massive increase in the service sector's dependence on the flexible labor of suburban youth. Sure, young people own cars—how else would they get to work?

11. The "good economy" of the skyrocketing stock market of the past several years is not a good economy for most Americans, but only for the tiny fraction that owns those assets: $1/200^{th}$ of the population owns nearly 40 percent of the stocks and bonds and about 55 percent of all private business assets. In 1995, Rifkin calculated that if working people had profited from the "boom" to the same degree that management did, the average factory worker would then have earned $81,000 a year. In fact, the income of working people has steadily declined, from a take-home median of close to $400 a week in 1979 to more

like $300 today, with accompanying substantial losses in health coverage, job security, job satisfaction, leisure time, and workplace dignity. Young people account for an overwhelmingly disproportionate share of the loss in wages. Even though time to degree is growing longer and fewer people are succeeding in earning one, holders of college degrees also earn less: the real wages of all college-educated workers fell almost 1 percent annually between 1987 and 1991, or at a rate similar to the decline in wages of workers not holding a degree (Rifkin 168–74; Mitchell 92–93).

12. I am of course drawing heavily on Jameson's identification of postmodernism with the logic of a stage in capitalism (late, global, hypercapitalism) and his consequent sense of the postmodern as the "dominant cultural logic or hege-monic norm" against which alternatives have to struggle: "I am very far from feeling that all cultural production today is 'postmodern,'" he writes. "The postmodern is, however, the force field in which very different kinds of cultural impulses—what Raymond Williams has usefully termed 'residual' and 'emergent' forms of cultural production—must make their way" ("Postmodernism" 6).

13. Butler's piece is on the one hand a useful and spirited defense of the transfor-mative work of the new social movements, which she observes have been in some quarters unfairly characterized as preoccupied with the "merely cul-tural." On the other hand, the standpoint from which she constructs her de-fense quite intentionally conflates all of the diverse positions seeking to frame a materialism after poststructuralism (what she dubs "a more serious Marx-ism") with the then-recent popular-positivist hoax by physicist Alan Sokal. Fraser's reply to Butler describes the importance of developing a productive encounter between the politics of recognition and concerns for redistribution.

14. Or in Žižek's terms, "bypasses the circuitous route of meaning" (*Enjoy* 122).

15. Nadel's response to Campion's film wonderfully argues that the film evokes the liberal utopia of the college dorm and like the television show *Friends* "not only valorizes dormitory-cafeteria life but also promises it need not end with gradu-ation" ("Search" 183). I would only add that Nadel must be describing the coed college dorm of a quite specific era, the early 1970s. I think the primary reason that Nadel and I disagree about *Wings* has to do with different generational experiences of youth, leisure, and normative representations of college life. Contemporary college students are really quite a lot like Merton Densher and Kate Croy: that is, they work; have persistent anxieties about their material circumstances; they live in other people's homes, have sex surreptitiously, and so on. The equation of college experience (much less young adulthood gener-ally) with dorm life is both class-specific and ultimately nostalgic, yearning for some other college life than that experienced by students today.

16. For instance: "Fine as [Bonham Carter] was in 'Room With a View' and 'Howards End,' she taps into deeper regions here. Never, it seems, has she played for such high stakes, juggled such complexity, darkness, and immediacy" (Carr).

17. The script compresses and rearranges the dialogue closing the novel (*Wings of the Dove* 399–403).

18. Ortner's article is largely concerned with the phenomenon of upper-middle-

class "kids" who in her view don't have the same reasons for concern as work-ing-class youth yet nonetheless experience "terror" and indulge in "whining." ("Whining" is the term employed by conservative columnists in the mass media who urge Xers to shut up, get a job, and stop living on the parental dole.) Drawing on Bourdieu's and the Ehrenreichs' observation that the professional-managerial class doesn't pass on economic capital but only the means of repro-ducing itself, she argues that elite Gen X experience is largely the result of "the anxieties of upper-middle-class parents" (434) who "have been terrorized by the media" and are deploying their unprecedented material resources in a desperate effort to keep their children from "sliding down class." I strongly agree with Ortner's emphasis on viewing "generational" phenomena in connec-tion with class experience and share her conclusion that the Gen X structure of feeling responds to working-class consciousness. And I think that Ortner's piece explains in part why most members of the X cohort don't like to see themselves generationally—i.e., for the same reasons that most people avoid self-definition by class origin. But I think that she perhaps unwittingly exagger-ates the size of the youth elite class by conflating elites with college-educated knowledge workers. Specifically, her model of who counts as a member of the elite fraction needs to be revised. For instance, she identifies the graduate students in the audiences of her lectures as elite exemplars, the prototypical group of "kids [who have] nothing to worry about." And indeed, she appar-ently writes this article in specific response to the graduate students' angry "howls of pain" at her thesis, that their anxieties are only false consciousness produced by "the media." Naturally, I don't think that her sense that my anxi-eties are really my parents' anxieties helps much. Like most of my cohorts, I lived in actual economic exploitation as a graduate student and in other capaci-ties as a cultural worker until the age of thirty-five. Ortner's absurd paternal-ism—that we "kids" had "nothing to worry about" because eventually we would find employment presupposes the parental mind-frame she purports to be discovering (i.e, what these young people will become when they grow up), instead of listening to the actual proletarianization of youth knowledge work-ers. Ortner psychologizes decades of lived experience, and thereby obscures it. Even more troublingly, her (incorrect) assumption that graduate students belong to the children of the upper middle class and live on parental handouts describes a growing reality and ultimately helps to normalize a disturbing trend: what has not been true is becoming so, and under the present state of affairs, increasingly only elites will be able to enjoy postsecondary education. For a more accurate study of the class status of the graduate student and knowledge worker, see Aronowitz and DiFazio (173–201).

19. "A few months ago, I would not have been drawn to inscribe myself inside this discourse: Generation X remained a strange land. But today, after some trek-king on the job market, the neurotic symptoms associated with Genexers are not foreign anymore" (Delvaux 171).

*Works Cited*

Aronowitz, Stanley, and William DiFazio. *The Jobless Future: Sci-Tech and the Dogma of Work.* Minneapolis: U of Minnesota P, 1994.

Bourdieu, Pierre. *Distinction: A Social Critique of the Judgement of Taste.* Trans. Richard Nice. London: Routledge, 1986.

Butler, Judith. "Merely Cultural." *Social Text* 15 (Fall–Winter 1997): 265–77.

"Business Data." Pages for Campion, *Portrait of a Lady;* Holland, *Washington Square;* and Softley, *Wings of the Dove. The Internet Movie Database.* <http://usimdb.com/Business?0120481>, <http://usimdb.com/Business?0120520>, and <http://usimdb.com/Business?0117364>. Accessed 20 Dec. 1999.

Caldwell, Gail. "Season's Readings: Critic's Choice: The Year's Best Fiction." *Boston Globe* 7 Dec. 1997, Sunday city ed.: G1.

Carr, Jay. "*Wings* Is Made to Soar." *Boston Globe* 14 Nov. 1997: D1.

Delvaux, Martine. "The Exit of a Generation: The 'Whatever' Philosophy." *Midwest Quarterly* 40 (1999): 171–86.

Ebert, Teresa. *Ludic Feminism and After: Postmodernism, Desire, and Labor in Late Capitalism.* Ann Arbor: U of Michigan P, 1996.

Fraser, Nancy. "Heterosexism, Misrecognition, and Capitalism: A Response to Judith Butler." *Social Text* 15 (1997): 279–89.

Gilroy, Paul. *The Black Atlantic: Modernity and Double Consciousness.* Cambridge: Harvard UP, 1993.

Grossberg, Lawrence. *We Gotta Get Out of This Place: Popular Conservatism and Postmodern Culture.* New York: Routledge, 1992.

James, Henry. *The Wings of the Dove.* New York: Norton, 1978.

Jameson, Frederic. "Marx's Purloined Letter." *Ghostly Demarcations: A Symposium on Jacques Derrida's "Spectres of Marx."* Ed. Michael Sprinker. London: Verso, 1999. 26-67.

———. *Postmodernism, or the Cultural Logic of Late Capitalism.* Durham: Duke UP, 1992.

Kelsh, Deb. "Desire and Class: The Knowledge Industry in the Wake of Poststructuralism." *Cultural Logic: An Electronic Journal of Marxist Theory and Practice* 1.2 (1998). <http://eserver.org/clogic/1-2/1-2index.html>.

Kinsley, Michael. "Back from the Future." *Generations Apart: Xers vs. Boomers vs. the Elderly.* Ed. Richard D. Thau and Jay S. Heflin. Amherst, NY: Prometheus, 1997. 18–21.

MacManus, Susan A. "The Nation's Changing Age Profile: What Does It Mean?" *Generations Apart: Xers vs. Boomers vs. the Elderly.* Ed. Richard D. Thau and Jay S. Heflin. Amherst: Prometheus, 1997. 110–39.

Maguire, Tom. "Conflicting Signals." *American Demographics* Nov. 1998: 19–20.

Millar, Jeff. "Deeply Felt *Dove* Soars." *Houston Chronicle* 14 Nov. 1997: 4.

Mitchell, Susan. *Generation X: The Young Adult Market.* Ithaca: New Strategist, 1997.

Nadel, Alan. "Ambassadors from an Imaginary 'Elsewhere': Cinematic Convention and the Jamesian Sensibility." *Henry James Review* 19 (1998): 279–85.

———. "The Search for Cinematic Identity and a Good Man: Jane Campion's

Appropriation of James's *Portrait.*" *Henry James Review* 18 (1997): 180–83.

Ortner, Sherry B. "Generation X: Anthropology in a Media-Saturated World." *Cultural Anthropology* 13 (1998): 414–40.

Rifkin, Jeremy. *The End of Work: The Decline of the Global Labor Force and the Dawn of the Post-Market Era.* New York: Putnam, 1995.

Rhodes, Linda Colvin. "Listening to Generation X." *Washington Monthly* Nov. 1998: 34–35.

Salmon, Richard. "Henry James, Popular Culture, and Cultural Theory." *Henry James Review* 19 (1998): 211–18.

Sadoff, Dianne F. "'Intimate Disarray': The Henry James Movies." *Henry James Review* 19 (1998): 286–95.

Zavarzadeh, Mas'ud. *Seeing Films Politically.* SUNY Series in Radical Social and Political Theory. Albany: SUNY, 1991.

Žižek, Slavoj. *Enjoy Your Symptom! Jacques Lacan in Hollywood and Out.* New York: Routledge, 1992.

———. *The Ticklish Subject: The Absent Centre of Political Ontology.* London: Verso, 1999.

## Filmography

*Notting Hill.* Dir. Roger Michell. Writ. Richard Curtis. Perf. Hugh Grant and Julia Roberts, Universal Studios, 1999.

*The Portrait of A Lady.* Dir. Jane Campion. Writ. Laura Jones. Perf. Nicole Kidman and John Malkovich. Polygram, 1996.

*The Talented Mr. Ripley.* Dir. Anthony Minghella. Miramax Films, 1999.

*Under Heaven.* Dir. Meg Richman. Writ. Meg Richman. Perf. Molly Parker, Joely Richardson, Aden Young, 1998.

*Washington Square.* Dir. Agnieszka Holland. Writ. Carol Doyle. Perf. Jennifer Jason Leigh, Ben Chaplin, Albert Finney, Maggie Smith. Hollywood Pictures/Caravan Pictures, 1997.

*The Wings of the Dove.* Dir. Iain Softley. Writ. Hossein Amini. Perf. Helena Bonham Carter, Linus Roache, Alison Elliott. Miramax, 1997.

# Content or Costume?

## James as Cultural Capital

*Dale M. Bauer*

My question—content or costume?—emerges from the ritual use of Henry James to depict the intellectual, or even esoteric, content of "art." James has been used, first, as a sign of cultural literacy, signifying that an audience can recognize James, appreciate the reference, and thereby belong to a "common culture." Thus, James is part of the "quantity of knowledge" we call cultural literacy, one that confers a status and a belonging associated with being "well read" or with being cultured. And secondly, James is used as cultural capital whose marking typifies the even smaller body of readers who actually "get" James's style. In Henry James's fiction, the major trope of cultural capital is irony, a social awareness of class and education that marks inclusion in a special group of people who "get it." As John Guillory explains it, cultural capital is a symbolic value that registers social class distinctions; it is "knowledge-capital" that operates as a "mechanism of social exclusion" (viii-ix).

Some movies produce their own cultural capital, say, Jane Campion's *The Piano,* which signals the ironizing of male power; other movies "borrow" the cultural capital of traditional "high art" or literature in order to validate a contemporary vision of America, especially its stratified social classes. In such cases, Jamesian irony does no cultural work, but the name "Henry James" does. He seems more unpopular than ever in college classrooms and remains high on the list of universally scorned novelists, despite his status on the Modern Library 100 best novels list. Why should James do the dirty work of signaling good taste for a culture that so little values his books?

Are these films "faithful" to James, to the cultural capital that accrues when readers know how to negotiate his style? What would be required to capture James's style on film? Do the contemporary renderings of James on film invoke his capital in order to advance contemporary social interpretations and to highlight class distinctions that the filmmakers may not wish to forward explicitly? Then why use James, when his name signals to audiences a nearly inaccessible style and a refusal of mass culture? This essay will address what the James films mean in terms of our contemporary culture's attitude toward books and literacy, as well as what the adaptations of James's novels signify in our culture.

While it is not surprising that filmmakers neglect Jamesian nuances of motives or of class discriminations, it is telling how James is constructed, 100 years later, as an analyst of mores and intentions, albeit as the conservative arbiter of value. The value that James holds for filmgoers is often spectatorial rather than narrative in kind. In representing James, as Diane Sadoff argues in this volume, filmmakers count on James's devotees and middlebrow audiences to "exercis[e] the middlebrow spectatorial skills of pleased absorption and character identification." Jane Campion's *Portrait of a Lady* and Iain Softley's *Wings of the Dove* suggest how James's intellectual and social currency serves as an affectation of *style,* a gesture rather than substance. One way to disclose that Jamesian capital is to recognize the way irony is deployed in these films, wherein the audience knows the inside joke, shares that capital, and takes satisfaction from the chance to demonstrate it. Jamesian irony means the interpenetration of appearance and reality, so that the capacity to distinguish them is debilitated. But films can't always make this subtle distinction between perception and representation, so how they manage the ironic interplay is key.

Jamesian irony promotes either identification or distance—the former if one "gets" James's point, the latter, if the reader is excluded from it.[1] Irony, in general, constitutes what Lori Chamberlain calls the "political relationship between the user and the audience being addressed or excluded. Even while provoking laughter, irony invokes notions of hierarchy and subordination, judgment and perhaps even moral superiority. It is subversive" (29). Irony produces the ambivalence with which James tantalizes and satiates his readers, what John Rowe calls the "formula" in late James: "burlesque and satire identify the aspects of the modern to be rejected; irony becomes the modern style that will endure" (121). This style is part and parcel of Jamesian content. Given his style, why is "James" used to mediate contemporary dramas of failed heterosexual romances, as in *The Portrait of a Lady* and *Wings of the Dove* or even in the Julia Roberts–Hugh Grant popular film, *Notting Hill*? The romantic hit *Notting Hill* (1999) invokes Henry James, both directly and indirectly, only to dismiss both his content and his capital. *Notting Hill* replays James's international scene, with the rich and glamorous but unhappy American actress falling for the modest and contented, though lonely, British bookseller. In this film, the star Anna Scott (Julia Roberts) is attracted to a handsome, diffident single guy who runs a predictably unassuming travel bookstore. Their on-again, off-again romance creates the tension that propels the plot; *Notting Hill* preserves the prototypical Jamesian class struggle between the British genteel middle class and the American flamboyant Hollywood embodied in the film star Roberts plays. That point of view is especially apparent when Hugh Grant's character pokes fun at the actress's new script, a submarine thriller, while he helps her run through her lines. When she stumbles over some of the military language in the script, he assures her that, after all, the thriller is not Austen or Henry James. When she wins an Oscar for her role in the alien-clone *Helix,* she has enough box office capital to do a James film. That she does so encourages the boyfriend in the illusion that his movie-star girlfriend takes his taste seriously. She must rise to her ex-lover's level of taste, inscribed in *Notting Hill* as his penchant for fine travel books and elegant prose. We don't have to know anything about his taste; we just assume that he has it, as cultural capital, and the movie doesn't discomfit the audience by forcing the issue of whether we actually know James.

The reference to the James novel on which the new star-vehicle is based is never made more explicit or specific than the brief scene in which Roberts appears in costume. James the social analyst and critic of middle-class taste never appears. "James" is reduced to an English countryside, a costume drama that is meant to ensure the heroine's newfound seriousness as an actress. Henry James is "noise," a simulacrum of content; its reverberations are invoked, but are not purely present.

By contrast, the lines from Ralph Waldo Emerson that initiate and inform the romance plot of Brad Anderson's *Next Stop, Wonderland* (1998) represent cultural content rather than cultural literacy. The Emerson aphorism about "Consistency" and "little minds" brings the hero (a plumber by trade) and heroine (a nurse) together in *Next Stop, Wonderland.* Henry James is an allusion in *Notting Hill;* in *Next Stop, Wonderland,* Emerson is substance.

Anderson's film explicitly employs the ironic use of cultural capital. Unlike "James" in *Notting Hill,* Emerson is not merely social capital for a literate girl who meets her mate. Rather, the movie is predicated on the aptness of Emerson since his transcendental philosophy appropriately critiques contemporary mating rituals. The heroine of *Next Stop, Wonderland,* Erin (Hope Davis), struggles to find a serious guy to replace the radical Marxist (as her mother classes him), who has just left her to pursue social justice on Native American reservations. The vehicle for this search is a series of blind dates in which the men try to impress her with their intellectual range, especially with their cultural literacy. Each of them flubs the famous Emerson dictum from "Self Reliance," ascribing it in turn to Cicero, W.C. Fields, and Karl Marx. The heroine is then convinced of the futility of her search and the impossibility of finding a literate man, someone who might really be civilized or at least sincere. Their confusion presents a sort of crisis of cultural literacy. Literacy in *Next Stop, Wonderland* promises a meaningful intimacy; without it, there can only be meaningless sex. Thus, the irony of the film depends on literary knowledge; otherwise, the suitors' mistakes are unrevealing and unfunny.

That is, the film demonstrates rampant cultural sexual anxiety as a result of anti-intellectualism. Director Brad Anderson counts on the art house identification with the heroine's intellectual preference versus the pretense at literary sophistication that Erin's potential suitors deliver. At the same time, the hero Alan, struggling with a persistent younger female student who insists they are dating, must contend with *her* resistance to intellectual exchange. When finally he invites her on a whale-watching excursion, she seems reluctant but makes an E. D. Hirsch–like claim—"I've read *Moby Dick*." Which is to say that her reading is cultural literacy employed for seduction, not the serious reading—the cultural or intellectual capital—of the hero and heroine, who meet in the last minutes of the film. He wants to go on the whale watch; she wants sex, just as Erin's scamming suitors do.

The movie relies on the irony that *we* know Emerson—it is the most recognizable of his lines—and depends upon our sympathetic grasp of the heroine's frustration with shallow men and shallower readers. When she finally does meet the hero, a 35-year-old student/plumber hoping to be a marine biologist, he not only knows the origin of the quotation, but he even corrects her own slight misquoting. He explains that Emerson really wrote, "A *foolish* consistency is the hobgoblin of little minds." Or, if we too have misremembered (or never really knew it), we are gratified by his gentle correction. The viewers' recognition of Emerson constitutes their cultural capital. In short, you have to appreciate this kind of distinction among possible lovers; otherwise, the movie's joke comes at the viewers' expense since we would be no better off than Erin's dates or the *Moby Dick*–wielding seducer.

In general, irony is the master's trope, the trope of power of cultural capital over and against those who have no such intellectual resources or, at best, a list-like cultural literacy. Irony as master trope itself engages us in the class struggle that leads us to side with the cultural elite over and against the culturally "challenged," i.e., those who dismiss the relevance of cultural literacy. Granted, *Next Stop, Wonderland* employs the comic irony of the romance, while the James novels on film rely more on tragic irony. The difficulty of translating James is in his irony since it risks alienating audiences who are excluded from the insider's knowledge.

In particular, James's irony works through dramatic juxtaposition, often of the sublime with the horrible. For instance, in *Portrait of a Lady,* James shows the "requirements" of Isabel's imagination when she assumes Osmond's configuration: "Her mind was to be his—attached to his own like a small garden-plot to a deer-park" (*Portrait* 636). Isabel's abstract thinking about the heights she might reach plays off Osmond's image of her containment. James's irony is a celebration of the capabilities of imagination and the perversity of its limitations. Its "really grasping" faculty—its power—can also lead to its manipulation, its delusions (qtd. in Holland 72). That we are allowed to see how Osmond contains her faculties gives the ironic force to their back-and-forth volleys. The ironic tension emerges when we see his vision in conflict with hers eventually smothered by Osmond's analytical skill. "Expression and betrayal," as Lawrence Holland contends, is the form that James's irony takes (288). Jamesian irony shows the utopian possibilities of the human imagination only to have those imaginative opportunities limited by the schemes of others.

## Campion's Symbolic Portrait

Jane Campion's *Portrait* is not concerned overmuch—if at all—with portraying James as James, whatever James represents to a variety of audiences. Instead, he is part of her effort to win an audience, and even converts, to her vision of sexual awakening among young women in the twentieth century. James's 1881 novel happens to be the main prop of this depiction.

You don't have to get James's irony to get Campion's film (in fact, it might help Campion if you don't). From the first scenes, we are struck with Campion's obvious refusal to play Jamesian irony. Instead, she gives us a highly symbolic version of the novel and her representation of its emphasis on sexual repression.[2] Refusing to reproduce James literally, Campion inserts her own project—configuring women's depression and silence—into the narrative. Campion's version causes us to speculate about the limits of translating James's ironic realism into film, which Campion refuses to do.

Campion's earlier film, *The Piano,* was publically attacked for including "Too Much Ironic Symbolism," a dismissal that Barbara Johnson argues is an attempt to celebrate rather than lament the heroine's muteness. In "Muteness Envy," Johnson counteracts this critical dismissal by showing how Campion ironizes the heroine Ada's silence (129–53). In another context, Johnson argues that the Western tradition seeks to "maternalize, terrorize, and sexualize the female body so that heterosexual monogamy is a woman's safest life choice" (173). But Campion rejects the possibility of such an audience preference for safety. Ada's marriage puts her in danger, thereby making her adultery all the more attractive. The film also rejects the patriarchal exchange of women between men that characterizes marriage: Ada makes her own arrangements—from the sexual exchange to untangling herself from the sinking piano.

As in *The Piano,* so in *Portrait:* Campion's goal is to combat the institutional silencing of women, and she returns to ironic symbolism to portray *her* James. In this case, Campion makes much of Isabel's silent grief. One of the most compelling scenes in Campion's film struck me as doing justice to a generally unremarked but poignant, though cryptic, moment in James's novel: Isabel's grief over the death of her infant son. Campion has Isabel (Nicole Kidman) fondle a casting of the baby's hand (the only one of Osmond's castings or reproductions that seems to serve a purpose), in a room as dimly lit as the scenes of Osmond's quarters in Florence, then Rome. Like everything else in Osmond's world, the baby too is copied, reproduced in something less ephemeral than human flesh. Given Osmond's penchant for copying, we can only surmise that he had the plaster cast made in the first place. As James himself writes, Osmond has "the hand of the master." (Or did Isabel order the cast, adopting early in the marriage her husband's habits and avocation?) Another hand—a much larger casting or sculpture—plays in a later scene: when Madame Merle and Isabel are wandering through a sculpture garden where they will have the momentous conversation in which Merle's treachery is revealed. Behind them is an oversized hand with one of the fingers pointed upward. There is something here, too, about the dead male child, metonymically reproduced and repeated—and prefigured, albeit much larger in these statues. These larger pieces overshadow the smaller plaster hand Isabel had caressed; they seem to represent the "feel" of Osmond's misogynistic threat, his control, his snuffing out her "too many ideas." There is visual tension between the small hand she can touch and grieve over and the larger fragments, copies, reproductions which seem all rather portentously to symbolize Osmond's menace.

Curiously, James devotes but two sentences to the death of Isabel's son: "She had lost her child; that was a sorrow, but it was a sorrow she scarcely spoke of; there was more to say about it than she could say to Ralph. It belonged to the past, moreover; it had occurred six months before, and she had already laid aside the tokens of mourning" (330). For James, Isabel's sorrow is borne in silence, without tokens of mourning. For Campion, on the contrary, Isabel's grief is linked to the symbol she caresses. Moreover, that grief is connected to the visual image of Isabel's private moment of mourning to the exchange when Merle intimates to Isabel her connection to Osmond. The image of the hand figures in less subtle ways, too: the male hands running over Isabel's breasts in the erotic fantasy sequence;

Goodwood's fingers, which caress Isabel's face; her own, which later trace his caress and which prefigure the erotic fantasy on her bed.

Why is the hand, or the touch, such a powerful symbol in Campion's film (besides the fact that it takes a little too literally the *Touchetts'* influence upon Isabel's life)? In running away from Goodwood's touch, as she does in the last scene in the film, Isabel reminds us that she associates touch with despair and grief—and also control. Of course, Osmond is everywhere associated with hands and touch, but of the more malicious kind. Campion's camera lingers on Osmond's hand as it is wrapped around Pansy's waist, almost touching his young daughter's breast. Campion hints at veiled incest here, and Osmond's insistence on his daughter's absolute obedience gives credence to the film's presentation of Osmond's utter malevolence. (For me, this is one of the problems of the film: there is little sense of Osmond's seductiveness, the attractions of his taste; Malkovich is certainly menacing enough, but perhaps too overwhelmingly *only* an evil figure. Campion's film doesn't make it clear why Osmond attracts Isabel, or why his taste alone would suffice to fulfill the "requirements of her imagination.") Perhaps Campion is continuing what she started in *The Piano*: she claims that the earlier film represents her first attempt to "writ[e] characters who don't have a twentieth-century sensibility about sex. They have nothing to prepare themselves for its strength and power" (qtd. in Johnson 144).

In one way or another, the film is less about repressed sexuality and more about failed reproductions. Much has been made of Campion's focus on female anxieties over sexuality, but it is the value of reproductions that I find at the crux of Campion's film: Osmond's obsession with copies, Isabel's interest in originals and in her own belief in self-reproduction, Ralph's investment in what Isabel "will make of herself." Campion represents reproduction through the visual symbols of plaster casts or, more symbolically, with the doll (its head covered in wrapping paper) that Madame Merle brings to Pansy in the convent; Madame Merle herself is the mother-surrogate for her own biological child, the failed reproduction that inaugurates the trauma of lost children and motherhood. The film also includes mechanical reproductions, such as we get in the newsreel version of Isabel's world travels. All of the represented "children"—Ralph, Pansy, even the dead baby boy's hand—turn out unfulfilled, empty, life-forms without function or continuance. Osmond endlessly copies, but Merle points out that his current copies are less interesting than his previous ones: he, too, can no longer reproduce well. Whatever we might think of Campion's symbols, her choice highlights the idea that reproducing is always dangerous, sometimes tragic—sometimes boring?

So, too, in reinterpreting Jamesian classics: Campion's emphasis on the difficulty of reproduction is a metacommentary on her "reproducing" the James novel. Ultimately, hers is no faithful copy. Campion sheds a feminist light on the Jamesian text insofar as she addresses her own darker vision of women's roles. The opening sequence in which young contemporary women offer comments and meet the camera's eye signals Campion's take on James: she refuses to play Isabel to Henry James's Osmond. Campion plays her own hand in refiguring James's mastery. Campion's symbols replace James's irony for her own trope: the metaphoric substitution of Isabel's desires.

### Wings of the Dove

While Campion stamps her signature on James, refusing to let his storytelling master hers, Softley's narrative is the more Jamesian. As Philip Horne argues about *Wings of the Dove* in "The James Gang," "to bohemianise and sex up the milieu—this Kate can kittenishly curl up on Densher's bed—is to lower the pressure of the novel's bottled-up sexual passion. Nevertheless, a daringly painful final scene of 'explicit' loveless sex unexpectedly captures, at the very last minute, some of the moral force of the original" (19).[3] Inevitably, the explicitness of Softley's and Campion's films must betray James's sexual subtlety. Even while sensationalizing James, Softley's "use" of him is less in competition with the Master than in concert.

Although it makes as many interpretive choices of its own as Campion's film does, *Wings of the Dove* delivers Jamesian content, along with the experience of the complex act of reading and identification that James demands in his late masterpieces and that he had been working out since *Portrait*. Perhaps it is Softley's willingness to confront James's major phase that makes me want to sympathize with his vision, since the major phase is so notoriously difficult, even if his unironic filmic reading of Milly's death and memory is disturbing. In keeping with Edgar Allan Poe's prescription for lyric poetry—the death of a beautiful woman as the most appropriate subject—the ending leads to a veneration of Milly's death, not an appreciation of its Jamesian irony. In the last scene, Merton Densher memorializes Milly to the extent that he leaves London and returns to Venice so that he can carry out what he promised to her: go to the places they'd been together. Yet Densher's return to Venice makes sense only if we take it on Softley's sentimental terms—even Poe had more irony than this.[4] By contrast, James's irony inheres in Milly's "turning her face to the wall" as the peculiarly American habit of allowing dead women power.

In the novel, Milly is more clearly manipulative than Softley's vision can encompass, since the novel shows her to orchestrate from the grave the end of Kate and Merton's affair. On the contrary, the film shows her to be an innocent girl falling in love, too dense to notice the passion between Kate and Merton. In the film, Lord Mark falls in love with Kate, and in the middle of one drunken night, tells her so as he caresses her in her bed. Disgusted, Kate sends him away and goes then to Milly's room and her bed, claiming it's too cold in the other. By making Milly too sympathetic, even guileless, Softley attenuates James's most pointed twists of our complicity with James's schemers: Kate, then Densher, finally Milly. In this scheme, Kate is left powerless since Softley honors the romantic tradition and ends the film with the commemoration of the dead woman's transcendence. Thus, Densher is more sympathetic, Kate infinitely less so, than in James's novel. Though it dwells on her brooding beauty, the film hates Kate. (The novel doesn't hate her, even if James hates Milly's illness and all that it represents: vulnerability, a barrier, the failure of intimacy. Even so, James the novelist transforms illness into a strength and a possibility.) Our identification with Milly in *Wings* is Softley's setup: she's the least ironic of the characters.

Actually, the simplifying of Milly's character is Softley's bargain with sin. He has to make Milly a naif in order to underscore the desperate treachery of Kate and Densher. That underscoring also means the rendering of their sexuality as a display. What is concealed throughout Henry James's novel is the life of passion he envied the French novelists' tradition of representing; here, Softley makes that passion present, a display that is thematized throughout the film.

In this sexual display, we are given the key subtext of Kate's and Merton's erotics: sexual spectacle. One singular addition is the scene where Merton kisses his older date to make Kate jealous; he has arranged this date to be able to follow Kate to Lord Mark's party since Aunt Maud has successfully separated the lovers for months. Both are especially aroused by sex in public, whether in the rain at the park or in the Venice streets after the Carnival. Their more traditional lovemaking—without social or sexual tension—leaves them spectacularly unsatisfied. Thus, it is the furtiveness that fuels their plot against Milly. In this first party scene, along with the up-against-the-wall sex, the chance of getting caught stimulates them, just as it has in the film's opening scene of their tryst at the underground station. Once they are caught, or once Milly's letter catches up with them, they are spent, all sexual intensity gone out of them.

In another interpretive move, Softley gives us the spectacle that James doesn't: the narration of the sexual commerce that Merton Densher demands of Kate. James leaves the crucial scene of their first sexual commitment offstage, since for Merton, once Kate agrees, "he felt, ever so distinctly

. . . that he was already in a sense possessed of what he wanted" (295). How would one depict Densher's premature self-congratulation? Instead, Softley illustrates their sexual connection as an act of the streets, somehow suggesting its vulgarity, its spectacle of publicity.

The last scene, however, stands in stark contrast to their hurried street sex in the emotional exhilaration after the Carnival.[5] In this light, the most graphic scene occurs after Milly's death, when Kate undresses in Densher's rooms and the lovers end up in bed. The whole balance of power has shifted away from Densher and his earlier playfully menacing proposition to Kate, "What if I didn't let you leave tonight?" Kate now controls the scene: not withholding sex, but offering herself as a way to bridge the psychic gap between them. In fact, Kate's nudity is a reminder of their cunning rather than their sensuality. Her undressing comes as a shock of banality, perhaps not to Merton but to the audience, rather than the shock of her un-Jamesian straightforwardness.

Something dysfunctional happens: Merton and Kate are distracted from their pleasure, and they both lie drained and despondent—in tears throughout the whole act. At that point, Kate asks Merton "on his honor" to forswear his love of Milly's memory. He can't, and they know that Milly's memory will come between them. Softley's irony of failed romance plays against Jamesian irony even as it pays inverted homage to Jamesian motives and their backfiring.

That is, Softley's filling in of Jamesian ambiguity lends him Jamesian capital insofar as he interprets the master's sexual suggestiveness. One of his interpretive choices, however, is out of synch with Softley's emphasis on sexual repression. While James doesn't name the father's disgrace, except to suggest how deeply Kate is affected by it, Softley does: an opium addiction, replete with Oriental exoticism—Asian men and women populating the scene of his abandon, adds concreteness to James's ambiguity. Instead of making Lionel Croy's dishonor the source of Kate's vague "family feeling," the film gives her a much more economic, less sentimental motive to try to marry for money—or to marry Merton off for Milly's money. Like Isabel's vivid grief over the dead son in *Portrait*, Kate's father's opium addiction is her reason for casting her lot with Aunt Maud. Her father needs the money to survive; in the novel, Kate's father casts her off, thereby leaving her free to decide on her own. Yet the movie shows the father's indebtedness to the shillings that Aunt Maud sends him weekly to sustain himself and his habit. So Kate's motivation in the film turns on some filial feeling rather than her own aversion to working-class or middle-class drudgery that the novel intimates.

So why present the father's crime *as* addiction? What if Lionel Croy's violation were some sort of sexual or domestic abuse? Or father-son incest, given James's dispatching of the unsettled, restless sons? Dead sons, as in *Portrait*, seem to trigger for James all the family trauma that precipitates the daughter's resistance, both Isabel's and Kate's. Unlike Campion's *Portrait*, Softley's *Wings* doesn't mention the dead sons. In this, Softley follows James's lead: "the dishonour her father had brought them, his folly and cruelty and wickedness" led to the failure of the family, along with the deaths of her two brothers (*Wings* 55), one by typhoid fever and the other by drowning while swimming. It's an odd, but appropriate detail—of long buried mourning and melancholia undergirding the entire Croy family's moroseness and neuroses.

Or is it to suggest, as Softley's film does, that Kate inherits her father's moral abandon? Her father tells her, "We're the same, you and I," unwilling to live in squalor, even for love. As Densher asks, "'What has he done, if no one can name it?'" Kate replies, "'He has done everything'" (57). What if Softley had represented Lionel's "crime" as homosexuality, in a conjecture that follows Eve Sedgwick's and Wendy Graham's analysis of homosexual panic in the novel?[6] In that case, Kate's scheming to marry might have seemed a repudiation of her father's homosexual "tendencies"; moreover, her relationship with Milly would have resounded with its own lesbian possibilities—a potential that resonates when Kate joins Milly in bed after Kate rebuffs Lord Mark's drunken advances. In the opium den, Lionel Croy lies with a young woman, thereby negating any association of his addiction with homosexuality.

Or is hers an addictive personality of its own? In large part, the scenes between father and daughter support the sources of Kate's motivation. While Kate is shown as loyal, even self-sacrificing for her father's sake, her addiction is to the luxury that her Aunt Maud provides and that Kate's sumptuous costumes symbolize. Her father refuses to allow her to pretend innocence of his failures, her mother's, or Kate's own. Softley presents Kate as determined to avoid squalor—of her father's or Densher's making. While Milly confesses to Densher that she believes in him, that his moment will come (or she will make it come), Kate has no such faith in his ability to rise in his career and do more than merely support her.

Softley proves to master James by representing the Master's ambiguity and complexity, even as the medium demands the kind of explicit choices Softley makes: opium addiction, Kate as villain, explicit sexuality. By contrast to Campion, Softley's rendering is more Jamesian insofar as he relies on filling in James's gaps rather than creating his own. What distinguishes them is the difference between mastering James and surpassing him. He interprets Jamesian silence as explicit eroticism, sexual shame, while re-

maining true to Jamesian cultural capital in showing the ironic sexual failure of Kate's plan to get Milly's money.

That shades of Emerson ("Consistency . . ."), Poe (the death of a beautiful
woman), Melville ("I read *Moby Dick*"), and James figure in recent films is
ironic indeed. While audiences might recognize James's name or his historical "style," they might not be aware of Jamesian content. What happens
to viewers when we "consume" the simulacrum—not the substance—of the
cultural capital that James represents?

Yet to readers attuned to these differences, to irony itself, a proper
quotation can equal a proper romance, thus reinscribing the "proper" in
what we mean by intellectual property. That the "proper," the idea for the
propriety, in James's narratives is important to his characters' motivations is
the irony that Campion and Softley both miss. They must miss it: otherwise, they risk losing the middlebrow audience that wants all the virtues of
such cultural capital without its exclusive politics. I imagine that this dilemma leaves us in an ironic position anyway: to be included in the circle
that "gets it," but also to exclude everyone else. How can a filmmaker be
simultaneously expansive and exclusive? This is where invoking James as
cultural capital gets tricky, for it means walking the line between incorporating and excluding an audience at the same time.

For an audience attuned to James's irony, his ambiguity, his tensions,
part of the pleasure in watching James on film is seeing what gets lost in the
translation. *Next Stop, Wonderland* presents the politically incorrect dilemma
of being an "insider": the suitors who do not know Emerson are haplessly
funny, while the two "insiders" who do know their Emerson are romanti-
cally attractive. In preserving Jamesian capital, we perpetuate a Hirsch-like
hierarchicalizing of cultural literacy even as we recognize its exclusionary
politics. We like such acculturation, except we want it without the responsibilities of its political weight, its obvious wielding of mastery. Should we
learn to embrace the "James" of *Notting Hill* as more accessible capital than
the more obscure Jamesian quality in Softley or Campion? And does this
mean undoing a middlebrow investment in cultural capital itself? As professional readers of James, both in print and on film, the gap between one
sort of capital and another becomes harder to deny and despite the best
intentions of Campion and Softley, even harder to bridge.

As you can see, I want all the pleasures of James's irony—recognition
of his ambiguity, depth, even seeing *The Ambassadors* in *The Talented Mr.
Ripley,* but more of the responsibilities, the moral complicity. I want to be
the heroine in *Next Stop, Wonderland* but not the snob appeal of being "in"
on the joke. Being a Jamesian "insider" but not an "excluder"—which is

hard because these films and their reception show that James is not for everyone, else why pride myself on my cultural capital and being able to spin off an essay on getting irony and, more important, how it works.

## Notes

I want to thank Sarah Edgington, my research assistant at the University of Wisconsin–Madison, and Ann Beebe, my research associate at the University of Kentucky.
1. In Booth's terms, "Irony is always thus in part a device for excluding as well as for including, and those who are included, those who happen to have the necessary information to grasp the irony, cannot but derive at least part of their pleasure from a sense that others are excluded" (304). Irony generates "collusion" between author and reader.
2. What would James's novel look like on screen had Merchant Ivory produced it? First, the movie would have been brighter, less ominous, than Campion's. Certainly, the casting would have been different. Perhaps the ubiquitous Helena Bonham Carter would have been Isabel, Helen Mirren or Anjelica Huston cast as Madame Merle, maybe even Ralph Fiennes as Osmond, or Daniel Day-Lewis as Ralph. I suspect that Merchant Ivory would have made a version of the movie as a tragedy of manners hinging on psychological realism.
3. As Horne does, Rowe also remarks upon the sexualization of James: "All of these films [the recent productions of James] bring to the surface erotic subtexts in James's fiction, even when these postmodern interpretations reach beyond the logic of James's text, in which sexual *secrecy* is crucial to social power" (196).
4. As Johnson argues generally, "Is it possible for a woman to have authority only on the condition that she be dead?"
5. Ann Beebe's reading of this scene in particular, as well as of the movie in general, informs this essay.
6. Graham explains the substitution of opium-addiction for "same-sex desire" as a botching of the complexity of James's "erotic tensions," especially among the women of James's novel (243).

## Works Cited

Booth, Wayne. *The Rhetoric of Fiction*. Chicago: U of Chicago P, 1961.
Chamberlain, Lori. "Bombs and Other Exciting Devices; Or, the Problem of Teaching Irony." *College English* 51 (1989): 29–40.
Graham, Wendy, *Henry James's Thwarted Love*. Stanford: Stanford UP, 1999.
Guillory, John. *Cultural Capital: The Problem of Literary Canon Formation*. Chicago: U of Chicago P, 1993.
Holland, Laurence. *The Expense of Vision*. Princeton: Princeton UP, 1964.
Horne, Philip. "The James Gang." *Sight and Sound* 8.1 (1998): 16–19.
James, Henry. *The Portrait of a Lady*. In *Henry James: Novels 1881–1886*. Ed. William T. Stafford. New York: Viking, 1985. 191–800.

————. *The Wings of the Dove.* Ed. J. Donald Crowley and Richard A. Hocks. New York: Norton, 1978.

Johnson, Barbara. *The Feminist Difference: Literature, Psychoanalysis, Race, and Gender.* Cambridge: Harvard UP, 1998.

Rowe, John Carlos. *The Other Henry James.* Durham: Duke UP, 1998.

Sedgwick, Eve. *Tendencies.* Durham: Duke UP, 1993

## Filmography

*Next Stop, Wonderland.* Dir. Brad Anderson. Writ. Brad Anderson and Lyn Vaus. Perf. Hope Davis and Alan Gelfant. Miramax, 1997.

*Notting Hill.* Dir. Roger Michell. Writ. Richard Curtis. Perf. Hugh Grant and Julia Roberts. Universal, 1999.

*The Portrait of a Lady.* Dir. Jane Campion. Writ. Laura Jones. Perf. Nicole Kidman and John Malkovich. PolyGram, 1996.

*The Piano.* Dir. Jane Campion. Writ. Jane Campion. Perf. Holly Hunter, Harvey Keitel, Sam Neill. Miramax, 1993.

*The Wings of the Dove.* Dir. Iain Softley. Writ. Hossein Amini. Perf. Helena Bonham Carter, Linus Roache, Alison Elliott. Miramax, 1997.

# "Hallucinations of Intimacy"

## The Henry James Films

*Dianne F. Sadoff*

> Popular culture does not . . . attempt to reproduce the
> psychological depth and density of texture of a novel by
> Henry James (for which we should all be truly grateful). . . .
> [The] complexity of "high" art is used first to establish its
> aesthetic superiority to "low," or obvious, art, and then to
> naturalize . . . superior taste. . . . Artistic complexity is a class
> distinction: [it] excludes the masses.
>
> John Fiske

> Academic high culture . . . constantly defines itself against the
> suspect pleasures of the middlebrow.
>
> Janice Radway

> I just didn't think [*The Piano*] would be nearly that popular. I
> thought it would be an art movie somewhere. Don't get me
> wrong, there's a part of me that wants to be popular too.
>
> Jane Campion

Not all filmmakers and critics agree with John Fiske's assessment of Henry
James's impossible—and unpalatable—availability for popularization. Nevertheless, moviegoers have recently rejected two James films as popular
cultural texts. While *The Wings of the Dove* crossed over from art house to
mainstream distribution, *Portrait of a Lady* and *Washington Square* did not.
Indeed, *Wings* garnered three academy award nominations, after which it
opened nationally in multiplex theaters, and is the last of the three to be
distributed on video; *Portrait* and *Washington Square,* on the contrary, opened
briefly in "selected cities," according to ads in the *New York Times,* played for

several weeks in university towns and large cities, disappeared, and went immediately to video. Reviews for the three films helped fuel modest success or induce failure. Not the reviews, however, but the films' uneasy position in a segmented industry accounts for their problematic reception. The audience for films of Henry James's novels, like the readership of the novels themselves, has never been a mass one.

Indeed, mass culture industries, Fiske says, seek to "appropriate" the people's culture even as the people "expropriate" the products of the industries. Despite Fiske's sentimental concept of cultural consumers, he is clearly correct that "while popular culture is never mass culture, it is always closely bound up with it" ("Popular" 331). The growth and diversification in the book and periodical industries in the late nineteenth century made fiction available for mass cultural production and for popularity. Yet given the demographic and appetitive diversity of the late-nineteenth-century audience for books and the late twentieth for films, and given the segmentation in both historical periods of the book and film industries, popular or "lowbrow" culture has now virtually eclipsed "highbrow" culture. While James's novels have entered the canon of high modern, elite culture, the films' status within a segregated culture industry might more appropriately be characterized as "middlebrow," a problematic cultural category whose industry functions are unstable and whose institutions diversifying. The failure of the Henry James movies is thus overdetermined. In a matrix of cultural forces, the questions of industry segmentation, commodity culture, and the rage for popularity converge to create two box office flops and one moderate success.

Yet Henry James craved popularity even as he despised—and despaired of achieving—it. James anxiously hoped to reach a mass audience even as he suspected its "vulgarity"; he craved "publicity" in the "public market of magazines, bookstores, and libraries" yet modeled "discretion" in his interactions with publishers; he manipulated his status as a transatlantic author in order to publish his tales simultaneously in British and American periodicals and then, again, to control copyright through the timing of book publication. Knowing his books a commodity, he recommended to other artists that they produce "vendible [and] *placeable*" artistic objects. Indeed, James was destined "to affront a publicity" he had the "weakness to loathe" (Anesko ix, 5, 11; Salmon 2–13). Nevertheless, Edith Wharton suspected that James had "secretly dreamed of being a 'best-seller'" (191). When *The Bostonians* and *The Princess Casamassima* flopped, he bemoaned to his friend, William Dean Howells, that after the promising receptions of *Daisy Miller* and *Portrait,* the two new novels had "reduced the desire, and the demand, for my productions to zero—as I judge from the fact that though I have for a good while past been writing a number of good short things, I remain irremediably unpublished" (*Henry James Letters* 209). In the face of his apparent eclipse, James acted like a modern professional writer dependent on publication for his income: he tried to increase his sales by hiring a newly created cultural intermediary, an agent, and sought the buzz and applause of live audiences in the theater—an endeavor at which he failed spectacularly (Anesko 127–30). In the face of the "devouring *publicity* of life," James bemoaned that, for the modern author, both personal life and professional work were objects available for public scrutiny and consumption (*Notebooks* 82; Salmon 78–79).

Yet James's struggle with the problem of publicity, or mass versus elite culture, was not his individual authorial problem. Historically situated at the moment when professional discourse was consolidating and mass culture emerging, when the book business was diversifying and the author emerging as a modern business man, when the institutionalization and "sacralization" of culture had begun to elevate once simultaneously popular and elite cultural forms (such as opera), James had to invent himself as author and in relation to his readership in a manner without historical and cultural precedent (Strychacz 5–22; Levine 83–168). Given his profound ambivalence about commodified culture and the "vulgarized" market for novels, James sought, in *The Art of the Novel,* to educate a "general reader." Indeed, in the late nineteenth and early twentieth centuries, such a reader— an intelligent, well-educated reader seeking absorption, pleasure, and intellectual stimulation—was being fashioned by the book-selling industry. The significant growth in commercial publishing, Janice Radway maintains, occurred when "changes in manufacturing" and in the "organization of the market economy were consolidated" and when, in addition, "complex technologies and new transportation methods" enabled extension of markets and commercial enterprises. After the advent of railroads and the development of machine-driven print technologies, cheap book production and information dissemination fueled the rise of newspapers, the emergence of the "employee-author," the "proactive editor," and a "book readers could use." As Radway demonstrates, new definitions of book, author, and reader challenged notions of intellectual property and the functions of cultural work. Institutions such as the Book-of-the-Month Club began to sell the "literary book" and to serve an educated generalist readership, Radway says, even as modern literary criticism developed to police and consolidate a "new high literary zone" (129–42). Although Henry James's novels and tales entered the latter category, as author he sought to serve the needs of the former.

The recent Henry James films are aimed at this middlebrow audience, at the "general" yet intelligent cultural consumer. All sought, in addition, to become popular art films. While films made for discriminating audiences of educated, often urban, consumers do not make "big money" according to film historians, independent filmmakers can recover their costs and make modest profits, even as they experiment with noncommercial products, through art house distribution (Sklar 293–95). The James novels seem tailored for this market niche. Full of eroticized perversity, innocent female victimage, and familial or marital distress, the stories seem culturally and historically transportable—as relevant to and usable by late-twentieth-century as late-nineteenth-century audiences. Whereas James's reader's desires are aroused by the texts' highly nuanced and psychologically complex narratorial situations, the films' spectator's desires get gratified by mise-en-scène and montage, by visualized scenes of masculine abuse, female ruination and spoliation. In the decade of feel-good art-house blockbusters, however, even the educated cultural consumer might (and did) choose the upbeat, post-Thatcherite *The Full Monty* over the ironic and only slightly perverse *Washington Square*. The art house filmgoer, once member of a specialized but highly coherent audience, now has a range of options as consumer. As the "independent-supplier" segment of the industry—in video and cinema—seeks to "adapt to shifting retailer buying patterns," the "higher-profile" art film must compete not only with A-list films but with B-movie titles, big box-office foreign films, and other genre titles (Wilson 1, 8). With a variety of products now available for a once-coherent market niche, competition for the cultural dollar of the intelligent generalist has intensified.

The social function of middlebrow culture has likewise become complex as print culture declines and visual culture expands its market position. Indeed, the hierarchy of the arts ranks cultural consumers, as Pierre Bourdieu has taught scholars of popular culture. Selecting a high-cultural text for consumption displays the buyer's taste and social position, confers prestige and distinction on the self-displaying cultured individual. A middlebrow text displays the middle-class longing to prefer legitimate cultural objects, a preference shared by authentically acculturated persons. The distinction conferred on high-culture consumers, no less in the United States than in Bourdieu's France (though in a different manner), confirms the status of the family of origin, is consolidated by the schools, and serves to consolidate and elaborate the social order (1–17). As my epigraph from Radway indicates, however, middlebrow cultural pleasures, when ranked against high culture's aesthetic, are by definition suspect. Whereas the consumer of high culture practices the skills of aesthetic self-distancing and detachment from the characters and events of a text and whereas the consumer of popular culture seeks material that she finds usable and then discardable, the consumer of middlebrow culture paradoxically seeks to be connected to expertise, learning, and culture even as she desires to experience the pleasures of attentive absorption. If the cultural text chosen is narrative—whether book or film—the middlebrow consumer enjoys identifying with the character(s), indulging a taste for romance, and taking pleasure in the process of consuming. The middlebrow cultural consumer, then, exercises her taste and displays her expertise when she selects a legitimate work of art, yet her choice is only possible because the art has been widely consumed by others and so popularized (323–28).

This is the cultural problem the James films address even as they seek to allay the anxieties such contradictions create. For the film adaptations of classic novels or dramas now crowding the cultural marketplace serve much as did the popularized classics peddled by the Book-of-the-Month Club in the 1950s: they nurture "middle-class longings for the prestige conferred by familiarity with high culture," as Radway maintains of middlebrow books; they create around the consumer the "aura of art" and confirm the "status of the cultured self." Like the readers of the Book-of-the-Month Club selections, the consumers of the James films may present themselves as "educated individuals" by showing that they know—or seem to know—the classics (321): the 1990s viewer of *The Portrait of a Lady, Washington Square,* or *The Wings of the Dove* need not have read the books.

The 1990s James movies, moreover, portray the middlebrow culture consumer's dilemma. James's narrator entices the reader into a high-cultural milieu, the emergent modern world of dysfunctional marriages and aristocratic or haute-bourgeois cosmopolitanism. Ralph Touchett is perhaps the perfect "cosmopolite"—he's "a little of everything and not much of any," Henrietta Stackpole slyly observes—, and Mrs. Touchett is the perfect "American absentee," the "amiable colonist" of Florentine and Parisian metropolitan cultures (*Portrait of a Lady* [PL] 81–82, 183). Indeed, cosmopolitanism and acculturation are intimately linked in these novels, for each portrays an American girl, fresh from provincial Albany or New York, who is wooed by an authentically or inauthentically acculturated cosmopolitan, European, or Europeanized man. While the American girl's marital choice may thus earn her the distinction and prestige of a highly cultured cosmopolitan husband, her destiny is sealed by her inability to distinguish the hanger-on expatriate from the legitimately cultured man—or by her refusal to care for the difference, through her national naivete. Isabel Archer's rejection of Lord Warburton's marriage proposal horrifies her uncle and fascinates Ralph Touchett; Catherine Sloper's European tour doubles her value on the marriage market despite her desire to wed a man with "luxurious tastes and scanty resources" (*Washington Square* [WS] 151). Although Milly

Theale's accidental and equivocal escape from the marital clutches of Kate Croy and Merton Densher produces the transcendent aura at which acculturation aims, the dove must die, leaving her memory to haunt and incapacitate Merton for marriage to Kate.

The American girl in metropolitan Europe thus stands in for the middlebrow cultural consumer, who seeks knowledge and expertise, learning and culture, but may not know authentic from inauthentic acculturation. She wants, with Isabel, desperately to "know something of human affairs"; with Catherine, to tour but not like Aunt Lavinia, to perversely and comically display her tourism to others; with Milly, to sate her starvation for culture, to spend the "unused margin" of her American spontaneity at the National Gallery—and so to become an acculturated woman herself, capable of receiving impulses and impressions, becoming acquainted with the classics, and so acquire cultural distinction (*PL* 143; *Wings of the Dove* [*WD*] 125, 244). Indeed, these films solicit a female spectator. "Have you called me here to look at you?" Morris asks Catherine testily. "I did want to look at you," she confesses; "you're beautiful." The spectator, too, looks at this gorgeous man, hoping, with her, that he wants not her fortune but her love. James's male protagonists appeal to book-readers, Hollywood seems to say, but only the American girl appeals to the middlebrow cultural consumer. Purchasing a ticket to *Portrait, Wings,* or *Washington Square,* the spectator buys appropriations of European culture that portray acculturation as a (marital and surplus) value, but only for females.

Still, nothing could be less middlebrow than James's highly nuanced narratorial situations. The directors of *Portrait, Wings,* and *Washington Square* seek to represent James's narratorial contract while satisfying filmgoers accustomed to exercising the middlebrow spectatorial skills of pleased absorption and character identification. Yet James's narrator's stance toward his characters and their story, his contact with his reader and with her delegate, the narratee, is vexed at best. James Buzard describes James's paradoxical disparaging of and imaginative participation in his characters' acculturational projects as demanding from the reader a "vacillation between irony and investment" (225). Indeed, *Portrait's* narrator's tone resembles nothing more than Ralph Touchett's "loose-fitting urbanity," which covers over sinister wisdom with a kind of metropolitan hospitality (234). The narrator's insouciant take on Isabel's character—her theories, her imagination, her desire for knowledge, her belief in her own finer mind and sensitive perceptions—imperceptibly slips, via free indirect discourse, into representations of Isabel's very theories, imaginings, and misreadings of herself and others; he elegantly invokes, enjoys, and pillories the high-class social buzz of perceptions and rumors about Isabel's learning and culture.

The reader, charmed by Isabel's ambitions and seduced by the subtleties of free indirect discourse, soon neglects the insistent repetitions of the narrator's seemingly sympathetic yet judgment-ridden prose. Repeatedly reminding us he's telling a tale, *Washington Square*'s narrator acknowledges the "awkward confession[s]" he must "make about [his] heroine": she's a romp, a glutton, a "commonplace child" (34–35). Yet that last perception belongs, through indirect discourse, to Catherine's father, onto whom the narrator often displaces his disparagement. Sloper "almost never addressed his daughter save in the ironical form," the narrator says, and when locked in combat with her over her choice of husband, Sloper—and the narrator—take pleasure in the "prospect of entertainment" she provides (46, 126).

James's narratorial contract thus seduces the reader into desiring intimate figural knowledge as a form of entertainment. His narrators engage readers by portraying their protagonists as literary portraits yet also as intimates: each American girl is "our heroine," and Isabel or Catherine thus performs for (and entertains?) us as we idealize her innocence but come to disdain her unknowingly self-displayed ignorance. The narrator coaxes us, paradoxically, into admiration of and pity for our newly intimate figural friends. Addressing her as "poor girl," the narrator patronizingly portrays Catherine Sloper as helpless and victimized, Isabel Archer as spoiled egoist. Ralph, our narrator's delegate in *Portrait*, sympathizes with Isabel's unhappiness even as he patronizes her: her masked and mechanical look, the serenity painted on her face; her function as "advertisement" for a happy marriage, as "representation" for Gilbert Osmond and his desires (330). Having flattered us, moreover, the narrator makes us complicit in our figural friends' suffering. Just as Ralph pities "poor Isabel," our narrator condescends to "poor Ralph," whose role as the "humorous invalid" makes his "disabilities . . . part of the general joke." But "we, who know more about poor Ralph than his cousin," become accomplices in condescension, in desiring secret knowledge of who's slept with whom, who's slapped whom, who can't perform in the bedroom (286). The complicit reader soon longs to know whether Isabel is as unhappy as all her friends think her; whether Osmond is really brutal; whether Madame Merle is his lover and Pansy's mother, as the reader suspects long before Isabel is told so.

In *Wings*, the shifting narratorial delegate foregrounds the links between knowledge and intimacy. For *Wings* is about the complex and unstable quality of intimacy, about how we know and see, and so value and desire, others. When Susan Stringham serves as narratorial delegate, she models this seeing, for Milly, who "works" on her associates' sympathy, curiosity, and fancy, can only be known to us "by feeling their impression and sharing, if need be, their confusion." We therefore join Susan and fall under the "spell of watching her." We track, pounce, spy, and scientifically observe Milly; our watching, like Susan's, is a "way of clinging to the girl," of taking pleasure in her comeliness. As Susan looks into an Alpine view of great beauty, sees her friend sitting at ease on the dizzying edge (much as does Catherine), a thousand thoughts roar in her ears, a commotion that "left our observer intensely still and holding her breath": it's a site and a sight of mortality (*WD* 130–35). Just so, we know our intimate friends through sights we imagine others have seen of them. After her visit to Sir Luke Strett, Milly waits for Kate's visit; she watches from the balcony as Kate arrives, and "a mute exchange, but with smiles and nods, took place between them on what had occurred in the morning." Milly suddenly sees, moreover, that the splendid and handsome image Kate presents to her "was the peculiar property of somebody else's vision," that the "fine freedom" she shows Milly she has also shown Merton Densher, that "a girl's looking so to a man could not possibly be without connexions"—including connection of and for herself. Like most events or dialogues in this novel, the narrator confesses, these scenes "lasted less than our account of them." Yet only the narrative stretch that he everywhere practices as narratorial strategy in *Wings* can represent the "vibration" of impression and intimacy (219–20).

As this discursive structure of impression and intimacy shows, however, knowledge and desire are always mediated in James's novels. Indeed, the American girl's acculturation occurs in metropolitan settings that invoke sexual predation, triangulation, and sadomasochistic pain—as though cosmopolitan culture were grounded in perversion. In each story, we see the American girl's manipulation by a friend, aunt, or parent; observe efforts to secure or transmit a dying girl's, father's, or uncle's inheritance; and watch sadistic sexual or marital relations. While *Washington Square* blocks intimacy and *Portrait* forestalls and disavows it, *Wings* indulges and saturates the reader with a sense of its pain. Merton and Milly watch each other at the game of intimacy, "she knowing he tried to keep her in tune with his conception, and he knowing she thus knew it. Add that he again knew she knew, and yet that nothing was spoiled by it, and we get a fair impression of the line they found most completely workable" (412). This layered structure of knowledge enables the narrator—and the complicit reader—to stand apart from, even as he participates in, the sadistic urge to hurt his American girl.

The absence of narratorial delegate makes the structure of sadism especially apparent in *Washington Square*, for as Catherine is sacrificed by her father, the narrator displays and imaginatively enjoys her suffering, as do we. Masculine aggression is everywhere apparent, even if denied and displaced onto others. Catherine's father threatens to abandon her on an Alpine cliff; she denies that Sloper might choke her with his own hand; he claims that he's fattened the sheep before Morris kills it; Morris thrusts the figurative "sacrificial knife" into Lavinia's hand; Morris feels a "vicious" and "cruel" desire to "abuse somebody" (154, 157, 175). In the film, by the end, Catherine lies in the street, abjected. In *Wings,* Merton's displacement of female narratorial delegates distances Milly from Kate's, Merton's, Susan's, and Maud's manipulation of her through Merton. Suffused with Milly's sacrificial aura, the novel's characters declare her "magnificent"; like them, we tolerate and enjoy her hurt and pain—her loss and gain—even as we, like Merton, try to excuse ourselves from responsibility for it. Engaged by the narrator and secured within the narrative contract, the reader is full of desire to know still more about these characters whose passions and perversions she's begun to fathom, to witness sadistic hurts even as she distances herself from her own complicity. This is high-cultural aesthetic pleasure at its best.

Soon, however, James's characters' perverse deceptions and manipulations, the narrator's condescension toward and pitying of their fragile virtues and inevitable missteps, seem unspeakably slimy to the contemporary reader. In *Portrait,* the narrator rhetorically generalizes Isabel's misfortunes by taking Ralph as his delegate. "Poor human-hearted Isabel, what perversity had bitten her?" he wonders ruefully, even as he "recognizes"— and identifies with, makes us a party to—Osmond's perversity (331). Isabel's portraitured happiness, moreover, becomes representative of marital unhappiness in general. "You could criticise any marriage," Ralph imagines; "it was the essence of marriage to be open to criticism" (286). Indeed, generalizing this criticism of marriage out of the novel and into the readerly world, the narrator implicates the reader in this perverse structure, makes us aware of our own posed and sham happiness. We, too, have become condescending, patronizing, cynical cosmopolites; we, too, have been bitten by perversity. How bored and mildly entertained are we by these unhappy marriages! Appalled and fascinated, we can't put the novel down.

Spectatorship is the operative trope for this complex and complicitous, high-cultural narratorial contract. The Jamesian narrator has a "taste for the *mise-en-scène,*" Buzard quips; viewing others as actors and himself as mere member of the audience, the narrator senses that "the job of director might suit him better" (264). In *Wings,* Merton finds himself reduced to "mere spectatorship" during Kate's "beautiful entrance": Maud's "managerial" look at her protégé, from head to foot; Kate's self-presentation as "distinguished actress" who can "dress the part," walk, look, speak, and in every way "express the part"; his own purchase of stall," all identify Kate as staged and presented—but as valuable, as merchandised, as commodified (271–72).

In *Portrait,* the scene that produces Isabel's long meditative vigil is full of tropes for her act of spectatorship: she receives "an impression," watches from the threshold a "sort of familiar silence," a "freedom" between old friends: "the thing made an image, lasting only a moment, like a sudden flicker of light. [Osmond's and Merle's] relative positions, their absorbed mutual gaze, struck her as something detected. But it was all over by the time she had fairly seen it" (342–43). This is a scene of spectatorship, deploying tropes for filmic images that flicker and cut to another frame. It's a scenario: a staged image that accumulates the significance of other images and invokes sexualized, retrospectively reconstructed knowledge. While Isabel fails to read this scenario rightly, we are less "innocent[ly] ignorant" (451). We, too, have been spectators, and—partially because we've witnessed other scenes of seduction—we draw the immediate conclusion that these two are lovers. And we long to see more scenes of Isabel's misery. We wish to witness an explosion: physical violence, marital abuse, sadomasochistic acts to match the sexual asides, maneuverings, and manipulations. We yearn to see Isabel sleep with Lord Warburton, who hangs around Pansy because he's still smitten with her stepmother; or with Caspar Goodwood, who seems to have given up his exemplary American business out of passion for a woman who spurns him. If we're readers, we're disappointed that we're treated, instead, to the cold sneers and silent treatments of a merely unhappy marriage—even if it is a massively failed coupling between the American girl and a charismatic, narcissistic aesthete.

If we're actual movie spectators, however, the films elaborate James's trope and indulge our sadomasochistic desires. Campion's *Portrait,* in particular, pictures abusive sexual scenes. After Ralph tells Isabel that Lord Warburton cares for her rather than her stepdaughter, cautions her that Osmond will accuse her of jealousy of Pansy, and asks her to "be frank" with him about her unhappiness, Campion cuts to Isabel's figure, crossing the threshold into her home, in shade, in slow motion, and then fades to black. Several scenes later, after Lord Warburton leaves Florence, the spectator's desire to see a fight gets gratified, as Campion's mise-en-scène visualizes the marital violence James's novel refuses to show. Shot in the film's pervasive cold blue light, with a virtually chiaroscuro palette, the scene's style is Gothic, complete with Renaissance mansion, walls shot asymmetrically. The action: a marital dispute in which a husband accuses his wife of humiliating him. As Osmond strides into the darkened drawing room, he grabs and piles pillows, then grabs and deposits Isabel on top of them, as though she were a bad daughter and he a chastising father. Isabel's figure is shot in parts, as an index of the violated, morselized body she might well become: the camera tilts up from her hands, corseted waist, and swinging handbag, over her slightly bared bosom and chokered throat to her face; zooms in on her torso, virtually slasher style, as Osmond moves to force her to stay put. Campion shoots Gilbert's hand over hers and, as he grabs her black glove, cuts to Isabel's face and we hear, almost before we see, the glove slap her; the same shot/countershot structure of hand and face pictures two more slaps. From a series of shot/countershots in close-up of Gilbert and Isabel as they argue, Campion cuts to a high-angle shot of Osmond's feet as he crosses the oriental rugs and black-and-white tile floor to his wife's figure—and trips her. The high-angle shot of her crouching on the black-and-white floor as he stands over her, the room seemingly lit through a draped and gauze-covered window fronted with a giant black candelabrum, portrays this visualized marital violence as Gothic, almost vampiristic, as a matter of power rather than sexuality. When Isabel stands, smoke rises behind her, Gilbert grabs her arm for the second time, and, as he verbally abuses her, aggressively nuzzles her cheek; at the scene's end, he malevolently and she submissively move slowly toward a kiss, then he disgust-edly turns his face aside. This Gothicized scene visually updates James for the 1990s, incorporating hints of slasher and vampire flicks into its scenario of female helplessness and masculine brutality. The postmodern viewer watches these acts with a certain Jamesian "unpleasant fascination" (*PL* 449).

As a heroine who chooses her husband unwisely yet, unlike contem-porary women, has few chances to leave him, Isabel is representative mod-ern wife. While James wrote his novel well after the British Matrimonial Causes Act of 1857, changes in the divorce law did not produce immediate social or ideological change. The separated or deserted woman was defined legally as a *femme sole* and so had equity rights over her property, but mar-ried women did not—and, in Henry James's awful irony, Isabel brought to her marriage a "fortune," to which she now has no right. "He married me for the money," she confesses to Ralph, in the novel's most intimate scene (478). The 1857 act, moreover, preserved the inequality of grounds on which to sue for divorce: men could sue for simple adultery, women only for "aggra-vated" adultery (which necessitated acts of incest, bigamy, desertion, or cruelty)—and, in another irony, James's Gilbert Osmond has given up adul-tery and is not physically cruel. In the heterogeneous United States, how-ever, divorce was less rigorously regulated—by church, civil, or judicial law—than it was in England. Areas settled by Protestants had formulated divorce laws during the colonial period; some colonies and states allowed legislative divorce well into the nineteenth century; informal marriage had become an established legal institution. The Western frontier states, more-over, took a laissez-faire approach to divorce; there, by 1860, "migratory divorce was already part of the American scene" (Glendon 34). Indeed, the

Western states' liberality caused a "divorce mill panic," which in the 1880s created increasing pressure for legal reform (Riley 108–29). All told, the divorce rate in the United States has been historically higher than that for other industrializing nations and has risen in every decade since the Civil War (Goode 16). Nonetheless, several decades into the twentieth century, divorce in the United States was still a "relatively uncommon event," and England remained largely a "non-divorcing society" (Glendon 198; Stone 371–90).

James would have known about the American divorce controversy personally. His father, Henry James Sr., Horace Greeley, and free love advocate Stephen Pearl Andrews had debated the fate of indissoluble marriage in the *New York Tribune* between November 1852 and February 1853. James Sr. argued for the availability of divorce, which served the "manifest public welfare"; Andrews, against any legal bond; Greeley, for the indissolubility of marriage (Riley 72). But the controversy was international as well. Indeed, as a self-consciously Anglo-American writer, James locates *Portrait*'s unhappy couple in Italy—alienated Americans in a Roman Catholic country, parent and stepmother to a second-generation American expatriate girl who has been convent educated, brought up by Italian nuns rather than by the unknown-to-her American expatriate, frenchified mother. These wandering cosmopolites live as outsiders in a country that confirms their own perverse yet permanent marital commitment. "Leave your husband before . . . your character gets spoiled," the modern American Henrietta implores; "with the off-hand way in which you speak of a woman's leaving her husband," Isabel responds, "it's easy to see you've never had one!" (417–18).

Isabel's story, as relevant to 1990s as to 1880s wives, is transportable across historical periods, narrative media, and national boundaries to address altered social circumstances. Anxiety about the failure of marriage and the family as social institutions, I would argue, mobilizes filmmakers' appropriation of James's novels. Although the film is set at English country houses and Italian Renaissance mansions, it translates a story about the unhappy but civilized Jamesian couple in "intimate disarray" into a picture that comments on contemporary dysfunctional partnership and the perceived problem of women's right to marital property. Written during the debate about the 1882 Married Women's Property Act, James's novel demonstrates the shift in sexual, marital, and reproductive ideologies that made it historically possible to scrutinize the links among gender, divorce, and property. And the debates about divorce and women's property in the British Parliament were nothing if not shrill. In 1857, conservative members worried that the possibility of divorce would make the people think marriage no more than "connubial concubinage" (qtd. in Shanley, "One Must

Ride" 366); in 1870, that a divorced woman's right to her property would "subvert the principle on which the marriage relation had hitherto stood" (Shanley, *Feminism* 73). By 1882, fears of unrestrained sexuality among women and the poor had largely subsided, the government joined in sponsoring the bill, and it passed with little debate (115–30).

It is not surprising, then, that filmmakers would appropriate this 1880s novel about a married woman's property to address the 1990s fear that marriage and the family are in crisis. This sense of peril creates shrill cries from across the political spectrum: that "deadbeat dads" who fail to pay alimony or child support should be jailed (they are, in Michigan), that kids demonize or overidealize stepparents, that divorce irrevocably harms children (see Chambers; Wallerstein and Kelly). I do not mean to deny that the rise in the annual rate of divorce since the 1960s has produced an alarming set of social problems—complex child custody arrangements, troubled individual relations and housing arrangements in the blended family, the state's problematic role in collecting alimony. The sense of doom that currently surrounds divorce, however, has been exacerbated by gender and economic anxieties. Female economic independence and new legal definitions of marital property—such as pensions, medical insurance, career assets, and entitlements to company goods and services—have endangered previously stable middle-class property-holding patterns. The 1970s invention of no-fault divorce in California, moreover, has made divorce available to the masses; most states' adoption of "community property" as defining ownership of marital goods and most courts' practice of equal or "equitable" distribution of such properties at dissolution has made divorce thinkable, especially for wives (Weitzman 110–42). Yet when social historians balance the divorce rate with statistics of marital longevity, the current sense of crisis can be contextualized by demographics and mortalities. Among currently marrying cohorts, only 40–50 percent will remain married after they've reached the age of fifty; given human longevity, however, marriages are neither more perishable nor of shorter duration in the 1990s than they were in the nineteenth century (Goode 16, Glendon 194–95, Sweet and Bumpass 172–210). As Andrew Cherlin says, "for the first time in our nation's history, more marriages [now end] every year in divorce than in death" (309). While a 1990s wife might find ending an abusive marriage as difficult as would Isabel, then, her access to legal options, economic rights, and institutional supports would make separation infinitely more likely.

Campion's film addresses the problem of marriage and divorce, introducing into James's story a certain "semiotic productivity" that enables spectators to use it in a variety of ways (Fiske, *Understanding* 142–56). While the opening credits roll, unseen women talk about their sexual pleasure in voice-over, a pleasure the viewer may read through the contemporary rhetoric of sexual dysfunction: the addiction to "being entwined with each other" that, at first fulfilling, becomes "negative"; the finding of a "mirror" so "loyal" that it shines back one's own image. A sequence of shots in both color and black and white then portrays women of many ages and races, dressed in the fashions of 1970s and 1980s, all presenting themselves to be looked at, looking back at the camera as though self-aware of their status as portraiture, as advertising for the film that follows. Soliciting an audience of baby-boomer and younger women, the film here displays its semiotic productivity, its willingness to be read not only as a feminist comment on divorce, but an endorsement of the 1970s discourse of female self-assertion, a 1990s parodic pop-psychology of dysfunctional coupling. Campion also problematizes James's conclusion; as Isabel turns from the door of the well-lit room and looks away from Gardencourt—the house of fiction?—she faces an unknown future rather than an almost certain return to her abusive husband. Although James's 1880s Isabel sees her destiny as necessarily living out the consequences of her badly made and manipulated marital choice, Campion's 1990s heroine is hardly "poor Isabel."

Despite its openness to multiple readings, however, Campion's film did not reach a mass audience nor was it popular. Although it solicited as spectator an educated and intelligent female consumer, *Portrait* is an art flick that encodes its own artfulness, its commodity status and market niche. A film about aestheticism and commodification, it calls attention to its own aesthetic through indexical troping, lighting, and mise-en-scène. The story's insistence—spoken by Ralph—that Isabel will be "caught" and "put in a cage" by her marriage to Osmond is everywhere indexed by the film's repertory of images. Here is a short catalogue. Spiderwebs: Isabel's umbrella, which Osmond twirls before her face; chandeliers, through which an overhead shot portrays a dinner party; patterns on rotunda and loggia floors; even Busby Berkeley style dancers, via a crane shot. Bars: multiple shots through balustrades as figures ascend stairs, or the camera tilts up, through, and over balustrades into gardens; the portico through which Ned Rosier balefully cries, "Pansy"; the foregrounded bars through which Ralph warns Isabel of her impending doom. Then, indexing the touch and its concomitant prophesy of marital violence, shots of hands, virtually always in close-up: "Don't touch," a guard intones as Henrietta strokes a recumbent effigy (shot at the Victoria and Albert Museum); Isabel clasps her hands by her face as she listens to a new friend play Schubert at Gardencourt; Madame Merle and Pansy entwine their gloved hands—one in black, one white—as they converse about (maternal) gift-giving; Osmond's hands, in detail shot, stroke his daughter's, while she sits, embraced and visually eroticized, on his lap, and he talks of their life together; Madame Merle clutches a gift-wrapped doll for the convented Pansy; Gilbert slaps (Campion 84).

Campion's mise-en-scène also indexes its status as art film. The director includes statuary: catacombs; morselized and giantized hands and feet (shot at the Capitoline in Rome); a life-sized statue stands beside Isabel, as Gilbert drones his love and the camera zooms alongside a catacomb wall with a death's head on it, the soundtrack gasping. Osmond, Ned, and Merle collect paintings, "bibelots," and "precious objects." Architecture serves as establishing shot, often framed asymmetrically, or shot as the camera pans, tilts, or rolls (Campion 84). Classical music plays on the soundtrack, especially Schubert's impromptus and quartets ("Death and the Maiden"). As an index of taste, Campion depicts embroidered and beaded gowns with trains and bustles, high-bourgeois drawing room decor—perfectly arranged objects on mantles; candelabra in the frame plane which the camera tracks past; accumulated Victoriana that hints at kitsch; the orientalized and lace collar-and-cuffed dressing gown Madame Merle wears to welcome Ned Rosier; the velvet, satin, and silk fabric so resplendent and textured it makes the viewer want to touch; the omnipresent mirrors that index self-reflection and its failures. The film's mise-en-scène, then, inscribes art and aesthetics into its scenario in part to signal its commodity status as art house film, in part, as product of independent filmmaking. Announcing itself "highbrow" culture, Campion's film separates itself from mainstream Hollywood fare, naturalizing the superior taste of the filmgoer who has selected this film as his or her cultural commodity. Yet its status as independent art film and its encoding of its artfulness and taste as beauty, made the film seem less than relevant to a middlebrow audience of cultural consumers used to the suspect pleasures, as Radway says, of spectatorial absorption, viewing for the story, and identifying with a romance heroine.

Like Campion's *Portrait*, Agnieszka Holland's *Washington Square* sought but failed to secure a middlebrow but discriminating spectator. While scrutinizing the middle-class cultural question of a woman's marital choice and its consequences, Holland's use of mise-en-scène and montage identify *Washington Square* as "highbrow." The opening sequence's establishing shots of Washington Square betray the film's bid for an art house audience. After an overhead shot of the square, the camera tracks down through the trees, dollies toward the house, tilts up and tracks through an opened window into the parlor, dollies around the room—cataloguing the perfect Victoriana of furniture and decor—into the dining room. On the soundtrack, a woman shrieks, and the camera quickly pans to the stairway, tracks up, up, and up several flights of stairs, pauses on a weeping servant girl, dollies into a bedroom, across a mirror, and up a woman's bloody body to picture death by childbirth. "Your daughter, sir," a nurse says, handing a baby to a black-garbed man. This breathtaking sequence shot identifies and ironizes the continuity that will mark this infant's life. Bereft of mother at her birth, Catherine Sloper first adores and then is locked in combat with her sadistic and punishing Victorian father. (In the book, Sloper declares that he is "not a father in an old-fashioned novel," as the narrator smiles to the narrator's [and readers'] sardonic amusement [83].) Throughout the film, repeated high- and low-angle shots depict the power struggle in which this father and daughter are "stuck like glue," as she seeks to marry the man of her choice and he attempts to prevent her—even after his death—from falling prey to scheming "adventurers."

Throughout Holland's film, the moving camera and lengthy sequence shots enable the director to eschew cuts and edits as she portrays the flow of life at Mrs. Elizabeth Almond's home and the refusal of it in Washington Square. When Sloper seeks Mrs. Almond's advice about his daughter's engagement, the mise-en-shot includes a room adjacent to and behind the parlor from which a little girl walks, moving through the depth plane into the screen plane; she whispers to her mother, who gives her permission for some unnamed activity. When Sloper stands, walking to the window on the right, the camera displays a hallway behind him, leading to the front door, through which a young woman walks, pauses, and then retreats. Seemingly extraneous spectatorial information is crucial here, for the infant Sloper examined in the sequence's beginning—and declared healthy—seems, figuratively, to grow, first to girlhood, then young womanhood, moving through the house and into her adult life. As Holland introduces this scene, the infant's young parents hand the baby over to grandmother (how differently from the servant's handing over of Catherine at her birth!) and leave through the front door. Mixing the effects of mise-en-scène and montage, Holland shoots their departure around doors, into halls, and seemingly through walls. When Morris Townsend courts Catherine in her father's parlor, on the contrary, the mise-en-scène is posed, composed, and formalized, the frame closed and the action static. When Morris and Catherine discuss her father's decision to disinherit her should they marry, the two lovers sit, hands in lap, with a closed secretary between them. In conventional two-shot and shot/countershot, Holland's stationary camera shoots Catherine in purple dress, perfectly posed against the perfect Victorian parlor's dark-green damask wallpaper, the mahogany secretary gleaming. Here, Holland's shot selection pictures the staid and stolid scene of Victorian courtship. Taken together, these two camera styles indicate Holland's maturity as a filmmaker, her knowledge of film conventions, and her high-cultural intentions.

Like Campion's *Portrait,* Holland's *Washington Square* represents the arts as an index of acculturation. First, the woman is framed, portrayed as portrait or representation. Three times, Catherine watches out her window, framed by its frame, with caged bird by her side, looking for her father (or, ironically, lover), then runs down the stairs, screaming "Father's home!" (or murmuring, "I've been missed"). In these scenes, Catherine's face dissolves into different stages of her girlhood: the crying girl who peed at the family party becomes older, though still bumbling girl, then poised young woman. Catherine's mother, dead in the opening shot sequence, appears throughout the film in pictures, hanging alongside other ornately framed women on the green and crimson damask walls. Later, Catherine is mirrored: she enters the mise-en-shot from outside the frame, reflected first in an ornately framed mirror near Morris; when she feeds her dying father, her face is echoed in another such mirror; trying out love, she kisses her image in a pier glass, laughing innocently as she thinks her first sexual thoughts. Rather than stand for female vanity, self-reflection, or beauty, however, these images index the framed woman as representation: Catherine, like these portraits of women, is stuck with her father and destined never to leave Washington Square, although she does not yet know it. The soundtrack uses the art song as index of acculturation. The young and nervous Catherine pees in her pants when trying to sing it at a party; she harmonizes the lovely song beautifully with her lover, at the piano, while a foolish Lavinia joins in ("la, la, la, la, la, la," while a rack focus highlights Sloper's sneer, in the background); a soprano performs it in Europe, as concertgoers gather, dissolving into the frame, and Catherine, becoming cultured, listens, weeping over sheet music; Catherine plays it, at the end, while the camera shoots her smiling, sardonically and knowingly, after she commands Morris never to see her again. The soundtrack's music represents culture with a capital C, and learning Culture, the heiress increases her value as bearer of Culture and as cultured object. Yet the film represents her ironized acculturation as fitting her only for a womanly life as spinster and surrogate nurturer.

Unlike Holland's *Washington Square* or Campion's *Portrait,* Iain Softley's independent (or "indie") film of *The Wings of the Dove* delivers what Radway calls the "suspect pleasures of the middlebrow." Softley's film reconfigures the American girl's marital choice as a sexual destiny, rewrites a story of multiple motives for matching Milly and Merton into a film about the heterosexual couple and its erotic adventures. The opening credits roll over a sequence that identifies the look as inviting sexual encounter. Merton follows Kate through a tube station; they get on a train; he sits then stands, seeming to invite her to sit; in shot/countershot, they watch each other; she exits and he follows her in shot/countershot, up stairs, into an elevator; the camera tracks up through floors as the elevator rises, each barred shot frames the couple kissing and finally, under cover of his hat, Merton feels her buttocks. "Kate," he whispers; "no," she says. Spectator absorption is guaranteed by this solicitous structure of the look. We, too, want to see more—under the darkened theater's cover. Softley translates the novel's complex plot into a romance, moreover, a melodrama that secures the spectator's figural identification: will Kate secure Milly's fortune for Densher, her lover? will Milly die so the lovers can live happily ever after? In Softley's movie, the "circle of petticoats" that finely entangles Merton becomes Kate's solicitation of Milly for erotic triangulation, with Lord Mark as besotted accomplice. As this enticement begins, our identification with Kate is tinged with arousal. Moreover, Helena Bonham Carter, the female lead, is a culture-film star. She is an image recognizable as herself and thus bears more aura than the character she plays; a type of the Merchant Ivory good-girl sexpot seeking to discover her erotic potential; a celebrity familiar for the high quality of her acting; a known quantity at the box office. Carter as star draws moviegoers to the theater, mobilizes the market, and helps ensure the investment of backers and the profits to production units. She is herself, as Richard Dyer would say, a "form of capital" in the movie business (9–72).

Softley's canny version of James exploits mainstream cinema's current appropriation of the conventions of pornography. But Softley's film merely hints at porno's "stock heroes, its story lines, its low-budget lighting and motel-room sets" (Hamilton B9). *Wings* invokes but outclasses hard-core porn by exaggerating its production differences from porn: using gorgeous costumes—complete with remarkable hats!—that seem to verge on the modern but recall the Victorian; lighting with chic blue or orange light to highlight cool or Mediterranean moods; casting a star who always performs in culture flicks. By playing elegant lighting and sets against porn tropes and story lines, Softley's film goes distinctly middlebrow—as porn has gone mainstream since the 1980s. Just as porn became feature length by "imitating other Hollywood genres with a vengeance," as Linda Williams argues, by attaching to other genres an "X-rated difference," Softley links his parodied porn flick to other mainstream genres. For *Wings* is a sort of sexual thriller. Most of the erotic scenes begin as one character follows another, in look-over-the-shoulder shot/countershot or steamy two-shot, through city alleys or up or down staircases; the staircase scenes recall Hitchcock's *Vertigo*—with spirals shot from overhead or from below, female feet leaving the frame and enticing the climbing (rising?) male up ladders—complete with Bernard Herrmann sound-alike music. The heroes, the story line, and the sex scenes all recall thriller chic. When Merton and Kate have sex by a canal in Venice, they are shot from behind, in medium long-shot, mid-cult

*Fatal Attraction* fashion, he standing while penetrating her (his shirttail out), she held up during intercourse by his hands, his thrusts, and her legs, wrapped around him. This phallic sequence starts with a shot of gondolas and blued window frame; heavy breathing heaves on the soundtrack. To top it off, Kate is crossdressed as a matador, for she and Merton have sex at the end of a sequence that shoots a costumed street festival, complete with gypsy music and dancing. (It's one of the film's several scenes of orientalizing music and exotic street spectacle: "culture" as the peasants' everyday life.) The masquerading Kate returns to Milly's mansion disheveled, tie undone and shirt open, to apologize to the bedded Milly for her antics, just as a slumming husband might do; "don't lie to me," the heiress retorts, as a cuckolded wife might.

Indeed, the sex in *Wings* always suggests a threesome. Softley inter-cuts scenes of Milly's seduction of Merton ("I'm going to make a fool of myself tonight, I know it") with Kate's looking at herself in a mirror, and her voice-over speaks her love letters to the man who's kissing another woman. "I see you touch her and I'm scared," she says, as Softley cuts back to Milly and Merton; "every time she looks at you and smiles," Kate voices over, as the camera cuts back to her reflected image, "don't forget that I love you more." In chic porn style, the third enhances a couple's pleasure. A little S/M adds more spice to the mix. When Merton follows Kate up a staircase and into a blue light at Lord Mark's party, she drills him about the "older woman" he has just kissed, a kiss shot from Kate's perspective. "Did it hurt?" Kate asks of her refusal to marry him. "Is that what you wanted?" he returns; "I hurt so much you can't imagine," she murmurs. They kiss; "I want you to go back and kiss *her*," Kate says afterwards, "with that mouth." This middlebrow appropriation of a soft-core porn motif suggests, more-over, that threesomes always involve not only same-sex rivalry but homo-eroticism. When Kate positions Milly and Merton in one gondola, herself in another, the sequence ends with a long shot of the girls, drunken and giddy, leaning over and touching across the barely lit, nighttime canal; "come closer," Milly giggles as Merton presumably watches. After Lord Mark drunkenly gropes the sleeping Kate in her darkened guest chamber, Kate visits Milly's room; the camera tracks up from the foot to the head of the bed, over Milly's blanketed body, to her face; a door closes on the soundtrack, and Milly wakes and invites Kate to join her. "What's wrong?" Milly asks; the two girls cuddle, as Milly puts her arm around Kate's back and they clasp hands around her breasts.

These girl-girl erotic scenes seem to demand a male spectator. Indeed, the "lesbian number" in pornography appeals to the male fantasy of himself making a third with the two women (Williams 140–41). Yet *Wings* inoculates the female spectator against the possibility—the fear?—of lesbian fantasy by representing women as appropriate viewers of explicitly sexual art of all erotic kinds. Softley rewrites Milly's National Gallery visit as an accidental stumble on a Gustav Klimt exhibit. Here, Milly encounters both Kate and Densher, as the lesbian number gets suggested. The camera tilts up "The Kiss," cutting to Milly as she looks at it; she spies Merton through a series of arches, then Kate arrives: they're together. "I want to show you something," Kate says, drawing Milly to Klimt's "The Danaë." Merton leaves the girls to look at the dazzling displays of breast, mouth, and touch; the huge, gilded, and fetishized buttocks and thighs. "It's not what you think," Kate denies, clinching the implication that the couple's erotic looking necessitates heterosexual touch; spectatorship, the scene seems to suggest, may also involve girl-girl identification when sexual arousal is linked to the look. When Kate follows Milly into a bookstore, she again draws her friend to art. They look at an etching of libertine cunnilingus *a tergo;* their laughter serves as aural match cut to the scene of Lord Mark's party, where the girls display their rebellious looking. That part of the bookstore's "reserved for men," Lord Mark remarks, threatening that he'd have thrown the girls out; "I saw them," the still innocent Milly says of the drawings; "have I suddenly become corrupt?" Shot in the film's pervasive blue light, this scene of revelry, drunkenness, and smoking mimics a twenties cabaret; the girls, dressed in shimmering blue gowns with one-feathered headbands, look like nothing so much as flappers. Announcing itself as set in "London, 1910" (although the novel was published in 1902), Softley's *Wings* uses costumes to suggest a historically unstable but definitely modern milieu, as women begin to liberate themselves from the taboos that surround sex. It's okay for women to watch—to take pleasure in—soft core, Softley suggests, activating the metaphor that mobilizes his own appropriation. Indeed, as the markets for adult films and porn video rentals expand, women, lesbians, and heterosexual couples have begun to consume a mainstreamed, even feminist, hard-core pornography (Williams 227–64).

Celebrity sex guaranteed *Wings* the middlebrow audience and big box office the other James films lacked. Whereas the eroticized scenes in *Portrait* endow Isabel with sexual fantasy, the high-profile star of *Wings* has sex with her screen lover. Campion shoots Isabel in autoerotic multiple-partner fantasy: she lies down, and the hands of two lovers appear, touching her breast, stomach, and thigh; Ralph Touchett lies beside, watching, spectator to Isabel's pleasure in the threesome, then stands; standing too, Goodwood attacks him; the lovers dissolve one by one from Isabel's fantasied ménage à trois. Isabel's home-movie travels across Europe—shot in grainy black and white, in the conventions of silent film and surrealist cinema, with a back-

ground of exoticized pyramids and women in veils—picture her as "nude,"
as a high-cultural image of the body made artful. But Softley climaxes his
film with a nude sex scene that brilliantly capitalizes on the novel's insistence that love is an expenditure, sex an exchange, and arousal a commodity. After the grieving Kate burns Milly's bequest letter, she enters Merton's
tiny bed chamber, sits on his bed, and removes her black corset. Naked, she
poses for his look as though she were a Klimt nude; "I'll never take her
money," he claims, sitting on the bed. They kiss; "I love you, Kate," he says;
she removes his suspenders, then his shirt. Softley shoots the lovers in
medium long shot, emphasizing whole body relations; Kate climbs on top,
stretches her fully naked body on her lover's, her buttocks softly curving; "I
love you, too." She sits up, moving on his penis; in shot/countershot, he
watches as she moves up and down; she throws her head back, in porn
iconography's sign of female orgasm—but, instead, she stops, and weeps:
"You're still in love with her." "She wanted us to be together," Merton assures her, in medium long shot through the brass bed's headboard, as the
camera (and his penis?) withdraws. Cut to the two lying beside each other;
the camera shoots her white face, in close-up, emphasizing facial reactions
and, so, emotion; Merton says, "I want to marry you without her money."
"Give me your word," Kate responds, "that you're not in love with her
memory." The soundtrack is silent; in extreme close-up, tears mark her
white face. She rises, the camera tracks up his chest to his face; he's still
silent. Cut to a montage sequence of Milly, laughing, then the girls touching
out of gondolas—"come closer!"—then fade to black. In detail shot of eyes,
nose, and mouth reclining, Merton's wide eyes weep as he continues to
remain silent.

    This culminating scene of failed sexual climax combines the conven-
tions of soft core porn that *Wings* appropriates. We watch the modern London girl climb on top of her lover, breasts bobbing; we watch her assume
the active role during intercourse, taking control of the sex act and so
breaking the taboo of female passivity. We hear of the third in the film's
threesome, the American dove who haunts this bed chamber and prevents
orgasm. We see her ghost in montage, reminding us of the girl-girl numbers. But most of all, it's a "money shot" gone awry: the male does not
ejaculate and so visually prove his pleasure; the female, whose pleasure is
central to this version of postmodern pornography, doesn't come; the emphasis on whole bodies and facial reactions highlights this money shot's
failure. And although the spectator knows that this sex scene is simulated,
she or he has yearned to see Helena Bonham Carter naked, takes pleasure
in viewing her fleshy body. Softley achieves this effect by shooting Bonham
Carter's breasts and face, buttocks and body, her whole body, so as to seem

to deny the possibility of body double: we see the star's real body, the camera proclaims. Indeed, the entire number, in which sex is enacted and money discussed, visualizes the novel's obsession with the intricate linkage of gain and loss. Merton steadfastly refuses to participate in a financial exchange through the hallucinated third, Milly, even as the dialogue reminds us that intimacy in *Wings* is always a matter of exchange, use, gain or loss, of working opportunities to enrich one's presentation, prestige, or pocketbook. The fetishization of Milly—her fortune, her beauty, her magnificence—characterizes a hallucinated intimacy in which sex is a commodity but the consumer never possesses the goods. Through the trope of the "money shot," this final scene in *Wings* foregrounds the problematic nature of heterosexual relations and sexual pleasure at the beginning—and end—of the twentieth century.

This cross between soft-core porn and indie film, finally, recalls the history of pornography's emergence and its eventual move into the mainstream. Pornography emerged, according to Williams, in the nineteenth century, with the 1857 passage of the British Obscene Publications Act—the same year as the Matrimonial Causes Act—and began to be consolidated in 1873, with the United States Comstock Law. A modern body of popular pornographic texts, then, appeared concomitantly with the first antiobscenity legislation (11–12). Linked to the emerging mass market for books, newspapers, and periodicals, this attempt to censor sex when women could first legally refuse it identifies one of pornography's cultural functions as the problematizing of sexual relations and heterosexual pleasure. In the twentieth century, moreover, pornography helped launch the art film as a genre, creating a marketing niche for erotica in the 1970s. With the 1972 debut of *Deep Throat* (Gerard Damiano), *Behind the Green Door* (Mitchell Bros.), and *The Devil in Miss Jones* (Damiano), porn became box office. Yet these new porn films, which followed a group of sex documentaries such as *I Am Curious—Yellow* (1968), aimed not simply to celebrate the sexual permissiveness associated with the 1960s sexual revolution, Williams maintains, but to depict the desire for greater knowledge about sex and sexuality. These seventies porn films, too, first pictured the problem of female pleasure; as a result, they appealed to a mixed-sex audience. As a popular genre, the new seventies pornography addressed the felt needs and experiences of its audience (Williams 87, 98, 154–55, Sklar 293–95). Soft core reached a wider audience with the *Emmanuelle* films and with the crossover of porn into high culture in *Last Tango in Paris* (Bernardo Bertolucci, 1972). In the 1990s, mainstream cinema has not only appropriated the tropes, storylines, and look of porn but has thematized that appropriation with nostalgia for the porn industry's decadence in *Boogie Nights* (Paul Thomas Anderson, 1997), with a rewriting of Arthur Schnitzler's decadent classic of ritualized sex, *Traumnovelle,* in *Eyes Wide Shut* (Stanley Kubrick, 1999). Kubrick brings mainstream porn full circle by casting Hollywood's power couple, Tom Cruise and Nicole Kidman, as bored marrieds seeking sexual adventure, by invoking 1970s stylized sex even as he appropriates a Viennese tale to comment on the impossibility of intimacy and fidelity in an era of excessive financial speculation and consumption, the postmodern 1990s.

Romance, melodrama, and nude sex scenes, then, when linked with the structures of stardom, made *The Wings of the Dove* a critical and box office success. Distributed by Miramax, the largest independent film distributor, *Wings* reached more screens—and  viewers—than did the other James movies, which failed to compete successfully for the intelligent cultural consumer's box office dollars. I do not mean to suggest that independent filmmakers must eschew high art or pander to middlebrow tastes in order to produce hits. Despite their differences as filmmakers, Campion, Holland, and Softley appropriate James's stories to address the perceived needs and experiences of contemporary moviegoers; the problems of sex, marriage, and divorce make these films of nineteenth-century novels relevant to 1990s viewers. The James movies all solicit an educated, intelligent spectator; all use the conventions of film—whether art film or soft-core porn—to reach a wide audience. Picturing female acculturation, they appeal to the middlebrow consumer's longing for legitimate cultural objects, for the distinction that accrues to the cultured self. Yet James's fiction continues, in the late twentieth-century United States, to indicate the vexed relationship of mass, high, and popular cultures. The uneasy position of the artist, whether author or auteur, makes acquiring a mass audience problematic within the cultural and economic matrix that is Hollywood. As Richard Salmon says, "If James refused to sever his links with the mass market, equally he wished to maintain his distance from it" (76). So, too, do Campion, Holland, and Softley, hybrid insider-outsiders, his postmodern heirs.

## Works Cited

Anesko, Michael. *"Friction with the Market": Henry James and the Profession of Authorship.* New York: Oxford UP, 1986.

Bourdieu, Pierre. *Distinction: A Social Critique of the Judgment of Taste.* Trans. Richard Nice. Cambridge: Harvard UP, 1984.

Buzard, James. *The Beaten Track: European Tourism, Literature, and the Ways to Culture, 1800–1918.* Oxford: Clarendon, 1993.

Campion, Jane. *Interviews.* Ed. Virginia Wright Wexman. Jackson: UP of Mississippi.

Chambers, David. *Making Fathers Pay.* Chicago: U of Chicago P, 1979.

Cherlin, Andrew J. "Marital Dissolution and Remarriage." *Diversity and Change in*

*Families: Patterns, Prospects, and Policies*. Ed. Mark Robert Rank and Edward L. Kain. Englewood Cliffs, N.J.: Prentice, 1995. 305–29.

Dyer, Richard. *Stars*. London: BFI, 1994.

Fiske, John. "Popular Culture." *Critical Terms for Literary Study*. 2d ed. Ed. Frank Lentricchia and Thomas McLaughlin. Chicago: U of Chicago P, 1995. 321–35.

———. *Understanding Popular Culture*. London: Routledge, 1996.

Glendon, Mary Ann. *The Transformation of Family Law: State Law, and Family in the United States and Western Europe*. Chicago: U of Chicago P, 1989.

Goode, William J. "World Changes in Divorce Patterns." *Economic Consequences of Divorce: The International Perspective*. Ed. Leonore J. Weitzman and Mavis Maclean. Oxford: Clarendon, 1992. 11–49.

Hamilton, William L. "The Mainstream Flirts with Pornographic Chic." *New York Times* 22 Mar. 1999: B9.

James, Henry. *Henry James Letters*. Ed. Leon Edel. Vol. 3. Cambridge: Harvard UP, 1980.

———. *The Notebooks of Henry James*. Ed. R. F. Matthiessen and Kenneth B. Murdock. New York: Oxford UP, 1961.

———. *The Portrait of a Lady*. Ed. Robert D. Bamberg. New York: Norton, 1995.

———. *Washington Square*. Ed. and intro. Brian Lee. New York: Penguin, 1980.

———. *The Wings of the Dove*. Ed. and intro. John Bayley. New York: Penguin, 1986.

Levine, Lawrence W. *Highbrow/Lowbrow: The Emergence of Cultural Hierarchy in America*. Cambridge: Harvard UP, 1988.

Poovey, Mary. *Uneven Developments: The Ideological Work of Gender in Mid-Victorian England*. Chicago: U of Chicago P, 1988.

Radway, Janice A. *A Feeling for Books: The Book-of-the-Month Club, Literary Taste, and Middle-Class Desire*. Chapel Hill: U of North Carolina P, 1997.

Riley, Glenda. *Divorce: An American Tradition*. New York: Oxford UP, 1991.

Salmon, Richard. *Henry James and the Culture of Publicity*. Cambridge: Cambridge UP, 1997.

Shanley, Mary Lyndon. *Feminism, Marriage, and the Law in Victorian England, 1850–1895*. Princeton: Princeton UP, 1989.

———. "'One Must Ride Behind': Married Women's Rights and the Divorce Act of 1857." *Victorian Studies* 25 (1982): 355–76.

Sklar, Robert. *Movie-Made America: A Cultural History of American Movies*. Rev. ed. New York: Vintage, 1994.

Stone, Lawrence. *Road to Divorce: A History of the Making and Breaking of Marriage in England, 1530–1987*. New York: Oxford UP, 1995.

Strychacz, Thomas. *Modernism, Mass Culture, and Professionalism*. Cambridge: Cambridge UP, 1993.

Sweet, James A., and Larry L. Bumpass. *American Families and Households*. New York: Russell, 1987.

Wallerstein, Judith, and Joan Kelly. *Surviving the Breakup: How Children and Parents Cope with Divorce*. New York: Basic, 1980.

Weitzman, Lenore J. *The Divorce Revolution: The Unexpected Social and Economic Consequences for Women and Children in America*. New York: Free, 1985.

Wharton, Edith. *A Backward Glance*. New York: Appleton-Century, 1934.

Williams, Linda. *Hard Core: Power, Pleasure, and the "Frenzy of the Visible."* Berkeley: U of California P, 1989.

Wilson, Wendy. "Many Changes Afoot among Independents." *Video Business* 10 Mar. 1995: 1, 8.

## Filmography

*The Portrait of a Lady.* Dir. Jane Campion. Writ. Laura Jones. Perf. Nicole Kidman and John Malkovich. PolyGram, 1996.

*Washington Square.* Dir. Agnieszka Holland. Writ. Carol Doyle. Perf. Jennifer Jason Leigh, Ben Chaplin, Albert Finney, Maggie Smith. Hollywood Pictures/Caravan Pictures, 1997.

*The Wings of the Dove.* Dir. Iain Softley. Writ. Hossein Amini. Perf. Helena Bonham Carter, Linus Roache, Alison Elliott. Miramax, 1997.

Latest James

# "Based on the Novel by Henry James"

## The Golden Bowl 2000

### Lee Clark Mitchell

The Merchant Ivory adaptation of Henry James's *The Golden Bowl* (1906) opens with a flourish: a Renaissance scene that is one of the more telling in Prince Amerigo's family history. Night shadows swirl as costumed guards march up stone stairs to an adolescent son in bed with his young step-mother. Both are dragged off as an older son accuses them in front of his father, the Duke, and a double beheading is then presented in shadowed silhouette at the hands of a grim-faced executioner. The voice-over intimates that the step-mother was not only lascivious but greedy as well, desiring more money and all but attaining it through her "charming sweetness." The scene quickly absorbs us through its dramatic compression, playing out deadly passions we barely understand, capturing an abrupt mix of ardor and desperation, of adultery entwined with incest, of severe consequences to actions lightly undertaken—all presented melodramatically. For those familiar with James's novel, the scene foreshadows something implicit yet never represented: Prince Amerigo's incestuous liaison with his wife's step-mother, Charlotte Stant. Later, a costume party hints at this historical prefiguration when Amerigo enters as a velvet-garbed Renaissance courtier, identified visually with his adulterous ancestor. And after Maggie Verver, Amerigo's wife, begins to suspect her husband and Charlotte, the foreshadowing is confirmed at a slide lecture on Amerigo's family history that at last explicates the opening scene—an explanation that prompts Maggie to blurt out to her friend Fanny Assingham, "What awfulness is there between them? Anything there shouldn't be?" We have now been given three hints, but—as if they did not suffice—Charlotte and the Prince are later surprised by Adam Verver in the dark, and looming shadows suddenly replicate the scene of Renaissance step-mother being dragged away.

Purists may chafe at an echoed sequence that appears nowhere in the novel (Maggie goes to the British Museum to research Amerigo's history, but we never learn what she finds). Yet this set of inventions is hardly an isolated instance in the film, where more than half the scenes have no parallel in the novel, and characters barely mentioned have life breathed into them in the film; Mr. Blint, for instance, becomes a flirtatious, ragtime piano-playing "Charles." Such poetic license is not only unsurprising, it forms a truth universally acknowledged about films "based on" well-known novels: Howard Hawks's *The Big Sleep* (1946) and David Lean's *Great Expectations* (1947), Stanley Kubrick's *The Shining* (1980) and Anthony Minghella's *The English Patient* (1996) are all imaginative adaptations that play fast and loose with "their" novels. By contrast, the various adaptations of Fitzgerald's *The Great Gatsby* or Nabokov's *Lolita* play just as fast, just as loose, but in each case inadequately and unimaginatively. Cinematic success or failure has never depended on fidelity to an original. The screenwriter of *The Golden Bowl*, Ruth Prawer Jhabvala, well understood this premise in explaining that "fidelity is not the first [thing]" she worried about in creating the screenplay, especially in light of her admission that "I didn't really expect anyone to have read the book."[1] Of course, reading the book *is* the first prerequisite to writing a credible screenplay, but even more so, to finding a cinematic language that works as analogue to the novel's literary language. Conventionally, screenwriters adapting novels strive to incarnate psychological processes, to externalize complex states of being, to enact in full view a fine gradation of thought and feeling. That is a tough demand to make of either the theatrical or the visual arts, arts that greatly appealed to Henry James.[2] Film adaptation thus seems to cry out for alternative sequences *not* in the original novel, if the reader's experience is to be recreated in the cinematic medium.

Yet it hardly need be observed that James stymies filmmakers, not only in his relative lack of interest in plot closure, but in his taste for dilations of psychological nuance—for people thinking about what others are thinking. And that preference makes James's three late novels radically untheatrical. *The Golden Bowl* in particular resists either paraphrase or dramatization in fundamental ways, since establishing what happens is always a matter of establishing first whose view is taken. Characters elude our interpretations (far more than even earlier James), and indeterminacy becomes so central to the novel that any version tends simply to import the reader's own moral assumptions. The novel preeminently confirms the French director Jacques Rivette's claim in 1974 that James is one of the "unfilmable" authors, who "can be filmed diagonally, taking up their themes, but never literally" (Horne 2). Even James himself remarked that the most salient feature of *The Golden Bowl* was "a certain indirect and oblique view of my presented action," and went on to describe it "not as my own impersonal account of the

affair in hand, but as my account of somebody's impression of it" (19). Or
as he rephrased the issue: "I have in other words constantly inclined to the
idea of the particular attaching case *plus* some near individual view of it."
The point is that a single-authored plot now fascinated James less than
multiple plots, overlaying each other, intersecting from different perspectives. Adapting *that* vision might have resulted in an interesting avant-garde
film, drawing on the apparatus and technology of film itself to reproduce
such multiplicity. But as other essays here attest, adaptations of James have
customarily relied on the straightforward style of narrative Hollywood, regardless of where they are produced.

Keep in mind that the metaphorical vertiginousness of *The Golden
Bowl*, in its approximation of individuals trying to parse hidden motives
and obscure desires, reduces the reader to a state where big epistemological
questions—What is happening? What does it mean? How should it be
valued?—are paramount. Grammatical habits themselves have shifted: the
indicative verbs of earlier novels give way to an increasingly subjunctive
mode in which supposition, desire, and contingency all seem to displace
statements of actual fact. The most characteristic figure of speech in *The
Golden Bowl* is the hypothetical simile ("as if"), which renders what is absent
present, intimating meanings even as they are rhetorically set aside.[3] Such
highly metaphorical language performs a complex double game, re-order-
ing conceptions to match real possibilities but also re-shaping those possibilities according to the imaginative strength of a reader's (and character's)
conceptions. As Ruth Yeazell has argued, James creates "a world in which
the power of language to transform facts and even to create them seems
matched only by the stubborn persistence of facts themselves"(3). The un-
easiness we feel in judging characters or plot in *The Golden Bowl*, then, is
precisely what makes the opening sequence of the Merchant-Ivory adaptation an interesting maneuver, since it provides a melodramatic swirl of
events that defies understanding, thereby heightening our self-consciousness about the vexed process of understanding itself. It adroitly bears out
R.P. Blackmur's view of the novel as "the most poetic [of James's late works]
in the sense of its language as well as its structure, and also the most shadowy" (151). Yet to the extent that the film *is* "based on the novel by Henry
James"—and that it requires closer correspondence to *The Golden Bowl* than
a purely invented sequence—we need to take the temperature of the novelistic scenes, and then of their cinematic avatars.

No more instructive sequence for James's narrative strategy can be
found than in the scenes that bridge the novel's two volumes, which follow
the Castledean's house party at Matcham. Charlotte and the Prince have
been urged by their spouses to attend it together, and, when the house

party ends, they stay over for what is planned as an adulterous excursion to
Gloucester—an excursion invisible to the reader as it is to everyone within
the novel. The first scene represents Fanny Assingham's recollection of having arrived from Matcham to inform Maggie of the Prince's delay, prompting
Maggie to return home from her father's house at Eaton Square in order to
await her husband—a gesture that captures Fanny's attention. The second
scene initiates Maggie's half of the novel, as she awaits Amerigo and contemplates her life. What makes this sequence of scenes immensely interesting—apart from tracing a turn in Fanny's sympathies and Maggie's development—is that we are privy to a series of fine consciousnesses, each trying to
understand the other.

The first scene begins with Bob Assingham waiting for his wife to
speak, couched as a complex boating metaphor that tells how Fanny is
"making for land. He watched her steadily paddle . . . and at last felt her
boat bump. The bump was distinct, and in fact she stepped ashore. 'We
were all wrong. There's nothing'" (297). The suddenness of Fanny's declaration breaks up the metaphorical conceit, causing Bob (and the reader) to
fumble until she specifies that she means nothing illicit has occurred between the Prince and Charlotte. Fanny's next step is to contemplate the
Prince's and Charlotte's neglect by their spouses, epitomized by Maggie's
having "her room in [Adam's] house very much as she had it before she was
married" (302). Gradually, Fanny begins to appreciate what has drawn the
two together—"to-day it was as if I were suddenly, with a kind of horrible
push, seeing through their eyes" (301)—and begins to sympathize. Sympathy is compounded by a measure of guilt, however, since Fanny is sensible
of her own entanglement in the affair; she introduced Amerigo to Maggie,
and promoted Charlotte with Adam. This insight leaves her distraught and
in tears, though Bob's "kindness and his comfort" finally allow her to realize that "Charlotte and the Prince must be saved" (305–6).

Fanny now turns her attention to Maggie, who awaits Amerigo's return at Portland Place. Maggie strikes her, Fanny confesses to Bob, as "beginning to doubt. To doubt, for the first time, of her wonderful little judgement of her wonderful little world" (307). For what had begun in the
separate marriages as "beautiful intentions all round" (315)—especially in
the "guileless idea of still having her father . . . in her life"—has ended with
Charlotte and the Prince becoming "mere helpless victims of fate" (315).
Maggie's leaving Eaton Square is the faintest register of her renewed self-
consciousness about the selfish desire that has led her to neglect the Prince:
"And now she knows something or other has happened—yet hasn't heretofore known what" (317). Maggie will have to find out even though she
"'was the creature in the world,'" as Fanny realizes,

"to whom a wrong thing could least be communicated. It was as
if her imagination had been closed to it, her sense altogether
sealed. That therefore," Fanny continued, "is what will now
*have* to happen. Her sense will have to open. . . . To what's
called Evil—with a very big E: for the first time in her life. To
the discovery of it, to the knowledge of it, to the crude experience of it. . . . To the harsh bewildering brush, the daily chilling
breath of it." (310)

This melodramatic litany erupts into the narrative, converting a commonplace adulterous passion into a moral and metaphysical crisis, giving a
sense of Fanny's inflamed imagination but more importantly of the issues at
stake in Maggie's newly aroused perceptions. As much to the point, the
sequence establishes Fanny's exemplary role for the reader as his or her
representative: abjuring categorical judgments in favor of simply appreciat-
ing why her friends act as they do. Her ardent sensibility notwithstanding,
the overall effect is of someone struggling to fathom a human mystery even
as she senses the harm that that effort may inflict. As she admits, "I perpe-
trate—in thought—crimes" (301).

The second volume opens "many days" later with the stakes dramatically raised, as Maggie newly considers her situation. Like much of the novel,
the scene is self-consciously belated, the retrospection of someone working to
ascertain what she has already seen. Immediately apparent, however, is a shift
in the power of that consciousness, as Maggie muses on the "outlandish
pagoda" now right in "the very center of the garden of her life" (327). This,
James's most famous metaphor, initiates a constellation of other tropes that
reveal Maggie's extraordinary capacity to create understanding based on the
smallest measure of phenomenal facts: "The pagoda in her blooming garden figured the arrangement—how otherwise was it to be named?—by
which, so strikingly, she had been able to marry without breaking, as she
liked to put it, with her past" (328). Maggie has continued to live in a state
of blissfully arrested development, marrying without yet having to "pay" for
the privilege. But what her husband's stay at Matcham has immediately
triggered is the curious desire "to do something just then and there which
would strike Amerigo as unusual" (331). In fact, her return to Portland Place
does affect him with "a kind of violence" (335) when he enters the room,
though the scene that ensues is entirely silent, consisting of her long internal
monologue—"Some such words as those were what *didn't* ring out" (337)—as
they look at each other expectantly.

An extraordinary power emerges from these scenes—Fanny contemplating the couples from afar, Maggie newly assessing her situation—that

engenders drama almost entirely on the basis of pure thoughts. Fanny's are expressed straightforwardly, aloud to her husband, while Maggie's are expressed to no one, in metaphorical leaps and bounds. The dramatic transition occurs as Fanny shifts from alarm at the behavior of Charlotte and the Prince to sympathy for their situation, while Maggie alters from a happy daughter in concert with Adam to a troubled wife unsure of how to approach her husband. The latter transition in particular is entirely internal and shades guilt and innocence together so thoroughly as to make any such distinction fade in importance against considerations of impetus and motive.

Hard as these two scenes are to represent cinematically, they are so centrally important that a film of *The Golden Bowl* cannot really get by without them. Not surprisingly, the adultery elided by James is put up on screen: Charlotte (Uma Thurman) and Amerigo (Jeremy Northam) appear in dishabille at the Gloucester inn, lounging until a kiss turns up the erotic charge and she mounts him fully clothed. As in Hossein Amini's screenplay for Iain Softley's *The Wings of the Dove* (1997), a now-familiar rule for adapting high culture texts is observed: adding explicit sexual encounters that were left by novelists to the reader's imagination. At this point, the film cuts abruptly to Maggie (Kate Beckinsale) waiting before a fire at Portland Place as Amerigo enters and asks "Why are you in the dark?" They converse in strained tones that register their mutual uncertainty, with Maggie clearly uneasy about her husband's account of the trip, pressing him about Gloucester cathedral and querying which king is buried there (a question that forms a motif of suspicion and is later repeated to Charlotte). Finally, she recalls a dream she had in his absence, "of being locked inside a beautiful pagoda, where I thought I was happy. Then something strange happened . . . a sound . . . a feeling more than a sound. I tapped the wall, and it was as if it pinged or had a crack. I thought I was trapped in there, and became frightened. Father must never know."

The invented erotic tumble, paired with a theatricalized "verbalization" of Maggie's interior monologue, creates a dyad that stands for the two bridge scenes in the novel. Fanny's and Maggie's prolonged meditations after the fact, as well as their consciousness of others' felt motives for action before the fact, become the basis for staging the fact itself: the actual domestic transgression with its social consequences. Even though the long scene in which Fanny and Bob try to understand the Prince and Charlotte is, as a dialogue, closer to theater than either the invisible adultery or the famous interior monologue, in such a cinematic context it is evidently misplaced. It is ostensibly "wrong" for presenting a complicating view, or refining any sense of pressures that have conspired against marital ideals; "wrong" for corroborating a long history of spousal neglect; "wrong" simply for initiating Fanny's sympathy. Instead, *The Golden Bowl* 2000 attends obsessively to the novel's lurid plot of adultery, with a single glaring eye that ignores James's strategy of introducing transgression *through* perceptions, of having acts themselves pale against a gradual consciousness of them. Ruth Prawer Jhabvala offers straightforward actions and events in a revision that, as it happens, was first proposed in patronizing tones to Henry by his brother, William:

> "Your methods and my ideals seem the reverse, the one of the other—and yet I have to admit your extreme success in this book. But why won't you, just to please Brother, sit down and write a new book, with no twilight or mustiness in the plot, with great vigor and decisiveness in the action, no fencing in the dialogue, no psychological commentaries, and absolute straightness in the style? Publish it in my name, I will acknowledge it, and give you half the proceeds" (Gard 392).

Henry's response, tongue in cheek, was to agree: "I *will* write you your book, on that two-and-two-make-four system on which all the awful truck that surrounds us is produced, and *then* descend to my dishonoured grave" (Gard 393).

Two and two makes four: That *is* the movies Hollywood style (though not necessarily "film" or "cinema"). Jhabvala's consent to William's proposal means attending to the sexual transgression rather than the anxieties it arouses—to the "shabby adultery," as Blackmur described the mere occasion for the novel, rather than the "poetic drama of the soul's action" that is its true subject (152). If William's call for "vigor and decisiveness" seems a prescription for an action-adventure movie, *The Golden Bowl* 2000 is another staple: the Hollywood melodrama of sexual forces unfettered by standard marital conventions, the postman who always rings twice. Adultery itself—though invisible in the novel—explains why the novel was considered ripe for cinematic translation at all, since it has never been widely read. Yet our delight in film adaptations of Edwardian novelists—Wharton, Forster, James—results not simply from their visually splendid voyeurism, nor from their emphasis on adultery and domestic unhappiness, but because characters of the Edwardian era still think chastity and marital fidelity *are* important, which may constitute the most exotic lure of all. What's clear when we return to James's novel is that he is less intrigued by lurid plot than lurid plotting, especially the prospective surmises, retrospective conjectures, and historical patterns by which individuals are constructed. The film sometimes captures what is beyond plot—for instance, in the opening fantasy, or in the scene between Charlotte and the Prince after their excursion to Gloucester,

Figure 26. Jeremy Northan and Uma Thurman in Merchant Ivory's *The Golden Bowl.* Arnaud Borrel.

meeting the next day in Mme. Tussaud's wax museum to consider their mutual guilt (see Figure 26). Here they supposedly feel safe from their social circle, even as the wax figures gradually seem to come alive, gazing watchfully at them, wonderfully embodying the adulterous couple's anxiety about being watched as well as what others might think or know. James's interior monologues have taken up residence in a collection of wax eyes.

Yet such scenes are exceptions in a film that shifts from epistemological melodrama, in its excesses of thought beneath the social surface, back to phenomenal melodrama, with its excesses of action played out onscreen. Where James presents unsettled figures divided against themselves—or as he later recalled them, "each of the real, the deeply involved and immersed and more or less bleeding participants" (20)—the film might be said to offer allegorical types, emblematizing anger (Fanny), mistreatment (Maggie), lasciviousness (Charlotte), or idealism (Adam). No one seems more than momentarily conflicted, and even the Prince shifts from a seduced figure to an abandoning one with few compunctions or reservations. Fanny Assingham, whom Anjelica Huston plays as a stern, self-certain moralizer, never admits responsibility for Maggie's introduction to Amerigo (that this *is* a responsibility would, in any case, be enigmatic to a twenty-first-century audience) and shows no distress at her own continuing involvement. Instead, she chides Charlotte and the Prince for appearing to spend time together, contradicting the novel's representation of her as someone notable for holding her tongue and for acting with anxious solicitude on behalf of her friends. The discreet but tortured Fanny—who does *not* say what's on her mind, who "came in fact within an ace of saying" (224) or "was on the point of replying" (233)—is never present in the film.

Jeremy Northam's Prince likewise is transformed into a more forceful figure, driving his own car (relegating his chauffeur to the back seat) or vigorously winning a bicycle race. This is a pumped-up version of the novel's restrained aristocrat who is so sublimely above emotion that when Maggie first intimates her suspicions, his failure to respond is described thus: "though he had in so almost mystifying a manner, replied to nothing, denied nothing, explained nothing, apologised for nothing, he had some-how conveyed to her that this was not because of any determination to treat her case as not 'worth' it" (478). The cinematic Prince is animated and incensed, responding to Maggie's angry accusations by joining the fray and shouting back. Jhabvala defended this transformation with her own erotic calculus, one that by implication devalues such Jamesian leading men as Gilbert Osmond, Owen Gereth, and Merton Densher: "Well, you can't have a languid central character, otherwise why would these two women be in love with him? You need some kind of driving force" (Horne 6). Where, one might ask, was the fieldwork that determined which women necessar-ily agree to such a claim? But that's the movies, once again. Our desires are shaped for us as gender clichés, in a gesture that abandons the darker, idiosyncratic characters peopling James's fiction. What distinguishes the novel's Prince is his phlegmatic willingness to let others attend to him, his realization that he can be handsomely objectified, even feminized as a fig-ure waiting to be possessed, a passive man over whom strong women battle.

While Fanny and Amerigo evolve into more forceful cinematic pres-ences, Maggie in a kind of reciprocal economy becomes at once less com-manding and inspiring. This is primarily a problem of casting, since Kate Beckinsale cannot express the mix of imaginative insight and quiet restraint that James invests in Maggie. Yet the problem is also linked to James's own narrative strategy, in the slow delay of our access to the consciousness of a clever woman who willfully neglects her husband for so long. The film makes it harder to see how she might be transformed from childlike naïveté into fearsome, even ruthless accommodation. And by focusing on marital drama rather than interpretive dilemmas, the film no longer gives us a Maggie thinking and wondering, trying anxiously to possess others rather than be possessed by them. Consider one of her mental images early in the novel's second half, imagining Adam and her in a coach being pulled by

Charlotte and the Prince: "She had seen herself at last, in the picture she was studying, suddenly jump from the coach; whereupon, frankly, with the wonder of the sight, her eyes opened wider and her heart stood still for a moment. She looked at the person so acting as if this person were somebody else, waiting with intensity to see what would follow. . . . what in particular would the figure in the picture do?" (342). Like countless other moments, this scene registers Maggie's intensely imaginative willingness to wonder about herself, to ponder what she might do by envisioning herself in strange situations and fantastic perspectives, all in terms of facts she does not yet know. Kate Beckinsale, by contrast, plays the role impulsively, even impetuously, and thus Maggie—not only with Fanny but with Amerigo—is reduced to a stereotypical wronged woman, miserable and outraged.

Of all the female characters, however, Charlotte endures the most unsettling transformation from novel to film. Her first appearance in an invented sequence in Rome establishes her ongoing passion for the Prince despite his impending marriage, and her unabated desire is displayed in every subsequent scene they share together. Charlotte becomes a merely two-dimensional figure, which was Uma Thurman's intention: "It's delightful to play someone who is kind of wicked, with no conscience, no guilt, no twentieth-century psychology wrapping her up. She is quite free" (Press notes 7). If the film alchemically translates Charlotte into a vixen after all, the irony is that the cinematic Charlotte bears a family resemblance to other ruthless women in James, beginning with Mme. Merle in *The Portrait of a Lady* (1881). Yet the difference is that, while both are remorselessly conspiratorial, Charlotte (as portrayed by James) so elicits compassion that generations of critics have found in her the novel's most sympathetic character.[4]

James's Charlotte engenders sympathy not only because of her scruples but because she is less selfish and more self-divided than Thurman ever tries to suggest. When we inhabit Charlotte's consciousness in the first half of the novel, as Ruth Yeazell observes, we are aware of "not a coherent viewpoint but a mind deeply and mysteriously in conflict with itself. Conscious pretense and innocent self-deception, fact and desire, the situation that Charlotte knows to exist and the situation she wishes to create—all merge in the elusive movements of James's prose" (9). But film does not let us "inhabit": in radical ways, it forces us to view from the outside figures who necessarily remain as opaque as they literally are on the screen. The novel's Charlotte expresses qualms to Adam—"Do you think you've 'known' me?" (195)—asking him to wait for a response to his marriage proposal until they hear from Maggie and Amerigo. And when the Prince's "grave" (208) telegram arrives, she offers it to Adam (an offer he politely declines), even knowing it would "have dished her marriage" (245). The reversal of this sequence in the film (Adam sends a letter to Maggie announcing their engagement) epitomizes all that has been turned inside out in the film's representation of character.

The film's gesture of flattening psychic interiors to make characters less self-divided continues in Charlotte's married pursuit of the Prince. The film follows the novel in having her finally visit him at Portland Place to exclaim about being left so often alone by their spouses: "What else can we do, what in all the world else?" (253). Yet James does not let them off from their openly adulterous response to such circumstances, and equates their moral hair-splitting to a parody of ethics, confirmed in the banal locutions they exchange as they finally "seal their pledge" with a passionate kiss (259). Whatever sympathy we feel for Charlotte, in short, is matched by an equal measure of disdain in a complex combination that is never approached by the film. The question worth asking, then, is what is at stake in the conversion of Charlotte into a vixen, a Lulu motivated by sexual desire with the wide eyes of moral blankness? Perhaps just as the film's Amerigo is the mythic "man of action," panting in his bicycle race, there to appeal to some exaggerated notion of "what women want," Charlotte is there because she represents what *The Golden Bowl* 2000 thinks men in the audience want. In the process, however, not only has James's ethically nuanced vision been erased, but his sense for the gradations of sex and gender has been reduced to romance novel stereotypes. Charlotte offers to run away with Amerigo, sentimentally agreeing to impoverishment all for love, thus defying the very premise of James's novel. And when Amerigo refuses, she becomes alternately mawkish and imperious, finally slapping him out of spite in a bizarre gesture that threatens to reconfigure the film as B-movie melodrama. Given this transformation for the worse, it seems appropriate that the film should end with Charlotte's triumphant return to America as Adam's wife.[5] Her excoriatingly private anguish in the novel, which Maggie perceives but will not alleviate, is transformed into public triumph.

If Charlotte's conversion into a species of "fatal attraction" seems strange, it is easily matched by Adam Verver's metamorphosis into a vigorous, idealistic, potentially violent master manipulator of everyone else. He is the most elusive, unknowable figure in all of James, as indicated by Gore Vidal's series of pointed questions: "What, finally, does Adam Verver know? and what, finally, does he do? . . . does Maggie lead him? Or does he manage her? Can it be that it is Adam who pulls all the strings?" (*GB* 12–13). Readers find him as bewildering as does everyone in the novel, and the chapter devoted to Adam alone (beginning Book II) confirms that even the narrator himself cannot make him out, "inscrutably monotonous behind an iridescent cloud" (131). Nick Nolte approximates this intended elusiveness through his acting style, but the screenplay repeatedly gives him lines that counteract this aloof air. His very history, invented by Jhabvala, provides a new motive for his collecting. He explains to Charlotte that he got his start from bituminous coal, employing immigrant workers twelve hours a day, seven days a week, all year long. And it is supposedly Adam's realization that "the workers have never seen anything beautiful" which gives him a mission—to bring his whole collection together for the "ungrateful citizens of American City." Charlotte baldly protests that "They want streetcars, not your museum," and Adam's forceful retort summarily defines his film character: "They may not want it, but they shall have it." Adam's history, in short, explains his idealism, which gives him a purpose larger than Maggie—something the novel refuses to do.

The film also gives us clear views of what Adams sees and allows us to impute what he must be thinking. This occurs most spectacularly when he opens a door to stumble on Charlotte in the dark with the Prince, melodramatically looming above them, hovering in the lighted frame. Adam's shadow all but absorbs the two figures, registering cinematically his awareness of their adulterous behavior. The scene is informed by the suppressed rage that Nolte emanates in the role, and Jhabvala finally confirms this temperament in a long, quietly threatening speech she has Adam make to Amerigo, in which he explains that his love of Maggie is the deepest thing about him. He recalls dining at a restaurant years before when a man looked at his wife too obviously, and Adam took a knife, "perhaps only a butter knife," to confront the man before being dragged out by his wife. "The first and last time in my life I ever failed to pay the check," he adds wryly.

This fiercely masculine strain resonates through the film, given Nolte's large, magnetically engaging presence. He is clearly a man capable of handling others directly rather than (as the novel represents him) a small, pot-bellied figure managing affairs unobtrusively from afar. James's Adam Verver is someone who "feared the idea of danger, or in other words feared, hauntedly, himself. . . . he lived in terror of having to" say no to others (134), which is part of the reason Maggie wants him to be married. Instead, Nolte plays Adam as an idealist and social egalitarian, vigorous and commanding as well as aware of his wife's adultery. "There is no ambiguity," Jhabvala feels, about Adam's knowledge, and he clearly "manipulates the entire situation—he and Maggie between them. He in silence, but he knew what everyone else was thinking." As Jhabvala adds: "He's immensely clever. A man doesn't become a billionaire and a patron of the arts if he's dim!" (Horne 5). Whether or not this prognosis is accurate, her version of Adam discriminates less than James's, as does her reading of his affiliation with Maggie.

Jhabvala simply denies anything incestuous about their relationship, or anything sinister in their treatment of others, since "the Ververs . . . are all
goodness, and Henry James painted them as goodness, in a way that an
earlier Bostonian knows goodness" (Horne 6).

But now, finally, for the one motif that is visible in the novel and
suppressed in the film: the father's and daughter's exclusive involvement
with one another. James repeatedly stresses that this state of affairs helped
lead to Charlotte's and Amerigo's adultery, yet the inability of *The Golden
Bowl* 2000 to imagine it as a contributing factor is reflected in the rarity with
which Adam and Maggie are shown alone together. On the contrary, the
first post-nuptial scene of either Maggie or Amerigo shows them at Portland
Place lovingly conversing together, succeeded by Charlotte at Fawns playing Debussy's "Sarabande" to Adam, followed in turn by a scene of Maggie
in Rome with Amerigo. Maggie only once leaves her husband to rejoin her
father—an incidence that hardly supports Charlotte's claim that "Maggie
thinks more on the whole of fathers than of husbands" (221). In short,
we're deprived cinematically once again of the causes for the marital drama
that unfolds.

All in all, this metamorphosis of James's cast of characters coupled
with the invention of so many scenes raises the question of what is achieved
by converting the "melodramatic" tenor of the novel—its metaphorical excesses and fantastic hypothetical style—into a melodramatic plot, without
recuperating those excesses in the domains that film uniquely possesses: in
sound effects, musical score, editing, cinematography, light and shadow.
One obvious answer is that by removing the "twilight or mustiness in the
plot" and relying upon "straightness of style" (as William James favored) the
film by default substantiates the wealth of cosmopolitan Americans living
in great houses. The account of a princely collector becomes a study of regal
opulence, exceeding all other Edwardian films in its focus on lavish interiors. The action is set in art-filled rooms with only occasional exteriors of
English castles (Belvoir Castle in Rutland), great country houses (Burghley
House, and Lord Northumberland's Syon Park in Middlesex; Helmingham
Hall in East Anglia), and Italian palaces (the Castello Massimo, in Arsoli).
The director James Ivory's supreme pride, in fact, seems to lie in set design,
in the great houses and extraordinary art he brought together for the film,
as though he imagined himself Adam Verver, collecting paintings by Poussin
and Holbein, Gainsborough and Teniers, Reynolds and Romney. And Ivory's
efforts are curiously echoed by those of Nolte's Adam Verver, who adores
Raphael, even Perugino, but also has nothing against using paintings for
wallpaper. When Charlotte inquires of the portraits at Fawns, Adam admits not knowing the names since "they came with the house"—a comment

corresponding to Ivory's description of cinematographer Tony Pierce-Roberts's efforts, who shot the film with anamorphic lenses that "often caused the backgrounds to go somewhat out of focus, suggesting a rich period decor without allowing too much distraction" (Ivory 3). Of course, film being film, background readily bleeds into foreground, with the visual surface serving as a primary reason for the film's potential appeal. Both John Bright, the costume designer, and Anna Pinnock, the set decorator, fill the screen with luxurious murals, rooms chock-a-block full of sculptures, paintings, and *objets d'art*, lush scenes all peopled with characters garbed in morning coats and evening wear, fancy frocks and designer hats, bejewelled arms and necks, and stick pins in ties always tied. These are all presented as if they were SUVs in a commercial aimed at an audience whose affection for such signs of affluent existence is largely unexamined and uncritical.

Confirming this hypothesis, Ivory claimed to have been heavily influenced by the paintings of John Singer Sargent (1856–1925): "Sargent gave visual expression to James's world of monied Americans living amongst titled, sophisticated people. His portraits often depict exactly the same cast of characters James was writing about. . . . Their visual references were similar, so their worlds overlapped" (Ivory 1–2). The very color register of the film was explicitly intended to invoke Sargent's vision: "It is . . . the frequent combination of certain colors—with strong yellows and ochers, set off by black, white, and pink—that strongly suggests Sargent" (3). Even without this testament to America's great society portraitist, the film clearly offers a painterly exploration of character and action, registering attitudes and values pictorially when it cannot in terms of action or dialogue. Or as Ivory flatly stated of sixteenth-century Helmingham Hall, "the story is in this" (Hodge E1). That half-architectonic, half-painterly focus helps explain why Jhabvala replaces the "official party" that opens Book III with a lavish costume ball at London's Lancaster House ("one of the few surviving private London townhouses . . . restored a few years ago," according to Ivory; "we found it totally sumptuous," 3). It allows John Bright to costume Charlotte as a seductive Cleopatra and the Prince as a Renaissance courtier. Another sequence that serves the same purpose is the invented Orientalist ballet at the post-Gloucester buffet dinner that enacts a drama of illicit female desire, male objectification, patriarchal domination, and self-annihilation—all themes binding together Jhabvala's interpretation of the novel. The ballet's swirling motion, moreover, suggests a visual rhythm that registers the pulsations of both character and plot, echoing Charlotte's pull—at least as Jhabvala imagines her—toward and away from the Prince.

If Ivory's cinematic style effectively translates James's setting into scenes that appear nowhere in the novel, it is salutary to recall that James himself rarely focuses on literal surfaces or provides close physical descriptions (unlike, say, Edith Wharton). As a writer, he was relatively indifferent to an opaque, phenomenal world that might be represented mimetically, and only truly energized by a transparency that gives access to the psychological processes no one can see.[6] His earlier novels may occasionally offer a realistic view of locales, though even Gardencourt or Osmond's Florentine villa (to pause only at *The Portrait of a Lady*) serve more as metonymy for character than as full pictorial descriptions. The gallery at Gardencourt that so fascinates Isabel is after all never described, nor are the numerous "spoils" at Poynton (excepting a Maltese Cross). Later, such realistic depictions are even rarer: Milly Theale's pointed comparison to Bronzino's portrait of Lucrezia Panciatichi or Strether's escape from Paris into a vista likened to a Lambinet landscape. This descriptive reticence makes it all the more remarkable that one of the few times James turns a pictorial eye on things in *The Golden Bowl* occurs in the Bloomsbury shop where Charlotte and the Prince seek a wedding present. The passage offers an extraordinarily comprehensive vision and for its rarity in James is worth quoting in full:

> Of decent old gold, old silver, old bronze, of old chased and jewelled artistry, were the objects that, successively produced, had ended by numerously dotting the counter where the shopman's slim light fingers, with neat nails, touched them at moments, briefly, nervously, tenderly, as those of a chess-player rest, a few seconds, over the board, on a figure he thinks he may move and then may not: small florid ancientries, ornaments, pendants, lockets, brooches, buckles, pretexts for dim brilliants, bloodless rubies, pearls either too large or too opaque for value; miniatures mounted with diamonds that had ceased to dazzle; snuff-boxes presented to—or by—the too-questionable great; cups, trays, taper-stands, suggestive of pawn-tickets, archaic and brown, that would themselves, if preserved, have been prized curiosities. A few commemorative medals of neat outline but dull reference; a classic monument or two, things of the first years of the century; things consular, Napoleonic, temples, obelisks, arches, tinily re-embodied, completed the discreet cluster; in which, however, even after tentative re-enforcement from several quaint rings, intaglios, amethysts, carbuncles, each of which had found a home in the ancient sallow satin of some weakly-snapping little box, there was, in spite of the due proportion of faint poetry, no great force of persuasion. They looked, the visitors, they touched, they vaguely pretended to consider,

but with scepticism, so far as courtesy permitted, in the quality of their attention. (115)

The description is so variously particularized as to overwhelm the reader, yet it builds by accumulation to suggest finally a breathless insufficiency. One gathers here something like a prospective rebuke to Adam's collecting sensibility or Ivory's visual imagination, suggesting desire could never be satisfied by mere possessions. The SUVs, James would warn us, are hardly worth the game.

At this point, then, we should return to the title of this essay to address the question implicitly raised by Merchant-Ivory: What does it mean to make "a film based on a novel by Henry James?" That qualifying attribution in the opening credits offers a pre-emptive strike; by stressing "based on," the film-makers ruefully confess to compromises for which they suspect a reproach. After all, *The Golden Bowl* 2000 is not *The Golden Bowl*, and the attribution therefore aims to defuse the very act of comparison. Yet since the film-makers assume the audience's ignorance of their source ("I didn't really expect anyone to have read the book"), this qualifying attribution appears like an odd gesture addressed to a coterie of hecklers—academics, intellectuals, James lovers—so marginal as to be entirely irrelevant. What guilt lurks here? Consider by contrast Amy Heckerling's *Clueless* (1995), which offers a brilliant updating of Jane Austen's *Emma* even though the novel is never mentioned. The resetting in Beverley Hills, the characters' names that are changed, the plot sequences invented and Valley-girl dialogue created: all bring the novel's myth into the twentieth century. Perhaps part of the difference is that James's novel, unlike Austen's, provides little to adapt, as a young Virginia Woolf realized right off: "The plot, if one can call it so, is of the slightest; an episode—an incident to be disposed of by the average novelist in ten pages or less" (Woolf 22). And with so little plot, the success of an adaptation resides in somehow converting other aspects of the novel into cinematic raw material.

It goes without saying that different adaptations of the same text remain different, and the advantage of having more than one film adaptation is that such differences expose possibilities in the original text not immediately apparent. Indeed, any adaptation opens up aspects of character (frequently through inventive casting), or clarifies plot (customarily through flashbacks and parallel editing), or modulates narrative pressures (by emphasizing visually muted scenes, often through the sound-track) that we hadn't necessarily appreciated in the original. Of course, bringing novels to the screen invariably means cutting scenes and revising dialogue, even while swatches of verbal description must be converted to visual images. But for

those devoted to the original, even poor adaptations—perhaps those especially—allow a reconsideration of what it is that keeps drawing us back to
the narrative, compelling a desire for it in another form. Adaptation establishes, in short, what is at stake in the novel, thematically and otherwise. In
the case of James's *The Golden Bowl*, the only other cinematic rendering is a
Masterpiece Theatre production aired in 1973, scripted by the BBC's long-
time great books adapter Jack Pulman and directed by James Cellan Jones.
By contrast with the Merchant Ivory film, this was clearly a bare-bones
production, with restrained costumes, uncluttered rooms, shot in under-
stated studio sets. The acting is reserved, without passionate embraces or
energetic expressions, and the camera matches this dramatic style with its
unadventurous recourse to a sequence of medium shots—thoroughly unlike the inventive mixture of long shots, tracking shots, and close-ups that
lend to the Merchant Ivory production a quick-moving dynamism comple-
mented by Richard Robbins's vibrant musical score. By contrast, the Masterpiece Theatre production has a characteristically flat (and silent) quality
that is distinctly televisual, very much of its time in the early 1970s.

   Yet this early production—proclaimed by Alistair Cooke, according to
one reviewer, as "the finest ever shown on Masterpiece Theater" (IMDb 1)—
enjoys some advantages over the Merchant Ivory film, and we might pause
at this point to consider their effect. The first advantage lies in casting.
Gayle Hunnicutt as Charlotte is no vixen but instead elegant, passionate yet
restrained, in love if also in financial straits, clearly a true friend of Maggie's
and aware of the moral dilemmas of her situation. Barry Morse's relative
sexlessness and wry indefiniteness as Adam allows us room to wonder; it is
hard to know what he knows or wants. Jill Townsend offers a brighter,
adept Maggie with mask-like discretion as well as a certain ruthless calculation. In a novel so clearly about people *acting* for each other, figuring out
what others know, this cast keeps the characters' secrets better. The second
advantage of the production is less easily matched: its four-and-a-half-hour
running time (meant to be viewed over six weeks) enables a closer approximation to the novel's sub-plots and minor scenes, giving in the process a
richer psychological tapestry.

   The production's third advantage, however, is the most critical: the
use of Bob Assingham (Cyril Cusack) as a narrator *in* the film, frequently in
voice-over as others act on-screen, informs us of their doubts and anticipa-
tions, their lingering questions and mixed motives. This conceit is established right off, with Bob seated in his club, facing the camera after the
credits have rolled: "I want to tell you a story. It's the most extraordinary
story you've ever heard. Extraordinary in a sense for what didn't happen
than for what did. More for what was never said than what was actually

spoken. It was the very silence of people who could so easily have given vent to their feelings. The fact that they did so little, when in the normal way one would have expected them to do so much, that makes the story curious, and I repeat, extraordinary. I was connected with the story only on the fringe, but Fanny was, you might say, in the thick of it, where, to be honest, she has a habit of being, and dragging me along with her. Not that I minded very much in this case. Because she demonstrates so much interest in other people's business." Jack Pulman's shrewd strategy was to establish from the beginning the idea of a story extraordinary "more for what was never said than what was actually spoken" and then to choose Bob Assingham to articulate "what was never said." Of the main characters, solely Bob is not involved in the story and can thus take the on-screen role played by Fanny in the novel, of narrator and, in Virginia Woolf's phrase, "official explainer" (383). In doing so, he nicely theatricalizes those aspects of the novel I admired in discussing Fanny's central scene above. Not only does this strategy capture the retrospective stance so often taken by figures in the novel as they ruminate about old incidents and dead conversations, but it defines Bob as a surrogate for the viewer (akin to Fanny's role in the novel), attempting to read the play of consciousness on others' faces. It even captures Fanny's emotional range in the novel, by allowing for different discursive registers as Bob both reports and comments on what others are thinking or saying.

The ploy may seem cinematically crude and easily parodied, though one could imagine a full-scale production that incorporated it as part of an imaginative, avant-garde reconceptualization of James's novel. Certainly the strategy corresponds to the reasons for James's delight in the novel's "indirect and oblique view of my presented action." That indirection more generally is part of what makes James so difficult for filmmakers, and capturing it on film requires the kind of cinematic technique that focuses our attention on the frame (and framer) even as it reinscribes elusiveness and indeterminacy back into the cinematic image. Consider the initial meeting of the Prince and Charlotte at Fanny's, as the camera lingers on them while Bob speaks: "They confronted each other, these two, across the room like two tormented creatures from a previous life. Now *what* that previous life had been in detail no one really knew, though Fanny professed to be sure of it. But that something *had* happened between them was certain. You could see it in the way the Prince was so markedly off-balance for the moment, and the way that Charlotte was so certainly on." This passage is closely adapted from the novel's anonymous narrator, but by making it Bob's speech, foregrounding his own role as narrator, an important dual thematic strain is sustained throughout: of people watching others, who watch others in turn; and of a rich psychological responsiveness lying under the masks that everyone dons.[7] Neither of these strains appears in the same scene from *The Golden Bowl* 2000, where Charlotte's desire and the Prince's past are both perfectly obvious.

"Other people's business," as Bob characterizes Fanny's "interest," is central to the novel, and his plaintive query early on—"why keep meddling?"—only prompts Fanny's response that one *does* meddle with those for whom one cares (99). Pulman's script deftly captures this interconnected quality in the novel, beginning with Bob's listening to Fanny's realization that she had helped create Maggie's marriage and must now "see that Charlotte gets a good husband as soon as possible" to help both Charlotte and Maggie (100). This is simply the inescapable consequence of living in James's late narrative world, where people are always interested in others, trying selflessly to assist, being "only too solicitous for each other's happiness." As Virginia Woolf waggishly observed: "The book, indeed, might be called a study in the evils of unselfishness" (Woolf 23). By contrast—and here again adaptations clarify each other—the Merchant Ivory production takes an opposite view of people, as individuals driven by their pasts (in Amerigo's case, melodramatically so), acting as autonomous agents, not particularly solicitous of each other's fate.

One index of the relative success of the Masterpiece Theatre production lies in its adaptation of Fanny's dialogue and Maggie's interior monologue, which bridge the novel's two volumes. Like Jhabvala, Pulman adds a scene at the Gloucester inn between Charlotte and the Prince, though Pulman echoes the novel's allusiveness by focusing only on their conversation over tea downstairs as they talk about taking a room. The film then cuts abruptly to the scene in London between Fanny and Bob, rendered nearly verbatim from the novel, evoking her uncertainty, her sense of responsibility, and her self-divided fear. The second scene, however, is worth a fuller description to suggest the striking effect of its use of dialogue, voice-over, and camera work. The camera first focuses on Bob speaking: "So Maggie waited, her heart I'm sure beating very fast." Then, as the camera shifts to Maggie, he slowly elaborates on what he believes motivates her in the decision to wait at Portland Place.

> She meant nothing reckless, nothing fundamental. She meant nothing more than that a discordant note had been sounded within her. How or why she didn't know. And that she had heard it, and that she'd wanted her husband to see that she had. It was late. It was no longer any question of that. The only thing was whether he might not have elected to stay on at Eaton Square. She'd left no message, another decision, and he might suppose that she'd already dined. And then again he might

have stayed on to be nice to her father, and that too would be utterly like him. All these thoughts must have gone through her mind as she tried to convince herself that what she was doing was the most normal thing in the world for a wife *to* do, to await her husband in his own home.

What is interesting here is the evocation of Bob's uncertainty as he in turn evokes Maggie's uncertainty about Amerigo, all within a context of her having acted at once uncharacteristically and unobjectionably. Throughout, the camera focuses on Jill Townsend's face as she waits, eerily motionless though slightly troubled, while Bob's voice continues on the sound track until the end of the scene, when his own face returns onscreen. Oddly, the ruminative power of this sequence seems (like many others) to negate the camera, making us concentrate on what is occurring mentally and emotionally (via voice-over) rather than physically (on-screen). In that regard, the film *does* make complex interior states of being visible, as, I argued earlier, any adequate adaptation of James must.

The Prince (Daniel Massey) arrives after the scene shifts from Bob to Maggie, allowing us to watch *her* watch his entry, observing (in Bob's words, again) "him visibly uncertain as to how he should find her. She hadn't known quite what she expected of him, but she hadn't expected the least shade of embarrassment." The camera then shifts back to Bob, who cautiously concedes: "yet that was written for a brief moment large upon his face. It had clearly made for him some difference, her meeting him alone and at home instead of elsewhere and with others. A difference that couldn't be measured by a simple disturbance in his routine. It was as if he harbored the impression of something markedly and pointedly prepared for him. And then it was gone." Again, Bob's voice-over elaborates meanings an actor might only faintly convey before Daniel Massey sits down without a greeting from Maggie. It is the next sequence, however, that forms one of the film's more arresting combinations, beginning with Bob intoning, "What she *might* have said, what she *longed* to say, I suppose, was," and then a quick segue into Maggie's own silent voice-over—taken again, as was the whole scene, nearly verbatim from the novel:

Why have I made this evening such a point of our not dining together? Well, because I've all day been so wanting you so all alone that I finally couldn't bear it, and there didn't seem to be any great reason why I should try to. You seem these last days, I don't know what, more absent than ever before, too absent for us merely to go on so. It's all very well and I perfectly see how

beautiful it is all around. But there comes a day when something snaps and the cup flows over. That's it. The cup all day
has been too full to carry, so here I am with it spilling it over
you, because it's my life after all, and I don't have to explain, do
I, that I'm as much in love with you now as on the first hour we
met, except there are some hours, which I know when they
come because they frighten me, that you are even more so, and
they do come, oh how they come, how they come.

Through all this, the camera points at a Maggie whose face remains entirely
fixed, until Bob breaks the frame with, "But of course she couldn't say that.
And how could she without making it seem more to him than she meant it to
seem?" In fact, the only words initially spoken *in* the scene are the Prince's,
expressing surprise that she's at Portland Place; they then chat about Gloucester,
and he dismisses himself with "I must go and bathe." As in the novel, the
jarring, unsettling impression is that he must wash off the smells of his interlude with Charlotte, leaving Maggie sitting alone as the room darkens and the
camera pulls back. The entire scene has achieved its effect of compelling us to
look at Maggie as she *thinks*, registering her emotional range before us, playing
out on Jill Townsend's face the slight, fleeting expressions of anxiety, longing,
and restrained insight that accompany her new understanding.

If the success of this adaptive strategy lies in its echoing the novel in
the domain of film, this is also paradoxically a flaw in the Masterpiece
Theatre production: its radical literalness. Notwithstanding the production's
considerable achievement, it never quite reproduces the effervescent, mer-
curial, dizzying quality of the novel nor converts a melodramatic epistemological vision into the commensurate cinematic experience that is achieved
at least twice in *The Golden Bowl* 2000. Yet if so faithful a transcription is
never in itself entirely sufficient, the Masterpiece Theatre production does
suggest what a necessary condition might be and what, more generally, can
be lost by an overly loose adaptation that fleshes out James's "slight" plot
into a lurid pot-boiler. With all due regard for the demands imposed on
conventional Hollywood films, the only reason for adapting *The Golden
Bowl* (unread as it may well be) is to transform Henry James's thematic concerns and narrative technique into another medium that might approxi-
mate his overall vision. That vision (if it can be put so bluntly) is the fundamental uncertainty of knowing another person—a vision narrated in a
fashion intended to lend the same truth value to literal and figurative meanings. Such a vertiginous combination leaves us with a series of accounts—
more or less convincing—about what has happened. To read the novel
carefully is to be in uncertainty at every level, but it is also to realize the

depth of Maggie's need to regain her husband, even at a cost to both Charlotte and her father. How does one adapt that vision to film? Perhaps the best way to think of such a possibility is much as James thought of revision itself—of seeing something again, renewing it in a different form. When revising his novels for the New York edition, he repeatedly confronted this issue, and in the last of the prefaces, written for *The Golden Bowl*, he pointedly asked: "What has the affair been at the worst, I am most moved to ask, but an earnest invitation to the reader to dream again in my company and in the interest of his own larger absorption of my sense?" (34). Perhaps "this process of re-dreaming," as James described it, might serve as the soundest guide for any successful film adaptation "based on the novel by Henry James."

## Notes

1. In response to an interviewer's query, "But fidelity, is that important?" Jhabvala responded: "Fidelity is not the first [thing]. No I don't think so. Like I said, the theme and the feel of the characters . . . the ambience and their relationships . . . that is what you try . . . but never, never literally" (Horne 2).
2. James's devotion to theater and his experience writing for the London stage are familiar biographical facts, but it is a lesser-known irony that he should have chosen the Preface to the New York Edition of *The Golden Bowl* to praise the visual arts, and in particular "Alvin Langdon Coburn's beautiful photographs," which appeared as frontispieces for the entire edition. James had carefully instructed Langdon on the sites and objects he wanted photographed, and took a strong interest in finding an adequate "optical symbol" for each volume (*GB* 24). For a discussion of James's avid interest in Coburn's efforts, see Edel, 334–38. It may be salutary to keep in mind the photographic critic Janet Malcolm's contrarian claims about "photography's inadequacy as a describer of how things are. The camera is simply not the supple and powerful instrument of description that the pen is" (133).
3. For a prominent example of a proliferation of this style—though it occurs throughout—look particularly at Maggie's image of her and her father's marriages as a coach with four wheels (341–45). Or see 387, where six such constructions occur in a single brief paragraph.
4. Leavis first made the dramatic claim that "Actually, if our sympathies are anywhere they are with Charlotte and (a little) the Prince, who represent what, against the general moral background of the book, can only strike us as decent passion; in a stale, sickly, and oppressive atmosphere they represent life" (178). A more recent version of this position is Vidal's "Introduction" to the Penguin edition: "When I first read *The Golden Bowl*, I found Amerigo, the Prince, most sympathetic. I still do. I also found—and find—Charlotte the most sympathetic of the other characters" (11–12).

5. By contrast, Amini's screenplay for Softley's *The Wings of the Dove* offers a largely sympathetic view of Kate Croy, constrained by financial desperation that is ever-present, ever complicating her moral dilemma.

6. In the Preface to *The Golden Bowl*, James describes the difficulty of finding a site for Coburn's photograph to the first volume, of the Bloomsbury shop where the bowl is for sale, which aptly confirms his writerly predilection: "The problem thus was thrilling, for though the small shop was but a shop of the mind, of the author's projected world, in which objects are primarily related to each other, and therefore not 'taken from' a particular establishment anywhere, only an image distilled and intensified, as it were, from a drop of the essence of such establishments in general, our need . . . prescribed a concrete, independent, vivid instance . . ." (25).

7. Here is the appropriate passage from the novel: "They stood together at all events, when the door had closed behind their friend, with a conscious strained smile and very much as if each waited for the other to strike the note or give the pitch. The young man held himself, in his silent suspense—only not more afraid because he felt her own fear. She was afraid of herself, however; whereas, to his gain of lucidity, he was afraid only of her. Would she throw herself into his arms or would she be otherwise wonderful? She would see what he would do–so their queer minute without words told him; and she would act accordingly. But what could he do . . . "It is too delightful to be back!" she said at last; and it was all she definitely gave him" (75–6).

## Works by James

GB—*The Golden Bowl*. Introd. Gore Vidal. New York: Penguin, 1987.

## Other Works Cited

Blackmur, R. P. "*The Golden Bowl* (Grove Press) (1952)." In *Studies in Henry James*. Ed. Veronica A. Makowsky. New York: New Directions, 1983. Pp. 147–160

Edel, Leon. *Henry James, The Master: 1901–1916*. New York: Avon, 1972.

———. *Henry James: The Critical Heritage*. Ed. Roger Gard. London: Routledge, 1968.

Hodge, Warren. "Celebrating the Capture of Another Glorious Space: Merchant and Ivory Know What They Like." *New York Times* 9 Nov. 1999, E 1-2.

Horne, Philip. "'It works diagonally': A Conversation with Ruth Prawer Jhabvala on *The Golden Bowl* and the Art of Adaptation." Merchant-Ivory Productions. <http://merchantivory.com/goldenbowl/ruth.html> 7 June 2000.

Internet Movie Database. Comments for *The Golden Bowl* (1972) (mini). <http://us.imdb.com/Title?0068075> Accessed 7 June 2000.

Ivory, James. Interview. Merchant Ivory Productions. <http://www.merchantivory.com/goldenbowl/news.html> Accessed 7 June 2000.

Leavis, F. R. *The Great Tradition: George Eliot, Henry James, Joseph Conrad*. Harmondsworth: Penguin, 1967.

Malcolm, Janet. *Diana & Nikon: Essays on Photography*. New York: Aperture, 1997.

Press notes for *The Golden Bowl*. Lions Gate Films, 2000. Jeremy Walker Associates,Inc. <http://www.jeremywalker.com/pages/films/filmset_golden.htm>

Woolf, Virginia. *The Essays of Virginia Woolf, 1904–1912*, Vol. 1. Ed. Andrew McNeillie. New York: Harcourt, 1986.

Yeazell, Ruth Bernard. *Language and Knowledge in the Late Novels of Henry James*. Chicago: U of Chicago P, 1976.

## Filmography

*The Wings of the Dove*. Dir. Iain Softley. Writ. Hossein Amini. Perf. Helena Bonham Carter, Linus Roache, Alison Elliott. Miramax, 1997.

*The Golden Bowl*. Dir. James Cellan Jones. Writ. Jack Pulman. Perf. Barry Morse, Gayle Hunnicutt, Cyril Cusack, Daniel Massey, Jill Townsend, Kathleen Byron. Masterpiece Theatre, 1973.

*The Golden Bowl*. Dir. James Ivory. Writ. Ruth Prawer Jhabvala. Perf. Uma Thurman, Nick Nolte, Kate Beckinsale, Jeremy Northam. Merchant Ivory Productions, 2000.

# The Rift in the *Loot*

## Cognitive Dissonance for the Reader of Merchant Ivory's
### *The Golden Bowl*

*Wendy Graham*

In *The Golden Bowl,* the mute machinery of cinema upstages the actors and their craft, as when Charlotte Stant, played by Uma Thurman, sobs into the sleeve of her dove-grey peignoir in her luxurious teal-blue boudoir at Fawns; the shimmering gilt lozenges bedizening this otherwise drab gown reinforce the film's intimation that marrying for money has not brought happiness to Charlotte, who seems more prisoner than mistress of her sleeping cabinet. While it is tempting to relate the form and function of costume and set design in this scene to James's own use of extended metaphor and metonymy in the text ("Golden Bowl," "Golden Isles," "golden bridge," "golden mist"), the Merchant Ivory method is iconic rather than analogical. The film mobilizes a set of esoteric signs or visual aids (gold, coins, masterpieces), which function as legible archetypes for a finite number of associations (power, wealth, lineage, taste). This is the method of pictorial, rather than literary, symbolism. In this film, we are confronted with a code, a system of explicit social conventions; in the novel, we encounter a hermeneutics or system of contingent signs. Since film generally makes use of both metaphor (substitution) and metonymy (synecdochic close-ups, camera angles), there is no clear reason why metaphor trumps metonymy in this adaptation of *The Golden Bowl* unless it is a question of genre. In "Two Aspects of Language," linguist Roman Jakobson argues that romanticism and symbolism rely on metaphor, whereas literary realism privileges metonymy: "Following the path of contiguous relationships, the Realist author metonymically digresses from the plot to the atmosphere and from the characters to the setting and the space and time. He is fond of synecdochic details" (111).

Advertising their venture to prospective investors, the team of Merchant Ivory described *The Golden Bowl* as "a passionate encounter between four people."[1] I think this plot summary usefully underscores the filmmakers' conception of the novel as character driven. Where Merchant Ivory departs from this scheme in lavishing attention on details of dress and milieu, the filmmakers have not digressed, in Jakobson's sense, to elaborate James's world and time. According to director James Ivory, the plan was to "suggest a rich period décor without allowing too much distraction."[2] The Merchant Ivory vision of life at the turn of the century is exclusive rather than panoramic.

Paradoxically, in their effort to get the look of the film right by consulting late nineteenth-century paintings and old photographs of "very rich Edwardian" interiors, James Ivory and his production designer, Andrew Sanders, have transformed everyday life into fantasy (Ivory). With their natural lighting effects, dense suffused color, and construction of sets as intimate spaces, primarily interiors, they have enhanced the wish-fulfillment aspect of James's narrative: the reconciliation of the Prince and Princess, whose marriage has faltered under the pressure of Prince Amerigo's proximity to his old flame, Charlotte Stant, who has become his stepmother in consequence of her marriage to "billionaire" Adam Verver, the father of Princess Maggie. While poignantly dramatizing Charlotte's plight as the spurned lover, the film has not done justice to the novel's reality principle, to its countervailing protest against American omnipotence and acquisitiveness. Certainly, the film communicates Adam Verver's menace, through the surliness of Nick Nolte's performance as well as anecdotal testimony to the character's past proclivity for violence, but it fails to illuminate the connection between his personal conduct and business practices. Nolte's Verver comes across as cold and calculating in his conduct towards Charlotte. His inexorable decree, mandating their return to America to oversee the construction of his museum, reduces her to tears. Curiously, when she cries out against being treated like one of Adam Verver's possessions and packed off to American City, her protest doesn't evoke a corresponding echo in the Prince, whose reconciliation with Maggie is presented as a romantic epiphany in the film: "Don't you understand? I love Maggie. I love my wife . . . more everyday."

The filmmakers' enhancement of Verver's character is offset by a diminishment of Maggie's cerebration and agency, which are minimized, literally condensed into a few scenes, whereas James devotes two hundred and fifty pages to her dawning recognition, resolution, and course of action. The cinematic Maggie's discovery of the golden bowl and its back story culminates in her strident emotional appeal to the Prince, "I want a happiness without a hole in it. The bowl without a crack," which miraculously

Figure 27. Anjelica Huston and Jeremy Northam in *The Golden Bowl,* Merchant Ivory Productions. Arnaud Borrel.

knocks him into position. James's Maggie is a force to be reckoned with well before this juncture, from the moment she realizes the lovers have arranged between themselves a system for not wounding her: "Baths of benevolence were very well, but at least, unless one were a patient of some sort, a nervous eccentric or a lost child, one usually wasn't so immersed save by one's request. It wasn't in the least what *she* had requested. She had flapped her little wings as a symbol of desired flight, not merely as a plea for a more gilded cage and an extra allowance of lumps of sugar" (355). In the novel, Maggie's epiphany is a blessing as well as a burden; she learns to know "Evil—with a big E," as the family confidante, Fanny Assingham, puts it, and exults in her newfound insight (310). Maggie's quickening of consciousness and emotional palpitation are not symptomatic of disillusionment, as the film suggests, but of freedom from delusion: "The cage was the deluded condition, and Maggie, as having known delusion—rather!—understood the nature of cages. She walked round Charlotte's—cautiously and in a very wide circle; and when inevitably they had to communicate she felt herself comparatively outside and on the breast of nature: she saw her companion's face as that of a prisoner looking through bars" (484).

Maggie has turned the tables on her adversary. By failing to acknowledge the subtlety and ruthlessness of Maggie's plan to wrest her husband from her rival's arms and send Charlotte packing, the film divests the Ververs of their common stock: perspicacity and opportunism, the unrestrained self-interest typical of nineteenth-century entrepreneurs operating in a free market: "It was a blur of light in the midst of which she saw Charlotte like some object marked by contrast in blackness, saw her waver in the field of vision, saw her removed, transported, doomed. And he had named Charlotte, named her again, and she had *made* him," James tells us (512). Trailing after her father from the age of ten into backrooms and back alleys where Adam risked "life, health, and the very bloom of honour" bargaining with disreputable persons over real and *ersatz* masterpieces, Maggie witnessed contests of nerve and skill that served as her tutorial in the art of turning every situation to her advantage (191). While the film cheerfully acknowledges Adam Verver's collecting mania as a form of "piracy," it downplays Maggie's declaration of her own self-interest. Wearing a demure white cotton nightgown, a girlish Kate Beckinsale surprises her papa in his study where he is brooding over the plans and model for his museum, which is transformed into a doll house by the nursery atmosphere of the scene. In such a context, how can Maggie's declaration of her own "selfishness" be taken at face value? Nolte simply laughs it off, "I'll let you know the day I feel myself to be your victim."

Frederic Jameson has suggested a paradigm for novels such as *The Golden Bowl,* in which "the wish-fulfilling mind sets out systematically to satisfy the objections of the nascent 'reality principle' of capitalist society and of the bourgeois superego," to an incorrigible fantasy demand, such as the illusion that romantic love will replace mercenary marriage in bourgeois society (183). By endowing his impecunious Prince with a rich father-in-law, an infatuated wife, and a mistress, the trappings of a medieval protagonist transported to the modern world, Henry James challenges the fantasy that romantic love can exist in a vacuum or overcome the tremendous obstacles presented by the social sphere. Divorced from his race and country, lacking a business pursuit or even a hobby, the Prince turns to adultery to assuage the bitterness of his coerced passivity: "If he, the great and the clever Roman, on the other hand, had an affair, it wasn't of that order; it was of the order verily that he had been reduced to as to a not quite glorious substitute....It kept before him again at moments the so familiar fact of his sacrifices—down to the idea of the very relinquishment, for his wife's convenience, of his real situation in the world; with the consequence thus that he was, in the last analysis, among all these so often inferior people, practically held cheap and made light of" (288).

Ultimately, there is a rift in the *loot,* and the fantasy that this grand mode of life is fulfilling comes to smash, like the golden bowl itself, on the domestic hearthstone. The marriage contract creates two classes of individuals in the novel: agents who have money and power and subjects who have masters: "The thing that never failed now as an item in the picture was that gleam of the silken noose, his [Adam's] wife's immaterial tether, so marked to Maggie's sense during her last month in the country. Mrs Verver's straight neck had certainly not slipped it; nor had the other end of the long cord—oh quite conveniently long!—disengaged its smaller loop from the hooked thumb that, with his fingers closed upon it, her husband kept out of sight" (553–54). Like the *Fugitive Slave Act,* the novel represents this master-slave relationship in its frankest form: human beings can be bought and human possessions have eternal obligations to their purchasers: "Mrs Verver and the Prince fairly 'placed' themselves, however unwittingly, as high expressions of the kind of human furniture required aesthetically by such a scene. The fusion of their presence with the decorative elements, their contribution to the triumph of selection, was complete and admirable; though to a lingering view, a view more penetrating than the occasion really demanded, they also might have figured as concrete attestations of a rare power of purchase" (574).

This is a more cynical account of Verver's aestheticism than the filmmakers have envisioned. Unlike the novel, the film displays nostalgia for an uncomplicated time in which good and evil tallied with the moral law. The viewer familiar with James's novel will undoubtedly experience a kind of *frisson* as the opening credits for *The Golden Bowl* dissolve into the dramatic action. Jhabvala has introduced and Ivory has rendered a darkly illumined scene of *cinquecento* adultery, incest, and murder, involving one of the Prince's stern ancestors, his son, and the youth's stepmother. The film effortlessly establishes a link between this historical *liaison dangereuse* and the relationships brewing among its protagonists through a spatiotemporal dissolve to the now ruined *Palazzo Ugolini,* where Prince Amerigo is in the act of relaying this gruesome tale to Charlotte Stant. Signaling her half-hearted acquiescence to the impending marriage between the Prince and Maggie Verver, whom Charlotte acknowledges as "your fiancée," Charlotte comments, "It would take Mr. Verver's millions to fix this up. Fortunately, he has them." The film establishes the mercenary motive for the marriage first and foremost. It does not grant the Prince space for the reflection he enjoys in the novel on the other merits of his alliance with the Ververs. Nor does it allow time to elapse, as in the novel, between the Prince's affair with Charlotte and his courtship and marriage.

The film's diegesis, its narration of the facts of the story, skews the audience's view of the situation in favor of the Ververs. They are the innocents preyed upon by the greedy and unscrupulous lovers. The lovers' contention that they've been driven into each other's arms by the mutually exclusive attachment between their respective *sposi* is treated as a sophistry in the film; however, in the novel, Fanny Assingham concedes that Maggie's "wish to remain, intensely, the same passionate little daughter she had always been" and her consequent neglect of Amerigo forged an alliance between her husband and stepmother such "as her grossest misconduct couldn't have done" (317). The Prince confirms this view when he complains of the grotesqueness of his situation, being "thrust, systematically, with another woman, and a woman one happened, by the same token, exceedingly to like"; as a "man of the world," he "blush[es] to 'go about' at such a rate with such a person as Mrs Verver in a state of childlike innocence, the state of our primitive parents before the Fall" (275). Intoning platitudes in defense of "Mr Verver's perfectly natural interest in his daughter" (224), Fanny is eventually jolted out of her complacency by her discovery of the priority that Maggie continues to enjoy in Eaton Square once Charlotte is nominally mistress there. Although she does not accuse Verver of an unnatural attachment to Maggie, Charlotte's assessment that paternal affection is "the greatest affection of which he's capable" goes well beyond the film's saccharine version of the relationship (224).

In her interview with Philip Horne, scenarist Ruth Prawer Jhabvala sidesteps the question of the novel's presentation of the Prince and Charlotte as themselves victims of the Ververs's rapacity: "But that has nothing to do with the character of the Ververs, who are all goodness." Jhabvala had specific misgivings about the novel's characterization of Adam Verver. Acting on the presumption that Verver's success as a captain of industry and a connoisseur implies a keen understanding of human nature, Jhabvala endows Adam Verver with a clarity about the state of his wife's and son-in-law's relationship that he lacks in the book. Adam's motive for holding his tongue is simply to spare Maggie. Jhabvala's confidence in Adam's perfect mastery of his predicament, that "in the book he manipulates the entire situation—he and Maggie between them," is reflected in the cinematography. Toward the end of the film, the camera lingers over Hans Holbein's portrait of Henry VIII, upon which Charlotte is discoursing both pedantically and tendentiously to an audience of house guests. Holbein captured Henry's domineering and ruthless character in this full-length portrait through the presentation of the King's physical bulk and immobility. Richly attired and fantastically bejewelled, the haughty King straddles the canvas, one arm akimbo, in a defiant and irreverent posture. Under Adam's superintending gaze, Charlotte calls the work "a chilling portrait of male assertiveness, and of the masculine ego in all its brutal physical strength and hardness. The subject matches the cold hardness of Holbein's style here, which brings out so well the King's defiance of all who stood in his way—including his numerous women, who, one by one, went to their doom." In the book, Adam is described as small, spare, and balding. Charlotte alludes to Verver's disinclination or incapacity for sexual intercourse when she says of her childless state, "It's not, at any rate . . . my fault" (256). In the screenplay, however, Jhabvala expressly revises this scene to pin the blame for Charlotte's infertility on the young woman herself: "Oh I've been to specialist after specialist—Sir Hubert this and Sir Winston that—and they all say the same." Nick Nolte, who frequently plays professional athletes on the screen, further lifts the onus from Adam by lending him virility, height, and a rugged charm. James's depiction of the character's unimposing physical appearance and ambiguous sexuality is belied in the film.

Yet the interplay between Holbein's portrait of Henry VIII and Verver's character is more complex. Although King Henry was something of a Bluebeard, he wore the cuckold's horns more than once. This historical allusion and the series of pictorial and imaginative tableaux—the *mise en abyme,* the ballet (*Scheherazade*), Fanny's impersonation of Mary Queen of Scots, a notorious adulteress, at a costume ball—keep adultery in the forefront of the viewer's consciousness. Significantly, the film's symbolic invocations of adultery focus on the male head of household; its dramatic episodes involving discovery, which advance the plot, tend to focus on Maggie.[3] (Of course, the golden bowl is treated as a symbol in the film: "happiness without a hole in it. The bowl without a crack," but it is instantly legible, iconic rather than potential.) This gendered contrast between the paradigmatic (associative) and syntagmatic (represented) levels of narration is the film's own invention, underwritten by a valorization of patriarchal omniscience and omnipotence. Patriarchy, as a transhistorical phenomena, appears unassailable in the film because it survives the humiliation of the wife's preference for a younger man and the challenge of youth.

Certainly, the film contradicts James's characterization of Verver as a man who resents being "perpetually treated as an infinite agent," who recognizes the "attribution of power" as a miscalculation deriving from the conventional association of money with power: his "finding it so taken for granted that as he had money he had force" (133). Absurdly, this misconception about Adam is the film's mantra. The film does not enact Verver's fantasy of being routed from his lair (the billiard room) by one of his daughter's house guests, a divorcée named Mrs. Rance who has set her cap for him, or so Verver fears. In the novel, he expresses an unmanly apprehension at the prospect of having to turn down Mrs. Rance, the Misses Lutch, or any number of conjectured petitioners for *his* hand. Verver is not idealized by the novelist. The ambiguity in James's portrait of Verver is not an instance of miscasting, as Jhabvala would have it, but a testament to the novel's realism and an echo of its social context.

Adam Verver has sublimated his passion for the female sex into fatherhood and the acquisition of wealth. Verver might have been the representative figure in Tocqueville's account of American life, for the habits of unremitting toil, prudence, and self-restraint have not been discarded once the goal of financial security has been attained; they have become fixed character traits. In his pursuit of pleasure, personal or aesthetic, Verver unconsciously adheres to the psychology of the market revolution, which promoted regular conduct and morality to produce conditions favorable to industry and to commerce: "Adam Verver had in other words learnt the lesson of the senses, to the end of his own little book, without having for a day raised the smallest scandal in his economy at large; being in this particular not unlike those fortunate bachelors or other gentleman of pleasure who so manage their entertainment of compromising company that even the austerist housekeeper, occupied and competent below-stairs, never feels obliged to give warning" (179). This is a sketch of a personality cut off from physical and sensual life, "a taster of life, economically constructed," a cerebral epicure: "It was all at bottom in him, the aesthetic principle, planted where it could burn with a cold still flame; where it fed almost wholly on the material directly involved, on the idea (followed by the appropriation) of plastic beauty, of the thing visibly perfect in its kind" (179).[4] James's insistence on the highly disciplined nature of Verver's psychic economy foregrounds the sublimation of untoward and inexpedient interests into worthier and more remunerative aims. In the novel, acquisitive cognition, "the spirit of the connoisseur" (139), is explicitly a refinement of competitive acquisition: "A wiser hand than he at first knew had kept him hard at acquisition of one sort as a perfect preliminary to acquisition of another" (143).

Verver continues to work doggedly, but he is no longer immersed in grimy industrial processes or in the "livid vulgarity" of investment: "getting in, or getting out, first" (143). He is the great benefactor, the man who will build his temple to culture high on a hill as the Puritan forefathers built their model communities, the man who will liberate the American people from "the bondage of ugliness" through the auspices of a "museum of museums, a palace of art" (143). Under the sway of highbrow associations (Keat's sonnet "On First Looking into Chapman's Homer"), Verver experiences a utopian vision "with a mute inward gasp akin to the low moan of apprehensive passion that a world was left him to conquer and that he might conquer it if he tried" (139). The trope of discovery links Verver with Keats's grand figure of Cortez in the presence of the Pacific, but Verver's conquest of the Old World calls to mind the sack of Troy as well as the doctrine of Manifest Destiny. The point is that the ecstacy gilding Verver's altruistic venture, a positive obsession with him, is narcissistically referred: "He was a plain American citizen staying at an hotel where sometimes for days together there were twenty others like him; but no pope, no prince of them all had read a richer meaning, he believed, into the character of the Patron of Art" (146). The upwardly mobile trajectory traced in this quotation, culminating in the title, "Patron of Art" ("pope" and "prince" are not capitalized), concisely illustrates the role of intellectual refinement in ameliorating a squalid background: "He had wrought by devious ways, but he had reached the place, and what would ever have been straighter in any man's life than his way henceforth of occupying it?" (142).

In the early nineteenth century, the republican ideology valorized the pursuit of money as an end in itself. Money meant status. When advances in entrepreneurial culture, transportation, and industry led to a proliferation of wealth at the mid-century, class stratification relied on new indices. Status accrued to those whose taste, manners, traditions, and acquisitions evidenced their inherited wealth or, at the very least, present abstention from labor. According to sociologist Thorstein Veblen, author of *The Theory of the Leisure Class* (1899), "this growth of punctilious discrimination as to qualitative excellence in eating, drinking, etc., presently affects not only the manner of life, but also the training and intellectual activity of the gentleman of leisure. He is no longer simply the successful, aggressive male— the man of strength, resource, and intrepidity. In order to avoid stultification he must also cultivate his tastes" (64). Veblen has laboriously outlined the social psychology of pecuniary emulation, in which the lower castes imitate the imputed social graces and intellectual cultivation of the higher grades and impugn the vulgarity of those beneath them. This is the historical logic determining billionaire Adam Verver's comparatively modest pride in his wealth as opposed to his utter intoxication with the notion of "the affinity of Genius, or at least of Taste, with something in himself" (140).

James declines to give an exposition of Verver's career as an abstemious self-made man; however, Verver's reflections on his first marriage suggest that sexual passion and romantic love were treated as encumbrances, excess emotional baggage that happily fell by the wayside as he ascended the ladder of social distinction. Veblen describes the American wife as her husband's chattel, the chief menial saddled with the obligation to uphold the family's repute through conspicuous consumption and leisure even when her husband continues to work hard to support this illusion of wealth, a situation especially prevalent in the middle class (68). "Daisy Miller" (1878) is an earlier study of the role of fashion and European travel in remapping the social geography that distinguishes the bourgeoisie from the leisure class. Hoping to present his attractive new acquaintance to his aunt, the narrator is obstructed by the "minutely hierarchical constitution of the society" with which persons of distinction, such as Mrs. Costello, self-identify. Had she seen an American family consisting of a mama, a daughter, and a small boy? "Oh, yes, I have observed them. Seen them—heard them— and kept out of their way" (*TJ* 164). The invidious gradations of distinction maintained between exclusive Old New York and promiscuous Schenectady, where Daisy's father has remained behind to superintend the operations of his factory, is threatened by the nouveau riche's accelerated acquisition of taste. Mrs. Costello's concession about Daisy, "she dresses in perfection— no, you don't know how well she dresses. I can't think where they get their taste," surprises the narrator: "But, my dear aunt, she is not, after all, a Comanche savage" (*TJ* 165). James musters a wonderful image of the dowagers of Old New York circling the wagons against the barbarian interlopers from the provinces.

In the transition from "Daisy Miller" to *The Golden Bowl,* James shifts his emphasis from the evolution of taste in dress, as a symptom of pecuniary emulation, to the acquisition of taste in art; collecting art is a further refinement of the original strategy for breaking into a higher pecuniary class. The first Mrs. Verver failed to sufficiently enhance her husband's renown through her conspicuous consumption and panache. Adam blames her for not realizing that antiques have more social cachet than clothing and, more sophistically, he accuses her of standing between himself and the attainment of taste on his first visit to Paris: "And they had loved each other so that his own intelligence, on the higher line, had temporarily paid for it. The futilities, the enormities, the depravities of decoration and ingenuity that before his sense was unsealed she had made him think lovely!" (141). The term "depravities of decoration" suggests a perverse and immoderate desire for personal finery. The phrase, "before his sense was unsealed," recalls a sinner redeemed from debauchery by divine intervention: "I was blind, but now I see." Verver has no memory of enjoying the honeymoon trip, which involved extensive forays into fashionable shops on the Rue de la Paix with "the frail fluttered creature at his side," in pusuit of "the costly authenticities of dressmakers and jewellers" (140). In spite of his fleeting acknowledgment that the art of the couturiers was "then wonderful to both of them," Verver divorces himself from his wife's outlook as a means of disavowing his bourgeois roots. He remembers her as a "broken white flower tied round, almost grotesquely for his present sense, with a huge satin 'bow' of the Boulevard" (140). In this evocation of his delicate spouse, pathos is less marked than a retrospective disdain. He sounds positively

grateful for the timely removal of "his wife's influence. . . . He even sometimes wondered what would have become of his intelligence, in the sphere
in which it was to learn more and more exclusively to play, if his wife's
influence on it hadn't been, in the strange scheme of things, so promptly
removed. Would she have led him altogether, attached as he was to her,
into the wilderness of mere mistakes?" (141).[5]

The migration of Verver's interests from the wider world of commerce
to the narrow channels of taste inflects his infatuated view of Maggie as
well: "daughter of his very own though she was, as a figure thus simplified,
'generalised' in its grace, a figure with which his human connexion was
fairly interrupted by some vague analogy of turn and attitude, something
shyly mythological and nymph-like. The trick, he wasn't uncomplacently
aware, was mainly of his own mind; it came from his caring for precious
vases only less than for precious daughters" (172). The trick of mind is
acquisitive cognition, which objectifies and appraises human specimens,
before installing them in a marble sepulcher, the museum of the mind.

I have digressed from my discussion of the film to gloss the many
permutations to the novel's characterization of Verver, such as his disinclination for society, which are winnowed in the Merchant Ivory *Golden Bowl*
to a select few. The film is careful to stand by its conception of Adam's
cosmopolitanism or worldliness, limiting evidence of his provincialism to
minor incidents, idiomatic speech, or a familiar turn of phrase such as "as
they say in American City." In the film, Adam doesn't recognize the gourmet
dishes prepared for his delectation at an English private residence (although he's probably hunted partridge and pigeon in the Midwest), and he
doesn't enjoy the "modern noise" accompanying the ballet. Nolte's Adam
might be taken for a Bowie-knife toting backwoodsmen masquerading in
dinner clothes; however, the filmmakers don't seem troubled by this rem-
nant of provincialism within a character who prides himself on his exemplary cultivation. What James calls Verver's "aboriginal homeliness" marks
him as a transitional figure in American history (237).

Even a consummate aesthete such as Henry James felt the stigma of
American provincialism early in his career as an art journalist. Reviewing
"The Duke of Montpensier's Pictures at the Boston Athenaeum" in 1874,
James takes the Duke to task for fobbing off minor pictures by second-rate
painters on a gullible American public eager for masterpieces: "Immaturity
and provincialism are incontestable facts, but people should never freely
assent to being treated as children and provincials" (*EA* 48). Consoling
himself with the notion that this transatlantic exchange of art has at least
broken the spell of American disjunction from Europe in the enjoyment of
collections, James sounds a lot like Adam Verver: "It has been proved that

there is no reason in the essence of things why a room full of old masters should not be walked into from an American street and appear to proper advantage" (*EA* 48). In the film, Adam is credited with a keen eye. He recognizes fakes. He regards his judgment as infallible: "You know I never act before I am sure." In the book, he takes great pride in his expertise as well: "no man in Europe or in America, he privately believed, was for such estimates less capable of vulgar mistakes" (139). However, his standard is lower than one would surmise from the film: "He cared that a work of art of price should 'look like' the master to whom it might perhaps be deceitfully attributed" (144). Americans had not, in 1903, attained the degree of sophistication that Merchant Ivory retrospectively attributes to them. In "On Some Pictures Lately Exhibited" (1875), James observes, "The day may come round again when we shall all judge pictures as unerringly as the burghers of Florence in 1500; though it will hardly do so, we fear, before we have, like the Florentines, a native Michael Angelo or an indigenous Andrea del Sarto to exercise our wits upon" (*EA* 68).

Private collectors began making bequests and loans of masterpieces to public institutions as of 1870, when the Boston Museum of Fine Arts, the Corcoran Gallery in Washington D.C., and the Metropolitan Museum of Art were founded. The Chicago Art Institute was founded in 1879. Harvard University established the first chair in Fine Arts for Charles Eliot Norton in 1873. Realistically, between 1870 and 1890, when Verver acquired his stupendous wealth, the industrious Midwesterner had few opportunities for perfecting his acquaintance with works of fine art and antiquities. James Ivory correctly typecasts Verver as "an American art collector of catholic but somewhat conventional taste." American connoisseurs, J. Pierpont Morgan, Henry Clay Frick, and Isabella Stewart Gardner, were used as models; however, unlike Verver, these collectors consulted experts (Gardner worked closely with Bernard Berenson and Norton; Morgan with Roger Fry; collectors of Japanese art and fine porcelain relied on the advice of Edward Sylvester Morse and Ernest Fenollosa). Adam buys exclusively antiques and masterworks. If taste and discernment were intuitive with him, rather than a hard-won acquisition of received ideas, however mysteriously acquired, he would be able to judge the merits of a Picasso as well as gauge the authenticity of a purported Raphael. Americans of the Gilded Age well understood that private collections were a status symbol, a nouveau riche ploy for gaining respectability. Even Morgan, a patrician by birth, was disparaged by Bernard Berenson for his showy and undiscriminating purchasing habits: "This afternoon I visited J.P. Morgan's house. It looks like a pawnbroker's shop for Croesuses" (Strouse 483). In its closing shots of Mr. and Mrs. Adam Verver's triumphant homecoming, effective black-and-white newsreel footage evoking turn-of-the-century America, the film displays a fabricated headline from the *New York Herald Tribune* proclaiming Verver an "American Croesuses." It is hard to know what to make of the parade of newsprint accolades that end the film, though not the book. Does Merchant Ivory seriously consider the comparison with Croesus honorific?

According to sociologist Pierre Bourdieu the invidious gradations of refinement associated with artistic culture depend on a sliding scale of effort, in which the pedant and the autodidact are equally remote from the ideal of unconscious acquisition: "In the final analysis, the tiny and infinite nuances of an authentically cultivated disposition where nothing is allowed to betray the effort of acquisition reflect a particular mode of acquisition" (65). The Prince instinctively recoils when offered the golden bowl; he can tell at a glance that the crystal goblet has a flaw because he's an aristocrat who has grown up among treasures. He has the requisite cultural capital for both seeing the art object and seeing beyond the object to the hidden order of significance it represents. This is very neatly expressed by James: "'Oh if I'm a crystal I'm delighted that I'm a perfect one, for I believe they sometimes have cracks and flaws—in which case they're to be had very cheap!' He had stopped short of the emphasis it would have given his joke to add that there had been certainly no having *him* cheap" (138–39). The Prince effortlessly embodies what Adam has striven all his life to become, a gentleman, an aesthete, an aristocrat. Verver's instantaneous perception of Amerigo's *value* reifies the abstract quality of nobility into something tangible and purchasable like a perfect crystal: "The aspirant to his daughter's hand showed somehow the great marks and signs, stood before him with the high authenticities, he had learnt to look for in pieces of the first order" (139). The Prince functions as a "semiophore" in *The Golden Bowl,* Krzysztof Pomian's term for an object that provides access to an invisible or absent realm (the past, the sacred) by rendering it metonymically visible and present (Bennett 35). By focusing on Verver's critical acumen, the film misses the point of the textual interplay between Adam's human acquisitions and art objects. Adam collects semiophores: "The infinitely ancient, the immemorial amethystine blue of the glaze, scarcely more meant to be breathed upon, it would seem, than the cheek of royalty" (191). The rare Oriental tile is a stepping stone to the *sanctum sanctorum.*

In the film, the Prince's subjectivity is flattened out, so that he glibly identifies with an object, a coin bearing the likeness of his ancestor, Amerigo Vaspucci, which he gives his future father-in-law as a betrothal gift.[6] In the novel, the coin functions as a metonym for the Prince's purchase price at the time of his marriage—"there had been certainly no having *him* cheap" (139)—and as a metaphor for the Prince's fate as a *"morceau de musée"* in Adam

Verver's collection (49): "It was as if he had been some old embossed coin, of a purity of gold no longer used, stamped with glorious arms, medieval, wonderful, of which the 'worth' in mere modern change, sovereigns and half-crowns, would be great enough, but as to which, since there were finer ways of using it, such taking to pieces was superfluous" (56). In the book, the Prince recognizes and then rationalizes the commodification of his personal value as the cultural capital that *he possesses,* "he was to constitute a possession, yet was to escape being reduced to his component parts," because he hopes to participate in the new world order like his ancestor, the famous explorer (56). The film's instincts regarding the coin may be correct, compactly summarizing the relationship between Adam and Amerigo as a collaboration between American wealth, energy, and business acumen and European cultural capital. In the film, the coin stands for the Prince *in absentia,* as when Adam, coin in hand, glowers at the embossed portrait of Amerigo's namesake, brooding over the misdeeds of his son-in-law. In detaching the coin from the full range of textual associations, however, the film obscures the novel's critique of Verver's acquisitions of human beings.

James's personal and professional preoccupation with works of fine art informs the film in a variety of ways. If James shares this passion with his protagonist, a patron of art with unlimited resources, how can the filmmakers be faulted for thinking that James favored Adam Verver? James understood Verver as a social type, whose aims may have been laudable, but whose actions were morally ambiguous: "Nothing perhaps might affect us as queerer, had we time to look into it, than this application of the same measure of value to such different pieces of property as old Persian carpets, say, and new human acquisitions" (179). He *is* a step up, morally speaking, from Gilbert Osmond, who coerces heiress Isabel Archer to finance his social climbing and to give free reign to his aesthetic appetites in *The Portrait of a Lady,* but in the final analysis, Verver is another heartless aesthete with a pretty daughter. Compared with the eccentric Osmond, Verver is a stereotype, a representative of the rising class of Americans experiencing the epochal aggregation of wealth and the pursuit of cultural capital at the turn of the century. Indeed, James's de-individualization of Verver better serves the novel's realism, as Verver's history follows the dynamic trajectory of the evolving bourgeoisie and reveals the underlying psychological, social, and economic forces directing its development in that era.

James Ivory can hardly be faulted for mimicking James's evocation of fine art and high culture as atmospheric or for fashioning the Ververs' milieu to his own taste, which is exquisite. However, I do want to insist that mere contemporaneity does not guarantee accuracy of historical presentation. To transcend the trappings of the costume drama, Ivory would some-how have to differentiate between antiquity, the middle distance, and the present as seen from the perspective of 1903. In his art journalism, James castigated the very artists with whom his "world vision" is conflated in the film. James Ivory describes the Belgian, James Tissot, as a painter of beautiful women. As early as 1877, Henry James finds Tissot's "sentiment stale" and queries, "What is it that makes such realism as M. Tissot's appear vulgar and *banal*, when an equal degree of realism, practised three hundred years ago, has an inexhaustible charm and entertainment? M. Tissot's pretty woman, with her stylish back and yellow ribbons, will, I am convinced, become less and less charming and interesting as the years or even the months, go on. Certain I am, at any rate, that I should not be able to live in the same room with her for a week without finding her intolerably wearisome and unrefreshing" (*EA* 254). Moving on to a portrait by George Frederic Watts, a fitting analogue to *The Golden Bowl* because the sitter "looks as if she had thirty thousand [in British sterling] a year," James praises the artist for capturing the taste of "no particular period—of all periods" with a style "distinctly removed from the 'stylishness' of M. Tissot's yellow ribboned hero-ine" (*EA* 255–56). James looks for a combination of imaginative elements, quality of workmanship, and "extreme solidity" or realism of presentation before praising a picture (*EA* 256). As one of the more brilliant members of a "large colony of foreign painters established in London, and basking in the golden light, not of the metropolitan sky, but of British patronage," Tissot personifies the link between cosmopolitanism and opportunism in James's view (*EA* 253).

Ivory's evocation of the work of John Singer Sargent is more felicitous. Sargent was James's favorite contemporary painter. Following the disastrous Salon of 1884, Sargent moved to London where James proved a staunch advocate. However, James watched Sargent's meteoric rise to prominence, primarily as a portrait painter, with a mixture of enthusiasm and misgiving. Writing of *El Jaleo* in "John S. Sargent" (1887), James claimed the picture of the Spanish dancer illustrated the "latent dangers of the Impressionist practice," which in the view of James's contemporaries consisted of a want of finish, a willful violation of the laws of anatomy and the tenets of flesh painting. James was concerned that Sargent had acquired so much technical facility with so little effort and at such an early age: "May not this breed an irresponsibility of cleverness, a wantonness, an irreverence—what is vulgarly termed a 'larkiness'—on the part of a youthful genius who has, as it were, all his fortune in his pocket" (*EA* 427). Extolling portraiture as the epitome of the pictorial arts, James was troubled by the superficiality of Sargent's efforts. Sargent's work excels in the area of "quick perception" and of short-hand notations, the signs by which objects are rendered in paint-ing, but it is missing the "faculty of lingering reflection" for James: "I mean the quality in the light of which the artist sees deep into his subject, under-goes it, absorbs it, discovers in it new things that were not on the surface, becomes patient with it, and almost reverent, and, in short, elevates and humanizes the technical problem" (*EA* 430).[7] Expressing a disinclination to tackle another James novel after *The Golden Bowl,* James Ivory remarks, "In a way I feel a bit like Sargent, who decided after a while that he didn't want to do any more portrait assignments. They had made his reputation, but he felt he'd done enough of them. What he wanted to do was something light and carefree, so he took up watercolors—and what watercolors they were! I think I could happily turn my hand to the cinematic equivalent." This comparison is fortuitous in that it aligns Ivory's method and conception of the task of adapting James's novel for the screen with the technique of an artist James found wanting in depth.

Remarking that "Sargent gave visual expression to James's world of monied Americans living amongst titled, sophisticated people," Ivory goes on to explain the affinity between the artist and writer, contemporaries whose backgrounds and milieu (both were part of the expatriate communi-ties in Paris and subsequently London) overlap; they were friends who could be said to share "visual references." In Ivory's opinion, Sargent's work represents the acme of turn-of-the-century cosmopolitanism, a term vari-ously indicating unerring taste, freedom from regional prejudices, and an acquaintance with the capital cities of Europe. James himself called atten-tion to Sargent's cosmopolitanism: "he has even on the face of it this great symptom of an American origin, that in the line of his art he might easily be mistaken for a Frenchman. It sounds like a paradox, but it is a very simple truth, that when to-day we look for 'American art' we find it mainly in Paris. When we find it out of Paris, we at least find a great deal of Paris in it" (*EA* 424). For James and his contemporaries, cosmopolitanism also sig-nified a freedom from provincial or bourgeois sexual mores. Writing in the journal *L'art* about Sargent's infamous portrait of *Madame X,* a figure whose lilac face powder and décolletage suggested the hot-house atmosphere of the boudoir, critic André Michel called the picture a "document of the 'high life' of this year of grace 1884" and prophesied that "future critics will see here our Parisian cosmopolitanism manifested in ideal form" (Ratcliff 87). James, hardly the narrow-minded prude for whom he's generally taken, was amused that *Madame X* had inflamed public sentiment against the artist in contrast to the racy examples of plastic art provided for the public's entertainment at the Salon in subsequent years. Only one of James's Americans is truly cosmopolitan, and that would be the stylish polyglot

Figure 28. John Singer Sargent, *Dr. Pozzi at Home,* 1881. Oil on canvas, 204.5 x 101.9 cm. The Armand Hammer Collection, UCLA Hammer Museum, Los Angeles.

Charlotte Stant. Fabulously rich people who travel extensively are not cosmopolitan as if by divine right. They must, at the very least, be able to sit through one performance of the *Ballet Russe* without, like Adam and Maggie Verver, blushing or contriving an early exit. Ivory's notion that Sargent illustrates "extremely cosmopolitan Americans living as millionaires in the most princely houses" treats the question of class as an open book or naturalized category. The Ververs happen to be members of the bourgeoisie who, by virtue of their new money, have stormed the gates of the American leisure class and the citadels of the British aristocracy. They would not be at home in Edith Wharton's New York where inherited wealth and lineage mattered.[8]

Ivory's rhapsodizing about the luxurious rich on the Merchant Ivory website carries over into the film, where a blank screen and neat white lettering introduces Adam Verver as "America's first billionaire." Variously described by Ivory as "cosmopolitan Americans," "millionaires," and "nouveau riche," "idealistic Americans like the Ververs" are said to seek "personal or artistic fulfillment" through art connoisseurship. That tidy depiction certainly isn't how a historian or a sociologist of the Gilded Age would frame the phenomena. Rather, Adam Verver's collection is *prima facie* evidence of his longing to achieve higher social caste for himself and his daughter through pecuniary emulation of aristocratic culture and marriage to a Prince. Furthermore, Ivory's invocation of cosmopolitanism (the *lingua franca* of high culture in the film) fails to take account of the vicious class and ethnic rivalries embedded in leisure class and nativist fears of amalgamation with the Other. In the novel, Adam and Charlotte visit an art dealer, Mr. Guterman-Seuss, whose small "tribe" (190) evinces the social evolution of "old Jewry" (192) from the "fat ear-ringed aunts and the glossy cockneyfied, familiar uncles," who have assimilated the local lingo, to the "head of the firm" who exhibits none of their "attitude of cruder intention" (190). The Bloomsbury antiquarian, who possesses the golden bowl, isn't identified as a "little swindling jew" until one hundred pages after his initial appearance (292). James's contemporary readers would have recognized him as a Jewish type, because of his profession, his extraordinary refusal to name his nationality when asked, and the fact that he's a polyglot, which implies that he's lived in the capitals of Europe. He lets the Prince and Charlotte know, to their great amazement, in "the suddenest sharpest Italian," that he has overheard and understood their intimate conversation (118). The film does not acknowledge this passage. The couple doesn't speak Italian, leaving the antiquarian's response absent as well. (Nor does the film make an issue of his ethnicity; the actor playing the dealer looks very British and has a *retroussé* nose.) In the book, Fanny Assingham is

Figure 29. Detail, John Singer Sargent, *Nonchaloir (Repose)*, 1911. Oil on canvas. Gift of Curt H. Reisinger, photograph © Board of Trustees, National Gallery of Art, Washington. Inset: Kate Beckinsale in Merchant Ivory's *The Golden Bowl* (2000). Arnaud Borrel.

linked to the antiques dealer through the word *revendeuse* (dealer in second hand merchandise) and the role they both play in fashioning and refashioning the romantic quartet (64). In the film, Fanny Assingham has a Southern accent, an unnecessary trial for Angelica Huston, because the scenarist has misconstrued James's description of Fanny. She only "*seemed*" to be "a daughter of the South, or still more of the East"; however, she is "neither a pampered Jewess nor a lazy Creole" (64). There is a method to this muddling of Fanny's roots; it enables the novelist to link her "false indolence, in short, her false leisure, her false pearls and palms and courts and fountains," her pecuniary emulation of the leisure class, with the upward mobility and self-interest of the Jew. Through Fanny, "the eyes of the American city looked out, somehow, for the opportunity of it, from under the lids of Jerusalem" (64).

The ethnic slurs carefully excised from the film are part of the novel's larger frame of reference: caste wars carried out through invidious comparisons and pecuniary emulation on an international scale. In fact, cosmopolitanism has a pejorative connotation in the novel. It is a sign of worldliness, but it is also the insignia of the Jew and the rootless parvenu. The Prince's younger brother has married a woman of the "Hebrew race, with a portion that gilded the pill" (53). Has the Prince married a parvenu's daughter for much the same reason? In "The Dread of the Jew" (1899), the editorialist for the *Spectator* points out that the talents of the Jews have been much exaggerated as a pretext for devising stratagems to keep them from competing on an even footing with Gentiles. He concludes, "Even the richest men in the world to-day are not Jews, but Americans" (339). Through "long centuries of enforced confinement to trade," Jews became habituated to commerce and "mounted too quickly to the top of the commercial ladder," where their success has occasioned suspicion and resentment (Morais 270). The fear that the "Jews of the world having obtained control of cosmopolitan finance, act together in the interests of their race, and inflict grievous injuries upon the nations" influences the popular perception of American capitalists as well ("Dread of the Jew" 338). "Soulless money-getters," who prefer an unobstructed path to prosperity, who desecrate the Sabbath, and preach non-intervention in America's global military conflicts, are the new Jews in poet Richard Hovey's 1898 assessment: "Let Rothschild-ridden Europe hold her peace" (qtd. in Lears 115).

The unparalleled economic clout of the Rothchilds in France and the political stature of Disraeli in Britain relaxed the ban on Jews in high society. In 1896, John Singer Sargent painted a portrait, *Mrs. Carl Meyer and Her Children,* evidently a cosmopolitan Jewish millionaire's family, that directly confronts the question of assimilation. In 1897, James called attention to Mrs. Meyer's ethnicity: "though her type is markedly Jewish, the tinting, is ever so delicate, of the space between her upper lip and her nose is not an effect of the shadow of the latter feature" (*EA* 511). To the discerning eye, the trace of a moustache is a token of racial difference. Similarly, her children have "shy olive faces, Jewish to a quaint orientalism, faces quite to peep out of the lattice or the curtains of closed seraglio or palanquin" (*EA* 511). Indeed, the peculiar green complexions of the children, the shading of the trio's upper lips, and their faintly arched eyebrows present a striking contrast to Sargent's rose-white complexioned matrons of the British gentry and his rich Americans. Yet, by virtue of the old figured and faded tapestry covering her Pompador couch, the gilt stool upon which she rests her feet, her extreme length of pearls, and other gorgeous accessories, Mrs. Meyer asserts her right to take her place among the high society women ensconced in the British portrait gallery, itself a portal to a realm of social distinction.

In keeping with Veblen's account of the social psychology of pecuniary emulation, the Ververs' acute distaste for vulgar revels and promiscuous social contact does not prove their innate refinement so much as their recent acquisition of taste and their unconscious fear of backsliding. In the novel, Adam Verver is implicitly ridiculed by the Castledean set for having pitched his standard absurdly high; he was "all geniality and humility among his own treasures, but as to whom the legend had grown up that he couldn't bear, with the height of his standards and the tone of the company, in the way of sofas and cabinets, habitually kept by him, the irritation and depression to which promiscuous visiting even at pompous houses had been found to expose him" (272–73). In the film, Fanny haughtily refers to the popular resort Baden-Baden as a place where the shops sell "vulgar" objects, such as pink shoes, to American tourists. In the novel, Fanny is mortified to discover that her "comparatively small splendour" marks her as socially insignificant at Matcham (273). In *The Golden Bowl,* James underscores his characters' relentless efforts to define their superiority—in an aesthetic or a moral sense—to their counterparts. Terms such as "vulgar" and "promiscuous" set up invidious comparisons between characters and define the "relative degrees of complacency with which they may legitimately be contemplated by themselves and by others" (Veblen 40). This complicated strategy of self-affirmation is necessary once conspicuous consumption as a technique for earning merit badges in the great bourgeois competition not to seem bourgeois has been exploded.

The cognitive dissonance occasioned for the Ververs and for Fanny Assingham by their fleeting contacts with the British aristocracy is highly significant. The Americans are gravely disappointed by the aristocrats' moral slackness and want of finish. The aristocrats fail to conform to their idealized notions of elite behavior: "What any one 'thought' of any one else—above all of any one else *with* anyone else—was a matter incurring in these halls so little awkward formulation that hovering Judgment, the spirit with the scales, might perfectly have been imaged there as some rather snubbed and subdued but quite trained and tactful poor relation" (272). This excerpt speaks to the higher freedom, the indifference to form, of people who don't have to curry favor or seek prestige. Lady Castledean, seen by Maggie as a hoydenish creature with "the biggest diamonds on the yellowest hair, the longest lashes on the prettiest falsest eyes, the oldest lace on the most violet velvet, the rightest manner on the wrongest assumption," is overdressed, insolent, false, and showy; nevertheless, her ladyship presumes to have kept "at every moment of her life, every advantage" (360). Who she is counts for more than what she does or has. The film takes particular pains to expose Lady Castledean's impropriety, especially in the two scenes where she and her lover, Mr. Blint, indulge in a riotous performance of the inane popular song "I'm Just a Silly When the Moon Is Full." Through her association with adultery, fashion, popular music, and gossip, Lady Castledean is denuded of cultural authority in the film. However, in the novel, her social position inures her against self-reflection and public ridicule. Without oversimplifying the novel's juxtaposition of innocent Americans and decadent aristocrats, I do see where this contrast leaves room for the Merchant Ivory solution, which is to proclaim the American contingent the new cultural elite. There might be another explanation for this juxtaposition. In Edith Wharton's *The Age of Innocence,* the New York Knickerbockers of the 1870s, many generations removed from their roots in the British aristocracy, are dismayed by the appearance and manner of a dingy Duke, whose conversation is no more distinguished than his clothing. Just as the leisure class has concocted an impossibly idealized image of the aristocracy, so has the bourgeoisie concocted an impossibly idealized image of the leisure class and the rank above them. Unlike the leisure class, whose legitimacy depends on its imputed descent from titled personages, the bourgeoisie is free to reject the standards of the higher pecuniary grades or to remake them in their own image. The Prince's purported authenticity, "He's perhaps one of the very last—the last of the real ones," is an ironic commentary on the bourgeoisie's powers of mystification and myth making, since a Prince without a country is a title without substance (320).

Merchant Ivory's romanticization of the Ververs' class background and lifestyle suggests, in keeping with Roland Barthes's description of canonical fiction, that "the bourgeoisie has obliterated its name in passing from reality to representation" or, more accurately, in passing from critical realism to heritage cinema (138). The film confirms Barthes's insight that "the bourgeoisie is defined as *the social class that does not want to be named*" (138). In keeping with Antonio Gramsci's notion that the bourgeoisie poses as an entity capable of continuous movement, capable of assimilating the entire society to its own cultural and moral level (Bennett 98), Barthes argues that this erasure of fixed identity is effected through the concept of nation, which was once a progressive idea, instrumental in the transition from monarchy to democracy, but which presently disguises the class interests of the bourgeoisie as the universal aims of the whole society. Gramsci's conception of the ethical state, which creates opportunities for "organic passage" from the lower social ranks into the bourgeoisie, envisions the museum as a tool of social engineering (Bennett 98). In 1857, the South Kensington

Museum lay the groundwork for the modern museum with an open admissions policy, Sunday and evening hours, cheap catalogs, adequate labels, and tour guides. Dedicated to the display of national handicrafts and the celebration of British industrial ingenuity, the South Kensington Museum functioned as an instrument of public uplift. As "spaces of emulation" in which the lower classes model the bourgeois virtues of sobriety, productivity, literacy, and culture (from their exposure to the middle and upper classes), museums further both liberal and conservative social agendas (Bennett 24).

James's *The Golden Bowl* is a minutely accurate anatomization of this process. Adam Verver's vision of the great American museum reflects specific class aims, the reconciliation of labor and capital, as well as the erasure of bourgeois hegemony through the improvisation of a newly inclusive national identity: "It hadn't merely, his plan, all the sanctions of civilization; it was positively civilization condensed, concrete, consummate, set down by his hands as a house on a rock—a house from whose open doors and windows, open to grateful, to thirsty millions, the higher, the highest knowledge would shine out to bless the land" (142–43). Sounding like an improbable cross between Emma Lazarus and Governor John Winthrop, author of "A Model of Christian Charity," Verver imagines a golden future for the blighted urban masses precisely because he has appropriated a glorious past for their communal enlightenment. America can take her place on the world stage once she acquires a deep history with European roots. The museum as "Greek temple" (143) facilitates the back-projection of America's cultural past, drawing affinities with the artifactual equivalent of the Elgin marbles and the ethos of civic pride, courage, and beauty they symbolize.

In 1873, James visited the Bethnal Green Museum, an early attempt at social uplift in the form of a district museum, far from Trafalgar square and open to the general public for a sixpenny fee and to the locals in the slum on non-paying days: "Half in charity and (virtually) half in irony, a beautiful art-collection has been planted in the midst of this darkness and squalor,—an experimental lever for the 'elevation of the masses'" (*EA* 28). On the basis of this review, I am pretty certain that James would not endorse the film's revisions to the character of Adam Verver, who admits to mistreating immigrant laborers at his coal works (12 hour days, 7 day weeks) and, incidentally, employing children, when he vows to give the working poor and the indigent something beautiful to look at. To be fair, Verver's plan of releasing the people of his adoptive city from "the bondage of ugliness" is voiced in the novel, but it is not a confession of guilt (143). Nor is it a profession of James's personal convictions. "The Bethnal Green Museum" may be read as James's proleptic rebuke to Verver's deluded notion that thirsty millions will find rest and refreshment in his palace of art; in his review, James wryly draws attention to a "group of Food Specimens, neatly encased and labelled,—interesting from a scientific, but slightly irritating from a Bethnal Green, that is, a hungry point of view" (*EA* 28). In the film, Charlotte expresses the utilitarian position that the masses "want their street-car, not your museum," but this view is dismissed as sour grapes because she doesn't want to be immured in American City. The filmmakers portray Adam's tenacious pursuit of his dream—"They may not want it. But they shall have it"—as heroic and idealistic. Merchant Ivory's *The Golden Bowl* is a fantasy and, better still, could be described as myth-making, because a myth "abolishes the complexity of human acts, it gives them the simplicity of essences, it does away with all dialectics, with any going back beyond what is immediately visible, it organizes a world which is without contradictions because it is without depth, a world wide open and wallowing in the evident, it establishes a blissful clarity" (Barthes 143).

The film's focus on the museum (a model of the building figures prominently in several scenes) bespeaks the film's investment in its own cultural capital as an art film and as an adaptation of a literary classic with a sophisticated visual repertoire. In his article, "Masterpiece Theatre and the Uses of Tradition," Timothy Brennan describes adaptations such as *The Golden Bowl* as attempts to "fuse together the apparently incompatible national myths of England and the United States": "In Masterpiece Theatre, national cultures are playing roles in a political melodrama: England playing the role of gentry; America, the entrepreneurial class" (103). Merchant Ivory's *The Golden Bowl* violates this rule in one peculiar respect; it denies the role of gentry to the Castledeans and transforms Verver's entrepreneurial background into a patrician past. When Lord Castledean bemoans Verver's usurpation of European treasures to enrich America's cultural climate, Lady Castledean replies, "You ought to ask some questions in Parliament. Make a *cause célèbre* out of it. Don't these things belong in British museums?" With the exception of the Lawrences and Reynolds, which appear in the music room of Verver's rented country estate in the film, the art works are no more indigenously British than they are American. Here, two rival imperialist powers vie for cultural ascendency. It seems a bit premature to cede pride of place to the Americans in 1903, but that's just what Merchant Ivory has done.[9] I think this choice has more to do with the realities of raising capital to get a film into production than with the historical context of James's novel. According to Gilles Deleuze, "what defines industrial art is not the mechanical reproduction but the internalized relation with money. . . . Money is the obverse of all the images that the cinema shows and sets in place, so that films about money are already, if implicitly, films within the film or about the film" (77). If this is true, Verver's billions exercised a fatal attraction for the scenarist, director, and producer of *The Golden Bowl*.

James himself was intensely alive to the role of cultural capital in the kind of transcontinental exchange he presents in *The Golden Bowl*. As an esoteric novelist hoping for a popular forum, James was not above advertising his own cultural cachet with the aim of drumming up sales and perpetuating a type of tasteful reader for his own work. Calling his material "one of those chances for *good taste,* possibly even for the play of the very best in the world, that are not only always to be invoked and cultivated, but that are absolutely to be jumped at from the moment they make a sign," James affirms the intercalation of art within the scheme of social prestige without demur (*AN* 289). However, James avoids naming, ascribing, valuing individual works of art in his novels—he won't recommend a list of classics to the ignorant or praise the accumulated knowledge of the elite. Certainly, he never thought to profit from "spinoff merchandise" inspired by his texts as Merchant Ivory has done. Fifty limited edition replicas of the golden bowl are available at Steuben for $14,000 apiece while supplies last.

## Notes

1. Ruth Prawer Jhabvala quoted in Horne, "'It Works Diagonally.'"
2. The film was shot with anamorphic lenses, which frequently caused the backgrounds to go out of focus. Ivory, "Imagining *The Golden Bowl*."
3. The one exception to this rule is the scene where Adam discovers the Prince and Charlotte conversing by candlelight beneath a portentous image, Verrio's depiction of the grim reaper plying his sickle among the sinners, which hangs above the staircase at Fawns.
4. Aesthetic consumption is a form of personal pleasure, which often mirrors or aggrandizes the purchasing power of the collector. In *Ways of Seeing,* John Berger explains that oil paintings depict objects that are, in reality, purchasable: "Works of art in earlier traditions celebrated wealth. But wealth was then a symbol of a fixed social or divine order. Oil painting celebrated a new kind of wealth—which was dynamic and which found its only sanction in the supreme buying power of money" (90). In Holbein's *Ambassadors,* the painting associated with James's novel of that name, all the objects are manufactured and rendered in such scrupulous detail that they cry out to be touched: "there is not a surface in this picture which does not make one aware of how it has been elaborately worked over—by weavers, embroiderers, carpet-makers, goldsmiths, leather workers, mosaic-makers, furriers, tailors, jewellers—and of how this working-over and the resulting richness of each surface has been finally worked-over and reproduced by Holbein the painter" (Berger 90).
5. James's account of Verver's rhapsody on Maggie's flowering under the twined

influences of marriage and maternity may appear, at first glance, to contradict my assessment of Adam's lack of emotional investment in marriage. But the father-daughter bond exists outside the nineteenth-century spermatic economy in which marital sexual excess could be blamed for diverting nervous energy that might more profitably be exercised in business endeavors. Notice of her early death exculpates the wife from any serious diminution of Verver's energy and capital, but Adam does "wince fairly still" recalling her pressure to purchase and to spend lavishly (140). Mrs. Verver's demise also promoted an incestuous bond between the father and daughter, who assumed the role of wife: "It was as if you couldn't be in the market when you were married to *me*. Or rather as if I kept people off, innocently, by being married to you. Now that I'm married to some one else you're, as in consequence, married to nobody" (162).

6. The betrothal gift prioritizes patriarchal ties (authority, emulation, taboo) over matrimonial relations. Reflecting on the difference his son-in-law has made in his domestic arrangements, Adam indicates that the anticipated awkwardness (angularity) of having a second male join the household has been averted by the unexpected "felicity of a contact" with the Prince's "practically yielding lines and curved surfaces" (137). The figures of speech, analogies with buildings and furniture, that frame this jest allow Adam to fantasize aloud about "rubbing against" the Prince's comfortable curves: "It's the sort of thing in you that one feels—or at least I do—with one's hand" (137). The implicit eroticism of this remark is striking. Shortly thereafter, James interrupts the conversation between Adam and the Prince to eroticize the latter's passivity, as if he were Danae on the receiving end of Zeus's passionate golden shower: "The Prince had taken the idea, in his way, for he was well accustomed by this time to taking, and nothing perhaps even could more have confirmed Mr Verver's account of his surface than the manner in which these golden drops evenly flowed over it. They caught in no interstice, they gathered in no concavity; the uniform smoothness betrayed the dew but by showing for the moment a richer tone" (138). "Golden drops" and "dew" frequently appear in Victorian pornography as poetic expressions for semen. The objectification of the Prince depersonalizes the sexual acts imagined and makes their articulation possible, if somewhat inscrutable.

7. The website decodes the film's visual glossary for the spectator unfamiliar with late nineteenth-century art. The website boasts a diptych of actor Jeremy Northam, sporting dark hair and a beard, whose physiognomy and coloring resemble Sargent's portrait of Dr. Pozzi, a womanizing physician rumored to be the lover of Madame Gautreau, the model for Sargent's *Madame X*. See figures 27 and 28. The film is quite clever about invoking *Madame X* through the sign of Charlotte's décolletage.

8. In her chapter on "The Gilded Age," Morgan biographer, Jean Strouse, handily summarizes the economic and social trends informing James's characterization of the Ververs's wealth and status: "A magazine article on 'The Owners of the United States,' published in 1889, claimed that the average annual income of the country's hundred wealthiest men was between $1.2 million and $1.5 mil-

lion—dwarfing the incomes of European royalty—while 80 percent of U.S. families earned less than $500 a year. Few of the new millionaires came from New England, none from the South: the huge fortunes of the late nineteenth century were made in railroads, industry and finance, in New York, Pennsylvania, Illinois, Ohio, and the West. . . . This tremendous concentration of private affluence had powerfully unsettling effects not only on the vast majority of Americans who were not rich but also on the nation's Old Guard elites. Boston Brahmins, New York Knickerbockers, and the residents of Philadelphia's Rittenhouse Square still had ample bank accounts and distinguished lineage, but power, and wealth in previously unimaginable amounts, now belonged to the 'new' men. Henry Adams regarded the inexorable advance of capitalists, bankers, 'goldbugs' and Jews (he used the terms interchangeably) with a scorn fueled by his own sense of eclipse" (215–16).

9. In 1911, James published a novella that takes the Castledeans's grievance seriously: "'The Outcry' deals with a question sharply brought home of late to the conscience of English Society—that of the degree in which the fortunate owners of precious and hitherto transmitted works of art hold them in trust, as it were, for the nation, and may themselves, as lax guardians, be held to account by public opinion"(CN 578). The Outcry features a family of embattled aristocrats, who are squabbling over a plan to sell one of the artistic jewels of their home, Dedborough Place, a kind of rural National Gallery, to an American art dealer, a Berenson type. Influenced by her love for an upstart art historian who cycles around England poking his nose into baronial vaults in search of masterpieces and claims to have found one at Dedborough, a daughter of the house is kicking up a row. In a letter to Wharton, James despairs over the general preference for this "inferior little product": "You speak at your ease, chère Madame, of the interminable and formidable job of my producing à mon age another Golden Bowl—the most arduous and thankless task I ever set myself; . . . and meanwhile, I blush to say, the Outcry is on its way to a fifth edition (in these few weeks) whereas it has taken the poor old G.B. eight or nine years to get even into a third" (HJL 4:591). It is the method not the "larger morality of the matter" that James disowns; unlike The Golden Bowl, which dramatizes consciousness, The Outcry, written for the stage and converted to its present form, is conceived as "a rapid, precipitated action, moving through difficulties and dangers to a happy issue" (CN 578). When James speaks of the treasures of the British private collections in The Outcry, of the Reynolds, Lawrences, Morettos and Rubens (Montavanos is apparently an invention, but a plausible one), he is citing the works of real artists; he even has an idea of what they cost. This is a significant departure from the descriptive ellipses of The Golden Bowl. In its handling of plot, action, and aesthetics, the Merchant Ivory production has much in common with The Outcry.

## Works by James

*The Art of the Novel.* New York: Scribners, 1962.
*EA—Essays on Art and Drama.* Ed. Peter Rawlings. Aldershot: Scolar,1996.
*The Golden Bowl.* New York: Penguin, 2001.
*HJL—Henry James Letters.* Ed. Leon Edel. 4 Vols. Cambridge:Harvard UP, 1974–1984.
*CN—The Complete Notebooks of Henry James.* Ed. Leon Edel. New York: Oxford UP, 1987.
*TJ—The Tales of Henry James, Vol. 3, 1875–1879.* Ed. Maqbool Aziz. Oxford: Clarendon Press, 1984.

## Works Cited

Barthes, Roland. *Mythologies.* New York: Hill, 1972.
Bennett, Tony. *The Birth of the Museum.* London: Routledge, 1995.
Berger, John. *Ways of Seeing.* London: Penguin, 1972.
Bourdieu, Pierre, and Alain Darbel. *The Love of Art: European Art Museums and Their Public.* Trans. Caroline Beattie and Nick Merriman. Stanford: Stanford UP, 1990.
Brennan, Timothy. "Masterpiece Theatre and the Uses of Tradition." *Social Text* 12 (Fall 1985): 102–112.
Deleuze, Gilles. *Cinema 2: The Time-Image.* Minneapolis: U of Minnesota P, 1989.
"The Dread of the Jew." *Spectator* 83 (September 9, 1899): 338–339.
Horne, Philip. "'It Works Diagonally': A Conversation with Ruth Prawer Jhabvala on *The Golden Bowl* and the Art of Adaptation." < http://merchantivory.com/goldenbowl/ruth.html>.
Ivory, James, "Imagining *The Golden Bowl*." <http://merchantivory.com/goldenbowl/ivory.htm>l.
Jameson, Frederic. *The Political Unconscious: Narrative as a Socially Symbolic Act.* Ithaca: Cornell UP, 1981.
Jakobson, Roman. *Language in Literature.* Cambridge: Harvard UP, 1987.
Lears, T.J. Jackson. *No Place of Grace: Antimodernism and the Transformation of American Culture 1880–1920.* New York: Pantheon, 1981.
Morais, Nina. "Jewish Ostracism in America." *North American Review* 133 (1881): 265–75.
Ratcliff, Carter. *John Singer Sargent.* New York: Abbeville, 1982.
Strouse, Jean. *Morgan, American Financier.* New York: Random, 1999.
Veblen, Thorstein. *The Theory of the Leisure Class.* New York: New American Library, 1953.

## Filmography

*The Golden Bowl.* Dir. James Ivory. Writ. Ruth Prawer Jhabvala. Perf. Uma Turman, Nick Nolte, Kate Beckinsale, Jeremy Northam. Merchant Ivory Productions, 2000.

The James Films and Critical Reactions

# A Henry James Filmography

*J. Sarah Koch*

It was as a graduate student studying literature at Oregon's Portland State University that I became involved with and enamored of the works of Henry James. Along the way, I took a class titled "Henry James on Film," which served not only to further affirm my interest in this author, but also to awaken an interest in screen adaptations of classic works in general, James's in particular. When I went looking for a full James filmography, however, I discovered that there didn't seem to be one. There are a number of sources that provide partial lists of James-based films and television fare (including the Internet Movie Database), but none of them was complete. Certain of the foreign adaptations (e.g., *Otra vuelta de tuerca* and *Georginas Gründe*) that have never been distributed in this country are not surprisingly left out of many American video guides, though they may be referred to on the Internet or in books on foreign-made films. Other adaptations, such as the earliest film *Berkeley Square* (1933), are listed in certain guides, even though they are apparently unavailable for viewing. (More about the issue of availability later.)

It is certainly clear, as evidenced by the number of James-based feature-films both recently produced and in production, that Henry James has enjoyed something of a revival. Merchant Ivory Productions is often given credit for beginning this trend with their 1979 version of *The Europeans*. Since then, we've seen their *The Bostonians* (1984) and *The Golden Bowl* (2000) as well as big screen productions by others of *The Portrait of a Lady, Washington Square,* and two versions of *The Wings of the Dove,* to name just a few. Over the years there have also been numerous versions of "The Turn of the Screw," the two most recent of which were released in 1999. *Presence of Mind/El Celo* represents a collaboration between the U.S. and Spain, while the other, a British production of *The American,* after debuting in the U.K. eventually appeared on ExxonMobil Masterpiece Theatre. With these, though, it would seem that the revival may be, at the very least, winding down. Apparently, the only James-derived screen- or teleplay scheduled for production at this

Figure 30. Heather Angel as Helen Pettigrew and Leslie Howard as Peter Standish in *Berkeley Square* (1933), the first James-based screen adaptation. Library of Congress.

point is a script of *The Spoils of Poynton,* prepared for the BBC by Sir John Mortimer (who also contributed dialogue to 1961's *The Innocents*).

It is well known that James, a theater devotee from his youth, had little success adapting his own works to the stage. However, since his day, other playwrights, including Ruth Goetz and Augustus Goetz, Michael Redgrave, John L. Balderston, and William Archibald, were able to manage the adaptation process, achieving the acclaim, and financial remuneration, that eluded him. James has also been drawn on as inspiration for operas, radio plays, and at least one ballet, though one could argue that James's work is especially well suited for the camera, as the late Leon Edel suggests in his preface to *The Complete Plays of Henry James:* "The appeal of Henry James's works for the theatrical and operatic stages, as well as for the cameras and video of our time, derives from three elements in his artistry: the modernity of his cosmic subjects, the depth and psychology of his realism, and his extraordinary visual sense. His observations were always acute and they were psychological. He had a sense of picture and scene, a belief that all the arts are one, and that the artist should never hesitate to experiment" (4).

My goal is to create an international catalogue of all the attempts to bring James to the screen, big or small. The results so far, though in themselves incomplete, include a substantial amount of product from the United States, Great Britain, Canada, France, Germany, Spain, Portugal, Sweden, and one joint Czechoslovakian–British effort (a taping of Benjamin Britten's opera *The Turn of the Screw*). At present this filmography represents 125 screen works generated by 46 of James's tales, novellas, and novels, including those films or television episodes that, though listed in certain reference books, are currently out of print or are simply unobtainable. This brings me back to a point I raised earlier regarding the apparent unavailability of particular renditions of James's work. Whereas many of the foreign films or television shows have never been released in this country, there were also many episodes made for early television, whether in the States or abroad, that were broadcast live and never taped, or if taped were later destroyed to make room for yet more product. (In the United States, especially in the first two and a half decades of television, there were dozens of drama anthologies, including those that featured adaptations of the classics. Much of this early work was esteemed strictly for its contemporaneous entertainment value and not considered worthy of preservation.) Even if the tape wasn't intentionally destroyed, it may have simply deteriorated before anyone thought to make a new and more durable copy. Although I originally had planned to designate certain titles as unavailable, I later chose not to, because what may seem to be unavailable today may be unearthed tomorrow. According to Rosemary C. Hanes, film and television research librarian with the Library of Congress, the library is involved in an ongoing process of uncrating and cataloguing early television materials from the United States. Besides this potential source there are, no doubt, others (including private collections) waiting to be discovered while some countries are still in the early stages of chronicling their television and cinematic output. All considered, then, it could be at the very least misleading to mark any of the items listed in this filmography as unavailable.

While compiling this inventory, I became intrigued by the recurrence of certain names (e.g., of adapters, actors, and directors) and by filmmaker's choices among James's stories. Considering that James wrote over one hundred tales and *nouvelles* and twenty novels, there is a great deal to choose from. The three most frequently adapted titles are "The Turn of the Screw," with sixteen versions, followed by thirteen of *Washington Square* and twelve of "The Aspern Papers." However, among the remaining eighty-four, there are also productions based on many of James's lesser-known works including "Glasses," "Lord Beaupre," and "The Tone of Time."

I would like to take this opportunity to thank those people who were especially helpful, and patient, in providing information and assistance. I

Figure 31. Robert Cummings as Lewis Venable and Agnes Moorehead as Julia Bordereau in the first filmed version of "The Aspern Papers." Library of Congress.

have already mentioned Rosemary C. Hanes and would also like to thank Casey Hoelscher of Development Source, as well as Lysa Sprindzuikate of the British Film Commission; director Gareth Davies; Canadian author and director of Dramatic Literature, Drama in Education and Theatre Studies at Brock University, Mary Jane Miller; Antonio Vicente Azofra (doctoral candidate, Valladolid, Spain); Cecilia Rosenow (doctoral candidate, University of Oregon); and author Marcella Farina. I also wish to express my appreciation for the work done by Larry James Gianakos in his five-volume history of the U.S. from 1947 through 1984, as well as that of Anthony J. Mazzella in his 1981 article for the *Henry James Review* titled "A Selected Henry James Artsography." Both of these were most useful, not only in providing information, but in offering me a means of double-checking certain facts.

    After much thought I decided the best way to organize such a catalogue for readers of James was so that the name of the original work appears first, followed by the subsequent films or television shows, listed in chronological order. I have also included abbreviations within a listing indicating that an award had been given. An award given to the film itself will be the last item listed, barring any added commentary regarding that particular title. The following key should help:

| | |
|---|---|
| A | best actor/actress |
| AA | Academy Award |
| D | best director |
| FJS | Franklin J. Schaffner tape collection (current location of collection unclear) |
| GG | Golden Globe Award |
| ISA | Independent Spirit Awards |
| LC | Library of Congress (indicates that the LC video archive contains a copy) |
| MFF | Montreal Film Festival |
| MTR | Museum of Television and Radio tape collection |
| N | nominated for an award but did not win |
| NBR | National Board of Review/D.W. Griffith Awards |
| NSFC | National Society of Film Critics |
| NY | New York Film Festival |
| NYFC | New York Film Critics Circle awards |
| NYT | *New York Times* |
| S | best supporting actor/actress |
| SFF | Sundance Film Festival |
| UCLA | copy in one of the UCLA archives |

## A Henry James Filmography

### "The Altar of the Dead" (1895)

The Green Room (*La Chambre verte*) (France). Inspired primarily by "The Altar of the Dead," but also by James's "The Friends of the Friends," "The Beast in the Jungle," and "Maud-Evelyn." Screenplay by François Truffaut and Jean Gruault. Dir. François Truffaut. Perf. François Truffaut (Julien), Nathalie Baye (Cecilia), Jean Dasté (Humbert), Jean-Pierre Moulin (Gerard), Antoine Vitez, Jeanne Lobre (Rambaud), Patrick Maleon (Georges). Le Films du Carosse SA/Les Productions Artistes Associés/UnitedArtists, color, 95 mins., 1978. Videocassette. MGM/UA Home Video, 1993. NY 1978. LC.

### The Ambassadors (1903)

The Ambassadors (U.S.; TV). Teleplay by Worthington (Tony) Miner. Dir. Franklin J. Schaffner. Perf. Robert Sterling, Judson Laire, Ilona Massey, Katherine Willard. Studio One, 60 mins., two airings: 15 May 1950, and 26 Feb. 1951. FJS: copy of second airing.

The Ambassadors (U.K.; TV). Teleplay by Denis Constanduros. Dir. James Cellan Jones. Perf. Alan Gifford (Lambert Strether), Bethel Leslie (Maria Gostrey), David Bauer (Waymarsh), Harvey Spencer, Roy Stephens. BBC-2, 45 mins., 14 Feb. 1965.

The Ambassadors (U.K.; TV). Teleplay by Denis Constanduros. Dir. James Cellan Jones. Perf. Paul Scofield (Lambert Strether), Lee Remick (Maria Gostrey), Delphine Seyrig (Madame de Vionnet), Gayle Hunnicutt (Sarah Pocock), Don

Fellows (Waymarsh), David Huffman (Chad Newsome), others. *Play of the Month,*
BBC-1, 95 mins., 13 Mar. 1977.

### *The American (1877)*

*The American* (U.S.; TV). Perf. John Newland, Tonio Selwart, Irene Worth, Alfred
Ryder, Leopoldine Konstantin, Neva Patterson, Augusta Roeland, Blaine Cordner.
*Philco Television Playhouse,* 60 mins., 30 Apr. 1950.
*The American* (U.S.; TV). Teleplay by Michael Dyne. Perf. Peter Graves (Christopher
Newman), Cloris Leachman (Claire de Cintre), Lili Darvas (Old Marquis), Ivan Triesault
(Urbain), Michael Hall (Valentin). *Matinee Theatre,* color, aired live 5 June 1956.
*The American* (U.K.; TV). Teleplay by Michael Hastings. Dir. Paul Unwin. Perf. Matthew
Modine (Christopher Newman), Diana Rigg (Madame de Bellegarde), Aisling O'Sullivan
(Claire de Cintre), Paul Hickey (Henri de Bellegarde), Brenda Fricker (Mrs. Bread).
*ExxonMobil Masterpiece Theatre,* WGBH/BBC, color, 90 mins., aired 3 Jan. 2001.

### *"The Aspern Papers" (1888)*

*The Lost Moment* (U.S.). Screenplay by Leonardo Bercovicci. Dir. Martin Gabel.
Photog. Hal Mohr. Music by Daniele Amfitheatrof. Perf. Susan Hayward (Tina
Bordereau), Robert Cummings (Lewis Venable), Agnes Moorehead (Juliana
Bordereau), Joan Lorring (Amelia), Eduardo Ciannelli (Father Rinaldo), John
Archer (Charles), Frank Puglia (Pietro), Minerva Urecal (Maria), William
Edmunds (Vittorio). Universal/Walter Wanger, bw, 89 mins., 1947. Videocas-
sette. Republic Pictures Home Video, 1989.
*A Garden in the Sea* (U.S.; TV). Teleplay by Michael Dyne. Perf. Dorothy McGuire,
Mildred Natwick, Donald Murphy. *U.S. Steel/Theatre Guild Hour,* 60 mins., July 1954.
*The Aspern Papers* (U.S.; TV). Teleplay by Michael Dyne. *Matinee Theatre,* color, aired
live 17 Nov. 1955.
*The Aspern Papers* (Canada; TV). Teleplay by Michael Dyne. Prod. and dir. Ron
Weyman. *Playdate,* 60 mins., 9 May 1959.
*The Aspern Papers* (U.K.; TV). Teleplay by John O'Toole. Prod. Rudolph Cartier. Sets
by Natasha Kroll. Perf. Beatrix Lehmann (Juliana Bordereau), Siobhan McKenna
(Tina), Edmund Purdom (Harvey Mornson), Clement McCullin (John Cumnor).
BBC, 18 Nov. 1962.
*Les Documents de Jeffrey Aspern* (France; TV). Dir. Raymond Rouleau. ORTF, 11 June 1968.
*A Mask of Love* (U.S.; TV). Teleplay by Sherman Yellen. Dir. Burt Brinckerhoff. Prod.
Barbara Schultz. Perf. Kathleen Nesbitt, Barbara Barrie, Harry Yulin. ABC's
*Matinee Today,* 90 mins., 7 Dec. 1973.
*Affairs of the Heart: Miss Tita* (U.K.; TV). Teleplay by Terence Feely. Dir. Derek Bennett. Perf.
John Carson (Charles Faversham), Beatrix Lehmann (Juliana Bordereau), Margaret
Tyzak (Miss Tita), Petra Davies (Mrs. Prest), Jane Bough (Olimpia). ITV, 20 Apr. 1975.
*Hullabaloo over Georgie and Bonnie's Pictures* (India/U.K.). Screenplay by Ruth Prawer
Jhabvala. Dir. James Ivory. Photog. Walter Lassally. Music by Vic Flick. Ed.

Humphrey Dixon. Costumes by Jenny Beavan, Purnima Agarwal. Perf. Peggy Ashcroft, Larry Pine, Saeed Jaffrey, Victor Banerjee, Aparna Sen, Jane Booker, Jenny Beavan, Aladdin Langa, the choir of the Sacred Heart of St. Mary's, Jodphur. London Weekend Television, color, 83 mins., Sept. 1978. Ivory, when asked if this film owed anything to "The Aspern Papers," declined to comment, but Neil Sinyard, in his book *Filming Literature,* takes for granted that it's based on that short story.

*Aspern* (Portugal). Alternative title, *Les Papiers d' Aspern.* Screenplay by Michael Graham. Dir. Eduardo de Gregorio. Perf. Jean Sorel (the "truth seeker"), Bulle Ogier (Miss Tita), Alida Valli (Juliana Bordereau), Ana Marta, Teresa Madruga. Color, 96 mins., 1981.

*The Aspern Papers* (U.S.; TV). Music and Libretto by Dominick Argento. Perf. Frederica von Stade (Tina), Elisabeth Soderstrom (Juliana), Richard Stilwell ("The Lodger"), with the Dallas Opera. *Great Performances,* 9 June 1989. LC.

*Los papeles de Aspern* (Spain). Screenplay by Rafael de Espana. Dir. Jordi Cadena. Perf. Nuria Hosta (Assumpta), Silvia Munt (Tina Bordereau), Amparo Soler Leal. 1991.

### *"The Author of 'Beltraffio'" (1884)*

*The Author of "Beltraffio"* (U.K./West Germany/France). Teleplay by Robin Chapman. Dir. Tony Scott. Photog. David McDonald. Music by John Scott. Staging by Marianne Ford. Perf. Tom Baker (Mark Ambient), Georgina Hale (Beatrice Ambient), Michael J. Shannon (James Sinclair), Stefan Gates (Dolcino), Catherine Willmer (Gwendolyn Ambient), Preston Lockwood (Doctor). Technisonor Production, 52 mins., 27 Mar. 1976.

### *"The Beast in the Jungle" (1903)*

(See also "The Altar of the Dead.")

*The Beast in the Jungle* (U.K.; TV). Teleplay by James Saunders. Dir. Bill Hays. Perf. Peter Jeffrey (John Marcher), Sian Phillips (May Bartram), Elizabeth Burger (Maisie), Tony Bateman (the Stranger), Valerie Lush (the Lady at Luncheon), Polly Murch (Jenny). ITV, 30 June 1969.

*The Cold Eye* (*My Darling, Be Careful*) (U. S.). Experimental film based on "The Beast in the Jungle." Screenplay by James Barth. Dir. Babette Mangolte. Perf. Cathy Digby (Kim Ginsberg), George Deem (Allan), Powers Booth (David), Saskia Noordhoek-Hegt (Illiana), Ela Troyano (Ella), James Barth (Frank), Maggie Grynastyl (Gertrude), Valda Setterfield (Bea). 16 mm, bw, 90 mins., 1980.

### *"The Bench of Desolation" (1909)*

*Affairs of the Heart: Kate* (U.K.; TV). Teleplay by Terence Feely. Dir. Gareth Davies. Perf. Eileen Atkins (Kate Cookham), Michael Bryant (Herbert Dodd), Yvonne Antrobus (Nan Drury), Bernard Lee (Mr. Drury), Robert Lister, Edward Dentith. ITV, 51 mins., 9 Mar. 1975.

*Le Banc de la desolation* (France; TV). Screenplay by Roger Grenier. Dir. Claude

Figure 32. Bonnie (Aparna Sen) as she looks out from the window of her palace in Merchant Ivory's *Hullabaloo Over Bonnie and Georgie's Pictures*. Library of Congress.

Chabrol. Photog. Jean Rabier. Staging by Guy Maugin. Music by Pierre Jansen. Perf. Catherine Samie (Miss Kate Cookson), Michel Duchaussoy (Herbert Dodd), Michel Piccoli (Captain Roper), Thalie Fruges. ORTF Cosmovision /Scott Free Enterprises of London, 52 mins., 13 Mar. 1976.

### *The Bostonians (1886)*

*The Bostonians* (U.S.). Screenplay by Ruth Prawer Jhabvala and James Ivory. Dir. James Ivory. Photog. Walter Lassally. Music by Richard Robbins. Ed. Katherine Wenning and Mark Potter. Costumes by Jenny Beavan and John Bright. Perf. Vanessa Redgrave (Olive Chancellor) (A/AAN) (NSFC 1984/A), Christopher Reeve (Basil Ransom), Jessica Tandy (Miss Birdseye), Nancy Marchand (Mrs. Burrage), Linda Hunt (Dr. Prance), Madeleine Potter (Verena Tarrant), Wesley Addy (Selah Tarrant), Wallace Shawn (Matthias Pardon), Nancy New (Mrs. Luna). Merchant Ivory Productions/WGBH/Rediffusion/Almi, color, 122 mins., 1984. Videocassette. Rhino Home Video, 1993. *NYT* 1984, 10 best films. LC.

### *"Covering End" (1898)*

*Affairs of the Heart: Grace* (U.K.; TV). Teleplay by Terence Feely. Dir. Michael Lindsay-Hogg. Perf. Diana Rigg (Grace Gracedew), Jeremy Brett (Captain Yule),

George Cole (Mr. Prodmore), John Welsh (Chivers), Celia Bannerman (Cora). ITV, 6 Oct. 1974.

### *"Daisy Miller" (1878)*

*Affairs of the Heart: Daisy* (U.K.; TV). Teleplay by Terence Feely. Dir. John Frankau. Perf. Daniel Massey (Frederick Winterbourne), Georgina Hale (Daisy Miller), Rosalie Crutchley (Mrs. Costello), Natasha Perry (Emily Walker). ITV, 6 Apr. 1975.

*Daisy Miller* (U.S.). Screenplay by Frederic Raphael. Dir. Peter Bogdanovich. Photog. Albert Spagnoli. Costumes by John Furness (AAN). Perf. Cybill Shepherd (Daisy), Barry Brown (Winterbourne), Mildred Natwick (Mrs. Costello), Eileen Brennan (Mrs. Walker), Duilio Del Prete (Giovanelli), Cloris Leachman (Mrs. Miller), James McMurtry (Randolph Miller). Paramount/Copa de Oro Pictures, Technicolor, 92 mins., 1974. Videocassette. Paramount Pictures. Corp., 1986. NBR 1974, 9th best English-speaking film. *NYT* 1974, 11 best films. LC.

### *"De Grey: A Romance" (1868)*

*De Grey* (France; TV). Screenplay by Roger Grenier. Dir. Claude Chabrol. Photog. Jean Rabier. Music by Pierre Jansen. Perf. Catherine Jourdan (Margaret), Yves Lefebvre (Father Herbert), Helene Perdriere (Mrs. De Grey), Daniel Lecourtois. ORTF, 52 mins., 20 Mar. 1977.

### *[Die Tochter]*

*Die Tochter/The Daughter* (West Germany; TV). Taken from Guy McCrone's play *Edenbrook's Daughter* (apparently never staged), which was based on various Jamesian motifs rather than any specific work or works. Dir. Volker von Collande. Staging by Karl-Hermann Joksch. Perf. Albrecht Schoenhals, Ursula Lingen, John van Dreelen, Gisela von Collande. NWDR Hamburg, 70 mins., aired 15 Feb. 1956.

### *The Europeans (1878)*

*The Europeans* (U.S.; TV). Perf. Zsa Zsa Gabor, Peter Cookson, Nico Minardos. *Matinee Theatre,* color, aired live 6 Jan. 1958.

*The Europeans* (U.K./U.S.). Screenplay by R.P. Jhabvala and James Ivory. Dir. James Ivory. Photog. Larry Pizer. Music by Richard Robbins. Ed. Humphrey Dixon. Costumes Judy Moorcroft (AAN). Perf. Lee Remick, Robin Ellis, Wesley Addy, Tim Choate, Lisa Eichhorn, Kristin Griffith, Nancy New, Norman Snow, Helen Stenborg, Tim Woodward. Merchant Ivory Productions, color, 90 mins., 1979. Videocassette. Connoisseur Video Collection, 1992. NBR 1979, 3d best English-speaking film. NY 1979. (N.B.: Among MTR's archives, this is listed as a 1985 production, not as the 1979 film it is. They are referring to its appearance on the 13 May 1985, *American Playhouse.*) LC.

### "The Four Meetings" (1877)

The Four Meetings (U.S.; TV). Perf. John Baragrey, Leora Dana. *Goodyear Theatre*, 30 mins., 8 June 1952.

### "The Friends of the Friends" (1896)

(See "The Altar of the Dead.")

### "Georgina's Reasons" (1884)

Georginas Gründe (West Germany/France; TV). Teleplay by Peter Adler, Volker Schlöndorff. Dir. Volker Schlöndorff. Perf. Elke Aberle, Joachim Bissmeier, Edith Clever, Eva Maria Meineke, Margarethe von Trotta, Danielle Palmero, Claude Giraud, Renee Regnard. Color, 65 mins. Released in France as *Les Raisons de Georgina*, airing there 10 Apr. 1976, and in Germany on 27 Apr. 1975.

### "The Ghostly Rental" (1876)

The Haunting of Hell House (Original title: *Ghostly Rental*) (U.S.). Screenplay by Mitch Marcus, L.L. Shapira. Dir. Mitch Marcus. Photog. Russ Brandt. Prod. Roger Corman. Ed. Daniel H. Holland. Original music Ivan Koutikov. Perf. Michael York (Prof. Ambrose), Andrew Bowen (James), Claudia Christian, Aideen O'Donnell. New Concorde/New Horizons Home Video. Color, 90 mins., 1998.
Le Redevance du fantome (France; TV). Dir. Robert Enrico. ORTF, 1964.

### "Glasses" (1896)

Affairs of the Heart: Flora (U.K.; TV). Teleplay by Terence Feely. Dir. Michael Ferguson. Perf. Gayle Hunnicutt (Flora Saunt), Anton Rodgers (Geoffrey Dawling), Patricia Routledge (Mrs. Meldrum). ITV, 6 Oct. 1974.

### The Golden Bowl (1904)

The Golden Bowl (U.K.; TV). Teleplay by Jack Pulman. Dir. James Cellan Jones. Perf. Barry Morse (Adam Verver), Gayle Hunnicutt (Charlotte Stant), Cyril Cusack (Bob Assingham), Daniel Massey (Amerigo), Jill Townsend (Maggie Verver), Kathleen Byron (Fanny Assingham). Six episodes. *Masterpiece Theatre*, 25 Mar.–29 Apr. 1973. MTR, LC.
The Golden Bowl (U.S.). Screenplay by Ruth Prawer Jhabvala. Dir. James Ivory. Photog. Tony Pierce-Roberts. Original music Richard Robbins. Ed. John David Allen. Set decoration Anna Pinnock. Costumes John Bright. Perf. Uma Thurman (Charlotte Stant), Jeremy Northam (Prince Amerigo), Nick Nolte (Adam Verver), Kate Beckinsale (Maggie Verver), Anjelica Huston (Fanny Assingham), James Fox (Bob Assingham), Madeleine Potter (Lady Castledean), Peter Eyre (Jarvis), Nickolas Grace. Merchant Ivory Productions/TFI International, color/bw, 126 mins., 2000.

### *"The Great Condition" (1899)*

*Affairs of the Heart: Elizabeth* (U.K.; TV). Teleplay by Terence Feely. Dir. John Sichel. Perf. Derek Jacobi (Bertram Braddle), Edward Hardwicke (Edward Chilver), Diane Cilento (Elizabeth Damerel). 50 mins. ITV, 13 Apr. 1975.

### *"An International Episode" (1879)*

*Affairs of the Heart: Bessie* (U.K.; TV). Teleplay by Terence Feely. Dir. John Sichel. Perf. Christopher Cazenove (Lord Lambeth), Anna Palk (Kitty Westgate), Geoffrey Whitehead (Percy Beaumont), Dorothy Reynolds (Duchess of Bayswater), Sinead Cusack (Bessie Alden). ITV, 10 Nov. 1974.

### *"The Jolly Corner" (1908)*

*The Jolly Corner* (U.S.; TV). Teleplay by Arthur Barron. Dir. Arthur Barron. Perf. Fritz Weaver (Spencer Brydon), Salome Jens (Alice Staverton). *American Short Story,* color, 43 mins., 1975. LC.

### *"The Liar" (1888)*

*The Liar* (U.S.; TV). Perf. Ilona Massey, Charlton Heston, Frederic Tozere, Susan Harris. *Curtain Call,* 30 mins., 27 Aug. 1952.
*The Liar* (Canada; TV). Teleplay by Howard Merrill. Prod. and dir. Paul Almond. *On Camera,* 30 mins., 1955.

### *"Longstaff's Marriage" (1878)*

*Le Fantome de Longstaff* (France). Dir. Luc Moullet. Perf. Helene Lapiower. 25 mins., color, 1996.

### *"Lord Beaupre" (1892)*

*Affairs of the Heart: Emma* (U.K.; TV). Teleplay by Terence Feely. Perf. Cheryl Campbell (Emma Gosselin), Jeremy Clyde (Guy Beaupre), Lally Bowers (Mrs. Gosselin), Valerine White (Mrs. Ashburg), David Yelland (Hugh Gosselin). ITV, 29 Sept. 1974.

### *"Louisa Pallant" (1888)*

*The Bitter Waters* (U.S.; TV). Teleplay by Zoe Akins. Dir. John Brahm. Photog. Lothrop Worth. Film ed. Marsh Hendry. Story ed. James J. Geller. Sound by J. Goodrich Jr. Set dir. William Ferrari. Perf. George Sanders (Charles Ferris), Constance Cummings (Louisa Pallant), Robert Vaughn (Archibald Parker), Cynthia Baxter (Linda Pallant), Celia Lovsky (Frau Traurnicht), Barbara Morrison (Mrs. Gimingham), Jerry Barclay (Herbert). *Screen Directors Playhouse,* 30 mins., 1 Aug. 1956. UCLA.

Figure 33. Robin Ellis as Robert Acton and Lee Remick as Eugenia in Merchant Ivory's *The Europeans*. Library of Congress.

### *"The Marriages" (1891)*

*The Marriages* (U.S.; TV). Teleplay by H.R. Hays. Dir. Delbert Mann. Perf. Henry Daniell, Margaret Phillips, Carol Goodner, Chester Stratton, Sally Gracie. *Philco Television Playhouse*, 60 mins., 22 Jan. 1950. UCLA.

*Affairs of the Heart: Adela* (U.K.; TV). Teleplay by Terence Feely. Dir. Michael Lindsay-Hogg. Perf. Anna Calder-Marshall (Adela Chart), Georgina Hale (Lola), Richard Vernon (Colonel Chart), Joseph Blatch (Godfrey), Timandra Alwyn (Beatrice), Amanda Townshend (Muriel), Vivian Pickles (Mrs. Churchley), Dorothy Gordon (Miss Flynn), John Rae (Ledbrook). ITV, 27 Oct. 1974.

### *"Maud-Evelyn" (1900)*

(See "The Altar of the Dead.")

### *"Nona Vincent" (1892)*

*Affairs of the Heart: Leonie* (U.K.; TV). Teleplay by Terence Feely. Dir. Christopher Hodson. Perf. Richard Morant (Allan Wayworth), Barbara Murray (Leonie Alsager), Derek Francis (Herbert Loder), Sheila Gish (Violet Grey), Rosamund Greenwood (Clara Grey). ITV, 23 Mar. 1975.

### The Other House (1896)

*Céline et Julie vont en bateau* (France). Released in the U.S. as *Celine and Julie Go Boating;* in Britain, *Phantom Ladies over Paris.* A very loose adaptation of *The Other House* and "The Romance of Certain Old Clothes." Screenplay by Eduardo de Gregorio, Juliet Berto, Dominique Labourier, Bulle Ogier, Marie-France Pisier, Jacques Rivette. Dir. Jacques Rivette. Photog. Jacques Renard. Ed. Nicole Lubtchansky. Perf. Dominique Labourier (Julie), Juliet Berto (Céline), Bulle Ogier (Camille), Marie-France Pisier (Sophie), Barbet Schroeder (Olivier). Les Films du Losange, Eastmancolor, 192 mins., 1974. NY 1974.

### "Owen Wingrave" (1892)

*Owen Wingrave* (U.K.; TV). Composer Benjamin Britten's two-act opera (op. 85), based on James's short story, commissioned by the BBC. Libretto by Myfanwy Piper. Dir. Colin Graham. Perf. John Shirley-Quirk, Benjamin Luxon, Janet Baker, Peter Pears, Heather Harper, Jennifer Vyvyan, Nigel Douglas, others. BBC-2, 110 mins., 16 May 1971.
*Un Jeune Homme Rebelle* (France; TV). Teleplay by Paul Seban. Dir. Paul Seban. Perf. Mathieu Carrière, Bernard Giraudeau, Muriel Catalá, Louise Conte. Technisonor, 52 mins., 17 Apr. 1976.

### "A Passionate Pilgrim" (1871)

*The Passionate Pilgrim* (U.S.; TV). Perf. Leueen MacGrath (Sister Elizabeth Wheeler), Richard Hart, Jane Seymour, Pat O'Malley. *Studio One,* 60 mins., 2 Oct. 1950.

### "The Point of View" (1882)

*A Point of View* (U.S.; TV). Perf. William Post Jr. *Cameo Theatre,* 30 mins., 16 Aug. 1950.

### The Portrait of a Lady (1881)

*The Portrait of a Lady* (U.K./U.S.; TV). Screenplay by Jack Pulman. Dir. James Cellan Jones. Perf. Richard Chamberlain (Ralph Touchett), Suzanne Neve (Isabel Archer), Beatrix Lehmann, Edward Bishop, Alan Gifford, Edward Fox, Felicity Gibson, Susan Tebbs, Sarah Brackett. Six episodes. WGBH, 1968.
*The Portrait of a Lady* (U.S./U.K.). Screenplay by Laura Jones. Dir. Jane Campion. Photog. Stuart Dryburgh. Music by Wojiech Kilar. Costumes by Jane Patterson (AA/N). Ed. Veronika Jenet. Perf. Nicole Kidman (Isabel Archer), John Malkovich (Gilbert Osmond), Barbara Hershey (Serena Merle) (S/AAN) (S/GGN), Shelley Winters (Lydia Touchett), Ralph Richardson (Mr. Touchett), Martin Donovan (Ralph Touchett), Mary Louise Parker (Henrietta Stackpole), Valentina Cervi (Pansy Osmund). Gramercy Pictures, color/bw, 144 mins., 1996. LC.

Figure 34. From left, Tyrone Power, Ann Blyth, Irene Browne, and Ronald Simpson in a scene from the past in *I'll Never Forget You*, based on James's *The Sense of the Past*. Library of Congress.

### "The Pupil" (1891)

*The Pupil* (U.S.; TV). Teleplay by Harry Granick. Perf. John Newland (John Pemberton), Sonny Rees (Morgan Moreen), Viola Roache, Neil Fitzgerald. *Philco Television Theater,* 24 Dec. 1950.

*The Pupil* (Canada; TV). Teleplay by Michael Dyne. Prod. Franz Kraemer. Exec. Prod. Robert Allen. Sound by Walter Michalik, William McClelland, Chris Christoff. Script ed. Doris Mosdel. Set design by Nikolai Soloviov. Costumes by Suzanne Mess. Perf. Albert Dekker, William Job, Edith Atwater, Michael Ray, Tudi Wiggins, Irena Mayeska, Edwin Stephenson. *Festival,* 90 mins., 5 May 1961.

*Ce que savait Morgan* (France; TV). Teleplay Luc Béraud, Marguerite Duras. Dir. Luc Béraud. Photog. Bruno Nuytten, Jean-Noël Ferragut, Olivier Lafevre. Ed. Chantale Coloner, Anne Boissel. Music by Alain Jommy, Jean Louis Richt, Stephane Van Den Bergh, Maurice Gilbert. Perf. Olivier Haccard (Morgan), Anouk Ferjac, Andrew Falcon, Jean-Pierre Besson, Catherine Mitry, Brigitte Roman, Pierre Baudry, Maurice Mirowsky, Jean Douchet, Michel Such, Arie Levi. PI Production/ORTF, color, 52 mins., 1974. ORTF, 1974.

*L'Élève* (France). Screenplay by Ève Deboise and Olivier Schatzky. Dir. Olivier Schatzky (D/MFF). Photog. Carlo Varini. Music by Romano Musumarra. Costumes by Yvonne Sassinot de Nesle. Perf. Vincent Cassel (Julien, Tutor), Caroline Cellier (Emma), Jean-Pierre Marielle (Armand), Caspar Salmon (Morgan), Sabine Destailleur (Louise), Sandrine Le Berre (Paula), Benny Pest (Jean). Blue Films/Ocelot Productions/La Sept Cinema/Rhone Alpes Cinema, color, 92 mins., 1995.

### *"The Real Thing" (1892)*

*The Real Thing* (U.S.; TV). Dir. Charles Haas. Perf. John Archer, Marjorie Lord. *Your Show Time*, bw, 30 mins., 11 Mar. 1949. LC.

*The Real Thing* (U.S.; TV). Teleplay by Elihu Winer. Dir. Charles Haas. Marshall Grant/Realm Television Productions, 1949. It is not clear if this ever aired.

*The Real Thing* (U.S.; TV). *Short, Short Drama*, 15 mins., 26 Feb. 1953,

*The Real Thing* (U.S.; TV). Perf. Brandon de Wilde. *The Web*, 1 Mar. 1953.

*The Real Thing* (U.S.; TV). According to Larry James Gianakos, this is the "Louis Auchincloss version [of James's short story, presumably] as adapted by A.J. Russell" (4:445). *Matinee Theatre*, 1 June 1956. N.B.: This information is in conflict with the episode listed in vol. 1 for *Matinee Theatre* and that date.

*Affairs of the Heart: Mary and Louisa* (U.K.; TV). This is actually a merging of "The Real Thing" and "The Tone of Time " (1900). Teleplay by Terence Feely. Dir. Michael Ferguson. Perf. Faith Brook (Louisa), Pamela Brown (Mary), Anton Rodgers (James Mallory), Liz Golding (Maggie), Leonard Kavanaugh (Saunders), Peter Myers (Major Monarch), Adrienne Burgess (Jemima), Douglas Wilmer (Leopoldo Visconti). ITV, 20 Oct. 1974.

### *The Reverberator (1888)*

*The Reverberator* (U.S.; TV). Teleplay by Louis Jacoby. Dir. Arthur Heller. Perf. Jacques Semas (Gaston Probert), Betty Lynn (Francie Dosson), Robert Burton (Mr. Dosson), Sally Moffat (Della Dosson), William Phipps (George Flack). *Matinee Theatre*, 23 July 1956.

### *"The Romance of Certain Old Clothes" (1868)*

(See *The Other House*.)

### *The Sense of the Past (1917)*

*Berkeley Square* (U.S.). Based on the unfinished novel *The Sense of the Past*. Screenplay by Sonya Levien and John Balderston. Dir. Frank Lloyd. Photog. Ernest Palmer. Music by Louis de Francesco. Art dir. William Darling. Perf. Leslie Howard (Peter Standish) (AAN), Heather Angel (Helen Pettigrew), Valerie Tay-

lor (Kate Pettigrew), Irene Browne (Lady Ann Pettigrew), Ferdinand Gottschalk
(Mr. Throstle), Beryl Mercer (Mrs. Berwick), Colin Keith-Johnson (Tom Pettigrew),
Alan Mowbray (Major Clinton), Juliette Compton (Duchess of Devonshire),
Betty Lawford (Marjorie Frant), Samuel Hinds (American Ambassador), Olaf
Hytten (Sir Joshua Reynolds), David Torrence (Lord Stanley). Fox Film Corpo-
ration, bw, 87 mins., 1933. NBR 1933, 10 best American films. *NYT* 1933, 6th
best film.

*Berkeley Square* (U.S.; TV). Adapted from the play of the same name by John L.
Balderston and J.C. Squire, based on *A Sense of the Past. Kraft Television Theatre,*
21 July 1948.

*Berkeley Square* (U.S.; TV). Teleplay by Joe Liss, from the Balderston/Squire play of
the same name. Perf. Leueen MacGrath, William Prince, Leslie Woods. *Studio
One,* 60 mins., 20 Mar. 1949.

*Berkeley Square* (U.S.; TV). Based on the Balderston/Squire play *Berkeley Square.*
Perf. Richard Greene, Grace Kelly, Rosalind Ivan, Mary Scott. *Prudential Family
Playhouse,* 60 mins., aired live 13 Feb. 1951.

*I'll Never Forget You* (U.K.). Remake of *Berkeley Square* (1933), released in England
under two titles: *Man of Two Worlds* and *The House on the Square.* Screenplay by
John L. Balderston and Ranald MacDougal. Dir. Roy Ward Baker. Photog.
Georges Perinal. Music by William Alwyn. Musical dir. C.P. Norman. Ed. Alan
Obiston. Perf. Tyrone Power (Peter Standish), Ann Blyth (Helen Pettigrew/
Martha Forsyth), Michael Rennie (Roger Forsyth), Beatrice Campbell (Kate
Pettigrew), Dennis Price (Tom Pettigrew), Raymond Huntley (Mr. Throstle),
Irene Browne (Lady Anne Pettigrew), Kathleen Byron (Duchess of Devonshire),
Robert Atkins (Dr. Samuel Johnson), Ronald Adam (Ronson), Felix Aylmer (Sir
William, physician), Jill Clifford (Maid), Arthur Denton ("loonies' driver"), Alec
Finter (Throstle's coachman), Tom Gill (Macaroni), Diane Hart (Dolly), Victor
Maddern (Geiger Man), Alex McCrindle (James Boswell), Gibb McLaughlin
(Jacob), Ronald Simpson (Sir Joshua Reynolds), Hamlyn Benson, Peter Drury,
Anthony Pelly, Catherine Carlton, Richard Carrickford, Rose Hewlett. Twenti-
eth Century Fox Corporation, Technicolor/bw endpieces, 91 mins., 1951.

*Berkeley Square* (U.S.; TV). Teleplay by Theodore Apstein (adapted from Balderston's
play). Dir. George Schaefer. Music by Bernard Green. Sets by Warren Clymer.
Perf. John Kerr, Jeannie Carson, Edna Best, Janet Munro, Mildred Trares, Norah
Howard, John Colicos, Jerome Kitty, Winston Ross, Frances Reid, Sheila Coonan.
*Hallmark Hall of Fame,* color, 90 mins., 5 Feb. 1959. UCLA.

*On a Clear Day You Can See Forever* (U.S.). Screenplay by Alan Jay Lerner, taken
from his play of the same name which was based on William Balderston's play
*Berkeley Square,* which in turn was taken from James's *The Sense of the Past.* Dir.
Vincente Minnelli. Photog. Harry Stradling Sr. Original music by Burton Lane.
Ed. David Bretherton. Costumes Cecil Beaton, Arnold Scaasi. Perf. by Barbara
Streisand (Daisy Gamble), Yves Montand (Dr. Marc Chabot), Bob Newhart (Dr.
Mason Hume), Larry Blyden (Warren Pratt), Simon Oakland (Dr. Conrad Fuller),
Jack Nicholson (Tad Pringle), John Richardson (Robert Tentrees), Pamela Brown

(Mrs. Fitzherbert), Irene Handl (Winnie Wainwhistle), Roy Kinnear (Prince Regent), Peter Crowcroft (Divorce Attorney), Byron Webster (Prosecuting Attorney), Mabel Albertson (Mrs. Hatch), Laurie Main (Lord Percy), Kermit Murdock (Hoyt III), Elaine Giftos (Muriel), John LeMesurier (Pelham), Angela Pringle (Diana Smallwood), Leon Ames (Clews), Paul Camen (Millard), George N. Neise (Wytelipt), Tony Colti (Preston), Jeannie Berlin (Girl in orphanage, uncredited), Richard Kiel (Blacksmith, uncredited), Judith Lowry (uncredited). Paramount Pictures/Paramount Home Video, Technicolor, 129 mins., 1970.

### *The Spoils of Poynton (1897)*

*The Spoils of Poynton* (U.K.; TV). Teleplay by Lennox Philips. Dir. Peter Sasdy. Perf. Pauline Jameson (Mrs. Gereth), Ian Ogilvy (Owen Gereth), Diane Fletcher (Mona Brigstock), June Ellis (Mrs. Brigstock), Gemma Jones (Fleda Vetch), Polly Adams (Maggie), Robin Parkinson (Arthur). *Masterpiece Theatre,* 4 episodes, color, 45 mins. each, 4–25 Apr. 1971.

### *"The Third Person" (1900)*

*The Third Person* (U.S.; TV). Teleplay by Warner Law. Perf. Judith Evelyn. *Matinee Theatre,* 14 Feb. 1958.

### *"The Tone of Time" (1900)*

(See also "The Real Thing," *Affairs of the Heart: Mary and Louisa.*)
*A Tone of Time* (U.S.; TV). Teleplay by Theodore Apstein. Perf. Sarah Churchill. *Matinee Theatre,* color, aired live 17 Oct. 1957.

### *["The Treasure Hunters"]*

*The Treasure Hunters* (U.S.; TV). Although this title is not listed in any James bibliography, Gianakos states that this was "adapted by Michael Dyne from the story by Henry James" (1:144). If it is James, it could, of course, be a retitled version of a number of his stories or novels (probably "The Figure in the Carpet"). Perf. Donald Cook, Roddy McDowell, Rex Thompson, Mary Ellis. *Goodyear Theatre,* 26 May 1957.

### *"The Turn of the Screw" (1898)*

*The Turn of the Screw* (U.S.; TV). Teleplay by Gore Vidal. Dir. Seymour Robbie. Perf. Geraldine Page, Robert Goodier, Rex Thompson, Cathleen Nesbitt, Nina Reader, Stanley Lemin. *Omnibus III,* vol. 18, bw, 36 mins., 13 Feb. 1955. LC.
*The Others* (U.S.; TV). Teleplay by Michael Dyne. Perf. Sarah Churchill, Tommy Kirk, Geoffrey Tune. *Matinee Theatre,* color, aired live 15 Feb. 1957.

Figure 35. Marlon Brando as Peter Quint in *The Nightcomers,* Michael Winner's prequel to James's "The Turn of the Screw." Library of Congress.

*The Turn of the Screw* (U.S.; TV). Teleplay by James Costigan. Dir. John Frankenheimer. Music by David Amram. Perf. Ingrid Bergman (Emmy/Governess), Hayward Morse (Miles), Alexandra Wager (Flora), Isobel Elsom (Mrs. Grose), Laurinda Barrett (Ghost of Miss Jessel), Paul Stevens (Ghost of Peter Quint). *Ford Startime,* NBC-TV, bw, appr. 70 mins., 20 Oct. 1959. MTR, LC; kinescope only, no viewing copy available at this time.

*The Turn of the Screw* (U.K.; TV). Benjamin Britten's opera, based on James's short story, performed by the English Opera Group Orchestra, conducted by Charles McKerras and Paul Hamburger. Dir. Peter Morley. Perf. Raymond Nilsson, Jennifer Vyvyan, Tom Bevan, Janette Miller, Judith Pierce, Arda Mandikian. Associated-Rediffusion, 60 mins., 25 Dec. 1959.

*The Innocents* (U.K.). Based on James's "The Turn of the Screw" and Archibald's play *The Innocents.* Screenplay by William Archibald and Truman Capote, additional dialogue provided by John Mortimer. Dir. Jack Clayton (NBR 1961/D). Photog. Freddie Francis. Music Georges Auric. Ed. James Clark. Perf. Deborah Kerr (Miss Giddens/Governess), Michael Redgrave (Uncle), Megs Jenkins (Mrs. Grose), Martin Stephens (Miles), Pamela Franklin (Flora), Peter Wyngarde (Peter Quint), Clytie Jessop (Miss Mary Jessel), Eric Woodburn (Coachman), Isla

Cameron (Anna). CinemaScope Twentieth-Century Fox/Achilles, bw, 99 mins., 1962. Chosen as the Film Festival Selection for the Cannes Film Festival, 1962. NBR 1961, 4th best film. LC.

*The Nightcomers* (U.S.). A "prequel" to James's "The Turn of the Screw," focusing on Quint and Jessel's relationship. Screenplay by Michael Hastings. Dir. Michael Winner. Photog. Robert Paynter. Music by Jerry Fielding. Perf. Marlon Brando (Peter Quint), Stephanie Beacham (Miss Margaret Jessel), Thora Hird (Mrs. Grose), Verna Harvey (Flora), Christopher Ellis (Miles), Harry Andrews (Master of the House), Anna Palk (New Governess). Scimitar/AE, Technicolor, 96 mins., 1971. LC.

*Le Tour d'ecrou* (France; TV). Teleplay by Paule de Beaumont. Dir. Raymond Rouleau. Perf. Suzanne Flon, Marie-Christine Barrault, Robert Hossein. ORTF, 25 Dec. 1974.

*The Turn of the Screw* (U.S.; TV). Teleplay by William F. Nolan. Dir. Dan Curtis. Photog. Colin Callow. Music by Robert Cobert. Ed. Bill Breashers, Gary Anderson. Perf. Lynn Redgrave (Jane Cubberly/Governess), Jasper Jacob (Miles), James Laurenson (Peter Quint), Eva Griffith (Flora), Megs Jenkins (Mrs. Grose), Kathryn Leigh Scott (Miss Jessel), Benedict Taylor (Timothy), John Baron (Fredericks), Vivian Bennet (Secretary). Dan Curtis Productions, two-part series, color, 118 mins., 1974. Videocassette. MPI Home Video, 1992. LC.

*The Turn of the Screw* (U.K./Czechoslovakia; TV). Benjamin Britten's third chamber opera. Libretto by Myfanwy Piper. Cond. Sir Colin Davis. Perf. Helen Donath (Governess), Robert Tear (Quint), Lilian Watson (Flora), Michael Ginn (Miles), Ava June (Mrs. Grose), and the Covent Garden Chamber Ensemble. *Great Performances,* 116 mins., Sept. 1984. LC.

*Otra vuelta de tuerca* (Spain). Screenplay by Gonzalo Goikoetxea, Eloy de la Iglesia, Angel Sastre. Dir. Eloy de la Iglesia. Photog. Andres Berenguer, Juan Gelpi. Music by Luis Iriondo. Sets by Simon Suarez. Ed. Julio Pena. Perf. Pedro Maria Sanchez (Roberto), Queta Claver (Antonia), Asier Hernandez Landa (Mikel), Cristina Reparaz Goyanes (Flora). Gaurko Filmeak, Eastmancolor, 119 mins., 1985.

*The Turn of the Screw* (U.S.; TV). Dir. Grame Clifford. Prod. Design Jane Osmann. Orig. music by J. Peter Robinson. Costumes by Robert Blackman. Ed. Conrad M. Gonzalez. Perf. Amy Irving (Governess), David Hemmings (Mr. Harley), Cameron Milzer (Miss Jessel), Irina Cashen (Flora),Olaf Pooley (John the Gardener), Bret Culpepper (Wyck the Groom), Balthazar Getty (Uncle), Micole Mercurio (Mrs. Grose), Linda Hunt (Narrator). Episode of *Nightmare Classics* produced by Shelley Duvall, color, 55 mins., 1989.

*The Turn of the Screw* (U.K.). Benjamin Britten's third chamber opera. Libretto by Myfanwy Piper. Dir. Claus Viller. Perf. Phyllis Cannan (Miss Jessel), Menai Davies (Mrs. Grose), Helen Field (The Governess), Richard Greager (Prologue/Quint), Sam Linay (Miles), Machiko Obata (Flora). Royal Opera House Covent Garden Suddeutscher/Rundfunk producers, 1990.

*The Turn of the Screw* (U.K./France). Screenplay by Rusty Lemorande. Dir. Rusty Lemorande. Photog. Witold Stok. Ed. John Victor-Smith. Perf. Patsy Kensit (Jenny/Governess), Julian Sands (Mr. Cooper/Uncle), Stephane Audran (Mrs. Grose), Marianne Faithfull (Narrator), Joseph England (Miles), Claire Szekeres

(Flora), Byrony Brind (Miss Jessel), Thomas Kryger (Jenny's father/Vicar), Albert Sasson (Psychiatrist), Doreen Mantle, Peter Whitman, Mickey Monroe, Anna Bolt, Laura Cox, Sara Mansfield, Tony O'Leary, Victoria Galbraith, Indigo River Mountain, Michael Tucek, Mark Choy. An Electric Pictures and Michael White production, color, 95 mins., 1992. LC.

*The Haunting of Helen Walker* (U.S.; TV). Teleplay by Hugh Whitemore. Dir. Tom McLoughlin. Photog. Tony Imi. Music by Frederic Chopin, Allyn Ferguson. Ed. Charles Bornstein. Perf. Valerie Bertinelli (Helen Walker/Governess), Diana Rigg (Mrs. Grose), Elizabeth Morton (Miss Jessel), Florence Hoath, Michael Gough, Aled Roberts, Paul Rhys, Christopher Guard. Color, 100 mins., 1995.

*Presence of Mind* (U.K.). Screenplay by Antoni Aloy, Barbara Gogny. Dir. Antoni Aloy. Photog. David Carretero. Prod. Jordan Leeann Leibert. Costumes by Yvonne Blake. Perf. Lauren Bacall, Harvey Keitel, Sadie Frost, Ella Jones, Dayna Danika, Nilo Mur, Augustin Villaronga, Jack Taylor, Tom Keller. CEO Films/Video Mercury Films. Released on video in Spain as *El Celo*. 1999.

*The Turn of the Screw* (U.K.;TV). Teleplay by Nick Dear. Dir. Ben Bolt. Photog. David Odd. Costumes Sheena Napier. Sets Pat Campbell. Perf. Jodhi May (Miss/the Governess), Pam Ferris (Mrs. Grose), Colin Firth (The Master), Caroline Pegg (Miss Jessel), Jason Salkey (Peter Quint), Joe Sowerbutts (Miles), Grace Robinson (Flora), Jenny Howe (Cook). Color, 100 mins., aired U.K. 26 Dec. 1999; U.S. 27 Feb. 2000.

### *Washington Square (1880)*

*The Heiress* (U.S.). Screenplay by Ruth and Augustus Goetz, based on their play taken from James's *Washington Square*. Dir. William Wyler. Photog. Leo Tover. Music by Aaron Copland (AA). Costumes by Edith Head and Gile Steele (AA). Art direction by Harry Horner and John Meehan (AA). Perf. Olivia de Havilland (Catherine Sloper) (A/AA) (GG/A), Ralph Richardson (Dr. Austin Sloper) (NBR/A, shared), Montgomery Clift (Morris Townsend), Miriam Hopkins (Lavinia Penniman), Mona Freeman (Marian Almond), Vanessa Brown (Maria), Selena Royle (Elizabeth Almond), Betty Linley (Mrs. Montgomery), Ray Collins (Jefferson Almond), Paul Lees (Arthur Townsend). Paramount Pictures, bw, 115 mins., 1949. Videocassette. MCA Universal Home Video, 1977. NBR 1949, 4th best film. NYFC 1949, 6th best film. LC.

*The Heiress* (U.S.; TV). Adapted from the Ruth Goetz and Augustus Goetz play, *The Heiress,* which was based on *Washington Square*. Perf. Marilyn Erskine, Vincent Price. *Lux Video Theatre,* 23 Sept. 1954.

*Washington Square* (U.S.; TV). Perf. John Abbott, Lurene Tuttle, Roddy McDowall, Peggy McKay. *Matinee Theatre,* 12 June 1958.

*Die Erbin/The Heiress* (Germany; TV). Based on Ruth Goetz and Augustus Goetz's *The Heiress.* Dir. Franz Josef Wild. Staging by Lutz Wintersberg. Perf. Willy Birgel, Elfriede Kuzmany, Alice Treff, Camilla Horn, Lothar Blumhagen, Walter Buschhoff. Bayerisches Fernsehen/Erstes Deutsches Fernsehen, 122 mins., first airing 10 July 1958.

*The Heiress* (U.K.; TV). Prod. Terence Cook. Perf. Jill Bennett (Catherine Sloper), Alec Clunes (Dr. Sloper), Bryan Forbes (Morris Townsend), Margaretta Scott (Lavinia Penniman), Noel Hood (Elizabeth Almond). BBC, 7 Sept. 1958.

*The Heiress* (Canada; TV). Teleplay by Lloyd Bochner. *Folio,* 29 Jan. 1959.

*The Heiress* (U.S.; TV). Teleplay by Jacqueline Babbin. Dir. Marc Daniels. Exec. prod. David Susskind. Prod. Jacqueline Babbin. Music by Robert Corbert. Perf. Julie Harris (Catherine Sloper), Barry Morse (Dr. Sloper), Muriel Kirkland, Farley Granger (Morris Townsend), Suzanne Storrs, Barbara Robbins, Mary Van Fleet, David O'Brien. *Family Classics,* CBS-TV, 60 mins., aired and taped 13 Feb. 1961.

*Arvtagerskan* (Sweden; TV). Translator/teleplay Gustaf Molander, from the play *The Heiress* by Ruth and Augustus Goetz. Dir. Josef Halfen. Prod. Design Lennart Olofsson. Perf. Ulla Akselson (Maria, housemaid), Jorgen Barwe (Arthur Townsend), Margareta Bergfeldt (Mrs. Montgomery), Berit Gustafsson (Mrs. Elizabeth Almond), Ulf Johanson (D. Austin Sloper), Jullan Kindahl (Mrs. Lavinia Penniman), Ulla Sjölblom (Catherine Sloper), Folke Sundquist (Morris Townsend), Mimmo Wahlander (Marian Almond). 1962.

*Washington Square* (U.K.; TV). Perf. Vincent Price (Dr. Sloper). 1969.

*Affairs of the Heart: Catherine* (U.K.; TV). Teleplay by Terence Feely. Dir. John Reardon. Perf. Lynn Farleigh (Catherine Sloper), Bernard Hepton (Dr. Sloper), Ian Ogilvy (Morris Townsend). ITV, 3 Nov. 1974.

*Washington Square* (France; TV). Teleplay by Jean-Louis Roncoroni. Dir. Alain Boudet. Perf. Magali Clement, Jacques François. A2, 28 July 1975.

*Die Erbin/The Heiress* (Germany; TV). Based on Ruth Goetz and August Goetz's play *The Heiress.* Dir. Franz Josef Wild. Photog. Gottfried Sittl. Staging by Peter Scharff. Perf. Heidelinde Weis (Catherine Sloper), Alexander Kerst (Dr. Augustin Sloper), Gustl Halenke (Mrs. Lavinia Penniman), Alexander Wachter (Morris Townsend), Elfriede Kuzmany (Mrs. Montgomery). Bayerisches Fernsehen/Erstes Deutsches Fernsehen, 113 mins., color, first airing 18 July 1982.

*Washington Square* (U.S.). Screenplay by Carol Doyle. Dir. Agnieszka Holland. Photog. Jerzy Zielinski. Music by Jan A.P. Kaczmarek. Perf. Albert Finney (Dr. Sloper), Ben Chaplin (Morris Townsend), Jennifer Jason Leigh (Catherine Sloper), Maggie Smith (Lavinia Penniman), Judith Ivey (Elizabeth Almond), Betsy Brantley (Mrs. Montgomery). Walt Disney/Caravan Productions/Alchemy Filmworks/Hollywood Pictures, color, 115 mins., 1997.

### *Watch and Ward (1870)*

*Nora* (FR; TV). Teleplay Nicolas Brehal, Edouard Molinaro. Dir. Edouard Molinaro. Photog. Michael Epp. Original Music by David Marouani. Perf. Beatrice Agenin, Philippe Bouclet, Daniel Cauchy, Didier Cauchy, Christine Chansou, Yvonne Clech, Maxine Drouot, Niels Dubost, Jean-Michel Dupuis, Andreas Elsholz, Laurent Jaubert, Ludovic Jean, Axelle Laffont, Richard Leduc, Carine Lemair, Jeremy Lippmann, Alexandrine Loeb, Leslie Malton, Julia Maraval, Pierre

Mermaz, Jacques Perrin, Delphine Quentin, Cedric Radjoy, Fred Rall, Bernard Renan, Lorena Sayler, Guillaume Verdier, Yves-Marie Ygouf. Progefi/Taurus Film, color, 1998.

### What Maisie Knew (1897)

*What Maisie Knew* (U.S.; TV). Teleplay David Davidson. Dir. Franklin Schaffner. Costumes Grace Houston. Sets A.A. Ostrander. Music by Ben Ludlow. Script Editor Lois Jacoby. Fort [presumably Ford] Theater, airing in 1950 or 1951.

*What Maisie Knew* (U.K. TV). Teleplay by Denis Constanduros. Fir. Derek Martinus. Perf. Sally Thomsett (Maisie Farange), Maxine Audley (Ida Farange), Paul Hardwick (Beale Farange), Penelope Horner (Miss Overmore), Ann Way (Mrs. Wix), Gary Raymond (Sir Claude), Yvonne Antrobus (Susan Ash). BBC, 3 episodes, beginning 1 June 1968.

*What Maisie Knew* (U.S.). Dir. Babette Mangolte. Perf. Epp Kotkas, Kate Manheim, Saskia Noordhoek-Hegt, Linda Patton, Yvonne Rainer, Philip Glass. An experimentalist adaptation, 55 mins., 1975.

*Ce que Savait Maisie* (FR; TV). Teleplay Edouard Molinaro. Dir. Edouard Molinaro. Photog. Michael Epp. Original Music by Claude Bolling. Perf. Patrice Alexandre, Andre Asseo (Maitre L'Herminier), Adeline Bodo (Rose), Evelyne Bouix, Alexandre Brasseur (Le valet), Brigitte Chamarande (Marthe), Sophie Duez, Stephane Freiss, Christine Gouze-Renal, Matthias Habich, Lucienne Hamon (Maud), Florent Hiliou (Le Controleur), Axelle Laffont (La Femme de Chambre), Patrice Laffont (Le Marchand de glace), Richard Leduc (Maitre Carmier), Laura Martel (Maisie), Jean-Baptist Martin (Doctor), Carine Noury (Annie's friend), Catherine Samie, Maurice Vaudaux. Progefi/Taurus Film, color, 1995.

### The Wings of the Dove (1902)

*The Wings of the Dove* (U.S.; TV). Teleplay by Howard Merrill. Dir. Worthington (Tony) Miner. Prod. Franklin J. Schaffner. Perf. Charlton Heston (Merton Densher), Stella Andrew (Millie), Felicia Montealegre (Kate Thayer), Ann Shoemaker, Berry Kroeger. *Westinghouse/Studio One Summer Theatre,* appr. 60 mins., 10 Mar. 1952. MTR, LC.

*The Wings of the Dove* (U.S.; TV). Teleplay by Meade Roberts. Dir. Robert Stevens. Perf. Dana Wynter (Kate Croy), James Donald (Merton Densher), John Baragrey, Inga Swenson (Millie Theale), Henry Daniell, Isabel Jeans, Lurene Tuttle. *Playhouse 90,* 90 mins., 8 Jan. 1959. MTR.

*The Wings of the Dove* (U.S.; TV). Teleplay by Rodney Gedye. Dir. Rudolph Cartier. Perf. Susannah York (Milly Theale), Wendy Craig (Kate Croy), Edmund Purdom (Merton Denver), Lana Marris (Susan Shepherd), Joyce Carey (Maud Lowder), Frederick Jaeger (Lord Mark). BBC, 7 Jan. 1965.

*Les Ailes de la colombe* (France; TV). Teleplay by Christopher Taylor, Jean-Louis Curtis. Dir. Daniel Georgeot. Perf. Nelly Borgeaud, Colette Castel, Annie Ducaux. ORTF, 11 Jan. 1975.

*Affairs of the Heart: Milly* (U.K.; TV). Teleplay by Terence Feely. Dir. Derek Bennett. Perf.
Rosalind Ayres (Milly Theale), Lois Baxter (Kate Croy), Gary Bond (Robert Morton),
Georgina Cookson (Maud Lowder), Stuart Wilson (Lord Mark). ITV, 16 Mar. 1975.
*The Wings of the Dove* (U.K.; TV). Teleplay by Denis Constanduros. Dir. John Gorrie.
Perf. Elizabeth Spriggs, Betsy Blair, John Castle, Suzanne Bertish, Lisa Eichhorn,
Rupert Frazer, Alan Rowe, Gino Melvazzi. *Plays of the Month,* 4 Aug. 1979.
*Les Ailes de la colombe/Storia di Donne* (France/Italy). Dir. Benoit Jacquot. Perf.
Dominique Sanda (Kate Croy), Isabelle Huppert (Milly Theale), Michele Placido,
Jean Sorel, Francoise Christophe, Odile Michel. 1981.
*Le ali della colomba* (Italy; TV). Teleplay by Vittorio Bonicelli. Dir. Gianluigi Calderone.
Photog. Giorgio Abate. Perf. Delia Boccardo (Kate), Laura Morante (Milly),
Paolo Malco (Merton), Laura Betti (Aunt Maud), Margherita Guzzinati (Susan),
Bruno Corazzari (Sir Luke). RAI, three-part series, 1981.
*The Wings of the Dove* (U.S./U.K.). Screenplay by Hossein Amini (AAN). Dir. Iain
Softley. Perf. Helena Bonham Carter (Kate Croy) (AAN; GGN), Linus Roache
(Merton Densher), Alison Elliott (Millie Theale), Michael Gambon, Alex Jennings,
Elizabeth McGovern, Charlotte Rampling. Renaissance Dove/Miramax Films, color,
101 mins., 1997.
*Under Heaven* (Video title: *In the Shadows.* Cable: In a Private Garden) (U.S.). Screen-
play by Meg Richman. Dir. Meg Richman (SFF:N). Photog. Claudio Rocha. Origi-
nal Music by Marc Nelsen. Ed. Debbie Zeitman. Costumes by Ronald Leamon.
Perf. Joely Richardson (Eleanor Dunston, based on Milly Theale) (ISA), Molly
Parker (Cynthia Loomis/Kate Croy), Aden Young (Buck Henson/Merton
Densher), Kevin Phillip (John), Krisha Fairchild (Mrs. Newhouse/Cynthia's
mother), Marjorie Nelson (Mrs. Fletcher). Banner Enterainment, color, 108
mins., 1998.

## Works Cited

Edel, Leon, ed. *The Complete Plays of Henry James.* New York: Oxford Univ. Press, 1990.
Gianakos, James, comp. *Television Drama Series Programming: A Comprehensive
Chronicle, 1947–1984.* 5 vols. Metuchen, N.J.: Scarecrow, 1978–1986.
Mazzella, Anthony J. "A Selected Henry James Artsography." *Henry James Review* 3
(1981): 44–58.
Sinyard, Neil. *Filming Literature.* New York: St. Martin's, 1986.

# Bibliography of Critical Work
# on James and Film

*Sarah Edgington and Steve Wexler*

We have attempted to offer a comprehensive survey of secondary sources regarding Henry James and film. Our bibliography features citations from major and minor newspapers, magazines, academic journals, and online texts dating from 1961 to 1999. Dissertations are not listed.

We relied on the following Henry James bibliographies: John Budd, *Henry James: A Bibliography of Criticism, 1975 - 1981;* Beatrice Rick, *Henry James: A Bibliography of Secondary Works;* Dorothy McInnis Scura, *Henry James, 1960 - 1974: A Reference Guide;* and Judith E. Funston, *Henry James, 1975 - 1987: A Reference Guide.*

Additionally, databases such as ProQuest (a cross-section of general periodicals including the *New York Times,* the *Wall Street Journal,* and the *Washington Post*); *Newsbank NewsFile* (an anthology of over 70,000 full-text newspaper articles selected annually from over 500 U.S. and Canadian newspapers); *FirstSearch* (providing access to periodical abstracts from over 1,500 journals via *Arts and Humanities Search, ERIC, Humanities Abstracts,* and *MLA Bibliography*); and the University of Louisville's online catalog all proved invaluable, especially for recent literature.

We would like to thank J. Sarah Koch and B. Joanne Webb for their assistance.

Allen, Jeanne. "The Innocents: The Sound of the Turning of the Screw." *Purdue University Fifth Annual Conference on Film.* Ed. Walther Maud. West Lafayette, Ind.: Purdue UP, 1980. 103–10.

————. "'Turn of the Screw' and *The Innocents:* Two Types of Ambiguity." *The Classic American Novel and the Movies.* Ed. Gerald Peary and Roger Shatzkin. New York: Ungar, 1977. 132–42.

Alleva, Richard. "Henry James Made Carnal." *Commonweal* 19 Dec.1997: 15.

Andrews, Nigel. "Henry James on Location." *Sight and Sound* 43 (1974): 215–16.

Andriani, Lynn, and Jonathan Bing. "Movies: Better than Cliff Notes." *Publisher's Weekly* 5 Aug. 1996: 411.

Ansen, David. "*Washington Square.*" *Newsweek* 13 Oct. 1997: 75.

Armistead, J.M. "Henry James for the Cinematic Mind." *English Record* 26.3 (1975): 27–33.

Ashton, Jean. "Reflecting Consciousness: Three Approaches to Henry James." *Literature Film Quarterly* 4 (1976): 230–39.

Badder, David. "Aspern." *Sight and Sound* 51 (1982): 45.

Bauer, Dale M. "Jane Campion's Symbolic Portrait." *Henry James Review* 18 (1997): 194–96.

Bell, Millicent. "The Bostonian Story." *Partisan Review* 52 (1985): 109–19.

Bentley, Nancy. "Conscious Observation of a Lovely Woman: Jane Campion's *Portrait* in Film." *Henry James Review* 18 (1997): 174–79.

Berardinelli, James. "*Portrait of a Lady:* A Film Review." 1996. *Reel Views Archives.* <http://movie-reviews.colossus.net/movies/p/portrait_lady.html>. Accessed 30 Sept. 1999.

———."*Washington Square:* A Film Review." 1997. *Reel Views Archives.* <http://movie-reviews.colossus.net/movies/w/washington.html>. Accessed 30 Sept. 1999.

———. "*Wings of the Dove:* A Film Review." 1997. *Reel Views Archives.* <http://movie-reviews.colossus.net/movies/w/wings.html>. Accessed 30 Sept. 1999.

Birdsall, Eric. "Interpreting Henry James: Bogdanovich's *Daisy Miller.*" *Literature/Film Quarterly* 22 (1994): 272–77.

Blake, Richard A. "*The Wings of the Dove.*" *America* 178.2 (1998): 20–21.

Bousquet, Marc. "I Don't Like Isabel Archer." *Henry James Review* 18 (1997): 197–99.

Bradbury, Nicola. "Filming James." *Essays in Criticism: A Quarterly Journal of Literary Criticism* 29 (1979): 293–301.

Branch, Beverly. "François Truffaut and Henry James: The Encounter of Two Master Craftsmen." *Transformations: From Literature to Film: Proceedings of the Fifth Annual Conference on Film of Kent State University, Apr. 7, 8, 1987.* Ed. Douglas Radcliff-Umstead. Kent: Kent State UP, 1987. 184–90.

Brown, Monika. "Film Music as Sister Art: Adaptations of the 'Turn of the Screw.'" *Mosaic* 31.1 (1998): 61–81.

Caldwell, Gail. "Disregarding Henry: Why Henry James's *Portrait of a Lady* Loses Luster on Film." *Boston Globe* 21 Jan. 1997: 1.2.

Carlson, Jerry W. "*Washington Square* and *The Heiress:* Comparing Artistic Forms." *The Classic American Novel and the Movies.* Ed. Gerald Peary and Roger Shatzkin. New York: Ungar, 1977. 95-104.

Carr, Jay. "Campion's *Portrait* Lacks James's Finesse." *Boston Globe* 17 Jan. 1997: D4.

———. "*Wings* is Made to Soar" *Boston Globe* 14 Nov. 1997: D1.

———. "Passionate *Wings of the Dove* Soars." *Boston Globe* 11 Sept. 1997: E3.

Cavell, Stanley. "Postscript (1989): To Whom It May Concern." *Critical Inquiry* 16.2 (1990): 248–89.

Chandler, Karen Michele. "Agency and Social Constraint in Jane Campion's *The Portrait of a Lady.*" *Henry James Review* 18 (1997): 191–93.

Chase, Donald. "Romancing the Stones: Adaptation of H. James's 'The Turn of the Screw.'" *Film Comment* 34 (1998): 68–71.

Clark, John. "Judging a Movie by Its Cover: With Audiences Seemingly Tiring of Formulas, Hollywood Has Become Less Wary of 'Difficult' Literary Adaptations." *Los Angeles Times* 1 Dec. 1997: F13.

Coleman, Joan M., and William P. Coleman. "*Wings of the Dove*." 21 Nov. 1997. <http://www.wpcmath.com/films/wingsdove/wingsdove.html>. Accessed 30 Sept. 1999.

Coleman, John. "Amusette." *New Statesman* 62 (1961): 854.

Coleman, William P. "*Washington Square*." 28 Nov. 1997. <http://www.wpcmath.com/films/washsquare/washsquare.html>. Accessed 30 Sept. 1999.

Crnkovic, Gordana P. "Interview with Agnieszka Holland." *Film Quarterly* 52.2 (1998): 2.

Crowther, Bosley. "Screen: *The Innocents*." *New York Times* 26 Dec. 1961: 15.

Dapkus, Jeanne R. "Sloughing Off the Burdens: Ada's and Isabel's Parallel/Antithetical Quests for Self-Actualization in Jane Campion's Film *The Piano* and Henry James's Novel *Portrait of a Lady*." *Literature Film Quarterly* 25 (1997): 177–87.

Dawson, Ian. "An Interview with Peter Bogdanovich." *The Classic American Novel and the Movies*. Ed. Gerald Peary and Roger Shatzkin. New York: Ungar, 1977. 83–89.

Dennis, Larry. "Spectres and Spectators in *The Turn of the Screw* and *The Innocents*." Ed. Walther Maud. *Purdue University Fifth Annual Conference on Film*. West Lafayette: Purdue UP, 1980. 96–102.

Donoghue, Denis. "Henry James, at a Theater Near You." *New York Times* 3 Jan. 1997: A27.

Ealy, Charles. "Merchant Ivory: Subtlety Instead of Explosions." *Dallas Morning News* 6 Oct. 1998: 1C.

Ebert, Roger. "Love's Labors." *Chicago Sun-Times* 10 Oct. 1997. *Newsbank*. Accessed 22 Mar. 2000.

———. "Movie Portrait Is Different 'Lady' from Henry James." *Denver Post* 17 Jan. 1997, 6:1.

"Evil Emanations." *Time* 5 Jan. 1962: 59.

Fancher, H. "Henry James on Film." *New York Times Book Review* 9 Feb. 1997: 4.

Ferenczi, Aurelien. "Adapter ou ne pas adapter: Films, television, theatre." *L'Arc* 89 (1983): 91–96.

Forbes, Allistar. "The Lesson of the Master." *Times Literary Supplement* (London) 10 Oct. 1996: 1331–32.

Francke, Lizzie. "On the Brink." *Sight and Sound* 6.11 (1996): 6–9.

Fraser, Kennedy. "Portrait of the Director." *Vogue* Jan. 1997: 144–49.

Garner, Jack. "*Washington Square*: Period Detail Reigns in Evocative Adaptation of Henry James Novel." *Democrat and Chronicle* 27 Nov. 1997. <http://www.rochestergoesout.com/mov/w/washin.html>. Accessed 8 Dec. 1999.

Gott, Richard. "We Must Stay True to the Real Henry James." *New Statesman* 127 (1998): 46.

Green, Jesse. "That Was No 'Lady': Pilfering Literature." *New York Times* 11 May 1997, late ed., 2:23.

Gregorio, Edouardo de. "Mes papiers d'Aspern." *L'Arc* 89 (1983): 97–99.

Grenier, Richard. "Movies: *The Bostonians* Inside Out." *Commentary* 78.4 (1984): 60–65.

Gritten, David. "Movies: From Hackers to Highbrow: Ian Softley Departs His Pop-Culture Past to Tackle a Henry James Classic, *The Wings of the Dove.*" *Los Angeles Times* 2 Nov. 1997: 4–1.

Gussow, Mel. "A Festival Celebrates the Dark Explorations behind Decor, Cuisine, and Henry James." *New York Times* 19 Feb. 1998: E1.

Guthmann, Edward. "Cast Gives Character to the *Square.*" *San Francisco Chronicle* 10 Oct. 1997: 1.

Hartl, John. "James's *Dove* Gets a Seattle-Flavored Update." *Seattle Times* 7 June 1998: M4.

———. "A Powerful *Portrait:* Campion's Retelling of James's Classic Is Difficult to Resist." *Seattle Times* 17 Jan. 1997: F1.

Haskell, Molly. "The Women of Henry James." *On the Issues: The Progressive Woman's Quarterly* 7.1 (1998): 56.

Hirsh, Allan. "The Europeans: Henry James, James Ivory, and 'The Nice Mr. Emerson.'" *Literature Film Quarterly* 11 (1983): 112–19.

Holden, Stephen. "A Pas de Trois across Moral Terrain." *New York Times* 7 Nov. 1997, late ed.: E1.

Holleman, Joe. "Novelist Henry James Goes Modern in Another Version of *Wings of the Dove.*" *St. Louis Post-Dispatch* 31 July 1998: E5.

Hornaday, Ann. "Review: *Washington Square* Fails to Breathe Much Life into Henry James Classic." *Baltimore Sun* 17 Oct. 1997: 1F.

Horne, Philip. "The James Gang." *Sight and Sound* 8.1 (1998): 16–19.

Howe, Desson. "Speak Softly: The Director Goes from the Beatles to Henry James." *Washington Post* 14 Nov. 1997: N52.

Hunter, Stephen. "Henry James, Take Two: A Half-Century Apart, Two Adaptations Speak Volumes about Changes in Film." *Washington Post* 12 Oct. 1997: G1.

———. "You Aren't Going to Sit for This Portrait." *Baltimore Sun* 17 Jan. 1997: 4E.

Ivory, James. "The Trouble with Olive." *Sight and Sound* 54 (1985): 95–100.

James, Caryn. "Films Inspired by a Master of Literary Delicacy." *New York Times* 25 June 1993: C1.

Jefferson, Margo. "*The Bostonians* Misses the Boat." *Ms. Magazine* 4 Oct. 1984: 33–44.

Kael, Pauline. "*The Innocents* and What Passes for Experience." *Film Quarterly* 15 (1962): 21–36.

———. "The Woman Question." *New Yorker* 6 Aug.1984: 68–72.

Kaplan, Fred. "Taking Wings." *Village Voice* 25 Nov. 1997: 100.

Kauffmann, Stanley. "A Civil War." *New Republic* 6 Aug. 1984: 26–27.

———. "Domestic Mischief." *New Republic* 20 Oct. 1997: 26–27.

———. "The Portrait Retouched." 23 Dec. 1996. <http://www.thenewrepublic.com/magazines/tnr/archive/1996/12/122396/kaufmann122396.html>. Accessed 13 Dec. 1999.

———. "Scheming, Then and Now." *New Republic* 1 Dec. 1997: 32.

Kempley, Rita. "Agnieszka Holland: A War on Stupidity: Polish-Born Director of *Washington Square* Faces Off against the Mindless Moviemaking Machine." *Washington Post* 12 Oct. 1997: G7.

Kendrick, Walter. "On Film: The Unfilmable." *Salmagundi* 121–22 (1999): 49–62.

Kirby, Joseph A. "Portrait of an Actor." *Chicago Tribune* 12 Jan. 1997: 1.

Knight, Arthur. "Innocents Abroad." *Saturday Review* 23 Dec. 1961: 38–39.

Koch, Sarah J. "A Henry James Filmography." *Henry James Review* 19 (1998): 296–306.

Kridler, Chris. "*Wings of the Dove* Is Rich, Sensual." *Baltimore Sun* 14 Nov. 1997: E3.

Lawson, Terry. "*Wings of the Dove* Star Says Henry James's Book Is a Tough Read." *Detroit Free Press* 10 Nov. 1997. *Newsbank.* Accessed 22 Mar. 2000.

Liggera, J.J. "'She Would Have Appreciated One's Esteem': Peter Bogdanovich's *Daisy Miller.*" *Literature Film Quarterly* 9 (1981): 15–21.

Long, Robert Emmet. "Adaptations of Henry James's Fiction for Drama, Opera, and Films: With a Checklist of New York Theatre Critics' Reviews." *American Literary Realism* 4 (1971): 268–78.

———. "Dramatizing James: *The Bostonians* as a Film." *Henry James Review* 6 (1984): 75–78.

Lyman, Rick. "James Follows Jane as Screen Writer of the Day." *New York Times* 7 Sept. 1997, late ed., sec. 2:66.

Lyons, Donald. "Theaters of Cruelty." *Film Comment* 29.6 (1993): 20–22.

MacDonald, Dwight. "*The Innocents.*" *Esquire* Apr. 1962: 24.

Maslin, Janet. "Clash of the Dazzling and the Meek, Again." *New York Times* 3 Oct. 1997, late ed.: E1.

———. "Henry James, Not Too Literally." *New York Times* 27 Nov. 1996: C1.

Mazzella, Anthony J. "A Selected Henry James Artsography." *Henry James Review* 3 (1981): 44–58.

McFarlane, Brian. "Bogdanovich's *Daisy Miller* and the Limits of Fidelity." *Literature Film Quarterly* 19 (1991): 222–28.

McGary, Pascale. "Le Mystère de la chambre rouge." *Word and Image: A Journal of Verbal/Visual Enquiry* 8.4 (1992): 351–61.

Menand, Louis. "Not Getting the Lesson of the Master." *New York Review of Books* 44.19 (1997): 19–20.

Millar, Gavin. "Two Worlds." *Listener* (London) 102 (1979): 25–26.

Miller, Jeff. "Big-Screen Bonanza: A Dark, Defiant *Portrait.*" *Houston Chronicle* 17 Jan. 1997: 1.

Miller, Laura. "Henry James: Losing It at the Movies." *New York Times Book Review* 19 Jan. 1997: 31.

Moon, Michael. *A Small Boy and Others: Imitation and Initiation in American Culture from Henry James to Andy Warhol.* Durham: Duke UP, 1998.

———. "A Small Boy and Others: Sexual Disorientation in Henry James, Kenneth Anger, and David Lynch." *Comparative American Identities: Race, Sex, and Nationality in the Modern Text.* Ed. Hortense J. Spillers. New York: Routledge, 1991. 151–56.

Morgenstern, Joe. "Film: Among the Predators and the Prey." *Wall Street Journal* 7 Nov. 1997: A17.

———. "Review/Film: What's a Funhouse like without the Fun? Just like 'The Haunting'—House Hams It Up, Leaving Logic, Emotions and the Audience to Fend for Themselves." *Wall Street Journal* 23 July 1999: W1.

Murphy, Kathleen. "Jane Campion's Shining: Portrait of a Director." *Film Comment* 32.6 (1996): 28–31.

———. "An International Episode." *The Classic American Novel and the Movies.* Ed. Gerald Peary and Roger Shatzkin. New York: Ungar, 1977. 90–94.

Nadel, Alan. "Ambassadors from an Imaginary 'Elsewhere': Cinematic Convention and the Jamesian Sensibility." *Henry James Review* 19 (1998) 279–85.

———. "The Search for Cinematic Identity and a Good Man: Jane Campion's Appropriation of James's *Portrait*." *Henry James Review* 18 (1997): 180–83.

O'Sullivan, Michael. "Impressionist *Portrait of a Lady*." *Washington Post* 17 Jan. 1997: D6.

Ozick, Cynthia. "What Only Words, Not a Film, Can Portray." *New York Times* 5 Jan. 1997, late ed., sec. 2:1.

Palmer, James W. "Cinematic Ambiguity: James's 'The Turn of the Screw' and Clayton's *The Innocents*." *Literature Film Quarterly* 5 (1977): 198–215.

Peers, Juliet M.J. "That's No Lady . . . She's a Post-Structuralist." *Quadrant* 41.11 (1997): 31–33.

Petrakis, John. "On the Wings of James: The Challenges of Bringing the Novelist's Work to the Screen." *Chicago Tribune* 16 Nov. 1997: 8.

Raguet-Bouvart, Christine. "*The Europeans:* La Traduction Cinematographie de James Ivory." *La Litterature anglo-americaine a l'ecran.* Ed. Gerald Hugues and Daniel Royot. Cahiers et documents 12. Paris: Didier, 1993. 1997-85.

Recchia, Edward. "An Eye for an I: Adapting Henry James's 'The Turn of the Screw' to the Screen." *Literature Film Quarterly* 15 (1987): 28–35.

Rickey, Carrie. "Odd Coupling: Hollywood and Turn-of-the-Century Author Henry James." *Philadelphia Inquirer* 23 Oct. 1997. *Newsbank.* Accessed 22 Mar. 2000.

Sadoff, Dianne F. "'Intimate Disarray': The Henry James Movies." *Henry James Review* 19 (1998): 286–95.

Schepelern, P. "James on Film." *Kosmorama* 26.148 (1980): 138–41.

Seiler, Andy. "*Washington* Aims to Square with James's *Heiress* Book." *USA Today* 15 Oct. 1997: D3.

Shargel, Raphael. "Spiced Up Henry James. *New Leader* 29 Dec. 1997: 32.

Sheehan, Henry. "Painting an All-Too-Conventional *Portrait of a Lady*: Review: Jane Campion's Movie of the Henry James Masterpiece Is Shockingly Dull." *Santa Ana Orange County Register* 24 Dec. 1996: F3.

———. "Thoroughly Modern James: Review: For Once, the Turn-of-the-Century Novelist Soars on Screen with this Passionate, Powerful *The Wings of the Dove*." *Santa Ana Orange County Register* 14 Nov. 1997: F7.

Shields, John C. "*Daisy Miller:* Bogdanovich's Film and James's Nouvelle." *Literature Film Quarterly* 11 (1983): 105–11.

Sklar, Robert. "A Novel Approach to Movie Making: Reinventing *The Portrait of a Lady*." *Chronicle of Higher Education* Feb. 1997: B7.

Smith, Dinitia. "Hollywood Trains Its Lights on a Master of Shadow." *New York Times* 30 Oct. 1996: C13.

Smith, Henry Nash, and Arthur Barron. "On Henry James and 'The Jolly Corner.'" *The American Short Story.* Ed. Calvin L. Skaggs and Robert Geller. New York: Dell, 1977. 122–27.

Sorensen, Sue. "'Damnable Feminization'? The Merchant Ivory Film Adaptation of Henry James's *The Bostonians*." *Literature Film Quarterly* 25 (1997): 231–35.

Stafford, William T. "An 'Easy Ride' for Henry James." *Books Speaking to Books: A*

*Contextual Approach to American Fiction*. Chapel Hill: U. of North Carolina P, 1981. 54–59.

Sterritt, David. "*Washington Square* Director Draws Parallels to Today." *Christian Science Monitor* 89.231 24 Oct. 1997: 12.

Stone, Alan. "Henry James at the Movies: With a Decadent Sensuality, *The Wings of the Dove* Reaches for the Galleries." *Boston Review* 23.1 (1998): 27–29.

Strickler, Jeff. "*Portrait* Is Haunting at a Distance: Director Seems to Make Sure Audience Stays at Arm's Length." *Star Tribune: Newspaper of the Twin Cities* 17 Jan. 1997: 9.

Taubin, Amy. "Squaring Off." *Village Voice* 14 Oct. 1997: 94.

Teachout, Terry. "Classics That Sizzle." *New York Times* 20 Dec. 1997: A13.

———. "Taste: How We Get That Story—Quick: Read a Novel or Watch a Movie? The Battle Is Over: Movies Have Won." *Wall Street Journal* 6 Aug. 1999: W11.

Telotte, J.P. "Children of Horror: The Films of Val Lewton." *Aspects of Fantasy: Selected Essays from the Second International Conference on the Fantastic in Literature and Film*. Ed. William Coyle. Contribution to Study of Science Fiction and Fantasy 19. Westport: Greenwood, 1986. 95–106.

Thomas, Kevin. "Gems of Merchant Ivory." *Los Angeles Times* 12 Mar. 1998: F10.

Thomson, David. "*Killing Time.*" *Esquire* June 1998: 54.

Tibbetts, John C. "A Masterpiece Takes Flight: *The Wings of the Dove.*" *Literature Film Quarterly* 26 (1998): 313–15.

Tintner, Adeline R. "Henry James at the Movies: Cinematograph and Photograph in 'Crapy Cornelia.'" *Markham Review* 6 (1979): 1–8.

———. "Truffaut's *La Chambre verte:* Hommage to Henry James." *Literature Film Quarterly* 8 (1980): 78–83.

Turan, Kenneth. "Campion Paints Bold *Portrait.*" *Los Angeles Times* 24 Dec. 1997: F1.

———. "*Washington Square:* A New Approach to an Old Address." *Los Angeles Times* 10 Oct. 1997: F1.

Vineberg, Steve. "The Responsibility of the Adapter: *The Bostonians* on Film." *Arizona Quarterly: A Journal of American Literature, Culture, and Theory* 41.3 (1985): 223–30.

Walton, Priscilla L. "Jane and James go to the Movies: Post Colonial Portraits of a Lady." *Henry James Review* 18 (1997): 187–90.

———. "'The Tie of a Common Aversion': Sexual Tension in Henry James's *The Other House*. *Henry James Review* 17 (1996): 11–21.

Weintraub, Bernard. "At the Movies." *New York Times* 31 Dec. 1997: E9.

Wexman, Virginia Wright. "The Portrait of a Body." *Henry James Review* 18 (1997): 184–86.

Wilmington, Michael. "James's *Dove* Charged with Sexuality." *Chicago Tribune* 14 Nov. 1997: A5.

———. "*Washington Square:* A Superb Adaptation." *Chicago Tribune* 10 Oct. 1997: A5.

Wynne-Davies, Marion. "'All by Myself in the Moonlight': Edith Wharton's *Age of Innocence*." *Kobe College Studies* 41.2 (1994): 1–14.

Zwinger, Lyndon. "Bodies That Don't Matter: The Queering of 'Henry James.'" *Modern Fiction Studies* 41 (1995): 657–80.

# Contributors

**Dale M. Bauer** is a professor of English at the University of Kentucky. She has published books on feminist theory and Edith Wharton and has edited Gilman's "The Yellow Wallpaper" and a collection of essays on Bahktin and feminism. Her current project is *Sex Expression and American Women,* a study of the cultural taboos surrounding sexuality from 1860 through 1940.

**Nancy Bentley** is an associate professor of English at the University of Pennsylvania. She is the author of *The Ethnography of Manners: Hawthorne, James, Wharton* (Cambridge University Press, 1995). Her study of the emergence of high literary culture in nineteenth-century America will appear in *The Cambridge History of American Literature,* vol. 3, *Prose Writing 1860–1920* (forthcoming).

**Marc Bousquet** is an assistant professor of English at the University of Louisville, where he teaches American literature and literary theory. He is working on *The Practice of Association: Participatory Culture in the Nineteenth-Century United States.*

**Karen Chandler** teaches American and African American literature and film at the University of Louisville. She has written on melodrama, African American personal narrative, and independent black film, and has published essays in *Arizona Quarterly, African American Review, Henry James Review,* and other journals.

**Sarah Edgington** is an undergraduate at the University of Wisconsin. She is majoring in sociology and women's studies with a concentration in analysis and research. She also writes poetry and is interested in exploring the ways in which poetry and fiction can function as sociological texts.

**Wendy Graham** is an associate professor of English at Vassar College, where she teaches American literature, culture studies, and literary theory. She is author of *Henry James's Thwarted Love* (Stanford UP, 1999), an exploration of James's imaginative and personal engagement with the notion of sexual alterity. Her recent work focuses on the relationship between Pre-Raphaelitism and Modernism. She is secretary-treasurer of the Henry James Society.

**Susan M. Griffin,** a professor of English at the University of Louisville, is the editor of the *Henry James Review* and editor and author of a number of works on James.

**Matthew F. Jordan** is a commonwealth postdoctoral teaching scholar in the humanities at the University of Louisville. His work explores the impact of film, music, and other popular media forms on the formation of cultural identity. He is currently finishing a book on French discourse on jazz.

**J. Sarah Koch** is a native and current resident of Portland, Oregon. She earned an M.A. in English from Portland State University in 1997, where her focus quickly became the works of Henry James. She is currently self-employed as a freelance proofreader, copyeditor, researcher, and writer.

**Anthony J. Mazzella** is a professor of English at the William Paterson University of New Jersey. His essays are included in a book on Alfred Hitchcock and in several volumes on Henry James, including the Norton critical editions of *The Portrait of a Lady* and *The Wings of the Dove.*

**Peggy McCormack** is a professor of literature and film in the English department at Loyola University in New Orleans. She is head of the Film Program at Loyola and a member of the board of editors of the *New Orleans Review.* She has published essays on American and British literature and film and is the author of *The Language of Money: Gender, Class, and Sexual Economics in the Fiction of Henry James* (UMI Research Press, 1990) and the editor of *Questioning the Master: Gender and Sexuality in Henry James's Writings* (University of Delaware Press, 2000).

**Lee Clark Mitchell,** Holmes Professor of Belles-Lettres at Princeton University, has written essays on a range of modern American authors. His books include *Witnesses to a Vanishing America: The Nineteenth-Century Response* (1981), *Determined Fictions: American Literary Naturalism* (1989), *The Photograph and the American Indian* (1994), and *Westerns: Making the Man in Fiction and Film* (1996). His present project involves the intersection of ethics and aesthetics in contemporary discussions of Henry James.

**Alan Nadel,** a professor of literature and film at Rensselaer Polytechnic Institute, is the author of *Invisible Criticism: Ralph Ellison and the American Canon* (1988), *Containment Culture: American Narratives. Postmodernism, and the Atomic Age* (1995), and *Flatlining on the Field of Dreams: Cultural Narratives in the Films of President Reagan's America* (1997). He is the editor of *May All Your*

*Fences Have Gates: Essays on the Drama of August Wilson* (1994), and he has won prizes for the best essay in *Modern Fiction Studies* (1988) and the best essay in *PMLA* (1993). His poetry has appeared in several journals including *Paris Review, Georgia Review, Partisan Review, New England Review, Sycamore Review,* and *Shenandoah.*

**Leland S. Person** is a professor of English and head of the English department at the University of Cincinnati. He is the author of *Aesthetic Headaches: Women and a Masculine Poetics in Poe, Melville, and Hawthorne* (University of Georgia Press, 1988). He has published extensively on nineteenth-century American literature, especially on Hawthorne and James, in journals such as *PMLA, American Literature, American Literary History, American Quarterly, Nineteenth-Century Literature, Arizona Quarterly,* and the *Henry James Review.* He has been president of the Henry James Society and is currently book review editor for the *Henry James Review.*

**Julie Rivkin** is a professor of English at Connecticut College, where she teaches courses in American literature, literary theory, and contemporary women. She is the author of *False Positions: The Representational Logics of Henry James's Fiction* and co-editor with Michael Ryan of *Literary Theory: An Anthology.*

**Diane F. Sadoff** is a professor of English and the chair of the department at the Miami University, Ohio. She has published *Monsters of Affection: Dickens, Bronte, and Eliot on Fatherhood* (Johns Hopkins University Press) and *Sciences of the Flesh: Representing Body and Subject in Psychoanalysis* (Stanford University Press). She has also coedited *Teaching Contemporary Theory to Undergraduates* (MLA Publications) and *Victorian Afterlife: Postmodern Culture Rewrites the Nineteenth Century* (University of Minnesota Press). She was a Guggenheim fellow in 1990–1991.

**Priscilla L. Walton** is a professor of English at Carleton University in Canada. She is the author of *The Disruption of the Feminine in Henry James* and *Patriarchal Desire and Victorian Discourse: A Lacanian Reading of Anthony Trollope's Palliser Novels.* She is coauthor, with Manina Jones, of *Detective Agency: Women Re-Writing the Hardboiled Tradition,* and the editor of the Everyman paperback edition of *The Portrait of a Lady.* She is also the editor of the *Canadian Review of American Studies,* a member of the advisory board of *PMLA,* and a member of the editorial board of the *Henry James Review.*

**Steve Wexler** is a graduate student at the University of Louisville and serves as an editorial assistant for the *Henry James Review.*

# Index

Illustrations are indicated with *italicized* page numbers.